Iₒₒₒₐₓₐᵤₓ (barcode text: I0083274)

TOURISM AND SPATIAL
TRANSFORMATIONS

Tourism and Spatial Transformations

Edited by

G.J. Ashworth

Professor of Heritage Management and Urban Tourism
Faculty of Spatial Sciences
State University
Groningen
The Netherlands

A.G.J. Dietvorst

Professor of Recreation and Tourism Studies
Centre for Recreation and Tourism Studies
Agricultural University
Wageningen
The Netherlands

CAB INTERNATIONAL

CAB INTERNATIONAL   Tel: +44 (0)1491 832111
Wallingford   Telex: 847964 (COMAGG G)
Oxon OX10 8DE   E-mail: cabi@cabi.org
UK   Fax: +44 (0)1491 833508

A catalogue record for this book is available from the
British Library.

ISBN 0 85198 981 0

Typeset in 10/12 Palatino
by Solidus (Bristol) Limited
Printed and bound in the UK by Biddles Ltd, Guildford

Contents

Contributors   ix

Preface   xi

1   **Tourism Transformations: an Introduction**
A.G.J. Dietvorst and G.J. Ashworth   1

I   **TRANSFORMATIONS BY PRODUCERS**   13

2   **Materializing the Imagined: on the Dynamics and Assessment of Tourist–Recreational Transformation Processes**
J. Lengkeek   17

3   **Evolution of Tourism on the Spanish Coast**
G.K. Priestley   37

4   **The Third Sector: a Secure Domain of Self-organization in Free Time or a Threatened Field of Social Action?**
J. Lengkeek   55

5   **Lost in the 'Jungle' of Northern Thailand: the Reproduction of Hill-tribe Trekking**
E.M.H. Binkhorst and V.R. van der Duim   69

6   **Mass Tourism and Problems of Tourism Planning
    in French Mountains**
    J. Herbin   93

II **FROM PRODUCERS TO MANAGEMENT OF THE
    PRODUCT**   107

7   **Transformations in the Concept of Holiday Villages
    in Northern Europe**
    W. Faché   109

8   **Tourism Planning in Urban Revitalization Projects:
    Lessons from the Amsterdam Waterfront
    Development**
    M. Jansen-Verbeke and E. van de Wiel   129

9   **Public Space in the Post-industrial City**
    J. Burgers   147

III **FROM MANAGEMENT BY PRODUCERS TO
    TRANSFORMATION BY THE CONSUMER**   159

10 **Tourist Behaviour and the Importance of
    Time–Space Analysis**
    A.G.J. Dietvorst   163

11 **Nature-based Tourism and Recreation:
    Environmental Change, Perception, Ideology and
    Practices**
    J. Philipsen   183

12 **Sports Tourism: the Case of Golf**
    G.K. Priestley   205

13 **Impacts of Festival Events: a Case-study of
    Edinburgh**
    C. Gratton and P.D. Taylor   225

IV **FROM TRANSFORMATION BY THE CONSUMER
    TO MANAGEMENT OF THE CONSUMER**   239

14 **Management of Recreation and Tourist Behaviour
    at Different Spatial Levels**
    H.W.J. Boerwinkel   241

15 **Managing the Cultural Tourist**
    G.J. Ashworth   265

16 **Managing Deviant Tourist Behaviour**
    B. Beke and B. Elands   285

17 **Managing the Impacts of Recreation by Agreeing
    the Limits of Acceptable Change**
    R. Sidaway   303

18 **The Role of Management Information Systems in
    the Provision of Recreation**
    P.D. Taylor   317

19 **Conclusion: Challenge and Policy Response**
    G.J. Ashworth and A.G.J. Dietvorst   329

Index   341

Contributors

G.J. Ashworth: *Professor of Heritage Management and Urban Tourism, Faculty of Spatial Sciences, State University, PO Box 800, 9700 AV, Groningen (The Netherlands)*

B. Beke: *Director, Advies- en Onderzoeksgroep Beke, Rijnkade 84, 6811 HD, Arnhem (The Netherlands)*

E.M.H. Binkhorst: *Staff Member Christelijke Hogeschool Noord-Nederland, Faculteit Economie en Management, PO Box 1298, 8900 CG Leeuwarden (The Netherlands)*

H.W.J. Boerwinkel: *Lecturer, Centre for Recreation and Tourism Studies, Agricultural University, Generaal Foulkesweg 13, 6703 BJ Wageningen (The Netherlands)*

J. Burgers: *Senior Lecturer, Faculteit Sociale Wetenschappen, Vakgroep Algemene Sociale Wetenschappen, Rijksuniversiteit Utrecht, Heidelberglaan 2, PO Box 80140, 3508 TC Utrecht (The Netherlands)*

A.G.J. Dietvorst: *Professor of Recreation and Tourism Studies, Centre for Recreation and Tourism Studies, Agricultural University, Generaal Foulkesweg 13, 6703 BJ Wageningen (The Netherlands)*

V.R. van der Duim: *Lecturer, Department of Sociology, Agricultural University, Hollandseweg 1, 6706 KN Wageningen (The Netherlands)*

B. Elands: *Research Assistant, Centre for Recreation and Tourism Studies,*

Agricultural University, Generaal Foulkesweg 13, 6703 BJ Wageningen (The Netherlands)

W. Faché: *Professor of Social Interventions in Leisure and Tourism (Agology), Initiator and Coordinator of the European Master's Degree in Leisure and Tourism Studies (Homo Ludens), University of Ghent, Henri Dunantlaan 2, B-9000 Gent (Belgium)*

C. Gratton: *Professor of Economics, School of Leisure and Food Management, Sheffield Hallam University, City Campus, Pond Street, S1 1WB Sheffield (UK)*

J. Herbin: *Professor of Physical Geography, Institut Alpine de Géographie, Université Joseph Fourier, 17, Rue Maurice Gignoux, F-38031 Grenoble (France)*

M. Jansen-Verbeke: *Professor of Tourism Management Studies, Faculteit der Bedrijfskunde, Erasmusuniversiteit, PO Box 1738, 3000 DR Rotterdam (The Netherlands)*

J. Lengkeek: *Senior Lecturer, Department of Sociology, Agricultural University, Hollandseweg 1, 6706 KN Wageningen (The Netherlands)*

J. Philipsen: *Lecturer, Department of Physical Planning and Rural Development, Agricultural University, Generaal Foulkesweg 13, 6703 BJ Wageningen (The Netherlands)*

G.K. Priestley: *Professor of Human Geography, Universitat Autonoma de Barcelona, Departament de Geografia, Edifiri B, E-08193 Bellaterra, Barcelona (Spain)*

R. Sidaway: *Research and Policy Consultant, 4 Church Hill Place, EH10 4BD Edinburgh (UK)*

P.D. Taylor: *Director, Leisure Management Unit, University of Sheffield, Hicks Building, Hounsfield Road, S3 7RH Sheffield (UK)*

E. van de Wiel: *Lecturer, Faculteit der Beleidswetenschappen, Katholieke Universiteit Nijmegen, PO Box 9044, 6500 KD Nijmegen (The Netherlands)*

Preface

Tourism and recreation have had, and still have, a considerable spatial and sociocultural impact on our society. The recent growth of the tourism industry has raised the question of limits of acceptable change, sustainable development, capacity and 'liveability'. It is now widely acknowledged that tourism and recreation transform, wittingly or not, landscapes, monuments, national parks, urban public spaces and local sociocultural characteristics.

This book grew out of a series of lectures framed in the international seminars on product development and regional planning for tourism and recreation as part of the European Erasmus Postgraduate Programme Homo Ludens (1991–1994). A primary purpose of these seminars was to foster contacts between researchers and to confront students with a spatial approach to tourism and recreation problems. To encourage the development of a coherent view, the so-called transformation model served both as a comprehensive and analytical tool to grasp the complexity of tourism and recreation processes and as a common basis of understanding for planning and intervention purposes. However, this volume is considerably more than a collection of the seminar papers. Each of the contributions has been substantially revised or in some cases totally rewritten following editorial suggestions, and other essays have been included to present a balanced book.

We owe a considerable debt to the cartographic staff of the Department of Physical Planning and Rural Development of the Agricultural University of Wageningen, especially Gerrit Kleinrensink and Adri van 't Veer. They produced most of the maps and figures.

We would not have been able to produce this book without the willing and creative input of its contributors, all of whom patiently followed the remarks and suggestions of the editors.

Greg Ashworth, Faculty of Spatial Sciences, University of Groningen
Adri Dietvorst, Centre for Recreation and Tourism Studies, Agricultural University, Wageningen

1

Tourism Transformations: an Introduction

A.G.J. Dietvorst[1] and G.J. Ashworth[2]

[1]Centre for Recreation and Tourism Studies, Agricultural University, Generaal Foulkesweg 13, 6703 BJ Wageningen, The Netherlands: [2]Faculty of Spatial Sciences, State University, PO Box 800, 9700 AV Groningen, The Netherlands.

Tourism and recreation are already big business in contemporary society. Their economic significance is considerable and for many countries the expenditure of foreign visitors makes a substantial contribution to the overall trade balance. It is no longer necessary, as it was a generation ago, to demonstrate that tourism and recreation make important contributions to economic development and social well-being. Not surprisingly the spatial and sociocultural impact is increasing and although recreation and tourism have long been considered to be 'clean' industries, for some regions at some times and for some activities the limits of acceptable impacts have been reached. Environmentally sensitive areas are being threatened and the issue of sustainable tourism has become important in recent years.

Public place-management authorities, at spatial scales from the local to the national, commercial enterprises in a wide range of recreation-related fields and individual consumers have all profited in different ways from the growth in these activities and anticipate further gains from their continued expansion. However, most tourism and recreation activities were previously regarded as marginal additions to existing local economies, societies and land-use allocation systems. There was a widespread assumption that their impact could be accommodated by the use of surplus or existing factors of production and in any event these were 'clean' activities in terms of their physical impacts. Growth has increasingly undermined these assumptions to the point where discussion now focuses upon such issues as 'limits', 'sustainable development', 'capacity', 'liveability' and the like, all of which can be subsumed in the necessity for choice and thus for policy intervention.

1

A Transformation Model

The necessity for a policy of intervention and its applications through planning and management requires a prior understanding of the nature of recreation and tourism and specifically of its dynamic character, for it is the possibility of intervening to manage the rate and direction of change that legitimates such intervention. In the past decades the time–space point of view is acknowledged as providing interesting insights into the transformation processes of economic and sociocultural phenomena (see for instance Giddens, 1984).

In order to emphasize the dynamic character of the tourism–recreation product development process and to have an overarching concept that integrates both supply and demand, the Centre for Recreation and Tourism Studies of the Wageningen Agricultural University developed the so-called transformation model (Dietvorst, 1992). This model shows the continuing transformation of the original tourism–recreation resource (whether a landscape, a monument, an urban public space, a national park or other elements) by activities and interventions by producers and consumers of many types, wittingly or not, for a variety of objectives. It embraces material practices as well as the role of image production and interpretation.

Why has the concept of transformation been chosen for analysing the dynamic character of tourism–recreation developments? The concept of transformation (to be defined as the changing of the shape, appearance, quality or nature of something) is used as a synthesized concept to express the importance of space and time in considering tourism and recreation. Space and time are basic attributes of tourism and recreation, because tourism and recreation presuppose movement. In fact the word tourist can be seen as a new word for traveller and without travel tourism and outdoor recreation are almost impossible. For a long time space and time have been treated and unthinkingly accepted as mere environments of action, although geographers and historians have paid much research attention to each of these fundamental attributes separately. Central to the idea of modernity is that of movement. Lash and Urry (1994, pp. 255–256) show how rapid forms of mobility have radical effects on how people actually experience the modern world, changing both their forms of subjectivity and sociability and their aesthetic appreciation of nature, landscapes, townscapes and other societies. It is obvious that the occurrence of time–space compression and the acceleration of social developments legitimate the choice of the concept of transformation as crucial for the analysis of tourism–recreation development.

Among the innumerable consequences of the general acceleration in the turnover times of capital, production and consumption, Harvey (1989) points out some relevant ones which support our arguments for using the concept of transformation as a central focus point in this book.

First, the acceleration mentioned has as a consequence an accentuation of the ephemerality of fashions, products, values and established practices. There is a shift towards what is called 'instantaneous time' with related phenomena like instant food, time-sharing, short-break holidays, last-minute bookings and so on. Producers are forced to respond fast to market shifts and short-term action seems to be more important than long-term planning. The volatility is apparent in the increasing significance of design, taste, fashion and image to manipulate the consumer market. The tourism industry especially specializes in the acceleration of turnover time through the production and marketing of images.

Secondly, the collapse of spatial barriers by modern information technology (the globalization trend) makes people more sensitive to local qualities. On the one hand the variety of local and regional uniqueness is diminishing: the same phenomenon is exploited in entertainment places all over the world (see for instance the presence of the so-called white-knuckle rides in theme parks). On the other hand local differences in entrepreneurial abilities or sociocultural qualities are emphasized: 'We thus approach the central paradox: the less important the spatial barriers, the greater the sensitivity of capital to the variations of place within space, and the greater the incentive for places to be differentiated in ways attractive to capital' (Harvey, 1989, p. 296). This explains why tourism regions seek to promote a distinctive image and to create an atmosphere of uniqueness that may prove attractive to visitors.

Thirdly, the time–space compression is connected to the 'three-minute culture' which does not leave enough time to follow a lengthy programme on the television. It results in a search for the instantaneous and a predominance of the visual over the written. Urry (1992) has stressed the increased importance of visual consumption or more generally aesthetic judgement, rather than one based upon reason and discourse. There is a shift from the 'Gutenberg generation' to the 'MTV generation'. The former was educated with the printed word and with logical, sequential thinking, the latter prefers crossing and fragmented stories (as in the 'soaps'): no linear logic, no consistency, no separation between private and public, between commerce and arts, between illusion and reality. No longer is the transformation of a genuine resource into a tourism–recreation product just a matter of material transformation, but increasingly also a symbolic transformation, in which the image takes precedence over the material product (the

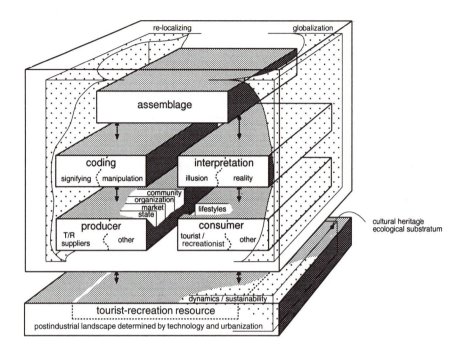

Fig. 1.1. Model of tourism transformations.

accommodation, the region as such) and the illusion is made up of a collection of visual and aural images. Zukin's (1991, p. 38) analysis of the post-modern urban landscape summarizes this transformation as follows: 'Spaces of production recede into the historic vernacular; more than ever, the urban landscape relies on image consumption.'

The principle behind the proposed transformation model is the assumption that people, through a variety of symbolic and material interventions, determine the transformation of the original physical and socioeconomic space valuable for tourism and recreation. The model (Fig. 1.1) shows the continuing transformation of the original resource by activities and interventions by producers and consumers. The main types of such transformations will now be described.

The Resource

The resource can be considered to be any element used in the creation of a tourism–recreation product. Normally a distinction can be made between resources for which no regulation mechanism is necessary and scarce resources. Scarce resources can be divided into:

- physical resources, i.e. land, water, vegetation, energy;
- labour;
- capital goods, i.e. resources converted entirely through human effort;
- sociocultural resources, i.e. historical and here-and-now patterns of social life, folk-ways, traditions, built environment, art, etc.

In creating the tourism–recreation product the physical resource (the landscape in the broadest sense) no doubt plays a crucial role. Technology and rationalization have exerted a tremendous influence on, for example, the actual morphology of the rural and urban landscape. Even the growing interest in nature and natural development presupposes an intensive technological intervention in existing natural systems. The sociocultural resources become more and more important as can be inferred from the tremendous interest in European societies in cultural heritage. We can conclude that the distinctions between types of resources are becoming blurred. Legislation, exploitation techniques, zoning, fencing off and specific management measures are increasingly directing the dynamics of the natural systems to achieve predetermined objectives. Four different but related transformations can be distinguished.

Material transformation by producers

Producers transform the original resource (such as the landscape or the city) by direct actions (building facilities, transforming coastal landscapes into resorts, transforming historic buildings into restaurants or museums, all kinds of planning activities, constructing cycle paths, etc.). Frequently a kind of non-intervention is possible when public authorities restrict or forbid certain activities. All kinds of public authorities, entrepreneurs, private organizations and local communities are involved in this 'production' process. The suppliers of the tourism–recreation product act upon other producers and are also subjected to the influence of activities of others in their region. The different functions compete for their share of the scarce space available. Owing to the current changes in farming practice in the European Union (EU), the European landscape is undergoing a process of transformation. In regions with economically marginal agriculture nature development and tourism compete to use the abandoned agricultural areas. In densely populated regions the urban usage of space has increased significantly and, although the population growth rate is diminishing, high-prosperity lifestyles need more and more space for living, working and leisure. In some regions resistance to the

extension (especially spatial) of the tourism industry is already perceptible and nature conservationists especially are worried about the
effect on nature and landscape of camp-sites, hotels and chalet parks.
In some parts of the world the concept of 'tourism urbanization' is
already appropriate (Mullins, 1992). Also the changing relationship
between the State and the market exerts an influence upon the
character and direction of the tourism–recreation development in a
certain area. Competition also occurs between tourism–recreation
regions and places in a struggle for a part of the market. The quality of
a region or a town becomes a significant production factor and places
compete using their assumed unique characteristics. Successful regions
are capable of organizing themselves whilst combining strong aspects.

Symbolic transformation by producers

It is widely acknowledged in the field of marketing that the acquisition
of product information is influenced by a personal interpretation of the
design or package. Because the tourism product often has a specific
spatial character, people's view of the environment and the resulting
mental image are subject to manipulation by producers. The producers
transform the physical structure of a region more or less indirectly
through coding. A certain coding is added to the already transformed
material resource. In many cases this is the real added value of the
tourism–recreation product (TRP), i.e. the illusion: resources are converted into products through interpretation (Ashworth, 1992). The TRP
is packaged, designed and assembled: a romantic holiday in Paris is
offered by a tour operator, peacefulness and a fascinating landscape
could be enjoyed in the southern part of France (according to the local
tourist board) and so on. The movement from any station in Europe to
Paris Gare du Nord as such is not a tourism product, but the
consciously promoted 'romantic weekend in Paris' is. Cycling in the
countryside is not a tourism product but the feeling of having a day off
is.

Lengkeek (1994) has argued that attractions are increasingly being
created in this way today: 'You should have been there … didn't you
visit the Bonnie and Clyde Shootout Area?' These attractions get a
'signifying' function in modern society because they are designated as
beautiful, worthwhile and funny. It is through coding that the producer
can manipulate the consumer market.

MacCannell (1976, p. 110) has elaborated this further in his considerations of the semiotics of attractions: 'Usually, the first contact a
sightseer has with a sight is not the sight itself but representations
thereof', and he has introduced the term 'marker' to designate the
information about a specific sight. Attractions are thus combinations of

sight and markers. Such markers 'authenticate' the sight and the experience: they may be just a locational designation but also include postcards, descriptions and guidebook entries. The attraction of the asylum of Saint-Paul-de-Mausole in Saint-Rémy-de-Provence is not found in the architectural particularities of a monastery built in the 12th and 13th centuries, but in the mere fact that Vincent Van Gogh here tried to recover from what has been most commonly diagnosed as an epileptic disorder. Here Van Gogh spent a considerable part of his final months, creating his famous paintings of cypress trees, olive groves and the ever-present barren Alpille Mountains. This story functions as the marker authenticating the dramatic character of the location.

A specific category of producers is the group of intermediaries (tour operators, travel agencies) because they do not transform the original tourism–recreation resource directly, although through the offering of package tours and other kinds of services they could be very influential in transforming the authentic character of destination areas.

Symbolic transformation by consumers

Consumers or visitors transform the physical structure of the region or the area visited by them through their distinctive interpretation of the product offered. According to Boorstin (1961) tourists do not even directly experience 'reality' but thrive on 'pseudo-events'. The mass tourist especially travels in guided groups and finds pleasure in attractions that others may regard as 'unauthentic' and contrived, gullibly enjoying the 'pseudo-events'. However, according to MacCannell (1989) all tourists embody a quest for authenticity, which may only be 'staged' (the constructed tourist attractions as for instance the 'authentic' folklore event). The motives, needs, preferences, etc. of tourists are, so to speak, 'matched' by them with advertisements in newspapers, the recommendations by friends and relatives, and former experiences influencing their decision whether or not to go for a day out or a holiday or a visit to a museum. This transformation or assemblage is indirect because the supplier reacts to the trends in the market, i.e. the behaviour of the visitors. Lifestyle changes are important explanatory variables here.

Adventure and challenge are no longer looked for in stories or printed material but increasingly in visualized fiction and personally sensed authentic experiences. Pictures, movies, television and CD-i replace verbal contacts or written sources. Sensory and more especially visual experiences are important today: visiting restaurants, theatres, pop concerts and museums are popular activities. Recent technological developments have transformed our culture into a much more visual one (Clark *et al.*, 1994). On the basis of research into trends in leisure activities, Knulst (1993) observes the development of a culture greatly orientated towards sensory experience. He considers the 'marriage between sports and tourism' as typical of this modern sensory culture. The modern tourist looks for active holidays abroad (mountain-biking, Alpine cycling, rafting and so on). Although participation rates for sport activities have grown for almost every age group, many people of mature age are looking for contemplation and *lieux de memoires*. They opt for a cultural return from their travel and use the educational opportunities of cultural tours to experience a mental pilgrimage to the past, which could be the route to Santiago de Compostela or equally the Beatles' cavern in Liverpool or Elvis' Graceland in Memphis.

Different lifestyles and/or recreation styles also compete for the use of the same space at the same time, leading to conflicts between local inhabitants and visitors for many facilities that are centrally important in much local policy for such areas.

Material transformation by consumers

The decision to take a walk in the neighbourhood or a holiday to Greece results in a contribution to the transformation of the physical and social structures of the areas visited. Space consumption, crowding, wear on infrastructure, deterioration of historic monuments, erosion in vulnerable landscapes, disturbance of birds and other animals, traffic congestion and all kinds of environmental impacts belong to the direct transformation of the original tourism–recreation resource. The concept of lifestyle, i.e. a confirmation of self-identity and role amongst one's peers (Ryan, 1991), plays an important role in the explanation of the variety of preferences and motives for leisure behaviour.

Fundamental to the understanding of each of the transformation processes described is the context in which they take place. In Fig. 1.1 the four transformations form just the surface reflections of much wider, complicated developments in society. The model focuses upon the spatially visible tracks of the transformations, but neglects the explanatory mechanisms. To reveal these the original model is extended by adding the dimensions of relocalization and globalization and the tension between flexibility and sustainability. The tension between sustainability and flexibility leads to all kinds of systems control and intervention. More insight is needed into the impact of these interventions in the complicated social reality, and the current debate on the shift in roles between the public and the private sector offers interesting viewpoints in this respect.

The relationship between the tourism production and resource systems is complicated by some aspects of the nature of tourism itself. Tourism makes extensive use of resources which are also in use for non-tourism activities. Equally the tourism product frequently serves additional non-tourist demands. This multi-use, multi-selling and multi-buying have numerous implications for interventions which are discussed below. Similarly tourism makes use of resources which are freely available (such as scenic landscapes) or which have been created and are maintained for reasons other than tourism (such as conserved cityscapes or museums). Consequently tourism producers frequently have little direct control over the resources they use, while resource managers have little direct influence upon tourist users of their resources. All this renders the relationship between the tourism production and resource systems both particularly prone to, at best inflexibility and, at worst, complete breakdown, and singularly difficult to manage in combination. However, doom-laden scenarios of an immanent 'resource crisis' (Ashworth, 1992; Jansen-Verbeke, 1994) must be balanced against another characteristic of tourism that emerges from the above description of transformations, namely that tourism can in effect create its own resources. An old town, a barren agriculturally valueless region or a backward stagnating culture can become a tourist-historic city, a scenic landscape or a distinct saleable cultural entity. Tourism has shaped resources where none existed before. The capacity of tourism to both create and destroy the resources it uses is a dichotomy dominating much of the discussion in subsequent chapters and a focus for further justification for intervention.

The constitution of meaning forms a part of processes like globalization and relocalization. The scale factor is very important for the analysis of the transformation processes. Especially important is the way the tourism–recreation development contributes to the creation of local and/or regional identity. Some of the tourism–recreation transformations are consciously produced, but others develop more or less unintentionally. At least some of the consequences are unforeseeable and unintended. The planning process cannot be totally manageable and in this complicated modern society unexpected results are becoming normal. To develop a successful intervention policy more unravelling of these impacts of the system is badly needed.

The dynamic character of the tourism–recreation transformations is determined by processes of symbolic and material reproduction. Symbolic and material reproduction was central to Habermas' theory of communicative action (1991, orig. 1981). He made a challenging attempt to integrate the contributions of various social scientists into a coherent social theory. Central in his thinking is the process of rationalization, the way the rationality or reasonableness of a form of social action can be increased. Habermas makes a distinction between the rationalization of purposive–rational actions (such as the managing of an industry) and communicative actions, such as the way people exchange notions on social relations. The first type of rationalization increasingly dominates the production processes in modern society. Society is structured as systems (political or economic) which are organized to optimize and sustain social relations with the objective of guaranteeing the physical existence of society, its safety, order and exchange of goods. Yet we cannot understand the functioning of these social systems unless we look at the creative roles of social actors, and the ways in which they construct, negotiate and reconstruct the social meanings of their world. The resulting communication processes constitute and validate the shared opinions about claims of comprehensibility, truth, credibility and rectitude. In acting communicatively the social actor achieves consensus and this world of consensus can be called the life-world. In exploring the concepts of system and life-world Habermas tried to show how each presupposes the other. However, he stated also that we are threatened today by the 'colonization of the life-world' by systemic rationalization processes. 'What has happened in modern society (and continues to happen at an alarming rate) is a selective process of rationalization – where purposive–rational rationalization prevails, encroaches upon, and deforms the life-world of everyday life' (Bernstein, 1985, p. 23).

Lengkeek (1994), in exploring the social foundations of leisure, suggests that the organization of the everyday social order continually leads to the production of another reality, the so-called 'contrastructure': 'everything revolves around it where matters of leisure and all other forms of what is not self-evident – games, humour, religion and science – are concerned' (Lengkeek, 1994, p. 237). This contrastructural reality is constantly exposed to encapsulation and exploitation by the rationally organized everyday world (see also Chapter 2). As soon as public authorities are concerned with the development of leisure or outdoor recreation facilities, they impose the internal logic of material reproduction (effectiveness and efficiency) upon recreational space. As in many other aspects of physical planning guidelines were sought: recommendations of x ha of public recreation space per thousand population, the land–water ratio in such projects and so on. Secondly, the 'contrastructural world' is a source of commercial exploitation (Lengkeek, 1994, p. 202). Many new contrastructural experiences become a prey of the market: trekking in the Himalayas, the romantic weekend in Paris or the existential experience in unspoiled nature areas. By constantly searching for niches in the consumer market the leisure dreams of many tourists become dependent on the logic of material reproduction.

Limitations of the Book

Every book has limitations which are either consciously adopted or are forced upon it by circumstances. The most important of these, at least of which we are aware, can be listed, as they form the structures that constrain all authors to a greater or lesser degree.

The experience of almost all of the authors is not only European but is strongly focused upon a restricted area of northwestern Europe. These are dominantly countries with mixed economies operating to varying degrees welfare–market economies with a substantial tradition of public planning intervention. This has implications in practice not only for 'who does what in recreation' (and 'who pays'), but for the existence of an organizational structure and instrumentation for intervention and, most important, an expectation among citizens that public bodies have a responsibility and justification for determining and pursuing some sort of public interest within this field.

The focus of this book is on the practice of intervention, especially intervention in pursuit of collective goals, rather than upon analysis as such. In part this is justified by the production over the last 20 years of a substantial body of academic work analysing various aspects of recreation or tourism as activities. In particular it is now possible to acknowledge the existence, as it was not a generation ago, of a distinct and conceptually mature economics, sociology and geography of leisure activities. The role of recreational enterprises within economies at levels ranging from the firm or project to the regional and national systems, the various roles of leisure within socialization and the spatial patterns are all now sketched in general terms sufficiently to create a common basis of understanding as an essential prerequisite for planning. What is still lacking, however, is a comprehensive and synthetic analysis of intervention itself: there are no recreation and tourism planning and management in the same sense as has been shaped for other sectors with a longer history of deliberate public intervention such as transport or housing. Certainly many issues directly related to recreation and tourism have not only been identified but are near the top of the political agendas of many public agencies and policies for these most certainly exist in abundance. The following chapters will refer to numerous policies for sport, cultural performance and collections, commercial tourism enterprises and social tourism, as well as for managing the economic, environmental and even cultural impacts of leisure developments. Not only are these produced by separate agencies at various scales, they are based upon discrete aspects of the analysis and rarely have much directly applicable relationship to each other. However, each of the contributors below has endeavoured to seek out such wider relationships.

Tourism and recreation can include an enormous variety of activities occurring within an equally wide range of environments and spatial scales. It was not our objective to attempt to cover all, or even a representative sample of these: we are content if the small selection of cases and applications is sufficient to prompt questions that apply much more widely or illuminate parts of the more general model. Each reader, we would hope, is in a position to substitute quite different illustrative cases, thus extending our model into fields unimagined by us.

References

Ashworth, G.J. (1992) Tourism in resource crisis: the need for new models, new concepts, new instruments. *Vrijetijd en Samenleving* 10(2/3), 69–87.

Bernstein, R.J. (1985) Introduction. In: Bernstein, R.J. (ed.) *Habermas and Modernity.* Polity Press, Cambridge, pp. 1–34.

Boorstin, D.J. (1961) *The Image – A Guide to Pseudo-events in America.* Harper & Row, New York.

Clark, G., Darrall, J., Grove-White, R., MacNaughten, P. and Urry, J. (1994) *Leisure Landscapes. Leisure, Culture and the English Countryside: Challenges and Conflicts.* Background Papers, Centre for the Study of Environmental Change, Lancaster University, CPRE Publications, London.

Dietvorst, A.G.J. (1992) Een model van toeristisch-recreatieve produktontwikkeling. *Vrijetijd en Samenleving* 10(2/3), 21–27.

Giddens, A. (1984) *The Constitution of Society. Outline of the Theory of Structuration.* Polity Press, Cambridge.

Habermas, J. (1991, orig. 1981) *The Theory of Communicative Action.* Vol. II. *The Critique of Functionalist Reason.* Polity Press, Cambridge.

Harvey, D. (1989) *The Condition of Postmodernity.* Basil Blackwell, Oxford.

Jansen-Verbeke, M.C. (1994) *Toerisme: Quo Vadis?* Inaugural Address, Erasmusuniversiteit, Rotterdam.

Knulst, W. (1993) Trends in het toeristisch consumentengedrag. Paper, Congress 'Vernieuwen in toerisme', NSC, Rotterdam, 2 Dec.

Lash, S. and Urry, J. (1994) *Economies of Signs and Space.* Sage Publications, London.

Lengkeek, J. (1994) Een meervoudige werkelijkheid. Een sociologisch-filosofisch essay over het collectieve belang van recreatie en toerisme. PhD thesis, Landbouwuniversiteit, Wageningen.

MacCannell, D. (1976) *The Tourist. A New Theory of the Leisure Class.* Schocken Books, New York.

Mullins, P. (1992) Cities for pleasure. *Built Environment* 18(3), 187–198.

Ryan, Chr. (1991) *Recreational Tourism: A Social Science Perspective.* Routledge, London.

Urry, J. (1992) The tourist gaze revisited. *American Behavioral Scientist* 36, 172–186.

Zukin, S. (1991) *Landscapes of Power. From Detroit to Disney World.* University of California Press, Berkeley, Calif.

I

Transformations by Producers

A logical beginning for a study of the transformation of the tourism–recreation product is to answer the seemingly simple question 'who produces this product?' which leads directly to the supplementary question 'what forces are powering the transformations?' The purpose of this section must be to introduce some of the answers to this question and to move from inventorizing producers to examining the differences in objective and the consequences of these differences in the transformation process. The transformations described in the introductory chapter can be seen as being driven by both the economic attitude of maximizing the economic profits of the tourism product provided by the commercial entrepreneurs and also the existential need of most people to escape from the world of everyday life. As a consequence of these decisive mechanisms recreation and tourism have increasingly become essential factors for change in both landscapes and societies throughout the world.

In Chapter 2 Lengkeek introduces the concept of counterstructure to elucidate the idea that recreation and tourism can be viewed not only as shallow amusement but as an attempt to bestow a new meaning to our tense and complex reality by constructing in a reflective mode a counterpart reality alongside the worlds of everyday life. The quest for some counterstructure is realized by materializing the imagined in specific holiday destinations, museums, rock concerts or survival weekends.

A long-standing and fundamental difficulty in tourism studies has been to identify segments of the tourism market. The core of the difficulty is that tourism can be segmented in a variety of different ways by different participants in the process and these classifications overlap. Relevant to the argument here are at least three different types of segmentation resulting in aspects of what is bundled together as tourism.

There are 'producer segmentations' (i.e. the packages of attractions and supporting services constructed by tourism intermediaries, the tour operators being the most obvious, which can be sold as similar, interchangeable products). These are the familiar holiday packages on offer from travel agents, the most easily recognizable producers within an industrial approach to tourism.

There are also, however, 'consumer packages' (i.e. those activities and services actually assembled by tourists which comprise their holiday experience). These are likely to be far more varied and may include a greater or lesser element of purchased producer packages, augmented and altered according to individual requirements. Logically from the viewpoint of the individual holidaymaker, it is the consumer who produces a unique product through the process of assembly from the various elements offered by both tourism and non-tourism facilities at the moment of consumption.

Thirdly, there are 'place-bound packages' (i.e. the functionally associated and spatially clustered selection of attractions and facilities that comprises the tourism place-product). In these packages services used by tourists may be also used by residents, and tourists may comprise only a marginal addition to the total users of many cultural facilities. Managers of spatial jurisdictions at various scales will produce tourism products based upon various synergies of resources.

To these three main types of producers can be added two further dimensions. First, a high degree of fragmentation is to be found within each of the above categories of producer. The tourism 'industry' is characterized by the existence of many small enterprises. There are of course major chains operating in some sectors, for example in hotels, travel agents and tour operators, but even here the market share of the largest producers is small in comparison with most other commercial sectors. Consumers are by definition producing individual holidays with evidence that these decreasingly share common characteristics. Even governments responsible for politically defined jurisdictions operate through different agencies on different spatial scales, resulting in a multiplicity of producing units competing and overlapping at different levels of the spatial hierarchy. Secondly, the tourism–recreation product is produced by publicly responsible agencies, private commercial enterprises and private non-profit-making associations. The consequences of this distinction in ownership, and thus objectives and frequently working methods, are quite different answers to the 'what', 'in what quantity', 'for whom' and 'where' questions.

The balance of responsibility between these sectors has in most countries evolved incrementally as a result of numerous separate decisions, made on criteria long forgotten, leaving a legacy that is difficult to justify on any logical grounds. Not surprisingly it has proved especially vulnerable to proposals for shifting this balance of responsibilities between sectors, a theme that dominates the initial contributions.

There are many consequences of the existence of this multiplicity of producers, each busy with the shaping of particular products for particular markets for a variety of goals intrinsic and extrinsic to the agencies themselves. These raise broad topics which by their various nature cannot be comprehensively covered but only exemplified in a few representative cases.

Priestley considers the government, mainly at the national scale, as the producer, not in the sense that state enterprises **are** concerned with the exclusive final delivery of tourism services to the consumer but as the coordinator and initiator of the pace and direction of change and the establishment of important public collective goals in tourism development. Tourism is viewed as an engine of regional, and ultimately national, economic development, in which the government uses tourism to achieve other objectives in the destination regions. The Spanish experience of planned national tourism development, however recent, is still relatively longer than many Mediterranean imitators and its lessons therefore are particularly apposite.

The role of a 'third force' that is neither public nor commercial in its institutional structure and objectives, namely the voluntary non-profit private sector which occupies a key important and generally underinvestigated position, is considered by Lengkeek using principally Dutch cases which stand as representative, at least for similar European societies.

A welcome counter to the Eurocentric bias of the preceding cases, Binkhorst and van der Duim describe the case of the increasingly popular hill trek as part of the holiday product on offer in Thailand. Here all three categories of producers can be identified and, even more useful, the quite different objectives of each of these leads to a range of possible conflicts. The visitors add this element of authentic culture and exoticism to their holiday package, while the national government tourism agencies see the hill tribes as a means of extending the Thai product on offer from Bangkok and the coastal resorts, thus reaping economic gains. The experience of the third element, the local producers, poses the most interesting questions. Entrepreneurs from both outside and inside the tribes operate the logistics of the treks using selected aspects of tribal custom to shape a product peopled by the tribesmen themselves. The product is a transformation derived from the tribal culture but in turn is transforming the resource from which it is created. This raises many policy issues whose ramifications go far beyond the well-being of the tourism industry and beyond the scope of this book, but which are an important context within which tourism development occurs.

Many of the above issues are brought together in Herbin's case of French mountain tourism, which, although ostensibly drawn at the regional scale, in practice raises issues of far more general relevance, especially the resolution of conflict between local and supralocal interests in tourism destination areas.

Herbin describes the various stages in the transformation of the natural resource in the French Alps. What had for centuries been regarded as merely a desolate barrier to communication was transformed into a major tourism resource through a combination of the aesthetic revaluation of such areas by the European Romantic movement of the 19th century, together with new transport and sports technology. The railway, the cable car, the ski and the bobsleigh vitalized a natural environment for the exploitation of a new form of tourism, 'winter sports', originally organized by and sold to western Europeans. Success over two generations has now resulted in the Alpine regions suffering from what are now perceived to be excessive numbers of tourists in winter (and to a lesser degree in summer) seasons. This resource–demand discrepancy is now resulting in many undesirable features. Intensive building activities have led to the multiplication of mundane unifunctional winter resorts. The natural resource itself is being modified: mountains too steep for skiing are changed with the help of dynamite; forests on slopes that interfere with an ideal ski-run are simply removed; and if snow is not available snow-guns ensure the desired leisure fun. All this raises many policy and planning issues that Herbin discusses in the context of interaction between the interests and goals of local populations, private investors, public authorities and not least the tourist. These raise matters of relevance not only to Alpine communities but to all natural resource-based tourism development.

2

Materializing the Imagined: on the Dynamics and Assessment of Tourist–Recreational Transformation Processes

J. Lengkeek

Department of Sociology, Agricultural University, Hollandseweg 1, 6706 KN Wageningen, The Netherlands.

Understanding Changes

Leisure phenomena such as recreation and tourism constitute important areas of praxis in public policy and market exchange. The tourist industry is worldwide one of the more dynamic production sectors. Recreation and tourism have far-reaching consequences, changing or 'transforming' radically our material and symbolic environment. The transformation model Dietvorst presents in the foregoing chapter illustrates relationships, structures and processes in this transformation. The question nevertheless remains how to understand and assess the transformations.

In The Netherlands, as in many modern societies, time spent on labour constitutes only a relatively small part of the total time-budget when compared to the time spent on leisure activities (SCP, 1994, p. 416). Our environment is of tremendous relevance to the activities and meanings that are related to leisure and this explains the extent of the transformation processes. It is remarkable that the implications for future developments and intervention are so difficult to assess. In order to be able to attempt such an assessment at least three conditions should be discerned. The first has been indicated by Lyotard (1984). He characterized our era as 'the end of the great narratives' and implied that this hampers our identification of large-scale challenges and solutions. The second is that most experts still have difficulties in turning free time into a domain of professional reflection and judgement. And thirdly, recreation and tourism are difficult to grasp as serious objects of study because they fall within the realm of the imagination – some might

17

scornfully say illusion – and tend to be associated with connotations of triviality, superfluity and unnecessary luxury.

In the current debates on this subject we can roughly identify two radically opposing positions. On the one hand we see a no-nonsense attitude towards maximizing the economic profits of product development: recreation and tourism are a major source of income and work, and in that respect a material and, sometimes the only, legitimate basis for spatial reconstruction and management. On the other hand from the ecological standpoint recreation and tourism are seen as threats to sustainability, because they involve large-scale impacts of human activity on the ecology: they even jeopardize the true meaning of nature. It follows, therefore, that they must be controlled just like any other source of pollution and destruction.

The analytical transformation model offers only a step in the assessment of what actually happens. Moreover, we need criteria that apply fundamentally to the evaluation of far-reaching material and symbolic implications of recreational and tourist action and the transformation processes they embody. In this chapter I will sketch some contours for the evaluation of this transformation. As an introduction to this complex problem I first give a brief overview of developments in recreational and tourist policy in The Netherlands. After this I will present a theoretical framework that leads to four different but related dilemmas. These make a possible context for the evaluation of current and future prospects.

Recreation and Tourism as Collective Concerns

Although nowadays it is difficult to be conscious of the historical roots of recreation and tourism, the debates in The Netherlands on the collective interest of leisure, on freedom and on the social value of leisure activities go back to ancient times and have a much broader cultural context. For two and a half thousand years Europeans have carried on an intense moral discussion about the way to fill existence. This drew on old Classical traditions: the tension between an industrious existence and a reflective life. The first was the realm of necessity, worldly and social. The second enabled privileged social groups to develop an intellectual and moral superiority which qualified them for a leading political role. At the same time too great a distance from the demands of everyday life was considered a threat to social reliability. Human transactions were judged on the basis of these two principles and were linked to human fulfilment and the continuation of society. What we now define as free time was looked on more as a morality relating to social involvement and distance than a concept of time.

In The Netherlands as well as in other European countries the moral debate was linked in the 19th century to two processes that appeared simultaneously. The one process has a cultural-historical background. From the ideals of the Enlightenment sprang egalitarian ideologies in which the recognition and elevation of the individual were central. The active uplifting of the general level of civilization, socialism and enlightened liberalism were directed to allow more social groups to participate in what were previously the prerogatives of the élite. Free time became defined as 'useful' time and necessary for development of a fully-fledged individual. In the tradition of Rousseau, free nature represented the ideal setting for true insight and true personal development (see for example Beckers, 1989).

The other process came from industrialization and the rational organization of production. Working hours and non-working hours were sharply differentiated. For factory workers this meant they lost autonomy over a great deal of their day (the bosses' time). This had to be compensated for with autonomy in free time (Beckers and van der Poel, 1990, p. 56). The struggle for free time was in fact a struggle for a fairer return for labour: a healthy decent life, social development and education, and autonomy over some part of one's time.

Achieving a reconciliation between the demands of a capitalist production system (such as cheap disciplined labour) and social values (human worth) was a central task of the modern State in development, as can be seen in the case of The Netherlands during the 20th century (Thoenes, 1962). The guarantees of rewards for labour (money, social security, free time) tended to take the sting out of the class struggle. The reconciliation consisted of promoting the conditions for economic development on the one hand and the provision of collective care and facilities on the other. The State also took upon itself the care of collective leisure facilities by means of legislation, as in the case of the regulations governing working hours and provisions. State intervention in free time took more comprehensive shape after the Second World War. Until the 1970s conservation of natural areas and the experience of nature were still closely related to each other. There was scarcely any question of a conflict between protecting nature and promoting recreation. Recreation in natural surroundings meant socially desirable compensation for the inadequate and austere living conditions of large groups of urbanites. There had to be light, fresh and pure air and a healthy life for everyone.

In the first decades after the Second World War the problem of recreation was stated in terms of compensation. The rebuilding of the ravaged nation, the urbanization, the industrial expansion, the rationalization of agricultural production and the extension of the traffic infrastructure that followed contributed to a loss of free open space and a decline in the physical quality of the environment. The creation of more dense recreational space became an object of primary national importance and the words used to define these issues were very much the same as those used today to refer to ecological issues. The main aim of outdoor recreation policy was to take care of the growing stream of day recreationists (the 'trek outdoors'), the acquisition of large-scale areas for 'green facilities' close to urban concentrations and the stimulation of development plans for regions and specific recreational activities.

In the 1970s a second period of outdoor recreation policy can be distinguished, characterized by its technical approach and the furtherance of common participation. Recreation was considered a collective good, a right for everyone. The main task now was how to find the planning instruments to fulfil these collective ambitions. The coming into being of inter-municipality cooperation, a necessary condition for claims on government grants, increased the complexity of public involvement. The legitimation of outdoor recreation policy became self-evident and was unquestioned.

A third period in the development of policy – that of commodification and strategic action – can be distinguished from the beginning of the 1980s. Suddenly in the 1970s economic growth had halted. Public policy faced other, urgent priorities. There was rapidly growing unemployment and efforts had to be made to start up the national economy again. 'Rolling back the Welfare State' has certainly not been a prerogative of The Netherlands. However, the Dutch State was particularly active in rethinking the tasks, possibilities and responsibility of the State. Recreational policy was stripped of most of its legitimation. Tourism became the equivalent of economic profit and benefit. The two positions I mentioned in my introduction became articulated and were only contested for strategic reasons: the economic and the ecological standpoint. The old answers to the question 'what is the social importance of recreation and tourism?' appeared to be obsolete. The question 'what are recreation and tourism really?' is scarcely raised for strategic reasons as long as 'money' provides a convincing answer. The reduction of the problem of recreation and tourism to the purely economic, its importance in terms of the amounts of money involved, silenced any debate on social meaning.

State and Market as Part of the Problem

The responsibility and position of the State have been specified in the professional Welfare State as 'something *for* society' and as a response to society, implying an outside stance by the administrative system. An 'outside position' has also been accorded to the production system which legitimates itself by providing goods according to expressed 'needs' or demand, and following changes in taste, possibilities and social values, as if real social change only takes place within a world of citizens and consumers. In capitalist societies the debate concerning the active role of both State and market has lost most of its political relevance and has been banished to the academic world. In this section I want to discuss the theoretical interpretation of change (and transformation) that includes the particular developments in both State and market as a part of the process of social change, and therefore as a part of the problems of contemporary society too.

Habermas (1989, 1991, 1992) explains the development of Western society as a process of rationalization. With the origin of modern capitalist society, State and market turned into separate subsystems of action, each characterized by goal-directed rational action. Administrative rule and money are the new transformations of power. This power no longer operates on the basis of ideology or beliefs but on the basis of amoral efficiency and effectiveness.

Habermas in his all-encompassing analysis of the transformation of modern society pointed to different processes of change. He sees society as dependent on two fundamental processes: communicative action and material reproduction. Symbolic reproduction, as the main implication of communicative action, equips us with common definitions of reality that enable communicative action and mutual understanding. He calls these shared conceptions of reality *Lebenswelt* or life-world. These conceptions refer to culture (shared traditions, common interpretations), society (social integration, norms) and personality (socialization, responsible and predictable individuals). Communicative action involves a circular process: life-world as common understanding is the basis for communication, but is also the result of communication. Material reproduction means maintaining and adapting physical and organizational or social structures. Action is goal-directed. Instrumental action establishes the most direct relationship between goal and realization. Coordination of goal-directed action is increasingly based on formalized means. Those formalized rules or money-based exchanges do not evoke continuing discussion: meaning and value are made clear and fixed. Because means do not depend on continuous communication or negotiation they further the efficiency of goal-directed action. Often one depends on others for realization: then success is unpredictable. Strategic action is the kind of goal-directed action that influences the social environment and favours success.

Increasing rationality as a central characteristic of social development comes down to administrative and economic action and rests to a growing extent on formal means. This allows a greater complexity of instrumental relations. Economic action implies maximizing the relationship between investments and profit with the help of technology. A system of rules allows the State to become a bureaucracy. As a consequence, State and market turn into more or less independent social subsystems. The good functioning of the subsystems requires the submission of social individuals. Power, formerly supported by symbolic meanings rooted in the life-world, is transformed into a depersonalized, amoral force. In the meantime the life-world also rationalizes. There is an increasing reflection on truth, rightness and expressive standards. People choose more consciously and critically. Paying the lowest price for the highest quality is one example of rationality.

A central dilemma in Habermas' theory is the threat by subsystems imposing their system 'needs' of rational functioning on the life-world and ruling out communication about good or bad, right or wrong. Nevertheless, the increased rationality and criticism of the life-world of the operation of the subsystems might oppose this threat. Where this opposition fails he speaks of 'colonization of the life-world'.

From the perspective Habermas offers, the developments in State and market are part of the changes our society is going through and are also part of the social problems we are confronting. If the efficiency and effectiveness of State or market organizations define the material shape and location, and even the symbolic aspects of leisure provisions, then we must critically involve State and market in the evaluation of these transformation processes. In this respect we are confronted with a multi-faceted problem of recreation and tourism: a heritage of large-scale and standardized areas; the change from a range of provisions and qualities deliberately offered on behalf of freedom of choice to consumer sovereignty limiting choice to the most successful results of exchange between market and powerful consumer groups; and finally the inability of officials to redefine the meaning of recreation and tourism as a collective concern. The unawareness of the challenge results in a loss of a normative basis which could be used to compare recreation and tourism to other spatial claims and functions.

Everyday Life and Other Realities

The most central challenge, ignored in the process of the rationalization of the subsystems of State and market, is still to deepen our understanding of recreation and tourism as features of social change. Only from a proper understanding can we draw any legitimation for intervention or non-intervention.

Various studies in the field of leisure have stressed the importance of recreational or tourist experiences as attempts to escape everyday life and to seek new worlds (Mannell and Iso-Ahola, 1987). Cohen, for example, introduced the notion of 'the centre out there' into tourism studies, a concept borrowed from Victor Turner's exploration of pilgrimage (Turner, 1973; Cohen, 1979). Most puzzling is the essence of the other world of experience. Why do we oppose other worlds to our everyday experiences?

If certain leisure activities such as recreation and tourism are alternatives to everyday life, the first question to be raised is 'what is everyday life?' The German sociologist Alfred Schutz (1973) concluded that individuals construct shared conceptions of reality in which phenomena become accepted as natural or self-evident. Moreover, this natural world relates to the conviction that our physical and social world, nature and society constitute a whole made up of processes that are determined by higher laws. Schutz has been inspired by the work of the philosopher Edmund Husserl (1980, orig. 1911), who called this conviction 'the natural attitude'. In the natural attitude, we suspend doubt about its existence. Husserl, and later Schutz, reasoned that reality in this sense is not identical with 'objective reality'. Man has no unequivocal means to determine objective reality. Husserl referred to Descartes, who accepted his ability to think as the only proof of his existence: '*Cogito ergo sum*'. Man attributes meaning to his inner and outer world. Only in this way is he able to 'know' these worlds. Of course our natural attitude is more fragmented than Husserl, many decades ago, could have imagined. We share many more convictions on a global scale as a consequence of time–space compression (Giddens, 1991). However, the post-modern proposition concerning 'the end of the great narratives' does not exclude the acceptance of personal or shared realities. The constructed reality appears as self-evident and inescapable, although our constructed reality shows tremendous differentiation. But when confronted with things that do not fit into our natural attitude we speak of abnormalities, miracles or interventions from the supernatural.

Schutz (1973, pp. 207–259) elaborated this line of thought in his paper 'On multiple realities'. From Henri Bergson he borrowed the idea that we construct different realities and that these vary according to the tension of consciousness (*attention à la vie*) that underlies a particular sense of reality. The highest tension of consciousness or state of 'wide-awakeness' means that the self is fully interested in life, in executing its plans and projects. In this state the self is directly confronted with empirical experiences. In the lowest tension of consciousness there is very little interest in this confrontation. Between these two opposing states there is, in principle, an unlimited amount of planes of consciousness or states of awareness. Correspondingly we can imagine varying 'finite provinces of meaning' and we bestow some specific sense of reality on each of them. In fact our experiences in any 'province of meaning' show a specific cognitive style.

To clarify the notion of cognitive style, we first focus on Schutz's interpretation of Bergson's *attention à la vie*. The tension of consciousness is linked to three types of action, each with different time perspectives:

- action as an ongoing process (*actio*);
- action as a performed act (*actum*);
- the anticipated, projected or imagined action.

The dimension of time is of crucial importance here. The conscious subject has constantly to process heterogeneous information. According to Bergson, our states of consciousness are not separate experiences. Experiences succeed each other fluently in time (Bergson, 1989, orig. 1903). The constant stream of experience is irreversible. But there is a change of quality in experience (nothing remains the same from one moment to next), and the past, the recollection, is constantly involved in the ongoing experience of time. The physical time, measurable by chronometers, and inner psychic time do not necessarily coincide. Physical or cosmic time is movement in time and space in the outer world. The inner time, or *'durée'* as Bergson called it, is connected with the past and the future by recollections and anticipations. Our everyday life processes are linked to a high tension of consciousness and a strong sense of *durée*. Time is extremely actual there. The more the organization of everyday life is tightened, the more this time dimension dominates: we feel harried.

Consciousness of our action arises when we step out of our ongoing process of acting in the present. We take a reflective glance at acts we have performed. But also our ongoing acting has been partly anticipated. Anticipations are imaginations of our acts as if they had already been performed. In both types of action, *acta* and anticipations, there is a reflective condition. As Schutz (1973, pp. 210 and 214) states, meaning is not a quality inherent in certain experiences which emerges in our ongoing acts, but the result of retrospection into the past or the (imagined as if performed) future.

The understanding of our own finiteness, the time perspective of our own, inevitable death, is one of the most fundamental incentives to take action and to evaluate our actions in terms of success or failure. At the same time, we suspend the overt sense of our finiteness within our everyday 'natural attitude'. According to Schutz this creates a specific composition of everyday reality, a 'cognitive style' that can be characterized along the following 'parameters':

- a high tension of consciousness;
- a specific 'suspension' of doubt concerning the finiteness of our individual existence;
- a prevalent form of spontaneity (based upon projects and characterized by the intention of bringing about the projected state of affairs);
- a specific form of experiencing one's self;
- a specific form of sociality, the common intersubjective world of communication and social action;
- a specific perspective of time and space.

Schutz mentions in his list of characteristics of cognitive style only time, but adds later in his discussion also a notion of space (and standard space), following the same line of thought.

This phenomenological discussion seems remote from policy for recreation or tourism. But other realities can be understood as a breaking away from the high tension of consciousness. In other realities we can even enjoy the suspension of doubt. We can turn to other experiences of sociality or return to a lower speed of time. Because most social scientists are as preoccupied as Schutz by the intriguing question of how social life and interpersonal coordination are possible at all, they have tended to focus only on everyday reality and leave the debate on the real essence and diversity of reality to the philosophers.

Many areas of experience can be understood from the perspective presented here. The religious experience transcends everyday notions by suspending earthly projects or finiteness. The worldwide habit of transcending the here and now by taking drugs changes our perception of reality by changing all our perception chemically. When children play they can transform dolls into living beings and themselves into dangerous animals. The joker, reversing things as they normally seem, can take control of the seriousness of the moment for a short period of time. The theorist detaches himself from the necessity of conceptions that are necessarily useful or workable in everyday life. The beach tourist closes his/her eyes and gets back to an inner *durée* that feels more appropriate and is less influenced by harried standard time.

The specific quality of other realities may be that they are not as empirical as the everyday cognitive style requires. Truth, or words, may even spoil the experience. In this way language as the instrument of everyday common sense loses much of its adequacy. Communication in these other realities depends partly on other vehicles: 'you know what I mean?' The drug addict giggles, believers indulge in speechless togetherness. In religious communication often impossible metaphors – laying your heart in Jesus' hands – add to empathical understanding. The scientist may even stretch the importance of language as the format of the formula much further than we do in everyday communication.

Other realities could be understood by their peculiar cognitive style, changing the 'normal' or 'natural' parameters of everyday life: another tension of consciousness; the suspension of doubt and a different position in relation to 'truth'; a different option for bringing about certain states of affairs or preventing them taking place; a different relation of the self to social roles and sanctions, and a specific awareness of subjectivity (the real me, freed from external claims); another feeling of sociality as a transcending mode of *'communitas'* or as ultimate privacy; a change of time perspective condensing or expanding the standardized *durée*; and a different sense of place.

Counterstructure and the Dynamics of Realities

Although everyday language may lose much of its usefulness, we may share our fantasies, our religious experiences or our interest in the past or the exotic to a large extent with others. Even scientists are locked up 'together' in their ivory tower. The communication within different realities follows specific media. Language may serve as a means allowing some sort of 'osmosis' between different realities. But interviewing our fellow recreationist never fully reveals the true experiences. The empathy in what the Germans call the *'Aha-Erlebnis'* may be more important for a communicative exchange in other realities, because there we are scarcely dependent on language for the coordination of action. Nevertheless, through different means of communication there are reciprocal influences within and between realities.

Other realities are not only possible and relevant as shared, intersubjective experiences. They are in some way historically and systematically linked to the cognitive style of the everyday, social and shared, cognitive style: as a distancing from certain parameters or as an allocation of meaning by altering or stressing some of the parameters. As an example we can formulate the hypothesis that in a modern era of excessive information and tense daily projects we turn also to a more reflective type of action, which explains romanticism, a growing historical interest or nostalgia. Recreation and tourism can be seen not only as some depthless amusement but as a diverse attempt to bestow a new meaning on our tense and complex reality by constructing in a reflective/projective mode a counterpart reality along the different parameters of cognitive style. This other style may reflect sheer beauty or beastly cruelty. As Cohen and Taylor (1992) stated, 'a murder a day keeps the doctor away'. There are many examples of leisure activities that refer to socially less acceptable but probably existential tendencies in human nature: cock- or bull-fighting, hunting, risking one's own or someone else's life, 'gun-fun', hooliganism, sexual fantasies, etc.

As far as other realities are shared provinces of meaning they are also structured. They are not coincidental. The self-evidence of our routines draws a boundary around everyday reality that we cross when we leap into another bounded and structured reality. Turner pointed to an analogous liminal aspect in pilgrimage. Pilgrimage is a temporary distancing from everyday life that places the individual 'in another existential context' (Turner, 1973, p. 192). There is this separation from the familiar situation, a transition and a crossing of a threshold 'in and out of time', and then the entering into the new situation (Turner, 1973, p. 214).

The transcending experience of the pilgrim coincides with physical distance and provisions (the *camino*, the lodge, the sanctuary). Turner used the concept of anti-structure to delineate the other world, organized around another 'centre' than our normal life. The anti-structure allows the individual to be in a different context. The comparison between pilgrimage and tourism, and the use of the metaphor of anti-structure are tempting. Sociologists in the field of tourism have nevertheless adopted Turner's viewpoint too simply (Cohen, 1979; Graburn, 1983; Boissevain, 1986). The problem with Turner's concept of anti-structure is that it remains quite unclear. How is the social structure of the hosting country linked to the experiences of the pilgrim or the tourist into one concept of anti-structure?

In the following part I will rephrase the concept of anti-structure in three steps: first a linguistic adaptation, then an attempt to connect the different layers of the 'host world' and the imagining guest brought together in one structured setting, and, finally, a clarification of the structural dynamics of other realities.

First, the term anti-structure does not sound adequate. The other reality is not necessarily 'anti,' that is opposed to, everyday life. The relationship between realities may vary from close by to very distant, positive to negative, but in principle they can be compared with melodies which sound at the same time. My suggestion is to follow what in musical terminology is known as 'counterpoint'. Adapting the term to the structural realms of non-everyday realities I propose the term 'counterstructure', consisting of two components stemming from the same linguistic Latin source. Counterstructural realities may vary according to different cognitive styles and corresponding states of affairs. Individuals can alternate with different perspectives or different 'melodies' which bring them into different symbolic and structural contexts. The other world might be radically different from normal life, opposing everyday values, indifferent to them, broadening our possibilities, or simply reflecting everyday habits within a mirror of a completely different setting. Because these settings or contexts have their own style and logic, apart from their mutual connections and interrelationships with everyday life, it is insufficient to research and evaluate counterstructural experiences in everyday terms alone.

Secondly, to what extent can we speak of a shared, counterstructural other world? Searching for certain experiences, putting everyday reality into parentheses and changing the cognitive style, travellers transform the outer world into tourist experiences. The greater the distance from home, the more drastic the transformation facilitated. Does this sensation produce a new structure, since most of the meaning of tourism is not primarily induced or even recognized by local groups, but only by interpretations made from a considerable distance, in some 'guest-land'? As far as the experience of the traveller is a purely subjective phenomenon, there are, in principle, no structural changes at all, only changes in the individual. As tourists we experience a change of world as soon as we cross the national border. The life elsewhere seems to be a fantastic play where actors underpin our sensations in the roles of greengrocer, labourer, farmer, waiter or mechanic. The so-called tourist product is both a product structured by different actors and the everyday here-and-now world of the host community. We can imagine that different layers of meaning cover the same objective elements. Realities and fields of interaction from different perspectives roof over each other. Nevertheless, they constitute together a state of affairs that changes over time in empirical and symbolic aspects. The same objective world, although impossible to know, gives the setting and limitations for the different intersubjective context of relevance. Even though we do not realize it we are part of someone else's worlds. We start to notice this context of relevance as soon as we feel urged to oppose a particular state of affairs or when we find out that we can profit from it. And as soon as we realize this we start to interpret this world and act according to the rules we try to establish together. In other words, whenever someone bestows meaning on my existence I can become part of the other's world, for better or for worse. Most people are part of several realities in this sense. It is the dynamic state of affairs that can be linked to the theoretical concept of structure (Bourdieu, 1989).

In the third place, there is more that can be said about the structural dynamics. If osmosis takes place between these different contexts of reality, their dynamics can be linked to internal and external processes. I will concentrate here on the internal processes. The concept of 'doxa' provides a key for understanding the internal dynamics. Doxa is, as Hannah Arendt formulates it, the opinion that is modelled in the intersubjective *discours* (Arendt and Gardner, 1989). In other words, the organization of the absolutely right. Doxa is what defines value and validity within strict limits of a specific context of interaction and shared meaning. In tourism and recreation it relates to the right appreciation, the real thing, the proper behaviour (aggressive or respectful), the right clothes (the boating shoes or the golf trousers) or devices (the sophisticated fishing-rod or grandma's bike), the true knowledge of attractions (understanding history or nature), and therefore the right people, us against them. Most leisure experiences have a traceable history of interactions and communications originally organized in settings of religious ceremonies (e.g. sports, theatre), clubs or other social groups.

Doxa draws its content from a source of knowledge that Husserl (1980, orig. 1911) specified as life-world (*Lebenswelt*), our shared pre-given and immense set of notions that can be mobilized within the perspectives of the 'and so forth' and 'I can do it again'. Doxa implies a thematization or typification of this life-world, in which certain notions become relevant and others not. The doxa defines any state of affairs as *the* state of affairs and is, therefore, the precondition for structure, i.e. counterstructure. Bourdieu (1989) developed his field theory from this idea. In his perspective, any social structure is built up around a joint definition of the situation, which defines not only the shared reality but also the values and the relative importance of the different positions of the participants in the interaction field. The definition or doxa has to be agreed upon. So, in every field there is a potential for a change of doxa that changes the values and as a consequence changes positions within the field. Doxa is the opinion of those in the position to be absolutely right. In Bourdieu's field theory every social structure of doxa and positions is an overt, implicit or possible struggle of people trying to get the maximum out of the values that are defined by the doxa. The means (or capital as Bourdieu calls them) to be successful in this struggle are limited and unequally distributed in the field. Bourdieu stretches his concept of capital from the economic to social and cultural resources. As soon as scarcity of some means has been overcome, the valued objectives devalue according to some economy of social action. The winners in the field then have to change the doxa in order to preserve scarcity and to maintain their positions. In this respect we might presuppose an ongoing struggle between claims on notions offered by the life-world.

The relevance of the field theory for the counterstructural point of view is threefold. The doxa determines an inside and an outside perspective, in fact the normal and the abnormal, as Foucault suggested (see de Folter, 1987). The doxa of everyday life defines 'otherness'. Moreover in everyday life some gateways to specific forms of otherness are blocked by status and power groups who consider that otherness as their prerogative. As an example, the leisure behaviour of social élites has always been an objective for lower-status groups. Lower-status groups also find their own territories in counterstructure.

Finally, beyond the limits of everyday life we can see a myriad of fields where people share not only their imaginations but also the right conceptions of how their imaginings should be conceived of, experienced and reproduced. Each field can be understood properly only in terms of its own doxa and dynamics. It is here that counterstructure offers 'other possibilities' as regards content. By bracketing everyday action it allows us a more reflexive condition (for example, a historical consciousness) or a more spontaneous involvement in ongoing action (conditioning a state of oblivion or direct sensation). The more our everyday reality is organized around rational principles, the more our counterstructure specifically works as an extension of, a response to and a commentary on it. Leisure is not so much a response to an everyday reality that is only specified in terms of work – leisure being non-work – it is a response to an everyday reality that is constrained by its own rationality.

Dilemmas of Materializing Possibilities

If we try to draw conclusions from the foregoing in order to evaluate transformation processes then we have to determine in advance that counterstructure (in all its various appearances) is a historically specified feature of a more and more rapidly changing (to avoid the term 'modernizing' or even 'post-modern') society. It is within the realm of counterstructure that we realize or materialize our other possibilities. In the quest for some counterstructure probably no one is excluded, not even the self-conscious intellectual despising trivial tourism, staying at home in his free time and burying himself in books and exclusive debates (Boorstin, 1963; Adorno, 1977). But the counterstructure is also an aim for the rational, organizational forces within our paramount everyday reality: the State and the market. The State attempts to control and regulate the counterstructural worlds, or even redistribute privileges of distancing. The market aims at the exploitation of counterstructure as a source of experiences and motives. But as soon as counterstructural experiences have become incorporated in the everyday reality they lose their specific meaning. Then the quest for counterstructure goes on, a search for new horizons, new possibilities, new provinces of meaning.

The question we face is what we should do with groups of people indulging in their worlds of other possibilities and therefore constantly transforming the state of affairs. I will now sketch four main dilemmas in relation to the transformation processes, which might offer a step towards deliberate legitimations and the resulting (non)intervention.

A gamut of possibilities

Diversity is a magic word nowadays, not only in marketing (filling every gap in the market), in public policy (in relation to emancipation of underprivileged social groups), in ecology (biodiversity) and in postmodern pluralist ideology. Nevertheless, it is necessary to know exactly why diversity is good. The rationale for diversity from the foregoing discussion is that worlds of otherness, the different opposing or coexisting fields, define their own rights of being from within and tend to reproduce themselves. Every world is seeking some space within the objective state of affairs. We must realize that they constitute worlds in themselves. Nevertheless, we do evaluate them from our everyday, paramount rationality that is organized around a high tension of consciousness, a specific suspension of doubt, dominated as a field by vested interests. As soon as we interfere from outside in counterstructural settings we do so in terms of instrumental policy, strategy or everyday ethics. But forbidding 'other' experiences evokes an escape to new areas. Constantly using 'other' experiences as a source for market production may drive the consumer crazy. The standpoint we take should depend on a proper insight into these processes.

The issue is important for both planning and research. For example, one question is how to actually access worlds of meaning that the policy-maker or the marketing expert wants to become involved in. This is an even more important problem for policy-makers because they are most distant from the fields in question. The marketing expert will try to intervene by a rapid process of trial and error. At stake is how to transform material resources such as space, infrastructure and objects according to counterstructural field values.

The dilemma of different existing worlds raises questions. Is it possible to satisfy the demands of a field of reality optimally and avoid a mix of opportunities that satisfies nobody's imagination? Another question relates to how compatible or conflicting different realities are.

The nature conservationist feels offended when confronted by the hunter who uses the same resource for his/her experience of otherness. Sometimes, however, a strategic combination in transforming resources can be found that enables a peaceful coexistence of different worlds of experience, or even creates the most feasible conditions for reproduction; the ecotourist spends money during his/her journey to the tropical rainforest, and provides a strong material basis for nature conservation.

Dominance of claims

Opportunities for some worlds of imagination dominate others. A main task for public policy might be to keep an open and critical eye on power groups that claim an absolute truth or exert an unduly strong influence, thus overshadowing the weak. The market only tends to favour the groups with the largest purchasing power, leaving other groups out or with a very limited freedom of choice.

An example can be derived from the previously mentioned tension between the ecological and the tourist perspective. Some opinion-leaders and experts in the nature movement tend to give absolute value to biodiversity and the self-regulating capacities of 'ecosystems'. As a consequence there are strict, even calculable limitations to other human impacts and imaginings. There is nothing against optimizing conditions for self-regulating ecosystems, somewhere, but not as a totalitarian concept that overrules everything else.

The thinking holds for the euphoria accompanying the commercial success tourism has had in opening up every corner of the world, signposting every road, planting the hotel and catering industry everywhere, and adding amusement parks as standard ingredients. There is nothing against commercial product development so long as it is not the predominating image and omnivorous principle.

The most important planning question is that the choice for certain options is well reasoned and not the automatic consequence of strategic alliances between power blocs.

The logic of State and market

As we have discussed in the context of Habermas' theory, modern society has developed two main mechanisms to pursue our objectives: the State and its organizations, instruments, rules and collective provisions, and the market as the organization of production and exchange. Many sociologists have indicated that the nation State and the capitalist market are most typical of modern everyday social reality, marking the change from *Gemeinschaft* to *Gesellschaft*. But the two mechanisms have their own logic of efficiency and effectiveness that favours their internal performance and the success of their means.

The rigidity of administrative organizations and the extreme dynamics of the market have impacts on transformation processes that derive not from social values but from their own logic. These must at least be assessed. The outcomes of their action are difficult to survey because both systems of action coordination get more and more complicated and interwoven. The collective goals disappear behind the complexity. The outcomes may contradict each other, even leading to what Ulrich Beck indicated as 'risk society' (Beck, 1992). The paradox is that the underlying system rationality eventually turns into its opposite. A logical option is to bring a critical and creative element into public service as the rational organization of our collective interests. The constant debate on our common future, not only ecological but also social and cultural, is the only entrance to rational control of our own means. The task might not be to tighten the state organization but to make it more transparent and flexible.

The third dilemma seems a truism but most officials either fail or are unwilling to see themselves as part of a collective problem.

Exhaustion of resources

Changes in society contribute to the exploration of more and more possibilities for creating other realities next to our paramount existence. Many resources that we transform for materializing the other realities lie in history, in nature, in the nature of the human animal or in the life-world of other people.

The discussion surrounding sustainable development concentrates on only a part of our resources. The moment that State and market are involved in the reproduction and transformation processes of counterstructure they impose inevitably their everyday logic and rationality on the other realities. They tend to absorb as it were counterstructural worlds into everyday reality. This is exactly the reason why tourists and recreationists so often loathe being placed in the context of tourism or recreation, as if in their quest for counterstructure they are drawn back into a shared, everyday world. The real naturalist hates to be called a recreationist. The tourist often prefers to be a traveller finding a not evidently preconditioned confrontation with otherness. Of course, we cannot speak of 'the' tourist or recreationist, as Cohen (1979) and many others have shown. Some seek otherness more than others.

Certain conditions for the experience of otherness are scarcer than others or disappear more rapidly in the process of material and symbolic transformation. Some conditions are appropriated by specific groups and other people are shut out. Other conditions are so often reproduced that they are literally 'devalued' and their meaning dwindles.

The real paradox is that the more we are faced with rapid change and rationalized worldly affairs, the more we look for our other possibilities, desperately reconstructing what has gone or what actually never existed. The quest for authenticity is, by definition, a quest for the unreal in terms of everyday reality. The other reality, by the same reasoning, loses its meaning when put under the thumbscrews of everyday life. Nevertheless, it is meaning that we seek in another sense of time, another place, another sense of sociality, or another relationship with the self. The quest for other possibilities seems to be an essential, anthropological aspect of man in the face of particular social changes. We depend on resources for meaning that are threatened in various ways.

Final Remarks

The four dilemmas have a strong interrelationship. Specific fields of counterstructure come to the foreground only when we push dominant fields aside. Some fields stay out of reach of the State or the market because they are not substantial enough to evoke any intervention. Some fields expand their claims at the cost of other fields because the State and the market make rational use of them.

The dilemmas are grounded in common sense: whose interest prevails and whose is threatened; what diversity allows for freedom of choice; what control does one have over one's own possibilities in the face of bureaucracy or free-market competition; are ecological and economic resources the only ones we should care about? The theoretical considerations delineate the problem more clearly. What we see is an important world of reshaped realities and imagination. Different imagined worlds, especially when they depend on material conditions and limited space, clash and perish.

Defining a problem is but a condition for finding a solution; it never guarantees that the solution is simple, if there is a solution at all. Thinking about our resources, as indicated previously, is a challenge to the furthering of our collective interest (by intervention or restraint) and a crucial objective for our common future. It deals with the symbolic aspects of our environment. In fact, this task requires an enlarged sense of rationality that goes beyond the goal-directed organization of State and market. The Dutch case showed the opposite happening. In spite of that we must find ways to reason and understand an all-pervading field of human action that still gets attention only in the margins of science, political thinking and philosophy.

References

Adorno, T.W. (1977) *Kritische Modellen. Essays over de Veranderende Samenleving.* Van Gennep, Amsterdam.

Arendt, H. and Gardner, R. (1989) *The Realm of Humanitas: Response to the Writings of Hannah Arendt.* American University Studies, Series 5, Philosophy, No. 83. Lang, New York.

Beck, U. (1992) *Risk Society: Towards a New Modernity.* Sage, London.

Beckers, Th.A.M. (1989) Van natuuridealisme tot gedisciplineerd vermaak. De ontwikkeling van de sector openluchtrecreatie. In: van Doorn, H. (ed.) *Handboek welzijn.* Samsom, Alphen a/d Rijn.

Beckers, Th.A.M. and van der Poel, H. (1990) *Vrijetijd tussen vorming en vermaak. Een inleiding in de studie van de vrijetijd.* Stenfert Kroese, Leiden/Antwerp.

Bergson, H. (1989, orig. 1903) *Inleiding tot de metafysica. Met een inleiding van Jan Bor.* Boom, Amsterdam/Meppel.

Boissevain, J. (1986) Tourism as anti-structure. Paper presented at the Anthropology Seminar of the University of Utrecht.

Boorstin, D.J. (1963) *The Image; or What Happened to the American Dream.* Penguin, Harmondsworth.

Bourdieu, P. (1989) *Opstellen over smaak, habitus en het veldbegrip.* Van Gennep, Amsterdam.

Cohen, E. (1979) A phenomenology of tourist experiences. *Journal of the British Sociological Association* 13(2), 179–201.

Cohen S. and Taylor, L. (1992) *Escape Attempts. The Theory and Practice of Resistance to Everyday Life.* Routledge, London/New York.

de Folter, R.J. (1987) *Normaal en abnormaal: enkele beschouwingen over het probleem van de normaliteit in het denken van Husserl, Schütz en Foucault.* Historische Uitgeverij Groningen, Groningen.

Giddens, A. (1991) *Modernity and Self-identity: Self and Society in the Late Modern Age.* Polity Press, Oxford.

Graburn, N. (1983) The anthropology of tourism. *Annals of Tourism Research* 10(1), 9–33.

Habermas, J. (1989) *De nieuwe onoverzichtelijkheid en andere opstellen.* Boom, Amsterdam/Meppel.

Habermas, J. (1991, orig. 1981) *The Theory of Communicative Action.* Vol. I, *Reason and the Rationalization of Society.* Polity Press, Cambridge.

Habermas, J. (1992, orig. 1981) *The Theory of Communicative Action.* Vol. II, *The Critique of Functionalist Reason.* Polity Press, Cambridge.

Husserl, E. (1980, orig. 1911) *Filosofie als strenge wetenschap.* Boom, Amsterdam/Meppel.

Lyotard, J.F. (1984, orig. 1979) *The Postmodern Condition: A Report on Knowledge.* Manchester University Press, Manchester.

Mannell, R.C. and Iso-Ahola, S.E. (1987) Psychological nature of leisure and tourism experience. *Annals of Tourism Research* 14, 314–331.

Schutz, A. (1973) *Collected Papers.* Vol. I, *The Problem of Social Reality.* Martinus Nijhoff, The Hague.

SCP (1994) *Sociaal en cultureel rapport 1994.* Sociaal en Cultureel Planbureau, Staatsuitgeverij, Rijswijk.

Thoenes, P. (1962) *De elite in de verzorgingsstaat: Sociologische proeve van een terugkeer naar Domineesland.* Publikaties Sociologisch Instituut no. 7. Rijksuniversiteit Leiden, Leiden.

Turner, V. (1973) The center out there: pilgrim's goal. *History of Religions* 12(3), 191–230.

3

Evolution of Tourism on the Spanish Coast

G.K. Priestley

Universitat Autonoma de Barcelona, Departament de Geografia, Edifici B, E-08193 Bellaterra, Barcelona, Spain.

The analysis of the evolutionary processes which have transformed the development of tourism in Spain offers a particularly clear vision of some of the processes involved in tourism–recreation product development in general. The tourism model proposed identifies a number of direct interventions by producers which contribute to the transformation of the original resource. These include all kinds of planning activities. In the case of Spain, the development of tourist facilities along the Spanish coast reflects the differentiated impact of both public and private institutions in transforming the area into a tourist region.

The analysis of their contribution can easily be made for three main reasons. In the first place, the resources on which tourism was originally based were unexploited and unspoilt at the outset (López Palomeque, 1988). The country was politically ostracized and largely ignored by the rest of Europe, and economic development was limited. Internally the nation's energies were directed towards recovery from the Civil War and priority for investment was given to industrial and urban development. Moreover, tourism development prior to 1936 had not affected Spain to any significant degree, unlike Italian cities of cultural and historical interest and the coasts of southern France. Secondly, as a consequence of Spain's role today as one of the world's major tourist destinations, the study of the processes involved in the evolution of product development can be carried out on a large scale. Finally, the essentially homogeneous nature of the tourism–recreation product offered, both spatially and typologically, facilitates the identification of these processes. Typologically, the product traditionally offered has been based on the 3S trilogy of sun, sand and sea. It is therefore understandable that, spatially, the development of domestic and international tourism alike has been concentrated along the Mediterranean coastal fringe and on the island archipelagos.

Evolution and Characteristics of the Spanish Product

Evolution of international visitor numbers

The large-scale, rapid expansion of tourism supply and demand dates from about 1950 (see Fig. 3.1 and Table 3.1). The rate at which the number of international visitor arrivals increased accelerated throughout the 1950s, reaching explosive dimensions after 1960, at a time when no serious competitors had yet emerged. Fluctuations in arrival figures began to occur in 1965, coinciding with increases in the cost of living in Spain between 1962 and 1973 (these peaked in 1963 with a 13.1% increase in the cost of living) which were reflected in a rise in prices paid by tourists. Spanish tourism suffered the consequences of the worldwide economic crisis of 1973 in 1974 and 1975. Growth recovered thereafter, but increases in hotel prices caused a further recession in 1979. Growth stability was regained and maintained throughout the 1980s until 1989. By then, however, the upward trend in visitor numbers was no longer matched by income from foreign currency receipts. There was, therefore, a decline in economic viability, a situation which has continued until the present. The hallmark events of 1992 (Olympic Games in Barcelona and Universal Exhibition – EXPO – in Seville) have only served to temporarily disguise the general tendency.

Characteristics of the supply of and demand for accommodation

Hotel, self-catering and camp-site accommodation comprise a total of 1,950,881 beds, according to official statistics. Of these 49.9% are hotel beds, 20.6% are beds in non-hotel establishments, and 29.5% are places available in camp-sites (Ministerio de Industria, Comercio y Turismo, 1992). In fact, the number of self-catering beds is considerably higher than statistics would indicate, as many apartments available for tourists are not declared as such. The quality of accommodation is in general low: only 16% of hotel beds have 4- or 5-star rating, while almost half of the total (48.8%) have 1–2-star ratings. Camp-site rating is also relatively low.

The type of accommodation supply varies widely between regions (see Fig. 3.2). For obvious reasons of accessibility by road from France,

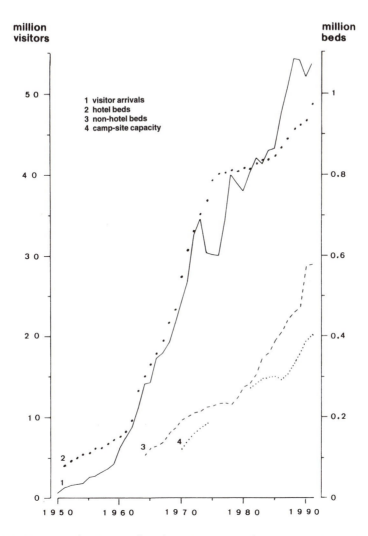

Fig 3.1. International visitor arrivals and tourist accommodation in Spain, 1950–1991.

camp-sites are concentrated along the Mediterranean coastline, extending from the French border as far as Valencia. Self-catering and hotel accommodation for short-term visitors constitute the supply on the island archipelagos, whilst these forms of accommodation are supplemented on the mainland coast by second homes, owned by both national city-dwellers and foreigners, and concentrated in certain areas, notably the Malaga, Valencia and Alicante coasts, and in Catalonia, where local ownership predominates.

Table 3.1. Tourism supply and demand in Spain, 1950–1991 (all statistics expressed in thousands). Sources: Ministerio de Información y Turismo, 1963–1974; Ministerio de Información y Turismo, 1975–1979; Ministerio de Industria, Comercio y Turismo, 1980–1992.

Year	Visitor arrivals	Hotel beds	Non-hotel beds	Camp-site capacity
1950	750	–	–	–
1951	1263	78.8	–	–
1952	1485	89.7	–	–
1953	1710	98.7	–	–
1954	1952	105.4	–	–
1955	2522	109.7	–	–
1956	2728	120.7	–	–
1957	3187	122.8	–	–
1958	3594	132.5	–	–
1959	4195	142.5	–	–
1960	6113	150.8	–	–
1961	7455	162.1	–	–
1962	8669	192.9	–	–
1963	10,932	263.9	–	–
1964	14,103	300.6	–	104.3
1965	14,252	328.1	–	120.8
1966	17,252	354.2	–	126.8
1967	17,859	384.0	–	135.8
1968	19,184	434.4	–	156.1
1969	21,682	465.4	–	171.2
1970	24,105	545.8	121.2	190.8
1971	26,758	612.3	–	–
1972	32,507	657.7	179.0	208.1
1973	34,559	699.4	–	211.6
1974	30,343	732.9	190.9	221.2
1975	30,122	785.3	–	224.0
1976	30,014	799.0	–	230.4
1977	34,267	803.7	–	232.2
1978	39,970	808.0	–	227.9
1979	38,902	806.6	–	246.4
1980	38,027	814.4	–	272.2
1981	40,129	811.7	270.9	280.6
1982	42,011	826.0	277.9	303.9
1983	41,263	834.5	292.7	344.3
1984	42,932	835.2	295.5	356.3
1985	43,235	843.3	298.0	385.4
1986	47,389	864.8	290.0	406.5
1987	50,545	886.7	304.0	438.0
1988	54,178	907.9	328.4	457.4
1989	54,058	918.6	335.8	470.4
1990	52,044	929.5	384.9	571.3
1991	53,495	972.8	402.7	575.3

Marked seasonality is characteristic of the pattern of demand, although this is less so on the Costa del Sol, and least marked in the Canary Islands. The majority of visitors arrive by road (although many of these are, in fact, day-trippers from France or are on their way through to Portugal and south-coast African ferry ports). Organized holidays make up 60% of all European visits to Spain. German and British visitors account for 60% of all overnight stays and 66% of air-charter travel, which is largely concentrated on the island groups.

Spatial Distribution of Tourism Facilities

The different forms of tourism facilities offered show clearly differentiated distribution patterns. Self-catering and hotel accommodation for short-term visitors is concentrated in a relatively small number of resorts, where high-density land occupation is often combined with high-rise building forms (Gaviria, 1974; Vasalló, 1983). The most notable examples are Benidorm (with over 200,000 beds), Torremolinos, Salou, Lloret de Mar and Calvia municipality (including the resorts of Santa Ponsa, Magaluf, Peguera), all of which can accommodate more than 100,000 visitors. Camp-sites, on the other hand, occupy, where possible, land adjoining long, unspoilt beaches or, alternatively, slopes leading down to unexploited coves. Second homes show a tendency towards a more ubiquitous location, extending the limits of existing coastal settlements, occupying formerly uninhabited beaches and coves, as well as wooded and even barren hill-slopes relatively easily accessible to the coast. In fact, the spatial impact of the low-density second homes in tourism (totalling 2,637,712 according to the 1991 census) is much greater than that of hotels in most areas.

The presence of additional tourism facilities as a means to diversifying the product and attracting visitors is of relatively little significance. It has already been stated that the Spanish tourism product is based on the sun, sand and sea combination, and few additional facilities are provided. The most notable exception is the construction of 38 golf-courses (28 eighteen-hole and 10 nine-hole courses) along 125 km of coastline in Malaga. In recent years there has been a rapid expansion of a relatively new type of tourist facility, namely marinas, which have been built in large numbers along the Mediterranean coast, especially in Catalonia. These, however, cater for domestic demand rather than the international market.

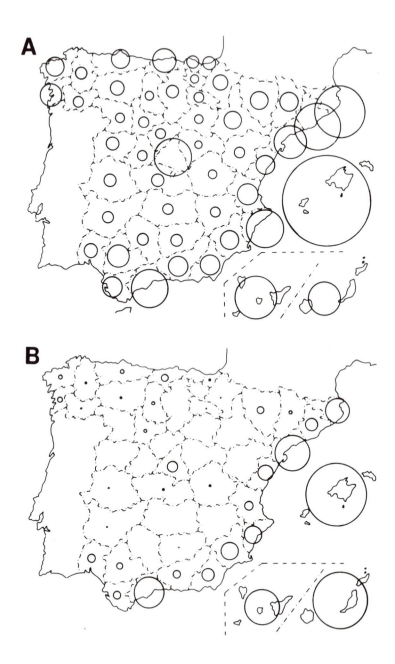

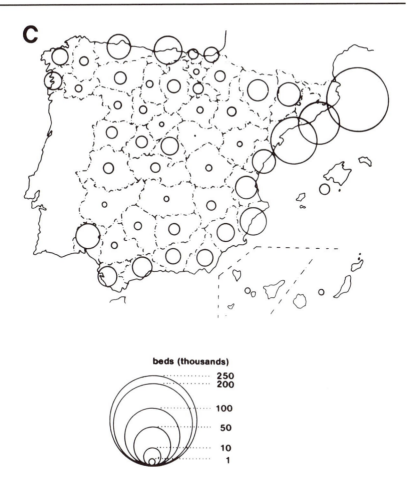

Fig 3.2. Distribution of tourist accommodation in Spain, 1992 (A = hotel beds; B = apartment beds; C = camp-site capacity).

Agents Involved in Shaping the Tourism–Recreation Product

Once the existing tourism–recreation product has been described, the next step is to identify the contribution made by each of the agents that together constitute the producers. In the case of Spain, three agents have played a major role in shaping the country's tourism–recreation product: the central government and, in recent years, autonomous regional governments after the transfer of legislative and administrative responsibilities; municipal authorities; and private investors.

National and autonomous governments

Two clearly differentiated periods of influence may be distinguished: the first, coincident with the period of the dictatorship of General Franco, which lasted until his death in 1975; and the second, with the period of democratic government, which has lasted from 1975 until the present, under the new Constitution.

1962–1975

Under the dictatorship of General Franco, the creation, in 1962, of a Subsecretariat of Tourism (Subsecretariado de Turismo) within the Spanish Ministry of Finance marked the official recognition of a tourism policy. Thereafter, tourism became one of the most tightly regulated sectors in the Spanish economy. Cals (1974) identified five types of measures through which the government exercised its control:

1. accommodation price authorization;
2. credits and loans;
3. provision of tourist accommodation;
4. development of infrastructures;
5. promotional campaigns.

Accommodation price authorization   Although both the maximum and minimum prices for accommodation were fixed by the government, only the maximum prices established were, in fact, of significance, as they were kept low in an attempt to ensure that they were internationally competitive. Control was excessive, as annual price increases were lower than the rate of inflation. The underlying objective, as in all tourism policy, was to achieve maximum numerical growth at any price. This policy had far-reaching effects on the tourism product, because it eventually led to the loss of the economic viability of international tourism. By as early as 1971 it was clear that the costs of services consumed by tourists were no longer compensated by the foreign exchange that they brought in. According to a report carried out by the Sindicato Nacional de Hostelería y Actividades Turísticas, a price rise of 68% would have been necessary to re-establish 1955 levels (Cals, 1974). Low prices tended to attract tourists with limited buying power, which was reflected in low average spending per tourist. As a result, hoteliers were unable to invest in plant renovation and modernization, or improve the quality of service by employing truly professional labour. The spectacular growth of the tourism sector in the early days enabled it to finance its own investments and, as a result, to develop parallel to and largely independent of the rest of the Spanish economy.

Credits and loans Financial support of the tourist sector was, in general, lacking. Measures typical of export sectors, such as tax rebates, export allowances and risk compensation, were not applied to tourism. Loans such as *Crédito Turístico* (originally known as *Crédito Hotelero*) were made available to the sector, but interest rates (7.25%) were not especially favourable. Only 15–35% of requests were granted annually and these only partially covered the cost of any single investment. By 1973, *Crédito Turístico* constituted only 6% of all government loans in Spain. This is one reason, and probably the most influential, as to why a large number of hotel companies fell under foreign control.

Provision of tourist accommodation The agencies responsible for government investment in tourist accommodation were INI (*Instituto Nacional de la Industria*) and ATE (*Administración Turística Española*). ATE was largely responsible for establishing and managing a network of hotels (*albergues* and *paradores nacionales*) aimed at opening up new areas to tourism. These hotels were normally of a high quality and often occupied historically valued buildings. By 1971 there were 82 *albergues* and *paradores*, and although most of them were running at a loss, a further 32 were planned for the period 1972–1975. Most of these were never built (or restored in the case of historical buildings) and there are now 83. Nevertheless, they constitute one of the most prestigous elements of the Spanish tourism product.

The influence of the INI on the tourism sector was greatest within the transport subsector. In 1954 the airline company Aviaco became part of the INI, and a sister company of Iberia (Spanish national airlines) in 1959. Aviaco's activities focused mainly on regular passenger flights and freight services, and although it was the first charter company to exist in Spain, it was only after 1971 that charter flights were developed on any scale, by which time companies from tourist-generating countries had already captured a large share of the market. The INI also established a road transport company, Atesa, which was at the same time a travel agency. As in the case of the air-charter sector, the travel agency controlled only a small share of the market, which was mainly controlled from the countries of origin of the tourists.

Development of infrastructures Government action in this field focused on two aspects: on the definition of necessary infrastructures associated with tourist accommodation, and on investment in social capital. These measures, however, came at a late stage of development, when the foundations of the tourist product were already in place. It was not, in fact, until 1970 that minimum infrastructure requirements were established, consisting of such basic necessities as the provision of drinking-water, electricity, access by road, parking facilities and the treatment and disposal of liquid and solid waste. New units had to satisfy these minimum requirements and pre-existing establishments were given 12 months to comply. Also introduced were measures to declare an area a 'saturated zone', where no further accommodation could be provided. The term was later modified to 'zone with insufficient infrastructures' hence eliminating the defence of aesthetic or ecological values. This measure could have served as an important instrument in controlling development, but it was never really applied.

In terms of investment, the huge gap between private and public investment was paralleled by a similar deficit in infrastructure. It was only with the government's Third Development Plan (*Tercer Plan de Desarrollo*), 1972–1975, that public investment in infrastructure was seriously contemplated. Investment was to total 7100 million pesetas, mostly allocated to road construction. Conflict was in fact increased by improving access.

Promotional campaigns   Government investment in promoting the tourist product was very limited. For example, in 1974 a total of 400 million pesetas (0.2% of foreign exchange earned through tourism) was allocated to promotional campaigns. Most campaigns reinforced the image of the summer 3S attraction and the predominance of tourism in certain large coastal resorts. As a consequence, they did not help to counteract the problems of high seasonality, high geographical concentration and uniform motivation. For example, the Malaga coast was named and commercialized as the Costa del Sol ('Sun Coast'). Even more recent campaigns, aimed to promote alternative forms of tourism, have insisted on the climatic component – 'Everything under the sun'.

Response to the 1973 economic crisis

It is important to examine the measures adopted by the government in the face of the economic recession which originated in 1973, in order to identify their repercussions on the Spanish tourism industry. The government decided to revalue the peseta in February 1973, after the devaluation of the dollar (a similar decision had been made in December 1971). This had disastrous consequences for the tourism industry, for profit margins dropped below economic viability levels and demand also fell as a result of the general crisis (Cals, 1974). Moreover, the tourism sector was excluded from the measures introduced to compensate for losses suffered in export sectors as a consequence of devaluation. The situation was further aggravated by the bankruptcy of Courtline, one of the major British tour-operators in Spain, in August 1974. In view of the foreseeable crisis, the government immediately announced a series of measures designed to alleviate the problems of the tourist sector. For the first time a halt was called to the 'numerical expansion at all costs' policy and the export nature of tourism was finally recognized. Measures taken by the government included: devising a plan to regulate tourism supply; drawing up the first National Plan for Hotel Modernization; granting loans both for making operational capital available and for investing abroad in order to minimize dependence upon foreign travel agents; reorganizing the government Ministry; modifying the regulations on the activities of travel agencies; creating a register of Tourist Export Companies (*Empresas Turísticas Exportadoras*). This could have marked the beginning of a change in tourism policy, but Franco died in 1975, marking the end of an era.

1975–1993

The change in the political system in Spain after Franco's death brought a change in tourism policy. During the first years of democratic government, however, the main priority was the establishment of the constitutional basis of the system. The new Constitution was introduced in 1978, under which regional autonomous governments were set up and many of the responsibilities of the former central government in terms of tourism policy were transferred to them. The first autonomous government set up was the Catalan Generalitat in 1979. Decentralization was accompanied by liberalization, for while the central government retained control of exchange rates and promotion at national level, maximum price control was abolished in 1978, and some state-owned companies were transferred to the private sector.

However, it must be remembered that the foundations and main characteristics of Spanish tourism were laid down during the Franco era and many were difficult to change. Several major defects were inherited. The division of the production activities of tourism services and infrastructure among different sectors of the economy and administration requires close coordination between policies in these different sectors so that tourism policy can be coherent and effective. Such coordination was never achieved under Franco. Coordination between privately and publicly financed services was lacking, installations and infrastructure were also inadequate and investment was unbalanced. Planning, where present, had also been uncoordinated. The lack of administrative coordination, public investment and planning had left development in the hands of private enterprise and speculation was, consequently, rampant.

Each new autonomous government has defined its own objectives and policies. Certainly the governments in the major tourist regions have been active in recognition of tourism as an important sector of the economy, thus correcting a previous basic misunderstanding. In general, as a first measure, they have produced White Papers on Tourism (Miguelsanz, 1983; Aguiló, 1987), and have reorganized tourism administration in an attempt to coordinate the different elements which together make up the tourism industry. They have also recognized the need for public investment and planning, for the legislation and regulation of tourist supply (in order to improve quality and to safeguard the environment), for the spatial, temporal and typological diversification of tourism, and for staff training. Each region hopes to create its own tourist image and promote its own differentiated product. The results so far are not too promising but readjustment is inevitably a slow process, as a consequence of the basic structural defects which existed initially and the recession in tourism demand in Spain in recent years.

Municipal authorities

Municipal tourism policy can be understood only in the light of general tourism policy, legislation – or lack of it – on matters affecting tourism development, and both municipal and private investment. The policy of growth at any price at a national level was also reflected at municipal level, where overdevelopment was permitted (Bote Gómez, 1990). The absence of adequate legislation meant that quantity was largely uncontrolled, as were quality and design. Serious spatial planning was also lacking (although some tentative measures had been contemplated in the Third Development Plan). Urban development plans (*Plan General de Ordenación Municipal*) did exist, but were seldom rigorously implemented. New urban development plans, updating previous ones, were drawn up in the early 1980s, after major tourist development, and tended to legalize the status quo, making only slight modifications. In fact, municipalities have full control of urban planning, the designation of natural conservation areas and the granting of building permits. In the absence of overall national or regional planning, each municipality was therefore free to plan for future expansion in terms of quantity, quality and location.

A further difficulty which municipalities faced was the lack of sufficient revenues. During the Franco era, local taxes were low and little additional income was forthcoming from the central government. Necessary infrastructure and public services were not provided by the latter and the municipal authorities were unable to finance their provision. Hence, in the face of potential competition from neighbouring municipalities, some opted for permissive policies and were open to speculative development by private investors, in order to acquire revenue through the granting of building permits. Under the new democratic government larger revenues became available to municipal authorities, especially after 1977. Up to 1969 income had been very low, but in 1970, the introduction of taxes on 'accommodation supply' helped raise income. In 1977, revenue increased with the introduction of new taxes on property (classified according to size and location), vehicle tax and refuse-collection charges. This new source of income contributed to the improvement of services and infrastructure. However, the deficit was still considerable. Lack of adequate planning in the past added further difficulties, and the allocation of revenues from the central government was largely (80%) based on permanent population figures with no allowance for the additional population that had to be catered for during the summer months.

Private investors

In the early stages of development, much investment was made by local residents – mainly fishermen and farmers – in the form of piecemeal modifications to existing property, but soon outside investors moved in. Investment came from both national (mainly urban) and foreign sources, and its destination was largely determined by the following considerations. Favourable conditions (lax building restrictions in terms of quality and density) offered to investors stimulated construction in certain resorts. The inertia of an already existing product, as well as short-term market strategies, interpreted mainly as foreseeable profits based on successful existing formulae, also attracted investment.

Typology of Tourist Resorts

The pattern of tourism thus established was essentially one of large-scale mass tourism based on linear concentration along the coast. However, as stated earlier (see also Fig. 3.2), the tourism–recreation supply is not uniform either at a macro (regional) scale or a micro (municipal) scale. The factors influencing these variations may be summed up as follows. A high level of development was usually attained in those areas where local investment (often small-scale) was made available at an early date, and accompanied by the permissive attitude of local authorities towards ensuing development on the part of outside investors. The development of, for example, Lloret de Mar on the Costa Brava followed this pattern. Only rarely did initiative come from elsewhere. Government initiative played an important role in only a few cases. The most noteworthy is the case of the Costa del Sol, where the hitherto unattractive and undeveloped coast became a major tourism destination with an important high-quality ingredient largely as a result of government assistance in tourism-product marketing and the encouragement of investment from private sources.

A low level of development has obviously been the result of the inverse operation of these same factors, of which the most important were the restrictions imposed on development by local authorities. Notable examples are Tossa, next to Lloret de Mar, and Sitges, paradoxically the two pioneer Spanish resorts, which have consciously limited development. In the case of potential resorts where local initiative was lacking early on, natural conditions have exercised an important influence on subsequent development. These factors include beach size, accessibility and the extension of surrounding land suitable for construction. However, a single local or outside investor could change or set the trend for the extent and type of future development. Such is the case of the luxury marina complex of Puerto Banus constructed near the already fashionable resort of Marbella on the Costa del Sol. It became the focal point of development in the surrounding area, including an exclusive element, known as the 'Millionaire's Mile', and an extension inland, where the construction of five golf-courses and their corresponding property developments have converted a barren unattractive valley into a high-quality recreation and tourism complex.

The major conditioner of the type of tourism which evolved is, however, the period of peak development (see Fig. 3.3). Accommodation was initially in the form of hotels – generally small, family-run enterprises. With larger-scale investment, hotel size increased and after 1970 mainly high-capacity hotels were constructed. During the early 1960s, small apartments for short-term renting were introduced, but rapidly rising building costs soon made them an unprofitable investment. Camp-sites, principally located on formerly deserted beaches, spread southward along the Mediterranean coast from the French border once the construction of the coastal motorway began in 1974.

After 1970, the second-home market increased rapidly, partly stimulated by foreign demand, but mainly in response to the demand from an increasingly prosperous and numerically growing middle class in the major Spanish cities. The type of construction was clearly influenced by consumer tastes and buying power. Spaniards preferred large individually designed detached residences (on part of the Girona coast) or low-density, low-rise apartment blocks (on the Tarragona coast), whereas foreigners tended to show a preference for small detached residences and terrace housing in condominiums (on the Valencia and Alicante coasts) or built to resemble 'typical' villages, often dotted around golf-courses (on the Malaga coast). In recent

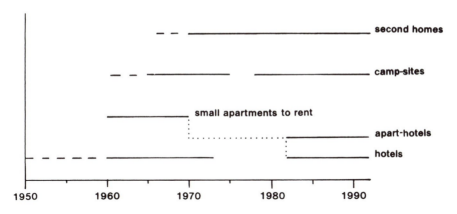

Fig 3.3. Typology of tourist accommodation in Spain, 1950–1992.

construction styles, terrace housing predominates. In fact, in many areas, the superimposition of low-density second-home complexes in tourist resorts has had a wider spatial impact than the provision of accommodation for mass tourism (Cals, 1982; Valenzuela Rubio, 1986).

Conclusions

Although the main characteristics of tourism were established during the Franco era, government action had no profound, far-reaching effect on the structure of the different subsectors which together comprise the industry. The tourism sector was used as an instrument of development policy, but was not really a component of this policy. It was never a priority sector, always marginal to 'serious' economic sectors. This mistrust of the stability of the sector was openly admitted, expressed in a report published in 1963 (Oficina de Coordinación, 1963), and was reflected in many ways. Public investment was limited. Medium- and long-term planning was absent and, as a result, the expansion of tourism took place without any selective criteria, the yardstick of management efficiency being the increase in the number of tourists. An independent Ministry of Tourism was never created. Adequate control of the quality of the product was lacking and this, combined with the ruinous policy of low prices, made it impossible for supply to maintain existing quality levels, let alone improve them at a later date. Training of employees was inadequate, and there was a parallel lack of interest in and funding of academic research in the field of tourism. Finally, the population at large often showed apathy and at times resentment towards the influx of tourists.

In these circumstances, municipal authorities could not be expected to assume serious planning responsibilities. The nation's priority was the development of large urban and industrial growth points, and even there, urban planning was often lacking. Additional difficulties were the limited financial capacity of small coastal towns and villages; the type of tourism promoted at national level which filtered down to community level; the total absence of points of reference from elsewhere in a pioneer context; the impossibility of taking into account social costs when economic development was desperately needed; and the absence of a collective consciousness of the consequences for the environment. As a result, the most important instrument in shaping the tourist–recreation product was personal initiative on the part of private investors, most of whom were intent on acquiring rapid returns on their investments. Municipal policy, where restrictive, was able to exert an influence on the extent, quality and type of development. Investment was market-orientated, but based on current consumer patterns or intuition rather than on the analysis of long-term market trends.

The influence of the timing of major development on the type of tourism which evolved has already been shown, but additional related factors involved in the shaping of the product can also be distinguished. The physical characteristics of the sites available often acted as a restrictive factor, for small bays surrounded by steep, rugged slopes were obviously not used for large-scale development. At a later date such slopes became attractive, when the demand for detached houses as second homes increased. Accessibility was also important at two levels. At regional level, proximity to the French border (for road transport) or to airports with adequate facilities for international air transport encouraged the expansion of nearby resorts. At a more local level, relatively easy access to coastal sites from main roads tended to accentuate the trend towards differentiated growth even further.

While second homes were spread along vast stretches of coastline and surrounding hills and valleys, accommodation for short-term tourists was largely concentrated in a relatively small number of high-density resorts, surrounding urban centres. The 3S product, based originally on picturesque fishing villages, deserted beaches and coves and rocky, pine-covered promontories was promoted as exactly this. Howevever, over the decades, the original resource has obviously been transformed. Fishing has been concentrated in certain ports, villages have grown and many promontories have been built upon. By contrast, the tourist image propagated has witnessed little change since the initial stages of tourism promotion. Of the 3S product, only the sun remains plentiful, for the sand is overcrowded and the sea is often contaminated and distant from the hotel. Fortunately for some, a fourth S (sex!) has been added in compensation, but is not advertised in brochures.

References and Further Reading

Aguiló, E. (ed.) (1987) *Libre Blanc del Turisme a Balears.* Conselleria de Turisme, Govern Balear, Palma de Mallorca, 2 vols.

Aranzadi, J.C. (1992) Plan Marco de Competitividad del Turismo Español. *Estudios Turísticos* 115, 3–10.

Barbaza, Y. (1966) *Le Paysage Humain de la Costa Brava.* Armand Colin, Paris.

Bote Gómez, V. (1990) *Planificación Económica del Turismo.* Trillas, Mexico.

Cals, J. (1974) *Turismo y Política Turística en España: una Aproximación.* Ariel, Barcelona.

Cals, J. (1982) *La Costa Brava i el Turisme: Estudis sobre la Política Turística, el Territori i l'Hoteleria.* Kapel, Barcelona.

Cals, J. (1983) El modelo turístico español. *Estudios Turísticos* 80, 15–19.

Cals, J. (1987) Turismo y política turística en España, 1974–1986. In: Velarde, H., García Delgado, J. and Pedreño, A. (eds) *El Sector Terciario de la Economía Española.* Colegio de Economistas de Madrid, Madrid, pp. 205–217.

Coya Sanz, M. (1975) Un análisis de la distribución espacial de la demanda. *Estudios Turísticos* 47–48, 139–177.

Dekker, B.R. and Hoekstra, D. (1992) *Un Futuro para la Costa Brava?* Faculty of Spatial Sciences, University of Groningen, Groningen.

Díaz Alvarez, J. (1988) *Geografía del Turismo.* Síntesis, Madrid.

Esteve Secall, R. (1991) *Un Nuevo Modelo Turístico para España.* Universidad de Málaga, Malaga.

Fàbregas, E. (1970) *Vint Anys de Turisme a la Costa Brava.* Selecta, Barcelona.

Figuerola, M. (1983) Importancia del turismo en la economía española. *Estudios Turísticos* 80, 21–30.

Gabinete de Estudios Económicos y Empresariales del Instituto Español de Turismo (1984) El papel del turismo en la estructura económica española. *Estudios Turísticos* 81, 3–19.

Gaviria, M. (ed.) (1974) *España a Gogo. Turismo Charter y Neocolonialismo del Espacio.* Ediciones Turner, Madrid.

Gaviria, M. (1990) España a la carta. *Estudios Turísticos* special issue, 77–85.

Gibert, A. (1972) *El Crak Turístico de la Costa Brava.* Cámara de Comerç, Girona.

Instituto Nacional de Estadística (1991) *Censo de Viviendas 1991: Avance de Resultados.* Instituto Nacional de Estadística, Madrid.

López Palomeque, F. (1988) Geografía del turismo en España: una aproximación a la distribución espacial de la demanda turística y de la oferta de alojamiento. *Documents d'Anàlisi Geogràfica* 13, 34–64.

Miguelsanz, A. (ed.) (1983) *Libre Blanc del Turisme a Catalunya.* Generalitat de Catalunya, Departament de la Presidència, Barcelona.

Ministerio de Industria, Comercio y Turismo, Subdirección General de Planificación y Prospectiva Turística-Estadística (1980–1992) *Anuario de Estadísti-*

cas del Turismo, año 19… Ministerio de Industria, Comercio y Turismo, Secretaría General de Turismo – Turespaña, Dirección General de Política Turística, Madrid (annual publication).

Ministerio de Información y Turismo, Secretaría General Técnica, Servicio de Estadística y Análisis de Datos, Sección de Estadística (1963–1974) *Estadísticas del Turismo, año 19…* Ministerio de Información y Turismo, Madrid (annual publication).

Ministerio de Información y Turismo, Secretaría General Técnica, Servicio de Estadística y Análisis de Datos, Sección de Estadística (1975–1979) *Anuario de Estadísticas del Turismo, año 19…* Ministerio de Información y Turismo, Madrid (annual publication).

Oficina de Coordinación y Programación Económica (1963) Informe del BIRF. In: *El Desarrollo Económico de España*. Industria Turística Internacional, Madrid.

Palomino, A. (1972) *El Milagro Turístico*. Plaza Janés, Barcelona.

Pearce, D.G. and Grimmeau, J.P. (1985) The spatial structure of tourist accommodation and hotel demand in Spain. *Geoforum* 16(1), 37–50.

Sanuy, F. (1983) El turismo y la crisis económica. *Estudios Turísticos* 80, 67–76.

Valenzuela Rubio, M. (1986) La residencia secundaria como factor de transformación y reordenación del sistema de asentamientos. Conflictos territoriales y retos urbanísticos. In: *Jornades Tècniques sobre Turisme i Medi Ambient* (17–19 setembre 1986, Sant Feliu de Guixols, Girona), pp. 107–128.

Vasalló, I. (1983) El turismo de masas en España. *Estudios Turísticos* 80, 3–14.

4

The Third Sector: a Secure Domain of Self-organization in Free Time or a Threatened Field of Social Action?

J. Lengkeek

Department of Sociology, Agricultural University, Hollandseweg 1, 6706 KN Wageningen, The Netherlands.

A World of Worlds

The variety of subjects, ideas and interests that lie at the heart of informal association are infinite and range from the stamp collector who mobilizes a philatelist association to those whose pursuit of collective interests has given rise to labour unions and political parties. There are many different ways in which people organize themselves in their free time. These range from small, very loose associations (a group of friends who regularly do things together) to nationwide umbrella organizations with millions of members and a professional, paid staff (e.g. a national sports union).

Clubs, informal groups pursuing joint leisure goals, groups involved in voluntary or welfare work and pressure groups, as well as all those groups that collectively plan activities in their free time, form a multi-faceted world. Every group creates its own world of meaning and has its own codes, symbols, behaviour, rituals and material assets.

This 'world of worlds' is so heterogeneous that we have been unable to find the concepts that adequately describe the phenomenon. Voluntary associations, leisure organizations, clubs, societies, mutual aid groups and self-organization are all concepts used in this context. However, they only seem appropriate for specific groups.

When Hoggett and Bishop began to study club life in two British communities in the 1980s, they were astonished: 'As our research developed, it seemed as though we had stumbled into an area of social life which was massive in its proportions, rich in detail and of fascinating complexity' (Hoggett and Bishop, 1986, p. 130).

This area of social life is not a hidden dimension of society: it is a neglected field of sociological interest and research. It is difficult to understand why the social sciences have shown so little interest in this colourful world of worlds. Research has been carried out, particularly in the USA, but, as Smith and Freedman (1972) put it, there is no grand, all-encompassing, and generally accepted theory of voluntarism, or even a respectable middle-range theory. For the most part, one finds a series of largely unrelated hypotheses dealing with various aspects of voluntary associations and with participation in them. In the 20 years since they wrote this, little has changed.

A most relevant question, nevertheless, is what the significance of this world of informal groups is in a changing society and what its relationship is to the evolving sectors of State and market. Here an attempt is made to present this generally underexposed element of the transformation model put forward in the introduction to this book (Chapter 1).

Position as 'Third Sector'

Writing in the early nineteenth century, Alexis de Tocqueville observed that there was an increasing disposition towards voluntary association in the New World. He saw voluntary associations as places where democratic principles could be exercised and these voluntary associations would provide a counter-force to powerful political institutions (de Tocqueville, 1971).

In 1893, Durkheim, thinking along the same lines, drew attention to the open space between the State and the individual. This space was filled by voluntary corporations, such as the trade unions that had replaced the old guilds and local, traditional relationships. The function of associations in social development is described in a similar way in the works of Tönnies (1954): the *Gesellschaft* (society) replaces the traditional *Gemeinschaft* (community) in the process of state formation and the development of the capitalist economy. *Gemeinschaft* is the realm of solidarity, the social order that is taken for granted, and which is doomed to disappear. The *Gesellschaft* is characterized by relations and corporations based on rational will (Martindale, 1961). These evolutionary perspectives raise the question of how to deal with the role of associations in a changing society. Are they lingering reminders of *Gemeinschaft* relationships embedded in symbolic meanings or are they just another kind of modern rational organization? At the First Conference of German Sociologists in 1910, Max Weber argued that it would be necessary to have a separate sociology of voluntary associations. This would have to focus on 'everything that lies between the politically organized and accepted power of national and local State and Church on the one hand, and the natural community of family relationships on the other', and would be a '*Soziologie des Vereinswezens im weitensten Sinne des Worts*' (Weber, 1911) – in other words, a sociology of a third sector. Weber's vision has not been fulfilled.

In The Netherlands, there was some short-lived sociological interest in voluntary associations in the early 1960s (Jolles, 1959, 1978; Abma, 1963). These authors worked within a structural-functionalist framework. Jolles conceived of 'association' as a functional, social technique, related in time and space to the problems of industrial society. In other words, clubs and similar associations were considered as being only temporary phenomena. They were meant to shelter people from the harsh reality of the production system. When a postindustrial society developed, the social techniques clubs offered would become obsolete, or new, more appropriate techniques would emerge. In this period, well-organized public services were ready to take over club provisions and services, and commercial goods and high-quality services were already starting to compete with club provisions.

Abma (1963) opposed this interpretation. He regarded informal interest groups as having a more permanent function. Clubs use their power either to change situations or to maintain a balance of power. In this sense they enhance the pluralistic character of modern society. The authorities accept club organizations as permanent partners and use them to carry out tasks and develop policy.

In the 1970s and 1980s strong state intervention could be seen in the field of outdoor recreation. In The Netherlands, this led to discussions about whether or not the significance of clubs would dwindle away altogether. In the same period, a great deal of voluntary work became professionalized.

Hoggett and Bishop (1986, p. 130) were even more pessimistic about losing their treasure, so recently discovered: 'We hope we have conveyed to the reader some of our sense of enjoyment at what we were privileged to experience and that we also succeeded in drawing attention to the precious and threatened nature of the territory.... It may well be, however, that the best we can do is to understand and appreciate better ... then leave it alone.'

The importance of the third sector often seems to be overshadowed by the growth in unorganized, individual free-time activities which has taken place since 1945. There is evidence both of growth and decline in organized club life within the various subsectors. In The Netherlands, club life continues to prosper and has even grown slightly. To understand the social meaning of this wonderful world of worlds and the changes that have taken place within it, we first have to clarify the phenomenon.

Concept of Self-organization in Free Time

At least four features are often used to define the phenomenon.

1. A determinable whole with a certain character or identity (name).
2. People with some organized interrelationships.
3. Certain objectives: these are primarily collective but they also cover individual interests as well.
4. An accomplishment that is based on unpaid exchange or labour, i.e. exchange that takes place in people's free time.

There is no clear-cut distinction between a voluntary association and formal organizations such as business enterprises and administrative bodies. The two forms merge gradually into one another. Voluntary association can involve elements of paid exchange, although relationships which are not based on payment predominate. They may exist because there was no commercial or administrative reason for an organized body of paid interrelationships. Alternatively, there may be an explicit wish to keep formal and paid relationships at a distance. The objectives of voluntary associations and formal organizations also merge into each other. Objectives can be located on a continuum between self-orientation and other-orientation. Self-orientation involves mutual exchange within the group. In informal organizations mutuality is based more on equality than in formal organizations. People produce and consume together what they themselves have made. Other-orientation implies altruism: helping other people, improving the well-being of others, indulging in non-paid services for the benefit of others, etc. Voluntary associations orientate their efforts 'voluntarily' towards collectively defined goals whereas the State depends on taxes and political procedures. Other-orientation is the most appropriate concept in defining 'voluntarism'. Self-orientation is best illustrated by club life. The phenomenon under discussion is based at least on two dimensions: that of self–other, and that of being minimally organized–highly organized (in perhaps partly paid functions). The last dimension can be refined into types of organization. Zimmer distinguishes at least three types: presidential societies (managed by a dominant leader), multi-divisional organizations (main role played by executive committees) and matrix-structured organizations (professionally managed, directed to target groups and based on volunteers) (Zimmer, 1992).

The self–other dimension can be differentiated into the fields of interest or legitimizing the action involved. A 'classical' entry into the area of legitimation is proposed by Habermas (1981), who distinguishes three areas: truth (corresponding to religion, knowledge, etc.), norms (morals, philanthropy, politics, ecology) and sincere expressiveness (art, culture, hobbies, enthusiasms).

Problems arise in defining this world of worlds. The complexity involved is hardly appropriate for a concept like 'third sector'. For the time being I would like to use the term 'third sector' in a negative sense, defined by what it is not. The third sector is the world of *non*-profit organizations (non-market in a strictly commercial sense) and of *non*-governmental organizations (non-state) ranging from barely organized structures to strongly formalized groups.

Whilst all types of organization can be found in the field of recreation and tourism, the self-oriented group is the most relevant. Sports clubs, groups of enthusiasts and conservationists provide for an impressive world of material leisure facilities, services, symbolic representations, and social pressure and influence. In the following section I will concentrate on this self-oriented aspect of the 'third sector'. As a full appreciation is beyond the scope of an introductory overview, I will focus here on one example of Dutch club life: water-sports clubs.

Water Sports: an Example

Water sports belong to water countries such as The Netherlands. After the Second World War, planners were quick to point out that the physical quality of the lakes and rivers in the Low Countries could be compared to the Swiss Alps as far as recreational and tourist potential was concerned. Historians claim that water sports or sailing for fun was invented in The Netherlands in the early 17th century (Jorissen *et al.*, 1990). At about the same time, a water-loving Lord Mayor of Amsterdam commissioned a shipbuilder to construct a small, fast sailing-vessel simply to enjoy the pleasures of sailing on the river IJ and through the harbours of Amsterdam. Dutch shipbuilders were among the most advanced in the world at this time and early scientific interest focused on the efficient use of wind power. The word 'yacht' is derived from the Dutch *'jacht/jagen'* – to go fast. This new type of boat became popular quickly, but it was only within the reach of a small, very wealthy élite. Because Protestant ethics strongly forbade idleness, this display of amusement and wealth on the water was camouflaged by public functions: yacht owners demonstrated their skill at festivities or when celebrities came on official visits. We know that a sea battle between yachts was staged as a welcome for Czar Peter the Great.

In 1660, when Charles I returned to England after his exile in The Netherlands, the Dutch authorities offered him one of these new playthings. The British nobility was more than enthusiastic about the little sailing-ship and it has been copied and improved on ever since. In 1720, British yacht owners founded their first club, the Water Club of Cork. Unlike the Dutch they sailed mainly on the open sea. The Water Club of Cork was a very exclusive society and drew up strict rules for internal hierarchy, conduct, clothing and admission. The club and its joint activities were modelled on those of the Royal Navy. Slowly, and within the confines of upper-class society, the idea of water-sports clubs began to spread. Royal protection and patronage was the height of social recognition and status. The most outstanding club in the early nineteenth century was the Royal Yacht Squadron.

In The Netherlands, the phenomenon of the water-sports club did not come into being until the mid-nineteenth century. Yacht owners competed, fought fake sea battles, and made joint manoeuvres on the water. These were, however, spontaneous or organized by local innkeepers. The situation changed in 1840 when King William II visited the already major port of Rotterdam. The royal barge was rowed by a group of young, upper-class water-sports enthusiasts from Rotterdam. The king's son, Prince Hendrik, himself a water-sports fanatic and a great admirer of the English court style, decided to found a Dutch Royal Yacht Club around a hard core of young Rotterdammers and model it on the British Royal Yacht Squadron. It is significant that he chose to use the term Yacht Club instead of the Dutch *Jachtclub*.

Prince Hendrik's aims went beyond competition. He saw club activities as both useful and pleasurable. In addition they could stimulate public interest and sympathy in nautical affairs. The Netherlands had lost her position as a sailing nation, and he felt that this had to be restored. It was also assumed that competition would have a positive effect on the production and perfection of boats. The club consisted of upper-class people from different parts of the country. Competing for 'honourable prizes before the eyes of the common people' meant they could display both their wealth and their privileges.

The Club's board consisted of prominent citizens from Rotterdam and Amsterdam, the two major cities. The Netherlands had had a strong tradition of regional diversity and autonomy and at this time was beginning to integrate itself into a unified nation State. The idea of a national club was, as yet, too ambitious. Within a few months conflict over equal representation on the board had produced a schism between members from Rotterdam and members from Amsterdam. The board split up and, in 1848, club members from Amsterdam founded their own *Koninklijke Zeil en Roei Vereeniging* (Royal Sailing and Rowing Club). It was the first local club. The national Royal Yacht Club collapsed but, within the space of four years, six new local clubs came into being. In 1890 local organizations decided to consolidate their interests and improve agreements on racing rules. They founded a loose bond of clubs and the Royal Sailing and Rowing Club of Amsterdam came to be the 'presiding club' (Jorissen *et al.*, 1990).

Unfortunately, the history of water-sports club life cannot be told here in any detail. It is, however, well documented. What is remarkable is that, with the creation of water-sports club life, a distinctive world came into being, rich in the symbols and objects of prestige, manners, taste and clothing and with specific technical knowledge. It was also a world in which there was a continuous struggle for success, recognition and power.

A few people of social position and authority dominated the water-sports world. The Amsterdam Royal Sailing and Rowing Club led this water-sports world for a hundred years, plotting, balloting and manipulating other clubs according to its whims. The world of water-sports clubs can be seen as a world apart. Upper-class groups positioned themselves at the top of a hierarchy, shutting out people of humbler backgrounds. They were able to accept or refuse participants as they wished. People of slightly lower status were allowed to join the water-sports world and they provided an acceptable reference group for those with a lower social position. On the one hand, the world of water sports offered a context for emphasizing social positions in a rapidly changing society and, on the other, it provided opportunities for upward mobility and a chance to secure a position amongst the élite. Style, values and positions were more or less dictated by a small, dominant group within this world.

It was not until immediately after the Second World War that the 'presiding club' had to give up its leading position. It is significant that the first democratically chosen chairman (in 1947!) was still the president of the Amsterdam club.

Gradually, the world of water sports changed. National income rose and boats and water sports became more accessible to the man in the street. The world of water sports expanded and, at the same time, developed into subworlds organized around specific water-sport activities and boat types. The introduction of surfboards meant the introduction of completely new values and style elements. Post-war, public-sector 'recreation-for-all' ideologies were detrimental to the exclusiveness and standards which had, until then, characterized the water-sports world. In addition, rising incomes led to a boom in boat production. New commercial harbours and water-sports facilities offered good opportunities for taking part in water sports. In this period un-organized water sports increased at a much faster rate than club participation.

Even so, water-sports clubs prospered and became increasingly important in promoting the interests of 'water-sporters' at national and local policy levels. The national, regional and local clubs began to function as a party. They were willing to discuss and cooperate with the authorities and, when necessary, to act as a pressure group working for better recreational facilities. Now, through mutual aid, they are able to offer alternatives to public facilities and market-bound consumption.

A Short-cut in Production and Consumption

Mutual aid implies the production and consumption of both material and non-material goods. Broekman (1985) has highlighted the problematic nature of using concepts such as consumption and production in the context of leisure. Spending time is, to some extent, interchangeable with spending money: you could buy goods or make them yourself. Broekman stresses the different satisfactions derived from each activity. Doing something yourself may offer direct satisfaction, because you like the act of doing. This satisfaction disappears if one just 'buys' the product of this activity. Broekman uses the concept of direct utility to refer to the direct satisfaction derived from the act of production. The concept of indirect utility refers to the act of production where the only aim is to get rewards for the results. These rewards may be payment or recognition, or the indirect utility which accrues to saving money that would otherwise have been spent buying the product. Indirect utility can be transferred, direct utility cannot. Using this conceptual distinction, Broekman differentiates between the following.

1. Production involving paid work for others (both official and 'black') or unpaid labour for others (indirect utility).
2. Productive consumption such as do-it-yourself activities done to save money (indirect utility).
3. Consumptive production or efforts for the sake of the act itself (direct utility).
4. Consumption, spending money or time in using the results of the efforts made by oneself or others (direct utility).

Direct utility is an important motive for club participation in water sports. Working together in building or maintaining the clubhouse and harbour provisions is a lot of fun. There is also satisfaction in working together for a shared hobby and doing such jobs as organizing competitions, training youth, helping and advising one another on the subject of boat maintenance, and exchanging knowledge on nautical issues. As Hoggett and Bishop (1986) put it, the club is not only 'a place to do', but also 'a place to be'. Mutual activities imply the creation of a certain atmosphere. Some work together for these reasons, others only pay contributions: the act of consumption may just be confined to being there and using the facilities. Clubs offer leisure opportunities: competitions, harbours, berths and jetties, sanitary facilities, water and electricity, winter storage, clubhouses and canteens, boat trailers and so forth. In 1985, according to official statistics, one-third of the 954 marinas in The Netherlands were managed and, in most cases, owned by clubs. Half of them were in the hands of commercial entrepreneurs.

Members of water-sports clubs are able to benefit from the fact that club facilities are cheap in comparison with commercial provisions. This is why many people become members. Some clubs fine members for not participating in mutual aid activities. In this way, members are induced to exchange money for time. In most clubs there are a few people – often retired or unemployed members – who do jobs either for an unrecorded payment or in return for the free use of facilities.

Different combinations of consumption and production are easy to find in water-sports clubs and are related to a variety of material and non-material aspects. I have already mentioned competition as a product. With the decline of competitive interest and an increase in the diversity of meaning, there is an increasing emphasis on the material aspects of accommodation, nautical training and legal and geographical knowledge. Sometimes examples of club-life products include uniforms, ties, 'the right shoes', manners, language, the way one expresses oneself and a preference for a particular type of boat. In this respect the club also reproduces class differences, lifestyles and identities. Social evenings or barbecues, for example, are organized with the intention of enhancing group identity and mutual solidarity.

Collectively aiming at direct and indirect utility presupposes interdependency. Utility refers to communicative functions (status/ identity) and to instrumental rationality (provisions, rewards). Interdependency is in delicate balance because the communicative affectivity of group symbols depends on ever-changing social values and the affectivity of influence on public services and the formal economy.

There are usually a board and several specialized committees within each club to direct collective and mutual activities. The success and spirit of clubs depend heavily on these committees. Club officials must have special skills and motives to function well. Many members of the board are selected for the skills they deploy in their professional positions, such as leadership qualities, financial expertise or technical insight. Sometimes clubs produce special skills themselves. All these skills provide a basis for power. Because the direct utility of efforts is important, expectations concerning rewards for efforts made within the group which imply the exertion of authority and power are often

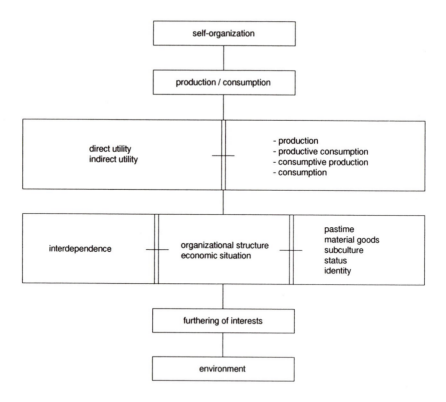

Fig. 4.1. Aspects of club life and the motives of club members.

unclear. The history of water-sports sclubs, just like the history of many other clubs, is a mixture of conflicts, disappointments, internal revolutions and splits.

Material and non-material production, the development of interdependency and the way boards give guidance to group processes constitute configurations which, to some extent, make each club unique. We may refer to the uniqueness of club 'ways' as 'subculture'. Old 'respectable' yacht clubs differ considerably in subcultural style from more recently founded wind-surfing clubs.

For water-sports enthusiasts the components of club life are as varied as the reasons for joining a club. Figure 4.1 provides a rough outline of the different aspects of club life and the motives of club members. Many authors have been puzzled by the way in which informal groups such as these have persisted over time. Olson (1981) in his search for 'the logic of collective action' made plausible the idea that individual contributions to an informal group depend on the share in the collective output of the group measured against the cost in money, effort or time to every contributing individual. Individuals tend to minimize their costs. Where the withdrawal of a contribution does not visibly affect the total output of a group, people are inclined to profit without contributing. Such groups, therefore, have a tendency to function 'suboptimally'. Sometimes it is all too obvious that clubs cannot operate as efficiently and as effectively as formal organizations. Nevertheless, groups tend to persist as long as some people have interests in the collective output of clubs. The contributions that are 'costs' for the one member may be profit or utility to the other. This means that there is always a good chance that there will be someone who will keep the club going.

When status considerations diminish in importance, the motive for cheap (self-produced) facilities continues to be a strong basis for club life. From recent research, it can be inferred that club facilities are twice as cheap as facilities provided by the market (Berntsen *et al.*, 1992).

Clubs and the Sociopolitical Environment

Local clubs have various relationships with the social environment. Traditionally, formal relations are few. Most relationships are established when club interests have to be defended against the outside world. Most more or less permanent relationships with the local environment are informal. For example, the chairman of the board is a prominent citizen and a close friend of the mayor. Because of this relationship he 'gets things done'. To some extent, however, there are formal relationships between the authorities and informal associations and there is regular exchange between them at national level. Public servants consult the national Water Sports Union (KNWV) on matters of planning and policy and the Union lobbies for changes in public policy. Both agree on sharing tasks.

The interconnection between the State and private organizations is a common phenomenon and its origin can be traced to the realm of industrial relations in the 19th century. Its function was to placate potential social turbulence. By admitting social organizations to structured cooperation, the State could control the masses. The Church also strongly advocated this approach. The working class, bound by ideological convictions through various associations, were kept in line. The concept of 'corporatism' has been used to identify this social technique.

Scholars such as Wilenski (1981) reintroduced this concept as neo-corporatism, an analytical tool useful in understanding the relations between the State, the economy and social organizations. Neo-corporatism implies that private organizations are directly involved in public policy and decision-making. In fact, totalitarian political systems tend to use clubs and voluntary groups as instruments for controlling people's lives and minds (de Grazia, 1981). The whole complex world of water sports and other, self-organized leisure activities was brought under central control during the German occupation of The Netherlands during the Second World War.

Neo-corporatism usually indicates large-scale exchange. The organizations involved can exert direct influence on public policy. In exchange they legitimate public action and control their rank and file. Wilenski applies this model to the interrelations between State, employers and trade unions. But it could also be applied to many leisure organizations and we find examples of attempts to influence governmental policies in the history of water-sports clubs. In club organization, we also find an increasing tension between the demands of the formal policy system (specific knowledge, skills, language, the right contacts, etc.) and the search for self-determination expressed by people themselves in the context of their own traditions, power relations and specific interests. The Water Sports Union is often seen as being too much a 'club', unable to respond professionally to the potential for developing water-tourism in The Netherlands.

By identifying the relations between the State and water-sports umbrella organizations as corporatist, we acquire a further perspective on the position of the third sector in a changing society. With the increasing tendency of local authorities to privatize public provisions such as marinas, corporatist relationships might also begin to encroach on local situations. In both cases, a permanent tension between exerting influence and being directed by the State can be observed. Most organizations feel torn between seeking public financial support and not compromising their position as a real third and independent sector.

Perspectives

In this chapter, the complex phenomenon of the third sector in relation to recreation and tourism is tied to the notion of self-organization in one's free time. The world of organized water-sports clubs has served as an example.

As far as self-organization is concerned, the third sector appears to be very much alive. To an important extent, recreational provisions and tourist environmental values are supported by organized groups of people spending their free time in a certain way.

In the absence of proper empirical insight, discussions on the third sector can easily be dominated by ideological presumptions. This has at least two corollaries. First, official policy and politics tend to manipulate or mould the third sector towards their own public goals. Recently, for example, the Christian Democrats in The Netherlands suggested returning public tasks to the community, to groups of people who were self-organized on the basis of a common solidarity. Second, we can see that there is an increasing interest in improving the way non-profit-making organizations are organized in order to ensure improved management, better input and output, and greater effectiveness. In this the third sector is supposed to follow the organizational model of the market. The very nature of self-organization and other-directed voluntary efforts counteracts these tendencies. This fact is not well understood and sometimes it is ignored. As a result both these efforts are bound to fail.

An understanding of the third sector involves two other notions. The concept of non-governmental organization definitely does not exclude collective or public interests. However, collective interests are organized on a more fragmented, flexible basis. Solidarity is bound to specific conditions and not to a general quality. In this sense, the third sector contributes to the democratic quality of a society that gives way to opposing powers. This does not imply, however, that voluntary associations or clubs as such function democratically *per se* or are 'more democratic than the formal political system'. As long as democratic conditions persist in society, people will organize themselves in order to articulate their interests, whatever their legitimate base.

The concept of non-profit-making organizations in a strict sense seems to be most inappropriate for the third sector. Considerable profit is involved, as I tried to show in my analysis of consumption and production in water-sports clubs. Returns can involve money or result in the saving of time and money. Returns can also take the form of respect, satisfaction, fun, tools and other assets.

In analysing the field of recreation and tourist policy, a first aim should be to understand the characteristic and complementary role of the third sector. When this has been done, it should be used in the best and most thoughtful way. A proper interest in the third sector will not harm the domain of self-organization in one's free time; it will, in fact, accentuate it.

References

Abma, E. (1963) Verenigingen in verleden, heden en toekomst. In: den Hollander, A.N.J., Hofstee, E.W., van Doorn, J.A.A. and Vercruysse, E.Y.W. (eds) *Drift en Koers. Een Halve Eeuw Sociale Verandering in Nederland.* Van Gorcum, Assen.

Berntsen, P., van Deijck, C., Lengkeek, J. and van Waarde, P. (1992) For profit: a comparison of commercial and club marinas. *Proceedings, VIII ELRA Congress 'Leisure and New Citizenship',* Bilbao, 9–14 June 1992.

Broekman, F. (1985) Productieve consumptie en consumptieve productie. *Vrijetijd en Samenleving* 3, 3.

de Grazia, V. (1981) *The Culture of Consent. Mass Organization of Leisure in Fascist Italy.* Cambridge: Cambridge University Press, Cambridge.

de Tocqueville, A. (1971) *Democratie en revolutie.* De Bussy, Amsterdam.

Durkheim, E. (1893) *De la Division du Travail Social. Etude sur l'Organisation des Société Supérieures.* Félix Alcan, Paris.

Habermas, J. (1981) *Die Theorie des Kommunikativen Handelns I and II.* Suhrkamp Verlag, Frankfurt.

Hoggett, P. and Bishop, J. (1986) *Organizing around Enthusiasms: Mutual Aid in Leisure.* Comedia, London.

Jolles, H.E. (1959) Het verenigingsleven in sociologisch perspectief. *Mens en Maatschappij* 34, 18–42.

Jolles, H.E. (1978) Sociologie van verenigingen. In: Rademaker, L. (ed.) *Sociologische Encyclopedie.* Spectrum, Utrecht/Antwerp.

Jorissen, F., Kramer, J. and Lengkeek, J. (1990) *Het Water op. Vierhonderd Jaar Pleziervaart in Nederland.* Hollandia, Baarn.

Martindale, D. (1961) *The Nature and Types of Sociologic Theory.* Routledge & Kegan Paul, London.

Olson, M. (1981) *The Logic of Collective Action. Public Goods and the Theory of Groups.* Harvard University Press, Cambridge, Mass.

Smith, C. and Freedman, A. (1972) *Voluntary Associations. Perspectives on the Literature.* Harvard University Press, Cambridge, Mass.

Tönnies, F. (1954) *Community and Society.* Transl. Loomis, Ch.P. Michigan State University Press, East Lansing, Michigan.

Weber, M. (1911) Geschäftsbericht. In: *Verhandlungen des Ersten Deutschen Soziologentages vom 19–22 Oktober 1910 in Frankfurt a. M.* Mohr, Tübingen.

Wilenski, H.L. (1981) Democratic corporatism, consensus and social policy. Reflections on changing values and the 'crisis' of the Welfare State. In: *The Welfare State in Crisis.* OECD, Paris, pp. 185–195.

Zimmer, A. (1992) Voluntary organisations. Ideography, evolution and structural change. *Proceedings, VIII ELRA Congress 'Leisure and New Citizenship',* Bilbao.

5

Lost in the 'Jungle' of Northern Thailand: the Reproduction of Hill-tribe Trekking

E.M.H. Binkhorst[1] and V.R. van der Duim[2]

[1]*Christelijke Hogeschool Noord-Nederland, Faculteit Economie en Management, PO Box 1298, 8900 CG Leeuwarden, The Netherlands;* [2]*Department of Sociology, Agricultural University, Hollandseweg 1, 6706 KN Wageningen, The Netherlands.*

'This is the jungle: freedom, no worries, we are far away from the city and everything is possible here.'

A trekking guide, Chiang Mai, quoted in Binkhorst, 1993.

Introduction

More and more tourists from highly industrialized countries find their way to less affluent and warmer destinations which comprise a 'pleasure periphery' on a world scale. These 'nomads of affluence', as Turner and Ash (1975) once called them, are searching for the 'extraordinary', whether it be 'tropical' beaches, 'unique' historical or cultural attractions, 'primitive' life or 'unspoilt' nature.

In Asia, Thailand has been at the forefront of this development. Although in 1960 the country did not even receive 100,000 visitors per year, tourist arrivals reached 4.8 million in 1989 and are projected to reach 8 million in 1996 (*Bangkok Post,* 2 March 1990). The rate of growth has been particularly spectacular since 1985.

Most of the tourists visiting Thailand arrive in Bangkok. The next most popular destinations are the city of Pattaya, the island Phuket and to a lesser extent Chiang Mai in northern Thailand. Approximately 10% of all foreign tourists to Thailand visit Chiang Mai. In the last 15 years this city has become the main centre for hill-tribe trekking. Though the first tourists reached the more accessible tribal villages more than 20 years ago, little by little 'hill-tribe trekking' has developed into an

Fig. 5.1. General map of Thailand with major touristic centres.

important tourist attraction, luring in excess of 100,000 trekkers a year.

However, as Leiper (1990) pointed out 'tourist attractions' do not actually operate or function. They are continuously (re)produced, by building huts or roads, performing traditional dances, providing food, producing and selling handicrafts or even opium, but also by adding certain codes to the original or transformed resource as 'primitive', 'authentic', 'exotic' or 'spectacular'. In other words, 'hill-tribe trekking' as a tourist attraction is constantly being transformed by the activities and interventions of all kind of producers. There are many professional 'experts' involved: tour-operators who are often international, local travel agencies, authors of travel guides, travelogue writers, guides, people working in hotels, restaurants or guest-houses, etc. They all try to organize and sell 'hill-tribe trekking' as a tourist experience or 'product' and therefore try to make it as 'attractive' as possible to catch the eye of the tourist. But 'hill-tribe trekking' will only be, and stay, a tourist attraction as long as hill tribes live in northern Thailand and tourists go trekking. Hence the local population and the tourists are an indispensable part in the reproduction of hill-tribe trekking.

In this chapter we will focus attention on four 'producers' who seem to accomplish an important role in the organization of hill-tribe trekking. We will analyse the way in which this tourist attraction is reproduced by trekking agencies in Chiang Mai, local trekking guides, local people and tourists. The results rest on a study of the literature and on fieldwork during a four-month visit to Chiang Mai and some hill tribes (Binkhorst, 1993).

Hill Tribes in Thailand

The term 'hill tribes' refers to ethnic minorities living in the mountainous regions of north and west Thailand. The Thais refer to them as *chao khao*, literally 'mountain people'. They are also called 'highlanders', in contrast to the Thai, who are called 'lowlanders'. Each hill tribe has its own language, customs, mode of dress and spiritual beliefs. Long recitations, committed to memory and passed on from generation to generation are, in fact, essential for continuing the culture. One thing is certain about the history of the hill tribes. They have been forced to migrate in order to survive.

Many of them migrated to the main area of the hilly north of Thailand: the exotically named Golden Triangle, along the borders with Burma and northwest Laos and the confluence of the Mekong and Mae Kok rivers. The mountains of northern Thailand form the outlying extremities of the Himalayan foothills. The hills of the Golden Triangle are beautiful enough on trekking holidays, but are nobody's first choice for a home. The land is poor for farming and the terrain difficult. The roads, even today, are inadequate and trails winding from ridge to ridge are the normal means of contact and transport. Dusty in the dry season, slippery with mud in the wet season, they link hamlet to hamlet across hundreds of miles of broken terrain. Their remoteness has also made them the stronghold of mainland Asia's last ethnic minorities: the hill tribes.

The Tribal Research Institute in Chiang Mai recognizes ten different hill tribes in Thailand and the total hill-tribe population in Thailand is estimated to be around 550,000, which is just 1% of the total Thai population (*Bangkok Post*, 1 May 1993). The six most often distinguished, largest, and most visited tribes are the Akha (Thai: *E-kaw*), Hmong

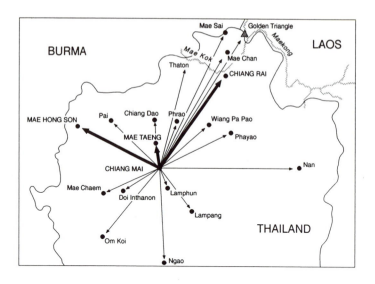

Fig. 5.2. Major destinations for hill-tribe trekking in northern Thailand in 1993.

(*Meo*), Karen (*Kariang*), Lahu (*Musoe*), Lisu (*Lisaw*), and Mien (*Yao*).

The official governmental policy appears to be the integration of hill tribes in Thai society. Hill tribes may retain their own customs and religion as long as they are loyal to the king and the law. However, in practice many resettlement, social welfare and educational pro-grammes are aiming at the assimilation of hill tribes in Thai society (Walker, 1986; Binkhorst, 1993).

Hill-tribe Trekking

Until recently, Thailand was the only country in which it was possible for travellers to visit hill-tribe villages and it is still the only country without travel restrictions. As a result, the six principal tribes who have settled in Thailand are by far the best known, but there are, in China and Burma in particular, many others. Their ethnic diversity and highly distinctive cultures make them some of the most intriguing and appealing minorities anywhere in the world.

Trekking in northern Thailand is directly related to the hill tribes, who are the main focus of a jungle trek. The trek, however, grew to be more than just a visit to various tribes. Now, it consists of a wide range of elements that form the total attraction. This means that the hill tribes are part of a broader and more widespread tourist experience. Tourists will visit the hill tribes among other 'sights' in Thailand (Pattaya, Phuket, etc.) or even Asia. On a smaller scale, the hill tribes are part of an experience consisting of, for example, jungle, elephant-riding, bamboo-rafting etc. Thus, a wide range of attributes creates what is finally gazed at by tourists. An individual tourist might set off from home with just one experience in mind, to see or do something specific, and might focus on that single experience for the duration of the trip. However, a far more common condition is that each tourist is involved with a range of sights or nuclei. This has been called the 'nuclear mix' (Leiper, 1990), referring to the combination of nuclei salient to the experiences of a tourist during a trip. Because some are more important than others, nuclei can be classified in a hierarchy, comprising primary, secondary and tertiary categories relevant to each tourist, or tourist typology.

Since the hill tribes are mountain people, the main nuclei which form the basis of the attraction are the people and the mountains, respectively, the hill tribes and the natural environment that surrounds them. Every day many treks set off from Chiang Mai to villages in the jungle to spend one or more nights with different tribes. What makes them so special?

Hill tribes seem to be able to live their life far away from the 'inhabited' world, each tribe in its own unique manner, within its own traditional practices. They live their life in an 'authentic' way, according to people from highly industrialized countries. Besides the hill tribes' authenticity, they look 'different' from any other people. They are 'extraordinary' (Urry, 1990). Their attractiveness rests on a combination of various elements: their way of life, primitive, in remote areas and close to nature; their appearance (clothing, many colourful ornaments); their customs, ceremonies, languages, traditional dances and songs, etc. All the elements are based on the cultural identity of the hill tribes. Thus, whether consciously or not, by living their life, hill tribes reproduce hill-tribe trekking.

Were it not for the hill tribes living in the mountains of northern Thailand, probably no tourism would have occurred in this region. Since they do live in these mountains, the natural environment is being more and more exploited. Hill-tribe tourism started with treks focusing on a visit to the tribal people: many hours of hiking just to visit different tribes. Soon the attraction was extended with natural elements which seemed to make the trek much more attractive. This is the natural environment as a whole in which the experience takes place: the jungle is exploited and functions as a 'multiple-use nucleus'. Rivers, bamboo and elephants are 'products' from the jungle and being used to transport trekkers from one village to another. Now, the natural environment provides more than just steep, slippery paths which are daily being conquered by tourists with a lot of 'blood, sweat and tears'. A more convenient and, in the eyes of the tourists, adventurous and 'real' jungle survival method of transport is offered by a ride on the back of an elephant or floating on a bamboo raft. The expansion of the hill tribes as an attraction even goes beyond local customs. Whereas elephants have always been used in the jungle for transport, bamboo has never been used for rafting by locals.

Among, or maybe around, the secondary nuclei such as elephant-riding and bamboo-rafting, a range of tertiary nuclei can be found. These consist of waterfalls (at least one is visited on almost every jungle trek) and to a lesser extent caves, hot springs and the pure beauty of the jungle flora and fauna. Orchid and butterfly farms and elephant-training camps are frequently visited, especially during tours in the Mae Taeng area, close to Chiang Mai.

Lost in the 'Jungle of Treks'

Tourists easily get perplexed in the 'jungle of treks' offered by over 200 different trekking agencies within Chiang Mai. As well as tourists who have already booked a trek as part of their trip, many travel on their own and stay in the north for maybe a week. They will probably have a quick look at the immense supply of trekking agencies in Chiang Mai's streets. Most of them, however, do not even shop around but buy a trek which is immediately offered at their guest-house when they check in. Surprisingly, although most treks consist of the same elements, they can vary greatly in terms of specific sights visited, tribes visited, and degree of difficulty or amount of walking.

Although trekking agencies all seem to offer the same 'different' treks, they can be distinguished in two touring systems, though partly overlapping. Cohen (1983) respectively called them the 'tribal village tour' and the 'jungle tour'.

Tribal village tour

The town tour encompasses the villages visited regularly by the one-day coach tours. It consists of a few nearby tourist-oriented villages among which Meo Doi Pui is the most prominent.

The excursion tour includes more remote but easily accessible villages, whether by coach, boat or car. These are typically visited during one- or two-day excursions from Chiang Mai or Chiang Rai.

Jungle tour

The standard jungle tour takes in a cluster of villages on the route of a standard three-day trekking tour. In 1983, Cohen reported a dozen small jungle tour operators in Chiang Mai offering this trek. In 1993, there was hardly any trekking agency without the standard jungle tour!

The special jungle tour encompasses the rest of the highland region visited by tourists, with treks to the extent of 15-day tours.

As Cohen (1983) pointed out, the four types of tours differ in some respects, for example the accessibility of the villages, the frequency of tourist visits, the temporal sequence of tourist penetration and its intensity. Jungle tours are based primarily on trekking, so they reach areas not readily accessible to motorized transport. Tribal village tours are to be found in the neighbourhood of Chiang Mai. The four types, however, continue to expand: villages visited 20 years ago on the special jungle tours might now be visited on the standard jungle tour or even on the excursion tour. The tourist's ideal, a village which has never been visited by tourists, is quickly disappearing!

> 'If you really want to see "something" you have to travel far away. For me it is impossible to enter the really remote areas: my age forces me to see the spoilt ones.'
>
> Woman (60) visiting the museum at the Tribal Research Institute, Chiang Mai, quoted in Binkhorst, 1993.

The standard jungle tour is the most common kind of trek. Except for differences of specific villages or rivers, it merely consists of similar elements along the route. Following a two- or three-night jungle trek, groups of four to twelve people get off pick-up trucks along the main road just a few kilometres before the first village. Trucks then drive on to the village site to deposit food and baggage. In the meantime, trekkers and two guides reach the village after a two- to three-hour walk. They look around and eat and sleep in the village. The control of communications between villagers and visitors is the task of the guide. The morning after, trekkers walk two to three hours again to the next village, have lunch there and will ultimately reach the second overnight village after a one- to two-hour elephant ride. Staying overnight in this village, they may then take a side trip to another village for a third night or, on shorter treks, go straight to the last day's feature, such as bamboo-rafting. After floating downstream for a few hours, they lunch and get on pick-up trucks that will take them back to Chiang Mai to the guest-houses they registered from (Michaud, 1993).

The Reproduction of Hill-tribe Trekking

The choice of going to Thailand and experiencing a 'hill-tribe trek' is largely based on anticipation. According to Urry (1990) such anticipation is constructed and sustained through a variety of tourist (post-cards, brochures and leaflets, travelogues etc.) and non-tourist practices (such as films, by hearsay, television, literature, etc.). However, this chapter primarily focuses on the (re)production of hill-tribe trekking in Chiang Mai and the surrounding main trekking areas itself. The role of trekking agencies, guides, local people and tourists on the spot will be highlighted.

Trekking Agencies

Over the last ten years tourism to the hill-tribe villages has escalated through the increase of tourists and trekking agencies (Village report, 1988). In 1977, there were a dozen travel companies. Dearden and Harron (1991/1992) reported over 54 companies offering trekking services in Chiang Mai in 1988. Estimates of the number of companies operating in 1993 are over 200, although not all of these operate independently. According to Cohen (1989), the small capital investment needed to start such enterprises and the rather minimal skills necessary to engage in routine jungle guiding offer few obstacles to escalation. The fierce competition between the companies in turn keeps prices low. However, the principal form of competition between the companies is qualitative. They vie with one another on the uniqueness and attractiveness of the routes and destinations they offer, the adventurousness and excitement of the tour itself, and the quality of their services. Hill-tribe tours were first advertised abroad in the non-conventional tourist guidebooks, directed primarily at the younger, enterprising, drifter-type tourists. More recently, however, such tours have been included in tourist packages of conventional travel companies such as Ralais Jumbo Tours, Neckermann, Cross Country Travel and Diethelm (Cohen, 1988a, b, 1989).

Trekking agencies who offer new hill-tribe destinations first have to find a new trekking route. Sometimes, roads or jungle paths need to be laid out in order to enter hill-tribe villages. When local families cannot accommodate all the visitors any more, bamboo huts are built to lodge tourists. These activities, specifically to serve tourists, complemented with, among other things, the construction of bamboo rafts and the supply of Thai and Western food on a jungle trek, are part of the way the original resource is transformed by these agencies. More interesting, however, is their role in what Cohen (1989) has termed 'communicative staging'. In general, the tourist's knowledge and image of the hill tribes are based on the information obtained from advertisements and pictures of treks at the guest-house or travel agency where they booked their trek, stories told by other travellers they meet along the way and maybe some information given in their travel guide. A few tourists will visit the hill-tribe museum at the Tribal Research Institute before they set off on a trek. Most tourists, however, get to know the tribes from the 'codes' given to them in advertisements by travel agencies. Cohen (1989) discerns three facets in the advertisements of the jungle companies: the image of the hill tribes to be visited, the experience of the jungle trek offered to the trekker, and the nature of the jungle trek. The image and the experience of the jungle trek will be described below. Since trekking guides play an important role in the nature of the jungle trek, the latter facet will be described when we talk about their role.

The Image of the Hill Tribes

> Come and experience these amazing people. Primitive hill tribe villages that are totally untouched and in their natural surroundings. See their culture and live among them in their timelessness. We will take you into the jungle, away from the normal trekking areas, to the world of the black Lahu and Karen peoples ...
>
> From a 1977 advertisement on the fence of a jungle company's stall in a guest-house in Chiang Mai, quoted in Cohen, 1989.

According to Cohen (1989) the hill tribes' image is expressed by several concrete epithets attributed to the tribes, like 'authentic', 'original', 'real', 'actual', etc. Moreover, some other characteristics ascribed to the hill tribes conjure up their authenticity, although under different guises; the principal one among these is 'primitiveness'. Primitiveness can almost be seen as the tourist trademark of the hill tribes. As well as this term, some other epithets are also used to express the same thing. They are 'primitive', 'simple' and 'unsophisticated'. 'Naturalness' is also a principal characteristic of the hill tribes, although it is hardly presented in the advertisements. It refers to the environment of the hill tribes, rather than to the people themselves. This characteristic is reflected in two epithets: 'natural' and 'harmony'. The presentation of the hill tribes as 'authentic', 'primitive' and 'natural' people is, however, not enough. To make them more attractive to trekkers, characteristics such as 'different', 'colourful', 'exotic', 'spectacular', 'unspoilt' or 'unchanging' and 'traditional' are also accentuated in the advertisements.

Finally, 'remoteness', both geographical and cultural, not only from the tourists' ordinary abode but also from the itineraries of routine tourist circuits, is one of the most frequently stressed characteristics of these people. Typical in this case is the exaggeration about the distance of places to be visited from Chiang Mai 'We are near the Burmese border, you can see Burma behind the mountains,' pretended one of the guides on a jungle trek only 40 kilometres from Chiang Mai, while pointing to the north (Binkhorst, 1993). By exaggerating the distance, an impression of much greater remoteness of the hill tribes is created.

In the advertisements, the attraction or the image of the attraction is displayed as colourful, primitive, natural, traditional, remote, unspoilt, etc. Cohen discerns three specific features of the image of the hill tribes as they are presented in the advertisements: selectivity, exaggeration and misrepresentation (Cohen, 1989). By being selective, only those characteristics of the tribes which have a tourist appeal are mentioned: the current problems and difficulties they deal with in today's Thailand are generally passed over. Furthermore, the appealing qualities of the tribes are advertised in an exaggerated manner, especially their remoteness, and possibly their 'unspoiltness'. Finally, the claim that the tribes are timeless or unchanging is completely contradicted by the current policy of the authorities to intervene in the life of the tribes, and by the processes of transformation which this policy has engendered (Cohen, 1989).

The Experience of the Jungle Trek

To enter hill-tribe villages, one usually departs from Chiang Mai conducted by a guide on a trek. The experience of the offered jungle trek is expressed as follows:

> What we can offer you: the chance to visit a variety of tribes in just a few days along picturesque scenic routes, to experience jungle nature and scenery, to enjoy unusual simple village life, to understand each tribe's customs and belief, to taste adventure with a most exciting and never to be forgotten boat trip.
>
> From a flyer for a trekking agency, Chiang Mai, quoted in Binkhorst, 1993.

This kind of advertisement includes many qualities of the tourist product offered by the trekking company. Following Cohen (1989) the most frequently offered 'qualities' are 'adventure', 'discovery', 'interest', 'enjoyment' and 'escape'. Of course the experience is 'non-touristy' too. Therefore trekkers are guaranteed to visit places where no one has been before: 'The Mae Taeng Route is non-touristy,' pretended one woman at a trekking agency. When asked which trek was chosen by most tourists, she said 'the Mae Taeng Route'. In fact this was the most popular trekking route at the time (Binkhorst, 1993). In these 'non-touristy' places, 'far away from the inhabited world', tourists are offered meals and drinks with fancy names such as 'jungle lunch' and 'tribal whisky'. Sometimes, this whisky is produced by the hill tribes themselves. However, in many cases it turns out to be whisky bought at Thai lowland markets.

Trekking Guides

Trekking guides are the intermediaries between the two parties involved in hill-tribe trekking. They are the link between the familiar and the unfamiliar and therefore play an important role in providing certainty to both tourists and locals. Jungle guides are an occupational subgroup whose appearance, conduct and values have been formed differently from the more urbane and conventional 'town guides', who conduct routine tourist excursions in and around Chiang Mai. Most of Chiang Mai's trekking guides are Thai males, with at least an early secondary level of education (Putsatee, 1992). The most important functions of trekking guides are the instrumental ones such as guiding trekkers in the jungle and mediating between them and the hill people at the tourist spot. They also perform an important communicative function in that they provide the trekkers with some information about the tribal people.

Because of the guide's presence he is the one who determines almost everything during the trek: the places to be visited, how and when they are visited, where to look, etc. By being the intermediary, he is able to give a specific 'code' to the original resource. Since tourists generally have little knowledge about the tribes and are in an unfamiliar environment, the guide is able to create the 'tourist's gaze' in some ways.

Some guides take the guide-training course set up by the Tourist Authority of Thailand (TAT). This course consists of 200 hours of study and many visits to various places and hill-tribe villages in the north of Thailand. As part of a new law concerning hill-tribe trekking, this training will probably be compulsory in the future. Some guides take a three- to five-day training course; some do not take any training. The training and other information resources are important factors determining what kind of information the guide obtains.

Guides as an Image of the Trekking Experience

Trekking guides are often presented as 'authentic' components of the trekking experience and consequently have a considerable influence on the nature of the jungle trek. As Dearden and Harron (1994) pointed out, they have become part of the visual show and a major factor in substantive and communicative staging of authenticity.

Many companies pretend that their guides themselves are tribal people. This should ensure the authenticity of their knowledge of the tribal people, as well as their competence in guiding the trekkers and communicating with the tribal people. 'We are the only tour company in Chiang Mai which is run by tribesmen, even our manager is tribal,' claims a trekking agency advertisement (Binkhorst, 1993). At the same time, more than one jungle company pretends to be the only one run by tribesmen, so it is obvious that their advertising is just one of those marketing efforts. Most of the guides, however, are Thai. According to Michaud (1993) the number of guides in Chiang Mai with genuine hill-tribe origins who regularly work for trekking agencies is less than 10%. The claim to an authentic knowledge about the tribes, warranted by the guides' origins, is one of the principal means of staging in hill-tribe tourism. Many guides, however, are 'instant guides' who know little about the hill-tribe cultures. They come from the city and look down on the 'primitives'. The advertisements generally highlight the competence and experience of the guides in jungle trekking. As against the promises from the advertisements, sometimes not only tourists but also local people complain about the guides' behaviour: 'Most of the guides treat us with discourtesy, causing bad feelings among the older people in our communities' (Villager, Ban Adu, quoted in Binkhorst, 1993).

Sometimes, by pretending that the guides are representatives of the tribal people to be visited on the trek, tourists are made to gain the impression of being a 'real' guest instead of just a visitor.

> 'In this Lisu village, we will visit my family, my aunt still lives there, it is really a good opportunity for you, you can be a member of my family.'
>
> Manager of a trekking agency, Chiang Mai, quoted in Binkhorst, 1993.

According to Cohen (1989), some guides may take a genuine interest in their guests, especially when they are new to the occupation. However, with time, a kind of staged personalism will be developed. Part of this staged personalism is also a specific image which the guide produces of himself. For example, one of the guides on a jungle trek was named 'Jungle John'; for daily use one could call him 'Jungle'. With his outlook as well as with his name, he created an image of himself as a real 'bushman': with a scarf tied around his head and high mountain boots, he looked like Rambo himself (Binkhorst, 1993). The guide's success and income depend to a significant extent on his reputation acquired by word of mouth. The more enthusiastic and positive about the guide tourists are when returning from a jungle trek, the better he will survive in this competitive occupation. So it is not far from possible that guides routinely 'stage' personal friendliness and interest in their clients.

Local People

Hill tribes do not just passively undergo the tourist arrivals in their villages but play an active role. By merely being there, dancing, giving massages, smoking opium, begging, etc., they constantly reproduce hill-tribe trekking. However, one should note that they themselves never chose to be a tourist attraction: they were more or less 'discovered':

> 'Some 17 years ago, tourists came to visit our village. They were tired of walking so they wanted to stay overnight. That was no problem: the house of the village headman was big enough, for 20 baht per tourist they could stay one night. Soon there were too many tourists: big groups with guides, so we could not shelter them anymore in the headman's house. After a while, we arranged a meeting because we thought it was not fair the headman earned all the money. We agreed on building extra huts next to each of our own huts so that all families could accommodate a group of tourists. However, another kind of competition came on: we had to reach the guides before they entered the village to offer our house. So during the day, the women take off to the waterfall from where tourists normally come, to talk with the guides and to offer her hut. Now, tourists and money are equally divided over all families.'

> Villager, Ban Adu, quoted in Binkhorst, 1993.

As tourism in northern Thailand grew in scope, hill-tribe trekking became more and more habitual and commercial. Jungle companies and hill-tribe families started to provide the trekkers with services such as food and accommodation, to make the trek bearable and enjoyable for them. As a result, commodification became a fairly interwoven aspect of the whole process.

Some 20 years ago, goods and services were part of the tribal peoples' hospitality. Now, guides have to pay for these goods and services. Until now, however, the average amount of money paid for one night for each tourist is 20–50 baht. This is the only fixed source of income for a hill-tribe host family. This is eventually complemented with the profit of selling soft drinks, handicrafts, jewellery, opium, performances of traditional dances and songs, massages, etc., all directly or indirectly contributing to the (re)production of hill-tribe trekking. From an average of 1400 baht for a two- or three-night jungle trek, however, an average of only 88 baht directly flows to hill-tribe host families. The rest of the price of the jungle trek paid by the tourist goes to guides, merchants at lowland markets or owners or drivers of pick-up trucks, longtail boats, elephants, bamboo rafts, etc.

Little by little, the rituals, goods and services have become a performance for money, and consequently their meaning has changed. The once 'authentic' public ritual becomes a staged performance, a cultural 'commodity'.

> 'We used to do this every night after we came back from working on the fields, then we were happy and sang and danced together. Now, these women first change their daily clothes into their traditional dress and perform the songs (which they could not even sing spontaneous) not because they are happy but for money.'
>
> Akha interpreter, Ban Adu, quoted in Binkhorst, 1993.

As Dahles (1992) points out, what tourists are confronted with is often not only the front stage of life, but also a rather decontextualized one. In this case, tribal dances, in which both natives and tourists play a role, are performed expressly for tourists as being authentic parts of the jungle trek. They are paid for by the guides although they will not say so in front of the trekkers.

> 'No, they dance because they are happy with you, we don't pay them because from the past my father is very good friends with the village headman.'
>
> Trekking guide 'Jungle John' in a Lisu village, quoted in Binkhorst, 1993.

The process of commodification also tends to affect the products themselves. As they become increasingly oriented to an 'external public', rituals may be shortened, embellished or otherwise adapted to the tastes of the tourists. Arts and crafts may also be changed in form, material and colours (Cohen, 1988a, b). Indeed, the handicrafts sold by the women in the village visited during fieldwork were made of cotton bought from factories at lowland markets instead of their traditional handspun and woven cotton. They were spurious, though good for money and jobs.

Money and Jobs

As Greenwood (de Kadt, 1979) states: 'The major impact of tourism on local people over the past 25 years can be summarized in one word: jobs.' In some villages money and jobs have indeed become very important to inhabitants, especially through the production and selling of handicrafts. The bulk of the production is sold to non-profit organizations and some of it goes to private shops, primarily in Chiang Mai and Bangkok. Villagers prefer to sell their wares directly to tourists, since they receive higher prices and incur fewer expenses than from sale to shops in town. Income from direct sales differs in villages, depending on what kind of tour is involved. In villages visited on the tribal village tour and the town tour, the selling of crafts can be good business, although it is becoming more important in the frequently visited jungle-tour villages as well. Especially when trekkers stop for a short period of time, fierce competition between the traders occurs. In Meo Doi Pui, the closest town-tour village to Chiang Mai, villagers have become middlemen for products of other highland groups and even for Thai or imported handicrafts. There, the 'front stage' (MacCannell, 1979), rows of souvenir shops, is spatially separated from the 'back stage', where the tribal people actually live their life. In addition to the overt, there is also a covert tourist space in Meo Doi Pui: tourists are brought into houses where old men apparently innocently smoke opium pipes, only to ask for a few baht or to attempt to sell them opium pipes when tourists take pictures (Cohen, 1983). However, to observe more of the 'real life' in Meo Doi Pui, you have to buy a ticket to enter a museum about hill-tribe life.

Whereas the direct sale of crafts to the tourists is practised primarily on the tribal village tour, hospitality is a source of income primarily for the jungle-tour villages. An average price of 20 baht per head per night (including rice and tea) is paid by the guides.

Villagers also provide a variety of other services for tourists, though on a small scale: for example, porterage of food and baggage, performances of traditional dances for which the dancers receive 30 to

60 baht a night, massages given by the tribal women, who earn an average of 50 baht per massage, or the sale of opium, of which the profit is generally spread over the guide as well as the owner. In some villages, a payment of one or two baht is asked for when photographs are taken, particularly of women in tribal dress or men smoking opium.

The growing and smoking of opium are still a problem in the hill-tribe villages. In 1958, the smoking and sale of opium were banned officially and in the following year the cultivation of poppy was also outlawed. Despite attempts to persuade the hill tribes to change to other crops such as coffee, opium is still produced in large amounts. During fieldwork many people spoke about the way villagers, even children, get addicted to opium. Since they show tourists how to smoke the opium pipe, they smoke with them. If the head of the family is not there, the women or even the children take over his job. Even without tourists opium would be smoked by some tribal people, but tourism stimulates it.

Tourists

If no tourist ever visited the hill tribes they would not be thought of as a tourist attraction. Whether by boat, raft or elephant or on foot, during a jungle trek tourists enter hill-tribe villages and gaze at the people and the environment in which they live. By sleeping in a bamboo hut especially built for them, drinking coffee and Coca-Cola from lowland markets, having 'tribal lunch', which may turn out to be Thai or Western, buying a shoulderbag, etc., tourists reproduce hill-tribe trekking over and over again. Thus, production and consumption of hill-tribe trekking by tourists take place at the same time. But there is more. Since tourists experience and nominate hill-tribe trekking as a tourist attraction, a bamboo hut is a 'real' tribal hut; ordinary food becomes a 'tribal lunch', hill tribes 'exotic' and north Thailand an 'extraordinary' environment.

Who are these 'Hill-tribe Trekkers'?

According to Cohen, from the 1970s on, the hill-tribe trekkers were 'alternative' youth tourists. Their interests and travelling style differed markedly from those of routine mass tourists. Owing to their growing numbers, a separate low-cost 'tourist establishment' emerged in

Chiang Mai. This consisted of low-cost guest-houses, eating-places and coffee-shops catering to the particular needs and preferences of this type of travellers (Cohen, 1989). Thus, hill-tribe tourism deals with 'alternative' low-budget travellers, on a scale close to that of mass tourism.

The bibles of alternative tourism, the Travel Survival Kits (Cummings, 1992), are guiding the low-budget tourists 'safely' from restaurant to restaurant, from guest-house to guest-house ('Chiang Mai Youth Hostel ... is clean, secure, friendly and their treks get good reviews').

Interviews with tourists undertaken in Chiang Mai in 1989 and 1990 as part of research done by Dearden and Harron (1991/1992) show that the socioeconomic profile for hill-tribe trekkers gives an equal split between male and female participants, with a mean age of 28 years. Almost 60% had university and college degrees, another 24% had attended college. About a third could be classified as professionals (doctors, lawyers, accountants, engineers, etc.), while 17% were teachers and 14% were still students. Europeans constituted almost 60% of the participants, North Americans 20% and Australians/New Zealanders 17%. Most were on an extended trip and were travelling independently. The total trip length exhibited a range from two weeks to five years, with a mean length of six months. The length of time spent in Thailand ranged from eight days to eight months with a mean length of 40 days.

The tourists described by Dearden and Harron (1991/1992) primarily join the so-called jungle tours. However, an increasing number of tourists visiting Chiang Mai or Chiang Rai are travelling by group tour and are visiting hill tribes only on a so-called tribal village tour. In other words, as hill-tribe trekking has become more and more popular, a wider range of tourists have been attracted and as a consequence new, more routine forms of production of hill-tribe trekking have been established. In the 1970s hill-tribe trekkers were small in number and adventureous, and boarded with local residents. But this 'counter-cultural reaction to routinized modern tourism', as Cohen (1988a, b) called it, had an ironical consequence. The search for the 'primitive' and 'unspoilt' offered local entrepreneurs the possibility 'for a covert and unsuspected "staging of authenticity"'. As numbers of tourists increased a growing demand for services and facilities and subsequently a more commercial visitor–host relationship emerged.

Not surprisingly, research by Putsatee (1992) shows that trekking tourists enjoyed not only gazing at hill-tribe culture, but participating in a wide variety of things such as visiting natural sites and attractions, and having 'adventures' and challenging experiences (elephant-riding, bamboo-rafting, etc.) which they could not find in general tourist areas or at home. As people keep demanding new out-of-the-ordinary experiences some tourists even decided to go trekking in order to have the chance to try illegal drugs and visit hill-tribe prostitutes, which they heard were not expensive. In fact the opportunity to smoke opium is taken frequently by many tourists. Some just try one pipe 'to know what it is', while others smoke until they are sick and fall asleep to wake up the next afternoon when hill-tribe life has already begun for many hours. Thus, tourists all give sense to the jungle trek in a different way. Depending on what one is looking for, they experience their own specific jungle trek.

> 'Oh, Tom, what was the name again of the people we were staying with last night, "Lagu", "Lafu", or something ?' He, exhausted from hiking and undergoing a massage, didn't want to think about it too much. He could only remember that the tribe which they visited the night before looked much 'cleaner' than this one. They had not been talking about the name of this tribe yet...
>
> Tourists, Ban Adu, quoted in Binkhorst, 1993.

Research by Dearden and Harron (1992, 1994) indicates that the hill tribes do indeed constitute the main motive for most people who want to go trekking, but post-trip satisfactions did not show that the hill tribes were the highlight of the trip. Table 5.1 shows that bamboo-rafting was the most satisfying part of the whole experience. The results suggest that the trekking clientele is primarily concerned with

Table 5.1. Motivations and satisfactions in hill-tribe trekking. (Source: Dearden and Harron, 1991/1992.)

Motivation	Percentage (n = 221)	Satisfaction	Percentage (n = 221)
Visit hill tribes	18	Rafting	15
Scenery	14	Visit hill tribes	14
Get away from city	12	Whole experience	14
Seek new experience	9	Hiking	13
Ride elephants	8	Trekking group	11
Raft	6	Elephant-riding	9
Hike	6	Nights in village	7
Adventure	5	Scenery	5
See Thailand	5	Drugs	5
Physical challenge	4	Adventure/other	7
Other	13		
Total	100	Total	100

the experience of hill-tribe trekking itself, with an emphasis on the recreational aspects, and less concerned with the authenticity of hill tribes *per se* (Dearden and Harron, 1994).

In summary, although often all hill-tribe trekkers are called 'alternative tourists', they all travel in what Cohen (1989) has called an 'environmental bubble' guided by Chiang Mai's 'tourist establishment'. The track which they think is 'off the beaten track' has gradually become a beaten track during the development of hill-tribe trekking. As a consequence, some tourists will not go trekking any more since they think it has become too commercial and 'too touristy'; others will go trekking because they think it is more accessible and convenient, being now surrounded by the tourist establishment which tends to all their needs.

Transformation of the Resource

Trekking agencies, guides, locals and tourists, among others, all contribute to the continuous transformation of hill tribes and their natural environment. Meo Doi Pui, the first hill-tribe village discovered by tourists approximately 20 years ago and now merely a handicrafts market, has little by little been turned into a museum. The traditional socioeconomic development of the village has slowly come to an end, as agricultural activities have been superseded by tourism. 'Why should we plough our fields while tourists come every day and provide our income?' (Hmong man, Meo Doi Pui, quoted in Binkhorst, 1993). The village of Meo Doi Pui has become a shopping area and tourists interested in traditional hill-tribe life can visit the hill-tribe museum. Tribal culture is being conserved in pictures, old tools and written information about a life before tourists and others changed it.

Dearden and Harron (1992) argue that the development of both individual villages and areas can be seen as a continuum. They depict villages in the early stages of visitors as 'explorer' villages with a minimal number and frequency of visits. Income and impacts are also minimal. Increasing numbers, frequency of visits and monetary hospitality may move a village along the spectrum to become a 'remote' village. If accessibility is restricted, and a three- or four-day trek is needed to reach the village, it may not proceed further along this continuum. However, easily accessible or especially interesting villages may develop into 'trekking' villages. Special facilities may be developed to serve the trekkers, such as a store selling consumer items and separate sleeping-huts. Several trekking groups might stay each night. Tourists thus undertake the jungle trek in a group instead of on their own, although they might be travelling through Asia or elsewhere as individuals, and significant amounts of money may be derived from providing goods and services for the trekkers.

When a village loses its traditional 'authenticity' and becomes less interesting for a visit, the village may decline in popularity as a trekking village, or it may experience rejuvenation. Increased visits in the rejuvenation stage will probably be within the 'rubber tyre' market, where visitors arrive in large numbers, by road, for a short stop. Rejuvenation, however, is not frequently seen in the north of Thailand. Rather, villages are ignored and traditional life is supposed to go on as if there had not been any tourists.

However, transformation of hill-tribe villages does not only depend on tourism: changes also occur through economic, social, cultural, political and ecological developments in northern Thailand. Influences from outside the community including modern consumer goods and modern culture are, together with the destruction of the forests, the two main causes of change in the hill-tribe villages. All the governmental policies aim at a progressive economic, social and political incorporation of the tribal people into the Thai community. For example, since the early 1970s, a hill-tribe radio station has broadcast music, news about Thailand and the rest of the world, educational and other programmes. Easier access to the villages because of better transport has brought many people into the hill-tribe communities, such as traders, government officers, community development workers and tourists, each contributing to changes in the hill-tribe societies. They also serve to make the villages less appealing to tourists, and add to the spreading of tourism to other villages and regions.

Conclusion

Jungle trekking in northern Thailand has developed commercially precisely at a time when lowland political, economic and cultural influences on the hill people were rapidly intensifying, gradually transforming their way of life. Moreover, the multiplication of tourist visits, while not necessarily having such a pervasive impact, none the less changed the nature of the relations between the tribal people and the trekking parties. These soon became less spontaneous and more commercial. Ethnic tourism can be a way of providing economic benefits which is thought to be quick and relatively painless for less developed communities. Of particular importance, however, is the question of who gets the jobs (de Kadt, 1979). Although the hill tribes are the primary nucleus in the hill-tribe attraction system, the tourist establishment is mainly in Thai hands. A fair distribution of income and, more importantly, the involvement of the hill tribes themselves in hill-tribe trekking are absent.

Tourism often fails to be environmentally benign and since its significant growth it has led to an increasing concern with its impacts on the physical environment. Prior to 1993, little attention was paid to this aspect in relation to hill-tribe trekking. The northern Thai Jungle Tour Club, a group of about 20 trekking agencies in Chiang Mai, focuses on trekking policies which take into account the effects of hill-tribe trekking. They seem to be aware of the environmental impacts. A principal environmental effect of hill-tribe trekking is the potential for the depletion of bamboo in areas close to principal rafting sites. After completion of the journey downriver, the rafts are abandoned since there is no economic way to return them to their starting-point. Although bamboo is very fast-growing, it remains unknown whether it can sustain the cutting rate. It is now being discussed whether it will be useful or not to substitute rubber for bamboo rafts. Although they are more expensive, they can be used longer and the costs can easily be retrieved from profits (Putsatee, 1992). The other principal environmental effect is related to the disposition of human waste. The hill-tribe communities have no waste-disposal facilities other than the biological disposal performed by domestic pigs or by water or burning.

Besides signs of soil erosion in the areas which have regular trekking routes, many trekking tourists and elephant trails, trekking activities have also caused harmful effects to the flora, waterfalls, water supply and natural activities of wild animals (Putsatee, 1992).

There is no national or regional policy regarding hill-tribe trekking and there is a lack of coordination among the authorities concerned with it. This results in problems related to the quality of management, guiding, natural environment and pre-tour preparations among tourists. A proper policy comprising organizational, cultural and natural aspects is necessary.

The hill tribes face a pressure on their cultures on a scale that they never experienced before. The root of the problem is that these minorities are running out of means of survival. There are no more hills and no more forests to which they can move. In an ideal hill-tribe settlement, the village is surrounded by a 'green belt' of virgin forest, replete with old teak trees, plenty of game for the men to hunt, and a wealth of herbs and plants for medicine, food and dyeing cloth. But they have moved further and further along the ridges. Now, in Thailand, they have reached the end of the ridge. As far as the eye can see from the top of the mountains, the lowlands are planted with rice and dotted with hamlets and villages. All of the lowlands are planted with other people's rice. There is nowhere else to go. There is not enough forest to allow old fields to regenerate, and, besides, illegal logging has denuded even more. This seems to be a time for a change for all the hill tribes. Their traditional solution to difficulties by moving away is now barely possible, and in some way they must accept a settled existence. Some communities will inevitably crumble and lose their identity, but it would be surprising if this were the fate of all. Hill-tribe culture is as it is because of adversity. Tribal identity is remarkably strong; it must be sufficient to help them adapt to life in modern Thailand. Perhaps with economic support, the hill tribes of Thailand may yet find a niche that allows them education, citizenship and a livelihood from farming without losing their cultural identity.

It may be clear that tourism is not the only force that involves changes to hill-tribe life, although it is easily blamed for affecting ethnic cultures. There are many forces bringing about changes in the hills, including missionaries, government programmes, bilateral aid programmes, United Nations projects and the penetration of media and market forces. The sum of these forces is to reduce the cultural heterogeneity of the hill-tribe people and incorporate them more into the fabric of northern Thailand.

References and Further Reading

Binkhorst, E. (1993) *Lost in the 'jungle' of Northern Thailand. Research into the (re-)production of hill tribe trekking by: trekking agencies, trekking guides, local people and tourists.* Essay, Centre for Recreation Studies, Wageningen Agricultural University, Wageningen.

Boyes J. and Piraban, S. (1992) *A Life Apart. Viewed from the Hills.* Silkworm Books, Bangkok.

Bradly D. (1991) *Thai Hill Tribes Phrasebook.* Lonely Planet Publications, Melbourne.

Cohen, E. (1979) Rethinking the sociology of tourism. *Annals of Tourism Research* 6(1), 18–35.

Cohen, E. (1983) Hill tribe tourism. In: McKinnon, J. and Bhruksasri, W. (eds) *Highlanders of Thailand.* Oxford University Press, Oxford/New York/ Melbourne.

Cohen, E. (1988a) Traditions in the qualitative sociology of tourism. *Annals of Tourism* 15, 29–46.

Cohen, E. (1988b) Authenticity and commoditization in tourism. *Annals of Tourism Research* 15, 371–386.

Cohen, E. (1989) Primitive and remote: hill-tribe trekking in Thailand. *Annals of Tourism Research* 16, 30–61.

Cohen, E. (1991) *Thai Society in Comparative Perspective. Studies in Contemporary Thailand,* vol. 1. White Lotus, Bangkok/Cheney.

Cohen, E. (1993) The study of touristic images of native people. Mitigating the stereotype of a stereotype. In: Pearce, D.G. and Butler, R.W. (eds) *Tourism Research Critiques and Challenges*. Routledge, London/New York, pp. 36–69.

Cummings, J. (1992) *Thailand. Travel Survival Kit*. Lonely Planet Publications, Melbourne.

Dahles, H. (1992) The social construction of mokum. Tourism and the quest for local identity in Amsterdam. Paper prepared for the workshop European Reactions to the Tourist Gaze, EASA Conference, Prague.

Dearden, P. and Harron, S. (1991/1992) *Trekking in Northern Thailand. Rural Development and Information Needs*. University of Victoria, London.

Dearden, P. and Harron, S. (1992) Tourism and the hill-tribes of Thailand. In: Weiler, B. and Hall, C. (eds) *Special Interest Tourism*. Belhaven Press, London.

Dearden, P. and Harron, S. (1994) Alternative tourism and adaptive change. *Annals of Tourism Research* 21, 81–102.

de Kadt, E. (1979) *Tourism Passport to Development? Perspectives on the Social and Cultural Effects of Tourism in Developing Countries*. Oxford University Press, Oxford.

Dietvorst, A. (1993) *Tourist Recreation Development and Spatial Transformations*. Centre for Recreation Studies, Coursebook 1993, Wageningen Agricultural University, Wageningen.

Grunfeld, F. (1982) *The Akha. Wayfarers of the Thai Forest*. Time–Life Books, Amsterdam.

Guntamala, A. and Puapratum, K. (1992) *Trekking through Northern Thailand*. Silkworm Books, Bangkok.

Hauser, J. (1992) *Thailand ANWB Reisgids*. Chevalier, Hendrik Ido Ambacht.

Khunaphante, P. (1992) Thailand: the preferable destination for the European tourist. Paper prepared for Tourism in Europe Conference, Centre for Travel and Tourism, Tyne and Wear.

Kunstadter, P. (1969) Hill and valley populations in northwest Thailand. In: *Tribesmen and Peasants in North Thailand*. Tribal Research Institute, Chiang Mai, pp. 69–85.

Leiper, N. (1990) Tourist attraction systems. *Annals of Tourism Research* 17, 367–384.

MacCannell, D. (1976) *The Tourist. A New Theory of the Leisure Class*. Macmillan, London.

MacCannell, D. (1979) Staged authenticity. Arrangements of social space in tourist settings. *American Journal of Sociology* 4(1), 589–603.

MacCannell, D. (1983) Reconstructed ethnicity. Tourism and cultural identity in third world communities. *Annals of Tourism Research* 11, 375–391.

Michaud, J. (1993) The social anchoring of the trekking tourist business in a Hmong community of North Thailand. Minority policy and practice in the Thai-speaking region. Paper for the Fifth International Conference on Thai Studies, London.

Odermatt, P. (1991) En waar blijft de lokale bevolking? Kanttekeningen bij het semiotisch onderzoek naar attracties. *Vrijetijd en Samenleving* 1, 27–47.

Putsatee, A.M. (1992) *Impact of Trekking Tourism on the Environment and Local People*. Mahidol University, Thailand.

Tribal Research Institute (1989) *The Hill Tribes of Thailand.* Chiang Mai University, Chiang Mai.

Turner, L. and Ash, J. (1975) *The Golden Hordes. International Tourism and the Pleasure Periphery.* Constable, London.

Urry, J. (1990) *The Tourist Gaze. Leisure and Travel in Contemporary Societies.* Sage Publications, London/Newbury Park/New Delhi.

van Teeffelen, K. (1990) *Te Gast in Thailand.* Stichting Toerisme en Derde Wereld, Nijmegen.

Village report (1988) Modern life and hill-tribes. *Thai Development Newsletter* 17, 53–58.

Villalba, N. (1986) *Dialogue Asia.* Christian Conference of Asia, Urban Rural Mission, Hong Kong.

Voogt, P. (1991) *Thailand.* Landenreeks. Koninklijk Insituut voor de tropen/Novib/NCOS, Amsterdam/Den Haag.

Walker, A. (1986) *Farmers in the Hills. Ethnographic Notes on the Upland Peoples of Northern Thailand.* Singapore.

6

Mass Tourism and Problems of Tourism Planning in French Mountains

J. Herbin

Institut de Géographie Alpine, Université Joseph Fourier, 17, Rue Maurice Gignoux, F-38031 Grenoble, France.

Introduction

In Austria and Switzerland tourism was already considered as an alternative to the decreasing prospects of the agricultural economy by the beginning of the 1900s. The development of winter sports facilities was characterized by local initiatives and more or less integrated into the local or regional economy. It was not until the end of the Second World War that tourism became of major economic interest in the Alpine regions of France and Italy. Project developers and large investors became involved in the regional economic development of these regions. In contrast to Austria and Switzerland, the participation of the local entrepreneurs is far less intensive in the modern ski-resorts in the French and Italian Alps, although this has begun to change in recent decades.

The Alpine regions in Europe today are inundated by over 50 million winter sports enthusiasts every season. A quarter, 25%, of the world turnover in tourism is realized in the Alpine regions, amounting to more than US$200 billion. The region is increasingly dominated by project developers, bulldozers are removing considerable parts of the mountainous forests in order to construct ski-pistes and the *ski sauvage* now threatens the remaining unspoiled areas.

This chapter will illustrate the sequence of planning policies mainly during the period since the Second World War as a clear example of the spatial impact of material transformations caused by the tourism industry. The first part of the chapter describes the strong policy of investment in tourism infrastructure pursued since the 1960s,

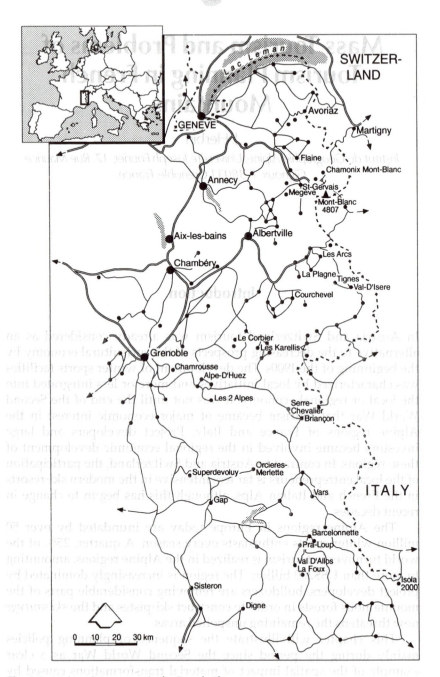

Fig. 6.1. Major winter resorts in the French Alps.

mainly in the Alpine massif, with the double purpose of meeting the demand for holidays or leisure activities (whether from local, national or foreign clienteles) and of providing a means of economic livelihood for local people, especially so that it was possible for them to remain in the region. After retracing the successive phases which marked this policy of tourism planning in the mountains, current problems caused by mass tourism and the policy reactions will be discussed.

The case discussed here, the French mountain zone, represents 21% of the surface of the national territory as it is administratively defined, including the Alps, Jura, Vosges, Massif Central, Pyrenees and the inland parts of Corsica, but contains only three million inhabitants (5% of the national population) (see Fig. 6.1).

The Main Phases of Tourism Planning Policies in the French Mountains

The village resorts: first form of tourist development in the mountains

Since the romantics and scientists 'discovered' the mountains in the late 18th century, until the eve of the Second World War, the first form of tourist development in the mountains – in France and surrounding countries – consisted in the spontaneous flowering of village resorts. Well-situated hamlets and villages on through routes and in the heart of great massifs which were explored by alpinists gradually became holiday resorts during the summer. The pre-existing nucleus was added to by chalets and hotels in an uncontrolled manner, as tourism was added to the traditional mountain economy. Rather quickly some of these resorts obtained a certain fame for a particular type of specialist tourism. These included:

- the early Alpine resorts (such as Chamonix or Pralognan), which developed mainly in the second half of the 19th century and which helped to modify the frightening image of the mountain;
- the health resorts (such as Aix les Bains, Saint Gervais, Barèges, Cauterets, Luchon, Le Mont Dore);
- the 'climate resorts' (Briançon, Villard de Lans);
- the winter sports resorts, developed with the construction of the first ski-lifts just after the Second World War.

The successive generations of resorts on unspoilt locations

The new resorts of the first generation

If we ignore the special case of the Mont d'Arbois in Megève (developed on a virgin site for skiing in 1920 on the initiative of Baron Rothschild) the first high resort was created on a new site in the French mountains in 1934, when the Alpe d'Huez developed on a mountain pass at a height of 2035 m, imitating the example of Sestrière, built in Italy ten years earlier. The first generation of new resorts, established higher in the mountains above the permanent habitat and allowing winter sports practice under the best conditions, appeared in France just before the Second World War (for example Alpe d'Huez, Méribel or Le Revard).

The new resorts of the second generation

The beginning of Courchevel in 1948, on the initiative of the department of Savoie, marked a turning-point in the notion of French mountain resorts, since it was the first to be developed according to an overall plan. Among the innovative aspects of this new resort, located on a virgin site, which were often used as later points of reference were:

- the decisive intervention of the local authority (the departmental council of Savoie), which assured itself in advance control of land and access roads;
- the implementation of an overall design plan by a team under the direction of the architect Laurent Chappis;
- the intervention of private investors developing, under strict guidance as to densities, roof heights and the like, individual plots.

The surprising success of Courchevel, which quickly became one of the largest mass resorts, encouraged the creation of other similar resorts (such as Chamrousse, Serre-Chevalier, Les Deux Alpes). A 'planning doctrine' for winter sports resorts had been established for the French mountains.

The new resorts of the third generation

The almost simultaneous development, in the 1960s and early 1970s, of some 20 'integrated resorts' (i.e. economically and environmentally integrated) on new locations is undisputedly the largest and most coherent planning operation that has ever taken place in the tourist planning of French mountains. The French experience (which included

La Plagne, Superdévoluy, Avoriaz, Flaine, Les Arcs, Les Ménuires, Le Corbier, Val Thorens, Tignes, Vars, Pra-Loup, La Foux d'Allos, Orcières-Merlette, Isola 2000, Les Karellis and many more) was imitated in other Alpine countries like Switzerland (Anzère) and Italy (San Sicario, Pila) and even in more distant regions such as the United States, Chile, Argentina, Japan and New Zealand. These resorts conformed to the doctrine called the 'Snow Plan', distinguished in legal-financial processes and general spatial and architectural archetypes.

In order to capitalize on the 'white gold' and to make French mountains a 'trap for foreign currency', this doctrine was elaborated and put into practice during the Fourth and Fifth National Plans (1960–1970) and continued with the 'priority options' of the Sixth Plan (1970–1975). The last foresaw the creation of some 150,000 international top-class hotel beds or 30,000 per year, in 23 new resorts and 20 old resorts, thanks to public subsidy and preferred loans for the development of infrastructure and for the acquisition of land. These quantitative objectives were achieved and even exceeded, thanks to the efficiency of the administrative instruments that were applied through the SEATM (Study and Tourist Planning Service for the Mountains) and the establishment of an interministerial structure in Chambéry. Such efforts aimed at the creation of new resorts, promising with much publicity and at a high cost to catch up with developments in Switzerland and Austria, especially in the number of foreign visitors.

The French State has played an important role in the preselection of the locations, the expensive construction of access roads, the procedure for land acquisition in the public interest, and the regulation of the relationships between the local authorities and the planners. Control and homogeneity were basic principles.

These principles for creating tourist complexes adapted to regular winter visits and entirely organized for the function of intensive alpine skiing need a continuous search for new areas, which must be extensive, snowy and high (most resorts are installed between 1800 and 2400 m).

The construction and selling of buildings (especially thousands of apartments or studios sold through various formulas such as joint property, time-sharing and the like) have constituted the 'hard nucleus' of those operations. In fact, the type of accommodation has stayed very monolithic everywhere, with only a smaller place reserved for hotels.

Architectural styles are constrained by strict zoning, traffic segregation, a unicentric concentration of collective functions, and a subsequent expansion in the form of satellites created lower (La Plagne) or higher (Les Arcs) than the mother-station, resulting in a microregional scale of planning for whole massifs or valleys (such as La Grande Plagne, Les Trois-Vallées, L'Espace Killy, Le Grand Massif, Les Portes du Soleil and La Forêt Blanche).

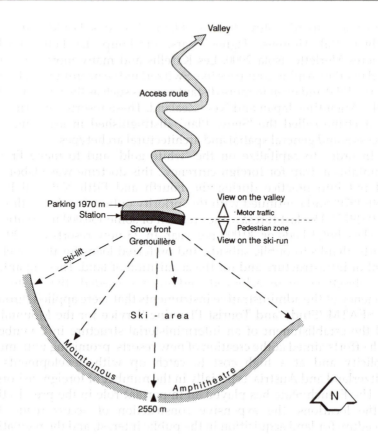

Fig. 6.2. Spatial structure of a modern winter resort.

The age of reconsideration

In spite of the success in terms of tourism visits (as much from national as from international demand) and the positive aspects that should clearly be recognized (especially the creation of many jobs for the mountain people), criticism of the policy of creating resorts in virgin locations has become increasingly heard. Without being officially stated, such policies were effectively abandoned by the mid-1970s, apart from some exceptions (especially Valmorel). The year 1977 marked a ministerial instruction on tourist projects in the mountains and a public debate on the Vallouise. The search for a new direction had begun, based upon a number of new considerations.

The justified criticism of the policy of the 'Snow Plan'

The profitability of resorts in virgin locations, which were full during the winter but little occupied in the summer, was in doubt. Policy was also blamed for the failure to integrate tourism into the local economy and society. The new resorts were located in the higher mountains, neglecting the lower slopes and the smaller village resorts.

The rise to power of the environmentalist movement

From the 1970s the environmentalist movements (like Club Alpin Français and Mountain Wilderness) started to denounce the excesses of such a policy, especially with regard to the damage to nature and the impact in the mountains of an urban culture. Several accidents, like the Val d'Isère catastrophe (where an avalanche killed 40 people) or that of Ravoire (where roads were swept away in a cloudburst), have reinforced the environmental arguments.

The new institutional context

Since the turning-point in 1977 several important institutional changes have modified the conditions of planning for tourism in the mountains. Notable in particular are:

- the 'mountain directive' which, without excluding completely development on virgin sites, nevertheless opposes the degradation of landscapes, insisting that new buildings should be in harmony with the existing settlements;
- the so-called 'UTN procedure' (*unités touristiques nouvelles*) established in 1979, which submits every large-scale tourist project to a thorough examination by a commission charged with authorizing it, under certain conditions;
- the 'Decentralization Act' of 1982, which diminished the role of the State and gave more room for the initiative and responsibility of the local authorities;
- the 'Mountain Act' of 1985, which improved conditions for self-development by communities by increasing their financial resources.

Changes in the snow market

Since the beginning of the 1980s important changes seem to have taken place in the winter sports market. Whereas it has long been dominated by the tyranny of supply, the market is now dominated by a tyranny of demand. Apart from some foreign markets (England, Spain) the broad demand for winter sports has indeed stagnated, especially on the French domestic market, which represents about 80% of the overnight stays in the winter season. This is a result of unfavourable weather conditions (three consecutive winters with poor snow conditions between 1987 and 1990): consequently the number of French people leaving for winter sports dropped to 7.1% in 1989–1990 compared to almost 10% in 1983–1984. It also seems that demand is diversifying: snow holidays are now not only for skiing.

Thus during the 20 years 1960–1980 the French winter sports resorts passed through a period of continuous growth, reaching 1.4 million beds in 1984, 3900 mechanical ski-lifts, creating 120,000 jobs and permitting 75 million overnight stays in winter with a turnover of 17 billion French francs. The development of mass tourism (for a summer clientele as well as a winter clientele) did not prevent the existence of a crisis which is at the same time structural (that is the adaption of supply to demand), a matter of product quality, functioning and management, financing and all in the context of economic depression and climatic change. In addition the well-known Alpine resorts have to cope with increasing competition from other suppliers. Eastern Europe may be underequipped but is a potential competitor with more stable climatic conditions. German project developers and investors are already busy renovating old-fashioned, formerly state-owned, hotels and building additional new facilities. Several regions, for instance the Tatra Mountains, offer cheap and competitive opportunities.

Mass Tourism and the Control of Space in the Mountains

The concept of space management leads to the examination of the problems of tourism planning in mountains for both quantity and quality. There are two main objectives.

- Avoiding using too much space. Because of the market seasonality of winter tourism the facilities are utilized only during relatively short periods. In order to improve the quality of the supply, additional facilities such as indoor sports halls and integrated leisure centres have been constructed, again consuming scarce available space. Traffic, with its noise and air-polluting emissions, has a tremendous impact on ecologically vulnerable areas. The cableways, ski-lifts and prepared ski-runs damage the natural habitat of the flora and the fauna and increase the danger of soil erosion.

- Avoiding the incorrect use of space. The previously natural environment has been transformed into partly urbanized scenery with often intrusive facilities. New forms of leisure activities such as helicopter-skiing, *ski sauvage* and steep-slope skiing pose an increasing ecological threat that requires more effective management of the natural resource.

The zones with a strong impact from tourism can be divided into two categories.

- Those important tourism resorts and their neighbourhoods which experience both a strong real-estate pressure and many winter and/or summer visitors.
- The natural zones in the massifs that are most desired by tourists or day-trippers (in particular the national parks and regional nature parks), where construction is regulated but nevertheless which have experienced increasing tourist numbers.

The following discussion is limited to the case of the larger tourism resorts and to the problems of their development control.

The costs of managing space for tourism

Apart from the poor sales in 1981–1982, the real-estate market was very active until 1988. Since then, in a generally retracting market, it seems that real-estate pressure (basically for studios or apartments for private use or for rent) has tended to concentrate on several areas and in several favoured sectors, such as:

- in the Northern Alps (La Savoie with the Olympic resorts of the Tarentaise, such as Val d'Isère, Tignes, Les Arcs, La Plagne, Courchevel and Méribel, the prestigious resorts of the Haute Savoie, such as Chamonix in Megève, Flaine and the Great Massif, Avoriaz and the Portes du Soleil, and, in Isère, the Alpe d'Huez and the Deux-Alpes);
- in the Southern Alps (Le Briançonnais);
- in the Pyrenees (La Cerdagne, which is under pressure from Spanish Catalonia, and the valleys of Luz and of Saint-Lary).

Parallel to this growth in real estate for leisure activities there has been a deterioration in resort centres, large or small. This deterioration especially affects the high stations, built on virgin sites in the 1960s. The public buildings have become old-fashioned, public spaces are neglected, and shops and services are highly seasonal. Renovation is necessary. The same problems can be seen in some summer resorts (particularly in the old health resorts) where hotels have often been transformed into studio buildings, been abandoned or are ruinous.

In the skiable areas the links between the higher stations and their large extensions on virgin areas have been weakened. Investment in ski-lifts, after having reached a record level in 1986, has now fallen to a much wiser level. The accent is henceforth on the improvement of already equipped areas, the modernization of ski-lifts, improvement of tracks, creation of installations for artificial snow, modernization of management and the improvement of reception quality and customer service. Diversification increases the winter season (with integrated leisure centres, cross-country skiing and the like) and the summer season (mountain golf, swimming-pools, network of paths and refuges). There is an increasing demand for the ATB (all-terrain bike), exciting water sports (rafting, hydrospeed, canyoning) and air sports (hang-gliding). Although the recent evolution of the winter sports market lowers real-estate pressure, it is still necessary to control the growth of the resorts and scattered and disorganized individual building. As the public is becoming more aware of environmental quality, this factor is itself a major tourism attraction. From now on tourism development and the quality of the urban and natural environment will be closely related, and more mountain resort managers will understand the necessity of investing in the environment.

The factors influencing the control of space

The evolution of demand

At the same moment that general demand has faltered, the demand for real estate, which determines the occupation of space, has considerably evolved. Plots are getting larger and less concentrated, as can be observed in a different context on the Costa Brava.

The behaviour of tourism producers

One of the main difficulties with the implementation of a broad development project in mountain resorts is the general absence of structural framework for tourism management on a local scale, which would permit public–private partnerships. The lack of such structures means that the tourist resorts are pulled between the divergent individual interests and group strategies of landlords, developers, hoteliers, estate agents, traders, summer residents and others. The tourist office does not have the legal and technical skills or the finance to play a coordinating role. Frequently the real-estate owner, even if he is still a farmer, tries to sell his properties as expensively as possible to developers; the developer rapidly completes his operation within the shortest time; the trader tries to resell land rapidly; while the summer resident, once installed in a region, and having contributed to its degradation, opposes new tourism development in the name of environmental protection. The sum of individual interests rarely coincides with the general interest of the resort, which requires a long-term vision. Purely individual solutions to the general problems, in the absence of the adequate decision-making structures found in Switzerland or in Austria, are largely responsible for the waste of space, the low quality of the tourist product offered, inadequacies in the field of promotion and ultimately poor financial results.

The instruments for managing space: the legal and regulatory framework

Tax law

Fiscal legislation is not an effective instrument for the management of space. Municipalities are not really urged to improve the volume of activities, but rather to favour real estate. Few stimulation measures, for example for spreading beds, have been attempted.

Land-use regulation

The 'mountain law' attempts the protection of agricultural land but the practical outcome of this wise set of principles depends on its application by prefects and mayors within the framework of land-occupation plans (POS – *plans d'occupation des sols*). In each resort the elaboration of such land-occupation plans can and must be the opportunity to implement a public project. The POS, however, is what the local council wants it to be, even if the State tries to enforce the national rules. After a dozen years of operation, the UTN procedure, which is decentralized and placed under the control of the prefects, exercises a real educational role so that some projects are modified or even withdrawn before their presentation. However, the protection of the environment still depends upon the interpretation of the prefects and mayors, which can be lax.

The protected spaces

Many official texts exist which allow statutory protection of an area. Some of those protections are obsolete, discredited and circumvented. More recent regulations are generally more respected but the means of management of these protected areas is often missing.

Incentive policies

The policy of so-called 'resort contracts' used in some plans can allow direct intervention in the management of space. This puts the accent on the quality of urban development, on long-term management as such and integration with private partners.

The 'Mountain Plan'

Announced by the French Minister of Tourism in 1991, this plan tackles the problem of space mangement in tourism resorts. It defines 'resort projects', forbids new alpine ski developments on new sites and examines the economic and financial balance of plans in regard to incentives to hotel investments, spreading of hotels and the quality of service.

These measures, imposed by the evolution of the winter sports market, should contribute some improvment. They do not, however, solve the problems of urban degradation.

Other possible solutions

Here intermunicipal 'coherence schemes' should be mentioned as these could have a considerable impact in tourism areas. They involve some smaller massifs or valleys presenting a clear community of interests in tourism development and establishing a 'development charter' for the medium term. The implementation of such a scheme could serve as a basis for the POS revisions and the UTN files. Permitting the local partners to reflect upon the appropriateness of the plans and their coherence, and the State to consider its precise obligations, could undoubtedly move in the direction of better planning policies on the microregional scale. At the moment one scheme of this type has been worked out, in the Haute Tarentaise; others are proposed, in the Mont Blanc area, for the Great Massif, in Oisan and in Cerdagne.

In the urban centres, policies for renovation of accommodation, shops or public spaces stimulated by the resort contracts should cover the Val d'Isère, La Clusaz and Saint-Lary. Others are in progress for La Mongie and Gourette among others. Comanagement of the natural peripheral spaces in a flexible manner is also needed and is currently being demonstrated in Vercors and Queyras. It is also important that the local people responsible for tourism become aware of the importance of the maintenance of a mountain agriculture and, if necessary, contribute to maintaining this activity, which is indispensable to the protection of a heritage of landscape beauty and to the quality of the environment that the tourists seek. In contrast to the German Alps this idea of agriculture as an environmental concierge is not yet well advanced.

Finally, the creation of development and resort management structures must be continued, because it is not enough to rely upon the goodwill of local communities in the face of individual initiatives. Such structures must not only permit the mobilization of new private resources and the better distribution of finance, they should also encourage all actors to participate in a common plan. It is clear that to succeed in the management of space in tourism resorts, both in the mountains and elsewhere, there must be a local collective leadership in a common interest, and a national State involvement for the long-term utilization of the national heritage.

From Producers to Management of the Product

The previous section illustrated something of the variety of producers involved in shaping the recreation–tourism product at various stages and in various spatial contexts. Such a description of the management of the tourism product immediately confronts the multiplicity of goals held by these diverse producers, which in turn frequently determines the purposes of management. The discussion of this management by producers is the theme of the following section. Three cases are considered here: first, the private commercial self-contained holiday resort; secondly, the use of tourism elements within multifunctional project development undertaken with a mix of public and private components; and, thirdly, the organization of public open space and its use for recreation within a broader range of uses.

A sectoral approach to tourism that attempts to isolate and identify the tourism facility, tourism as an economic sector and indeed the tourist as an individual consumer has proved a useful tool of analysis. It rapidly becomes both misleading and effectively impossible to apply when tourism is considered in wider contexts.

The three chapters in this section consider three such contexts which progressively include a wider range of variables. First, Faché describes the tourism enterprise that endeavours to provide as far as possible a self-contained and comprehensive holiday package. This is Center Parcs, the lineal descendant of the British interwar 'holiday camp'. This is a context where the producers of the tourism product have the most effective control over all the elements that comprise the experience (even the vagaries of the weather are replaced by a controlled internal climate), although the consumer, of course, still largely determines what, in what quantity and in what sequence the components are assembled. Equally other users of the same space or facilities are effectively excluded. This near-complete control renders product management easier but carries the disadvantage that the single producer is solely responsible for the provision of all facilities which service only a single tourism market.

In contrast Jansen-Verbeke and van de Wiel's study of urban waterfront development places commercial tourism projects within a context composed of both other such projects, which together form a composite product, and also other commercial and non-commercial land uses. Not only is space shared with non-tourist uses, the facilities often make little distinction between tourist and non-tourist customers. In addition tourism is expected to serve a much wider variety of purposes on the waterfront. Not only do specific tourism facilities provide specified tourism products for purchasers, they also contribute two important, if less tangible benefits to purchasers and non-purchasers alike within the area as a whole. These can be summarized as 'animation', i.e. keeping the area both 'alive' and 'lively', especially in the evening, by generating pedestrian traffic in public spaces, and 'cachet', i.e. helping establish a tone or atmosphere which extends from the recreational facilities to cover by association the whole waterfront.

Finally, Burgers' chapter analyses the changes in the use of public open space and its relationship to, as well as consequences for, policy. The coverage of uses has now become so wide as to have been largely ignored until recently with its ubiquity concealing its importance. Here the recreation and tourism product becomes diffuse, merging into non-tourism products, and management passes from the individual facility to public agencies and from simple and easily identifiable commercial considerations to much broader issues of the public interest in the management of multifunctional public spaces.

7

Transformations in the Concept of Holiday Villages in Northern Europe

W. Faché

Department of Social Interventions in Leisure and Tourism, University of Ghent, Henri Dunantlaan 2, B-9000 Gent, Belgium.

Introduction

Not long ago holiday villages with hundreds of beds were called 'large-scale holiday projects' in northern Europe (Becker, 1984). Yet none of those 'large-scale' holiday villages would be classified as such nowadays. At the present time holiday villages in temperate countries have thousands of beds and a gross area of a hundred or more hectares, and account for investments of millions of dollars (up to US$130 million) – in other words, a mega-scale approach. This trend started in the early part of the 1980s.

The enlargement of the holiday villages went together with fundamental innovations bringing about a fundamental change in the seasonal nature of tourism. These innovations are such that holiday villages are becoming extremely important options for short-break holidays. Moreover, developments in holiday villages provide some insight into the type and scale of tourism that could exert an important influence on tourism trends in northern Europe in the future.

There is not just an increase in the scale of the holiday villages, there is also an escalation in numbers. Currently three large operators are building large-scale holiday villages in northern Europe and plan to open new ones every year. These three are: Center Parcs, Gran Dorado and Sun Parks. But, apart from these three operators, plenty of other more or less separate initiatives are emerging. In northern Europe we counted 91 projects being either developed or planned in the next five years.

Finally, we can state the fact that these large-scale villages are successful. This holds especially for Center Parcs International, the

European market leader. They let villas in 14 holiday villages in four countries (The Netherlands, Belgium, France and the UK) with a total capacity of 47,774 beds. The unit occupancy rate exceeded 90% in all their resorts during each month of 1990 (Fitzpatrick Associates, 1993). There is an average of 3000 people staying in a village at any one time of the year. In the Benelux villages 72% of the guests were repeat visitors, having stayed in a Center Parcs village once or more before. The percentage of loyal guests (those who have stayed at one of the villages five times or more) was 28.3. This means that this group is as large as the group of first-timers (28.6%). Of those visitors having stayed at Center Parcs before, 56% had returned within a year (Konings, 1992). According to a survey in The Netherlands, the following visitor groups are the most strongly represented: the 25–39 age group (62%), families with young children (41.9%), average (33%) and above-average (45%) income groups (Center Parcs, 1991).

Despite fundamental innovative developments and the success of the large-scale villages, only a few studies have appeared on particular aspects, e.g. the ecological impact of large-scale holiday villages (Strasdas, 1991) and transformations, innovations and the evaluation of these transformations by the guests (Faché, 1987, 1990).

In this chapter the innovative developments which have affected holiday villages and the variations in village concepts will be reviewed. First, a definition of the current use of the term 'holiday village' must be given. In an international context there is little agreement about the use of the term. The following characteristics can be seen as essential:

- the holiday village is purpose-built and for the exclusive use of holiday-makers;
- a holiday village has been planned as such and has been designed as an architectural entity, with a village-like environment;
- a holiday village is an integrated resort with low-rise accommodation units (e.g. villas), recreation, eating, drinking and shopping facilities and leisure services;
- the dominant type of accommodation is self-catering units that contain kitchen facilities, one or more bedrooms and often a separate living-room.

Three Generations of Holiday Villages

Holiday villages developed between the two World Wars and since then have undergone many innovative transformations, making them an important option for holiday accommodation. We can pinpoint three stages in this development which justify the description 'three generations of holiday villages'.

The first-generation holiday villages

The precursors of the first generation were the holiday camps, literally camps of tents, which developed before the First World War. The most significant development concerning these holiday camps took place in 1936, when Billy Butlin opened the first of the Butlin holiday camps in Skegness, England. The Butlin holiday camps consisted of villages of chalet-style accommodation (not tents) with modern sanitation, communal catering facilities and extensive on site amusement and high-class entertainment for working-class families at an all-inclusive price. The keynote of the holiday camp was organized entertainment and activities on site with serviced accommodation (Ward and Hardy, 1986). The holiday camps, such as those established by Butlin, and two other noted entrepreneurs of the day in Britain, Fred Pontin and Harry Warner, were enormously successful before the Second World War and in the early post-war years.

> This prosperity resulted in Britain from a number of factors including the coming into effect of the 1938 Holidays with Pay Act, the high levels of employment, and the reduced age of marriage and high rate of family formation. In 1948 one in twenty of all holiday-makers in Britain stayed at Butlin's. The holiday camp was a symbol of the post-war society, reflecting the modernist architectural style of the period.
>
> (Urry, 1990)

Billy Butlin's early attempts to introduce his holiday camp concept abroad failed, but the holiday *village* concept has been successful on the Continent.

In the 1950s there was a shift in the villages towards 'self-catering': the residential units were equipped with kitchen facilities. Residential units, designed for families with children, generally contained four to eight beds.

The location of the village of the first generation was very important. Existing natural attractions serve as the resource base for these villages: a lake or a waterfront setting, a unique landscape or areas which offer outdoor recreation facilities for such sports as boating or golf. In most of these holiday villages there are also a limited number of outdoor recreational facilities within the village itself. Examples of such facilities are tennis courts, midget golf, a soccer and volleyball field, a traditional, rectangular, open-air swimming-pool, and a children's playground. A restaurant and a small grocery store are usually provided as well. The most distinctive characteristic of these holiday villages of the first generation is the fact that both their chalets and their recreational facilities can be utilized only during the summer months. Thus, the early holiday villages remain highly seasonal (Becker, 1984; Ward and Hardy, 1986; Boyer, 1992).

The second-generation holiday villages

During the 1960s a totally new breed of holiday village emerged in northern Europe: the four-season holiday village. These holiday villages of the second generation originated when indoor leisure facilities, such as indoor water leisure centres, indoor tennis courts, etc., were introduced in the villages as well. Apart from this fundamental difference from the holiday villages of the first generation, another major innovation of the second generation must be cited as well. In holiday villages of the second generation the stone-built villas with self-catering facilities were now also suitable for winter occupation, thanks to their construction and central heating.

But the most spectacular aspect of the second-generation holiday villages was the introduction of a whole new breed of leisure pool. The Dutch company Center Parcs first introduced the innovative 'subtropical water paradise' in 1980 at the new holiday village Eemhof in Zeewolde (near Amsterdam, The Netherlands). The success of so many large-scale second-generation holiday villages as (short-break) holiday provision can be primarily attributed to the presence of these indoor water-leisure centres, which constitute the centrepiece of these holiday villages and are their unique selling proposition.

These 'indoor water-leisure centres' differed greatly from the 'leisurized pool', which is a conventional pool with added fun features (e.g. slides, whirlpool). The purpose-built indoor water-leisure centres had the following common characteristics (Faché, 1989).

A varied aquascape

The new indoor water-leisure centres were much larger. Where a traditional pool had a water surface of approximately 250–375 m², it became quite common for indoor water-leisure centres to have 800–1200 m² of water surface, and sometimes even more. Moreover, there was no longer a rectangular water surface, but a variety of shapes and forms of water areas, so that a varied waterspace came into being. Water areas were fringed by a variety of tropical vegetation: palm trees and other subtropical and tropical plants.

More diversity of leisure features

In water-leisure centres a wide range of leisure activities was possible, thanks to a great diversity of features: simulated waterfalls and waves, water-slides, wild water channels, rapids, jetstreams, floating carpets, hot whirlpools, water-cannons, children's pools, outside heated pools and other facilities which contributed to the excitement and movement in and with water. In addition to this, there were numerous facilities for activities outside the water, like a solarium, a sauna, a Turkish steam bath, etc. Water-leisure centres also introduced large 'beaches', where one can relax in deckchairs and loungers, just as if one were at the seaside. There were also waterside cafés and terraces.

As eating and drinking constitute a significant leisure component, spaces for these activities are important leisure facilities. In other words, under a giant transparent double-skinned plastic dome, opportunities to play, to eat, to drink, to socialize, to relax and just watch the world go by are all being incorporated increasingly into the design of the new water-leisure centres.

Agreeable temperature

On the beaches and terraces one can comfortably sit in a bathing-suit because the ambient temperature is pleasant: at least 27°C (cf. traditional pool: 22–25°C). In a water-leisure centre there are various water areas with different temperatures, ranging from 29 to 36°C (cf. traditional pool: 23–24°C).

In addition to the indoor water-leisure centre, the large-scale second-generation holiday villages also have within the village itself a broad range of other indoor and outdoor recreational facilities for tennis, squash, badminton, fitness training, midget golf, golf, skiing, surfing, sailing, canoeing, bowling and children's games. This extensive range of indoor and outdoor leisure facilities is the key element of such holiday villages.

As a result of these innovations Center Parcs has become one of the best-known exponents of an all-season tourism product (Fitzpatrick Associates, 1993). Thus the holiday operators came to terms with the cold weather and rain in countries with a temperate climate. There has been a tendency on the part of tourism specialists and practitioners alike, at least in recent years, to assume that features of climate are the determining factor shaping the pattern of seasonal activity (Boyer, 1992; Allcock, 1994). The transformations in holiday villages demonstrate that seasonality can be combated. With the growth of second holidays and short breaks over the last decade, these indoor holiday villages became a significant provision for short-break holidays during all seasons of the year (Faché, 1994).

The conceptual development of holiday villages did not stop with the second-generation villages. The indoor-resort concept caught the imagination of the architects, who further and further extended the indoor facilities. This led to the development of the third generation of villages.

The third-generation holiday villages

With the holiday villages of the third generation, the Mediterranean holiday village centre was imported to regions with a temperate climate. Center Parcs were the ones to introduce a totally new concept by opening in 1987 a holiday village (Vossemeren in Belgium), with a Mediterranean village centre under a transparent heated dome. Under this dome three different areas can be found: a large 'subtropical water paradise', as described above, a leisure sports centre and a 'Parc Plaza' (named Gran Place in the case of Gran Dorado and Sun Terra Park in the case of Sun Parks).

The Parc Plaza is an important component of the indoor village centre. In a subtropical setting one can find restaurants, a café, a discothèque, bowling-alleys, terraces, gardens with living tropical trees and plants, a pond with real tropical vegetation and birds (for example, flamingos), and shops. The temperature in the Parc Plaza is 22° to 23°C.

A third significant component of the village centre is the indoor leisure sports area, with courts for tennis, squash, badminton, volley-ball and table tennis, a fitness centre and a beauty salon.

Water-leisure and leisure sports, casual social activities, eating, drinking, walking and leisure shopping are no longer compartmentalized in different locations. All these activities are possible in an indoor 'Mediterranean' resort.

In addition, a greater variety of accommodation options is offered. There are bungalows, for two, three or up to ten persons. Alongside bungalows, some holiday villages have also integrated on-site three-storey hotels. With this innovation the concept of holiday villages has come full circle. The first-generation villages attempted to provide an alternative to hotel holiday accommodation. Today they are completing the circle themselves, by building hotels as part of their village complexes.

In the development of large-scale year-round holiday villages in which a super indoor water-leisure centre is an essential component, Center Parcs has acted as a catalyst as witnessed by the villages which have been built or renovated – all with (subtropical) water-leisure complexes – in different countries. The most striking examples are the Gran Dorado villages (formerly Vendorado) in The Netherlands and

Germany, the Sun Parks villages in Belgium, the 'Vandland' Projects in Denmark and the upgrading of the Butlin holiday centres in Britain.

The arrival in 1987 of Center Parcs' holiday village in Sherwood Forest (Nottingham) implies also the introduction into Britain of an up-market holiday village and the introduction of new standards into British holiday centres (Holloway, 1989).

> The first-generation holiday camps (Butlin's, Pontin's and the like) are being forced to upgrade their facilities. The Rank Organization, in particular, has invested £90m over three years as part of a five-year £170m programme to redevelop its remaining five Butlin centres and give them a more up-market image, which has been generally successful in winning sales after a decline in trade for holiday centres during the early 1980s.
>
> (Holloway, 1989)

A key feature of Butlin's investment programme has been the development of 'Waterworld'. The Butlin's Minehead camp, for example, now renamed Somerset World, has had £10m spent on a water-leisure complex with new deluxe accommodation and a themed show bar. A sum of £25m has been invested in the Butlin's camp in Ayr (Scotland), upgrading the accommodation and creating a subtropical water world with a simulated beach (Bentley, 1988). In other countries (Belgium, Holland, Germany) major holiday village operators have undertaken similar projects, although not on the same scale.

The Center Parcs policy of continuously innovating and upgrading its facilities to the level of the newest sites will ensure that their catalyst role continues (Bentley, 1988).

An evolution to highly self-contained villages

The above-described evolution from first- to second- and third-generation holiday villages can be characterized as an evolution to highly self-contained resorts that offer all that their guests require in terms of indoor and outdoor recreation facilities, restaurants and shops on-site within the village itself, which means that a leisure world is created within the village.

A survey (Faché, 1987) among people who spend a short-break holiday in second- or third-generation holiday villages shows that these highly self-contained villages are preferred on the following grounds.

The presence of intramural recreation facilities saves the time of having to look for recreation in the vicinity of the holiday village and of reaching the extramural facility. Particularly during short-break holidays (weekend or mid-week breaks) this is an important consideration.

Table 7.1. Three important year-round holiday village operators in Northern Europe.

Holiday villages	City/Country	Opening year	Surface (ha)	Number of bungalows	Number of hotel rooms	Number of beds
Center Parcs						
De Lommerbergen	Reuver, NL	1968	35	502		2303
Het Vennenbos	Hapert, NL	1970	48	524		2890
Het Meerdal	Horst, NL	1971	71	655		3258
De Huttenheugte	Dalen, NL	1972	105	677		3401
De Eemhof	Zeewolde, NL	1980	65	701		3946
Erperheide	Peer, B	1981	47	616		2833
De Kempervennen	Westerhoven, NL	1983	132	649		3361
Het Heijderbos	Heijen, NL	1986	83	717		3814
Sherwood Forest	Nottinghamshire, UK	1987	150	709		3806
De Vossemeren	Lommel, B	1987	93	650	58	3742
Les Bois Francs	Verneuil s. Avre, F	1988	300	738	89	3832
Elveden Forest	Suffolk, UK	1989	164	683	89	3916
Les Hauts de Bruyère	Chaumont s. Tharonne, F	1993	110	634		3458
Longleat Forest	Wiltshire, UK	1994	150	600		3214
Gran Dorado						
Loohorst	N	1979	50	500		3050
Heilbachsee	G	1982	26	460		2344
Weertenbergen	N	1985	40	496		2790
Zandvoort	N	1990	28	407	124	2392
Port Zelande	Grevelingen, NL	1990	23	720		3780
Sun Parks						
Oost-Duinkerke	B	1982	50	675		3380
Vielsalm	B	1984	33	377		1995
Den Haan	B	1989	35	557		2792
Rauwse Meren	Mol-Rauw, B	1994	33	598	50	3220

Moreover, many people would not play tennis or midget golf or go swimming during their holidays if they had to go off the premises, since they cannot assess the quality, do not know what kind of reception they will have, etc. In other words the intramural amenities' threshold is very low.

But the most important motivation relates to the wide diversity of leisure options in second- and third-generation holiday villages enabling each member or subgroup of the family (for example, husband and wife, father and son) to undertake their own activities. This has proved to be an important motive, especially for families with children. Children usually enjoy themselves on their own in a holiday village. So it is not surprising to hear parents commenting: 'If the children have a good time, we can also have a splendid short-break holiday.' Moreover, since most holiday villages are fenced off and no car traffic is permitted in the park (except on days of arrival and departure), children can play freely without risk, and there is no need for permanent parental surveillance. Freedom for the children also means freedom for the parents in their activities. For families with children this is a major advantage of holiday villages. A holiday with the children does not mean that the parents are burdened.

Notwithstanding the fact that highly self-contained villages offer an extensive range of amenities within the village which meet the expectations of the guests, holiday-makers do leave the premises during the course of their stay.

Based on research on the action radius of guests in different holiday villages (Wolf *et al.*, 1981; Faché, 1987; Voskens-Drijver *et al.*, 1987; Eeckhout, 1991), we can conclude the following. The number of people undertaking activities outside highly self-contained holiday villages depends on the size of the recreational facilities inside the village and the touristic attractiveness of the village's surroundings. In a holiday village with numerous indoor and outdoor recreational facilities (viz. Sun Parks, Den Haan, Belgium) but close to a beach resort, 75% of the guests had at one time or another left the village for a short or a long trip, for a walk or for entertainment on the beach (Eeckhout, 1991). In contrast, in holiday villages offering the same level of intramural recreative facilities but situated in a touristically less attractive area not more than 35% of the guests left their holiday village (Faché, 1987; Voskens-Drijver *et al.*, 1987). Still, in both cases recreational facilities on-site within the village remain important, especially the indoor facilities.

Variations on village design approaches

The description of the second- and the third-generation village can create the impression that all these villages look alike. This is not the case. They are mutually divergent in many respects. An important variation is the *design approach*. We can distinguish three different holiday village designs.

According to the first concept, the holiday village groups single- and two-storey villas on an estate in an area which is highly attractive for tourists (for example, near the coast). By clustering the villas a large number of units can be concentrated on a confined space, and as a result the villages can be situated in areas with highly attractive natural surroundings or in a popular tourist area. A good example of this concept is Gran Dorado's Port Zelande at Grevelingen (opened in mid-1990). The source of inspiration for this village, the North Sea, 30 km from Rotterdam, was the Mediterranean Port-Grimaud (Dewailly and Flament, 1993). The village site is only 23.3 ha, with 722 bungalows and hotel-apartments, which are built close together, forming a harbour village with a marina (Fig. 7.1).

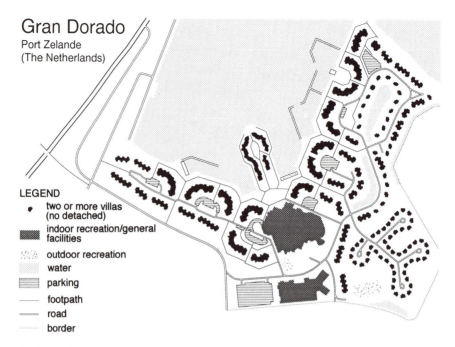

Gran Dorado
Port Zelande
(The Netherlands)

LEGEND
• two or more villas
  (no detached)
▰ indoor recreation/general
  facilities
⠿ outdoor recreation
  water
▤ parking
— footpath
═ road
⋯ border

Fig. 7.1. The spatial structure of Gran Dorado's Port Zelande (The Netherlands).

The village centre is entirely covered over, and is comparable to Center Parcs' covered village centres. Holiday-makers must rely on Grevelingen lake for leisure activities such as surfing, water-skiing, sailing, canoeing and skin-diving. This is a salt-water lake 11,000 hectares in area, 7000 ha of which is navigable. It is closed off from the North Sea by the Brouwers and Grevelingen dams. Holiday-makers can sunbathe and walk along the wide North Sea beach, which is connected with Port Zelande by a pedestrian bridge.

Entirely different from this is the concept of the scattered villas. This second design approach uses a strict division of the land into small parcels, with detached villas and small private gardens separated from one another by some trees and shrubs. According to Fischer (quoted by Harfst and Scharpf, 1982), 'this approach spoils the countryside without making good use of the open spaces'. A typical example of this concept is the third-generation holiday village Sun Parks, near the resort of Den Haan in Belgium, which was opened at the end of 1989, with 537 detached villas on a 40 ha site. This village was built on the polder behind the broad coastal band of wooded dunes (Fig. 7.2).

The third design approach consciously avoids obvious partitioning.

Sun Parks
Den Haan (Belgium)

LEGEND
- • one villa
- ▓ indoor recreation/general facilities
- ∴ outdoor recreation
- water
- ▤ parking
- — road
- ·· border

Fig. 7.2. The spatial structure of Sun Parks' Den Haan (Belgium).

The villas are clustered. The extensive open spaces between the villa clusters, suitable for leisure activities of all kinds, enable the holiday village to be designed in harmony with the landscape, integrating the existing trees and shrubs. This third concept aims at an arrangement of the villa clusters, taking such elements into consideration as the sunny side, view, location with respect to the open spaces and the natural lie of the land (Fischer, as quoted by Harfst and Scharpf, 1982). The Center Parcs villages are typical examples of this approach, e.g. Sherwood Forest, Nottinghamshire in the UK (Fig. 7.3).

Resort landscaping: placeness gaining importance over placelessness

Holiday village landscapes play an important role in marketing both the villages and the guests' holiday experiences. In this section the landscape 'themes' in villages will be identified and analysed. It is thereby posited that landscape concepts will be a key to gaining the competitive edge during the boom in the large holiday villages in northern Europe, as is already the case for international hotel resorts, as analysed by Ayala (1991).

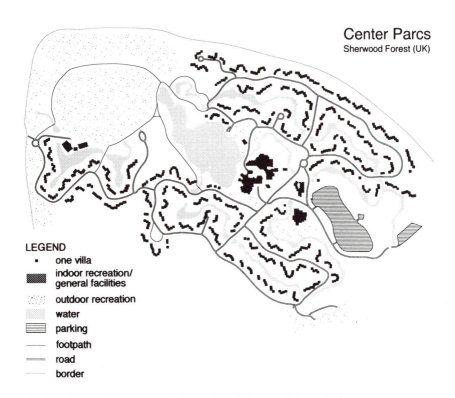

Center Parcs
Sherwood Forest (UK)

LEGEND
- ▪ one villa
- ▦ indoor recreation/
  general facilities
- ░ outdoor recreation
- ░ water
- ▤ parking
- ── footpath
- ══ road
- ⋯ border

Fig. 7.3. The spatial structure of Center Parcs' Sherwood Forest (UK).

In analysing the landscaping in second- and third-generation holiday villages it is important to distinguish between indoor and outdoor landscaping. Let us first analyse indoor landscaping. The dominant theme here is the 'tropical holiday world'. In the same way that the French Riviera has been 'tropicalizing' its vegetation since the 18th century by introducing exotic plants, northern European holiday villages are now doing this with their indoor leisure centres.

The indispensable element in this, the palm tree, became in the 20th century the emblem of *dépaysement* in Europe. It is a symbol of the sun and the 'warmth-seeking' holiday-maker (Dewailly and Flament, 1993).

This indoor tropical illusion can be a high-quality artificial environment, as is the case in many of the Center Parcs villages. In the subtropical water paradise highly valuable, living tropical trees and bushes from Asia, Central America, Brazil, Florida, Africa and southern Europe are displayed to convey lushness and exoticism. In Center

Parcs' village Erperheide (Peer, Belgium) over 600 species of plants originally from Africa grow, including seven varieties of palms, and small plants such as papayas, mangos, avocados, various bamboos, lianas, orchids, passion flowers, etc. There are a number of very special trees such as 60-year-old Sahara date palms from Egypt. The trees bear real bananas, oranges and dates. The various areas of greenery form a long line threading its way through the entire water-leisure complex alongside the pools, terraces and waterside cafés. Apart from the tropical plants, large amounts of stone were used to build rockeries and cobbled paths. The same botanical splendour is displayed in the Parc Plaza of Center Parcs villages, where, moreover, exotic animals live near a pond.

In this pseudo-tropical landscape people – according to our interviews – during a short-break holiday experience the illusion of being abroad. Not only viewing the tropical landscape but also feeling the tropical heat – making it possible for both adults and children to linger on a terrace in bathing-suits or play in the water without catching a cold – creates an environment that induces a feeling of well-being and enjoyment, as appeared from our interviews.

In contrast with the Center Parcs, Gran Dorado and Sun Parks villages where the landscape is composed of natural plants, there exist other villages where the palm trees and other tropical plants are synthetic, in other words a synthetic tropicality (e.g. Lalandio, Rodby, Denmark). It can be assumed that the importance of the landscape quality will grow depending on an increasing number of people coming in contact with the originals of the tropical or exotic landscapes that have been substituted in many resort developments (Ayala, 1991). Tourists are becoming more discriminating as they travel more widely and gain both confidence and knowledge (Stabler, quoted in Ayala, 1991).

A second theme goes back to the springwater bath of ancient Greece or Rome. The healing, relaxing and invigorating power of water remains the focus of some saunas which are part of the water-leisure centre. Some saunas trade on the vitality of that heritage by introducing Greek and Roman motif into their landscapes, thus inducing the illusion of ancient spas. A large pool area with 'Greek' columns and statues dominates the sauna in the Center Parcs village Eemhof (Zeewolde, Netherlands) and in the Sun Parks village Den Haan (Belgium). A similar theme can be found in international hotel resorts (Ayala, 1991).

Both these indoor landscape themes are easy to replicate. They set a marketing line vulnerable to competition and obscure the resort's exact location on the map. Villages built around an artificial tropical environment need not be located near a tropical sea since technology permits the 'tropical fantasy' to be constructed anywhere (Urry, 1990).

The indoor landscapes of the second and third generation of holiday villages can be characterized by what Relph (1976) called placelessness or sameness, in which different locations both look and feel alike.

In contrast to the indoor landscape, the outdoor landscape situated within the boundaries of the holiday village is in most of the villages not intentionally designed to create an environment that will induce an 'extraordinary' experience. None the less, competitiveness in the holiday village boom in northern Europe will be influenced by the individual village's ability to market and actually deliver an experience which is called 'extraordinary', in the sense of Urry (1990): 'tourist experiences which are, by comparison with the everyday, out of the ordinary ... minimally there must be certain aspects of the place to be visited which distinguish it from what is conventionally encountered in everyday life'. In the subtropical water paradise people experience particularly distinct pleasures involving different senses. But, as appeared from our interviews, people are also looking for other extraordinary experiences during their short-break holiday (Faché, 1987). Since people live and work for the most part in an urbanized, unnatural environment, many try to satisfy their need to experience nature during their holiday time. Providing the opportunity for tourists to have contact with nature, through view and closer physical contact by walking and cycling in a natural environment, is important in emphasizing the tourist's experience of being in a different environmental setting (Inskeep, 1991).

There are different ways in which this nature experience can be facilitated. A holiday village can be located near a nature park which is accessible for the village's guests. But Center Parcs makes an effort to facilitate this experience inside the village itself by creating a woodland and water landscape. The design principles applied by Center Parcs (1991) for this landscape of their newest villages are as follows.

- An evergreen landscape. A proportion of evergreen trees provides a green 'backdrop' to the village throughout the year. As a result, Center Parcs prefers sites comprising mature conifer woodlands. There are additional reasons for this preference.
- Conifer plantations often have a relatively poor diversity of indigenous flora and fauna and thus minimum ecological value, and yet they often have considerable potential for ecological enhancement.
- The mature trees provide excellent screening for the new village during construction and operation, helping to conceal and integrate buildings within the landscape from the outset.
- A proportion of mature trees is considered essential to lend the village the appearance of a country retreat all the year round.

- The critical age of the existing trees allows them to be selectively thinned out and interplanted with younger trees during the development period; these new trees will then have time to mature before the established ones have to be felled. Continuity of the woodland can thus be retained, ensuring that the village blends into the surrounding landscape.
- New artificial lakes and a network of informal waterways and pools form a second feature of the landscape. Not only providing for outdoor recreation, these water areas play a vital role in contributing to an increase in wildlife diversity.
- Variety of flora and fauna within the village itself. This is achieved, once the site for a holiday village has been selected, by having a team of ecological experts identify in detail any habitats of special note within the conifer plantation. These may consist of remnants of broad-leaved woodland, damp areas or diverse glades. Once identified, these areas are key determinants in influencing the lay-out of the village at a later stage. Equal weight is placed on identifying opportunities for incorporating existing habitats and creating new ones. The conifer plantations that already exist at the site are enriched with broad-leaved trees and shrubs, glades and especially a variety of new water habitats. At Sherwood Forest holiday village, for example, over 500,000 native trees and shrubs were planted, improving habitat quality and thereby attracting a greater diversity of wildlife. Water-courses were similarly planted with native and semi-native aquatic plants, and fish were released in the lakes.
- A landscape design approach responding to the *genius loci*, the spirit of the place, in contrast to a landscape design which is placeless. This design approach means that the village relates closely to the character of its woodland site. Tree and shrub planting is limited to species compatible with the soil types present and the natural vegetation of the surrounding countryside.
- Architecturally distinctive man-made elements blended into the forest environment with a minimum visual impact on the wider countryside. The single-storeyed villa clusters, the village centre with its dome, the car park, features such as timber bridges and the informal network of paths and cycle-ways are carefully located, preserving the character of the terrain and as many trees as possible, and ensuring minimum visual impact on the wider countryside.
- Individual privacy in a natural environment. The linked system of single-storey villas, the location of the villas in a woodland environment and the running up of forest trees to the edge of the villas creates privacy and close contact with nature.
- Tranquil forest setting through limiting traffic movement. The

village is designed with a single-width, one-way road circuit for access and servicing. Visitors' cars are only permitted beyond the car parks at the entrance to the village to load and unload on arrival and departure days, Mondays and Fridays. During the rest of the week bicycles take the place of motor traffic within the village.

- An extensive forest environment within the village. To ensure that 500 to 700 bungalows and other buildings, roads and car parks are blended into the forest, and that there is sufficient unbuilt-up space for attractive surroundings, informal waterways, glades, etc., all of which can contribute to the enjoyment of the sights and sounds of nature, a large site is essential.

For Center Parcs land has become the 'edge' value, and they have moved to the acquisition of larger areas of land in order to capture the woodland and water theme for their newest resorts (see Table 7.1). Center Parcs believe that 120 to 200 ha is an ideal size. The same land-acquisition trend can be observed in international resort hotels (Ayala, 1991).

A second outdoor landscape theme is the beach and marina. Beaches and associated marinas for sunbathing, swimming, boating, windsurfing, sailing and other water-recreation activities are the major attractions. The holiday village Port Zelande (Gran Dorado) located at the Kabbelaarsbank between the North Sea and the Grevelingen lake has opted for this theme. A yacht harbour for 650 boats is partly integrated into the village landscape. The landscape themes woodland and beach/marina can be characterized by what Ayala (1991) called 'placeness', which connotes distinctiveness inherent to places.

In contrast to the indoor landscape theme – tropical fantasy – which actually is a brand-name image for the whole category of second- and third-generation holiday villages, the outdoor landscape concept becomes more and more a key to gaining the competitive edge. Center Parcs' newest villages are intentionally designed to accentuate this brand-name recognition.

Variations on Location of Holiday Villages

In the initial period 'indoor holiday villages' were seen as 'footloose' since their major attraction – the indoor tropical fantasy – was an artificially created environment. Gradually the outdoors too became an important leisure feature. With Center Parcs the landscape within the village became an important point of focus, while with Sun Parks and Gran Dorado it was the broader surrounding landscape of the village, in other words the site of it. They prefer attractive tourist areas, e.g. a seaside resort (Den Haan, Oostduinkerke, Zandvoort and Grevelingen). The tourist image of the area is for these companies a major site selection criterion and a part of the product image.

Center Parcs, on the other hand, avoids tourist areas and prefers to seek out sites in economically underdeveloped regions with no tourist amenities. In such areas, the holiday village is the one and only tourist attraction.

Center Parcs chooses sites with the following features.

- A surface area of 100–200 ha, to accommodate 600 to 700 housing units.
- A mixture of woodland and open country, in the ratio 70:30, so that the village centre and the lakes can be constructed without loss of trees, whilst integrating and concealing the villas within the existing woodland.
- The existing tree population should be of low economical value, and as far as possible have the recreational qualities typical of Dutch pine forests, i.e. mature but not too dense conifer woodlands.
- Almost flat terrain, so as to avoid the necessity of extensive excavation and changing the landscape.
- Good road access without having to construct new roads off the site, and without imposing a traffic overload on the surrounding villages. In addition, good motorway connections are desirable to provide quick and easy access to the village.
- Urban through roads should be avoided as far as possible (Center Parcs, 1991).
- Sites should as far as possible be municipally owned, in order to keep claims upon private property to a minimum.

Apart from these, there are also other factors determining the choice of location. Recognizing the great importance of tourism as a growth sector, national and local governments have offered substantial financial assistance when a holiday village is to be 'planted' in a certain area.

The Dutch government has granted investment subsidies (the so-called IPR) to 'De Huttenheugte', 'De Eemhof' and 'De Lommergergen', all three of which are located in economically underdeveloped areas. In Belgium, the investment subsidy also played a part in the choice of location for the two Center Parcs holiday villages. Central government granted a 25% subsidy to Erperheide, which is located in a redevelopment area. Subsidies were also granted by the EEC, through the Belgian government, for the construction of Vossemeren in another redevelopment area. The English Tourist Board also awarded a subsidy of over £1.5m for the construction of Sherwood Forest holiday village.

Referring to the above-mentioned selection criteria the immediate environment of several of the initial Center Parcs villages was not especially interesting for holiday-makers (e.g. an agricultural area). But Center Parcs currently rather prefers sites close to or within a nature area, which in Bisbingen (Germany) initially met with resistance from ecological activist groups. If the village environment is an interesting one (such as a nature park), the specific environmental setting can be the dominant theme with the village landscape, thus reinforcing and complementing the environmental features (Inskeep, 1991).

Future Prospects

Large-scale projects and the environment

As described above, the evolution of holiday villages is marked by their ever-increasing scale. It is necessary to mention the fears concerning the negative effects of these large-scale holiday villages on the environment (Strasdas, 1991). Large-scale holiday projects should not be rejected as recreation facilities, however, since they do concentrate large numbers of leisure-seekers in one area, so relieving other areas. It is quite possible to design these projects in an environmentally and socially acceptable way (Hoplitschek *et al.*, 1991). But, before permission is given for the 'implantation' of a holiday village, an extensive survey into its effects on the environment must be carried out.

Innovations in accommodation and service

In second- and third-generation holiday villages, innovations mainly related to the collective recreational facilities. This trend will continue, but innovations in the future will mainly concentrate on accommodation and service. The higher the standard of living at home, the more demands people make on their holiday home. Holiday-makers are making increasing demands as regards the comfort and leisure amenities of holiday homes. In addition, a wider diversity of accommodation is essential. Lastly, holiday villages do not entirely come up to feminist aspirations, since domestic activities continue during the holiday, especially for women. Alongside the 'cocoon trend' in leisure time, a need for a 'short-break holiday product' is emerging, combining a hotel-level service (breakfast served at the bungalow, cleaning during the stay, laundry and baby-sitting services, etc.) with the privacy and home comforts of a top-quality bungalow (Faché, 1987).

Importance of all-weather facilities for short-break holidays

The conceptual development of the indoor holiday villages can be important for the future. Resorts have traditionally been seasonal operations. By introducing extensive all-weather recreational facilities holiday villages have become four-season resorts. This development is important for the resort operator as well as for the resort guest. The resort guests in northern Europe will want fewer weather risks with their holidays (Opachowski, 1989).

Will holiday villages with an ever-expanding covered artificial leisure environment be a model for the future development of indoor resorts in regions with a temperate climate and unpredictable weather? It is hard to say to what extent third-generation villages, with their all-weather facilities, actually compete with 'cold-water' resorts, as no research statistics are available. One thing is certain: these holiday villages provide a great many people with an opportunity for a short break close to home, without too much inconvenience from unstable weather and a relatively long journey to reach a sun, sea and sand destination.

References and Further Reading

Allcock, J.B. (1994) Seasonality. In: Witt, J.F. and Moutinho, L. (eds) *Tourism Marketing and Management Handbook*. Prentice-Hall, New York.

Ayala, H. (1991) Resort hotel landscape as an international megatrend. *Annals of Tourism Research* 18, 568–587.

Becker, Ch. (1984) Neue Entwicklungen bei den Feriengroßprojekten in der Bundesrepublik Deutschland: Diffusion und Probleme einer noch wachsenden Betriebsform. *Zeitschrift für Wirtschaftsgeographie* 28(3/4), 164–185.

Bentley, J.L. (1988) *Center Parcs*. PAVIC, Sheffield.

Boyer, M. (1992) Le Caractère Saisonnier du Tourisme entre Tradition et Modernité. In: Jardel, J.P. (ed.) *Le Tourisme International entre Tradition et Modernité*. Laboratoire d'Etnologie, Université de Nice.

Center Parcs (1991) *Nationaliteiten Overzicht 1986–1990*. Center Parcs, Afdeling Marktonderzoek, Rotterdam.

Dewailly, J.-M. and Flament, E. (1993) *Géographie du Tourisme et des Loisirs*. SEDES, Paris.

Eeckhout, K. (1991) Time budget research in Sun-parks De Haan. Masters thesis, University of Ghent.

Faché, W. (1987) *Advies voor een recreatiebeleid van Center Parcs*. Universiteit Gent, Gent.

Faché, W. (1989) Innovative indoor water-leisure centres in temperate countries. *Society and Leisure* 12, 341–359.

Faché, W. (ed.) (1990) *Shortbreak Holidays*. Center Parcs, Rotterdam.

Faché, W. (1994) Shortbreak holidays. In: Seaton, A.V. (ed.) *Tourism. The State of Art.* Wiley, Chichester.

Fitzpatrick Associates (1993) *All-season Tourism: Analysis of Experience, Suitable Products and Clientele.* Commission of the European Communities DG XXIII Tourism Unit, Brussels.

Harfst, W. and Scharpf, H. (1982) *Feriendörfer.* Landesamtes für Umweltschutz Rheinland-pfalz, Oppenheim.

Holloway, J.C. (1989) *The Business of Tourism.* Pitman, London.

Hoplitschek, E., Scharpf, H. and Thiel, F. (1991) *Urlaub und Freizeit mit der Natur.* Weitbrecht, Stuttgart/Wien.

Inskeep, E. (1991) *Tourism Planning.* Van Nostrand Reinhold, New York.

Konings, E. (1992) *Factoren die de Terugkeerintentie Verklaren bij Center Parcs.* Katholieke Universiteit Brabant, Tilburg.

Landscape Design Associates (1990) *Center Parcs, an Environmental Approach to Short Break Holidays.* LDA, Leeds.

Lavery, P. and McKeough, P. (1989) Indoor resorts in Europe. *EIU Travel and Tourist Analyst* 1, 52–68.

Opachowski, H. (1989) *Traumziele und Urlaubstraüme.* BAT Freizeit-Forschungsinstitut, Hamburg.

Relph, E. (1976) *Place and Placelessness.* PION, London.

Strasdas, W. (1991) *Ferienzentren der Zweiten Generation.* Institut für Landschaftspflege und Naturschutz, Universität Hannover und Technische Universität Berlin.

Urry, J. (1990) *The Tourist Gaze.* Sage, London.

Voskens-Drijver, M.E., van der Made, J.G. and Bakker, J.G. (1987) *Effecten van Verblijfsrecreatie op het Natuurlijk Milieu. Een onderzoek in de provincie Noord-Brabant.* Landbouwuniversiteit, Mededelingen 10 Werkgroep Recreatie, Wageningen.

Ward, M. and Hardy, D. (1986) *Goodnight Campers! The History of the British Holiday Camp.* Mansell, London.

Wolf, K., Jurczek, P. and Schymik, E. (1981) *Urlaub in Feriendörfern. Ein Strukturanalyse am Beispiel hessischer Feriendörfer.* Studienkreis für Tourismus, Starnberg.

8

Tourism Planning in Urban Revitalization Projects: Lessons from the Amsterdam Waterfront Development

M. Jansen-Verbeke[1] and E. van de Wiel[2]

[1]*Faculteit der Bedrijfskunde, Erasmusuniversiteit, PO Box 1738, 3000 DR Rotterdam, The Netherlands:* [2]*Faculteit der Beleidswetenschappen, Katholieke Universiteit Nijmegen, PO Box 9044, 6500 KD Nijmegen, The Netherlands.*

Introduction

Tourism can be the catalyst of radical changes in the economy, morale and appearance of a city in a critical stage of transition. Urban policies aiming at revitalization of particular downgraded urban areas are increasingly taking into consideration the potentials of tourism and leisure. A policy focusing on tourism as a vehicle for urban renovation cannot be equally successful in every context. The scale of the city and the site and situation of the renovation area make all the difference, as well as the political views held on urban renovation and priorities (Owen, 1990).

There is definitely a set of preconditions which need to be assessed in order to give tourism this 'catalyst' function. This chapter intends to look more carefully at the process of urban renovation plans in relation to tourism as a vehicle for revitalization.

Many different cities have turned to tourism as the lever for new initiatives. In the renewed masterplan of Rotterdam, several projects include tourism and leisure facilities (Jansen-Verbeke, 1992). The waterfront development especially is strongly inspired with plans for 'new' tourist activities. Smaller cities in The Netherlands, such as Nijmegen, have also recently invested in the development of an attractive waterfront, the 'Waalkade'. This small-scale urban renewal has added positively to the liveliness and attraction of the city of Nijmegen. Studies on the tourism impact of this project are now in progress. In fact lessons can be learnt from projects in many places. The point we intend to focus on is the planning process and the environmental context of the project, both

129

the policy context and the spatial functional context.

The recent experience with the Amsterdam waterfront development plans offers an interesting case-study, which will be discussed in the light of more general conclusions. In this urban renewal project, the role of tourism was not a major concern at the start; despite the fact that in most redevelopment plans for older port areas, tourism is considered to be a useful vehicle, this potential only came in view at a later stage of the planning process. A dilemma exists between regarding tourism as a core element in the redevelopment scheme and regarding it merely as an added value in the creation of a 'new' urban environment. This gradation in views reflects the political views as well as the social and economic carrying capacity of the city. The role of tourism in the plans will be focused upon, with a prime concern to analyse the present and potential linkage pattern between the 'old city' and the redevelopment area along the waterfront. In addition the lessons which can be learnt from the public–private approach in development planning will be commented upon.

Waterfront Developments: Some General Characteristics

The common element in all waterfront development projects is the fact that nowadays the interface between the port and the city has changed dramatically. In many historic cities (until the 19th century) there was a close relationship between city and port in terms of both spatial urban structure and functional association. The industrialization of the city (in the 19th century and the beginning of the 20th century) brought an expansion of the port activities, with a considerable spatial impact and to some extent a functional dissociation between city and port activities. Modernization of the port infrastructure (mid-20th century) increases the functional and spatial gap between city and port. Traditional waterfront areas and ports lose their function in favour of new development areas and become urban areas with a less distinct structure and function (Hoyle *et al.*, 1988). The functional association with the city is gradually disappearing. In many cases this evolution leads to a stage of urban decline in the waterfront area. The necessity grows to redesign the spatial structure and reconsider the functional integration with the city.

The present responsibility of urban planners primarily lies in finding new functions for old forms (infrastructure, warehouses, etc.) and in redeveloping waterfront areas in spatial, functional and visual harmony with the city. However, the most important challenge is to do this in an original way, without copying other waterfront development projects.

Obviously this process of a changing interrelationship between city and port is not unique. However, the way the redevelopment process is managed and implemented is unique, taking into account the geographical, economic, social and cultural context, the national and local policies concerning urban redevelopment and the involvement of public and private partners. Waterfront development projects seem to be the current answer to a common set of urban problems. The uniqueness of each site is emphasized, although the methods of achieving the objectives might be very similar (Murray, 1990). Despite this statement about uniqueness, there is a strong inclination towards imitation among, for example, Baltimore, London Docklands, Manchester, the Clyde project in Glasgow, Düsseldorf, Antwerp, Rotterdam Waterstad, Amsterdam and many other cities.

In large metropolitan areas, such as London and New York, the role of tourism and recreation in recent waterfront developments is rather modest. However, in smaller metropolitan areas, like Rotterdam and Amsterdam, the role of leisure functions in the redeveloping docklands could be or become relatively more important.

Compared to the existing tourism facilities and cultural amenities in the city of New York, the leisure function of the waterfront is modest. The South Street Seaport is the tourism core in the redevelopment of the New York Docklands. Although not fully implemented yet, a naval museum is the major attraction in the project. In the immediate surroundings old warehouses and residential quarters have been transformed into shops. In the summer both tourists and downtown workers (during their lunch break) are using the area. But customers for the planned luxury shops are missing. The main problem of the waterfront is that it is rather an isolated area which attracts coaches full of people in the summer but is not integrated into the inner city (Rietveld and van der Ven, 1991).

The London Docklands project is mainly an office and residential waterfront development. The project is based on two flagships. The first, Canary Wharf, is nominated as the New Manhattan, a large office court which can compete with the central business district of London. The second, the Royal Docks, embraces not only new housing facilities and a business park but also leisure functions, as a vast regional shopping centre and an exhibition centre. The distance between the Docklands and the inner city is substantial. In fact the leisure functions of the Docklands project are primarily defined only as a supporting element for the project (Harmens *et al.*, 1992).

Both the New York and the London waterfront redevelopment projects contain leisure functions but their relation with the inner city is weak. The two Dutch waterfront developments of Rotterdam and Amsterdam are on a smaller scale, but the leisure potential is relatively high, the spatial and functional relations with the inner city are strong and the development of a leisure function can substantially contribute to the existing facilities.

The Rotterdam waterfront development is mainly concentrated in 'Waterstad'. The core of the project is the old inland harbour. An open-air naval museum is the major attraction of this area. Some other projects are situated along the embankment of the Nieuwe Waterweg, Rotterdam's connection with the North Sea. The main concern is the fragmentation of the project and the missing (pedestrian) links between the attractions and the inner city (Jansen-Verbeke, 1992).

In each case-study, the characteristics of the external planning context need to be taken into consideration. In addition, the incubation climate for the launching of new projects and the carrying capacity of the city in terms of tourism development might be very different.

Amsterdam Waterfront: Site and Situation

The urban form of Amsterdam is characterized by being developed only to the south, the main barrier in the north being the waterfront. The waterfront along the IJ has played a crucial role in the past economic development of Amsterdam. An additional stimulus has been the location of the main railway station in the area. However, the construction of the railway, at the end of the 19th century, has isolated the waterfront from the rest of the city. The focus of urban development tended to be on the southern fringe of the city, so in many respects the inner city turned its back on the river. This barrier has been consolidated, despite the more recent urban development in north Amsterdam.

The plan area is most heterogeneous, including not only a derelict industrial and port area, but also the railway complex, the eastern docklands, the open water area and the main square in front of the central station. In fact the core area of the redevelopment area, in terms of location and functional uses, consists of three different islands (Fig. 8.1).

At the east end the development area is limited by the eastern commercial docklands. These quays were once the commercial gateway in the colonial sea traffic. After the opening of the North Sea canal, which offers a shorter connection with the open sea and the closing off of the Zuiderzee, the port activities of Amsterdam moved in a western direction. The infrastructure no longer meets the demands of modernized port traffic.

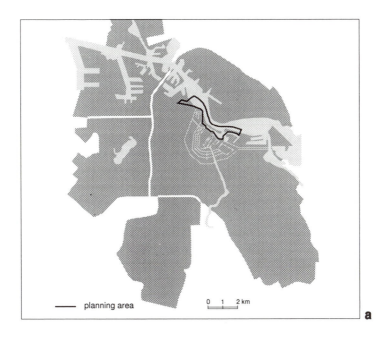

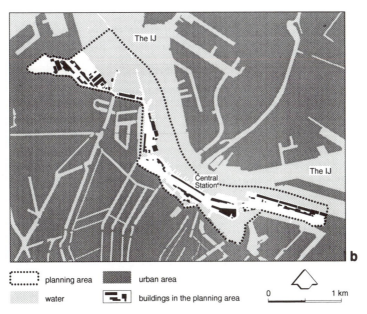

Fig. 8.1. (a) The IJ waterfront in the urban context of Amsterdam. Source: Masterplan, Amsterdam Waterfront Financieringsmaatschappij, 1992.
(b) Location of the redevelopment area. Source: Nota van Uitgangspunten, Gemeente Amsterdam, 1991.

Taking into account the central urban location of this area in relation to the railway station and to the inner city of Amsterdam, there were several arguments to open the discussion on a revitalization programme. The challenge now is how to turn the tide and develop the area into a high-quality location.

The Process of Defining the Objectives

The first initiatives were taken in the beginning of the 1980s; a plan for redevelopment of the eastern docklands was made with the main objective of restoring the functional links between the inner city and the waterfront. There was a strong plea to manage this project in an integrated way. Two major elements were included in the plan: a promenade along the south bank and new linkages with the inner city (Goldberg, 1991). Views on the objectives shifted from modest ambitions (limited to a subarea) to ambitions on a higher level which implied an expansion of the planning area.

The ambition was to turn the area into a high-quality location which could generate an injection of cash into the economy of the city. The prospect of a high-standard residential area was also rather attractive. In 1989 a first official report by the local authorities was issued: 'Nota van Uitgangspunten' (a report on the starting conditions and preconditions of redevelopment). The report outlined the policy for new destination plans and infrastructural changes in the development area and included a first attempt to clearly define the objectives, which were to:

- strengthen the position of the inner city by strategically developing a location of high quality. This means new functions in the waterfront area;
- develop a high-quality urban environment (competitive in terms of international standards) by developing a functional mix and accessibility, complementary to the inner city;
- exploit the opportunities of water-based activities for residents and visitors;
- stimulate the synergism with the inner-city functions (e.g. retail trade).

In 1991 an adapted version of the local policy views concerning the development project was reported. The option for an integrated development plan now included specific objectives.

In the first place, the position of the inner city and the policies to develop an urban area, closely connected with the inner city, were now considered in an international framework. In the second place, it was assumed that this high ambition would be implemented by creating an urban environment of a high quality, largely using the additional assets of a waterfront. In the third place, the future development needed to be balanced carefully against the possible impact on the existing urban system and structure. Special attention needed to be paid to the physical and functional impact on the small-scale inner city of Amsterdam.

The 'integrated' approach implied a systematic assessment of functional changes, spatial and infrastructural development, taking into account the current social forces. The most characteristic point of this report was the option of a multifunctional development. For each subarea, the proposal included a combination of economic activities (mainly offices), residential functions and, in addition, leisure functions.

Views on the optimal balance between the different space uses were continuously changing, which indicated the lack of a long-term planning objective of the local authorities.

The Public—Private Approach

The incubation time for this project was a long one, but at the beginning of 1991 the aims of this ambitious project became clearer and, above all, widely caught the public interest. The key problem, of course, was and still is finding the financial resources to implement such a large-scale plan. In order to guarantee the financing of the waterfront project, a public–private partnership was institutionalized. In February 1991 an official agreement was signed between the local authority board of the city of Amsterdam (the public partner) and a private partner, the Internationale Nederlanden Groep, a holding of a large Dutch insurance company and a Dutch bank group. The public and the private partner were each to participate on a 50:50 basis in the newly created company Amsterdam Waterfront Financieringsmaatschappij (AWF). The responsibility of this working company was to draw up a comprehensive and integrated plan for the development area, including a detailed programme for each function and a business plan.

To some extent the views being developed could function as a self-fulfilling prophecy, but only to the extent that the interference of external factors had realistically been anticipated. In order to establish a forum in which strategic views could emerge, the planning process included a number of workshops, to which were invited representatives of the different stake-holders and a panel of advisers and researchers. In this process of developing a 'programme scenario' different disciplines and experts were involved. The research agenda included a wide range of issues such as:

- the business functions in the waterfront project;
- a housing development plan;
- public attractions (cultural, recreational, tourism);
- commercial public amenities (shops and catering);
- office premises.

In addition, the above results were tested in terms of marketing feasibility, socioeconomic impact, physical building possibilities and the economic issues.

The scientific monitoring of the entire process was in the hands of a group of urban planners and sociologists from the University of Amsterdam. They organized the workshops and created the agenda for a continuous discussion.

In September 1992, the AWF published its masterplan, including the spatial scenario, for the development of the IJ bank. In several respects, the proposed masterplan differed from the initial official report and appeared to be far more ambitious. The size of the office space was increased to 700,000 m² and the proposals for the building density in the area around the Central Station exceeded the given limits. A systematic mixture of economic, residential and recreational functions, one of the main points of departure in the earlier plan, was abandoned. Nevertheless, much attention was paid to the potential attraction of the area.

One of the eye-catchers in the masterplan was the progressive architectural concept for the station roof. A spectacular roof was to cover and to link the Central Station and the riverbank. This construction would offer space for a large number of public facilities, such as a public library, a mega-cinema, a modern auditorium and a promenade along the IJ embankment. This prestigious building was to be connected with the inner city by means of the already existing tunnels but also by a flyover of 25,000 m² which was to include an exclusive high-quality shopping mall. The plan of the architect Koolhaas aimed at a high density of office premises in an area of 350,000 m² at the east side of the Central Station. Both the shopping mall and the office quarter were to be located above the complex of railway tracks.

At the beginning of 1993 the financial company published a financial and economic scenario and an overall business plan for the development of the IJ bank. This was followed by a debate in the local council, which was to approve or reject the plan. Since the business plan did not take into account every initial guideline and only partially reflected the current policy views, an intense political debate was the result. In fact, not only did the development of the IJ bank depend on the approval of the council of Amsterdam, but the financing for the project had also become a major bottleneck. The private partner withdrew from the project, because of the marginal profits. Other institutional investors, pension funds and project developers were reluctant to participate in the project.

As a reaction to this failure, the council of Amsterdam drafted a new plan, far less ambitious than the Koolhaas plan and in fact taking into account even fewer guidelines of the Nota van Uitgangspunten. So the planning process is still going on, albeit with far less ambitious options. Despite the changes, the potential role of tourism and recreation remains a key issue.

Tourism and Leisure Function in the Perspective of Urban Revitalization

A strong emphasis on tourism and leisure was not included in the first outline of the plan. Gradually the potential of public attractions as magnets for other investors came into focus. From the very beginning of this planning process, an integrated approach was seen as a sure way to connect spatially the different functions in the area, and to generate a pattern of synergism between urban facilities.

The leisure function was looked for in the sectors of culture, art, tourism and recreation. The recreational opportunity spectrum of the inner city of Amsterdam consists of a spatial clustering of a wide variety of leisure facilities. One of the major attractions of this leisure environment is in fact the historical setting. Within this setting a number of public attractions have developed into an urban, cultural tourist product.

Amsterdam plays a dominant role in the cultural life of The Netherlands. The clustering of cultural amenities also includes public attractions in the fields of art, music, theatre and cinema. The construction of these public attractions in a historical setting explains the strong position of Amsterdam in the national and international tourism market.

The image of a historic city with a lively cultural programme, with a spectrum of interesting museums, canals, bridges and architecture, is a strong asset. Nevertheless, the position of Amsterdam as an urban tourism destination is now seriously threatened. Recent research work even indicated the start of a downgrading process in comparison with other European cities (KPMG, 1993). A clear indication of this is the declining number of international visitors, the shortening of the average stay and the negative image-building. In many ways the time is ripe to reconsider the tourism potential of Amsterdam and a new *élan*, related to the waterfront development plan, is needed right now. Developing new attractions has become a rather unlikely scenario. This leaves the challenge of the upgrading of existing attractions.

The actual dispersion pattern of 'places of interest' for tourists is not considered to be optimal. Although most sightseeing attractions in the historic city are within walking distance, the spatial connectivity pattern is rather weak. In addition, there are some weak points to be identified in terms of the lack of tourism-supporting facilities such as high-quality shopping and diversified catering facilities.

Regarding both of these defects, the redevelopment plan for the IJ waterfront offered some new perspectives. Existing amenities can be given an additional emphasis in combination with the new amenities. However, there are conditions attached to the implementation of an integrated public function. Although the scale of the redevelopment area is rather compact, the necessity to plan for a clustered pattern of public attractions is strongly emphasized. Spatial proximity of the elements is seen as an essential condition of an attractive site with an urban environment which encourages a longer stay. The opportunities of a synergetic interaction between the different urban functions need to be assessed systematically.

Prior to this detailed urban analysis of functional interaction, the current views on the role of tourism and recreation in Amsterdam were researched. Different scenarios were tested amongst a selected group of key persons.

The first scenario was the least ambitious one and included the opportunity of improving the recreational quality of the urban environment, especially for the urban residents. The second scenario emphasized the leading role of Amsterdam as a national cultural trendsetter. The third and most ambitious scenario proposed to raise Amsterdam to the level of international urban tourist destinations. Parameters for each of these scenarios were tested amongst a diverse panel in terms of the strengths and weaknesses of Amsterdam, and of potentials and strategies concerning spatial management and marketing. The result of this brainstorming indicated the carrying capacity of Amsterdam to support each of these levels of ambition. The conclusion was very clear: the second scenario was most strongly favoured.

Spatial Analysis of the Tourist Functions of Amsterdam

The way in which the tourist function is embedded in a multi-functional urban environment and the above scenario of 'Amsterdam as a cultural top city' becomes a key issue. The location pattern of existing public attractions determines in many ways the options for the new development.

New developments of public attractions need to fit into the existing pattern of tourist space use in Amsterdam. The issue of spatial integration was given a high priority; the spatial and functional connections between the historical city and the 21st-century part of Amsterdam were studied in detail. A spatial analysis of the present tourist attractions in Amsterdam was the first step in order to understand the current patterns of urban space use, the zoning of tourist areas and the pattern of connecting routes between interesting sites.

The spatial pattern of the tourist attractions (the core elements) and the supporting facilities are to a large extent the heritage of the past. Few spatial planning views have been included in this process of urban development. However, more recently the spatial implications of this tourism-opportunity spectrum have caught the attention of urban planners and tourism marketeers. Understanding the tourist-attraction system by analysing the spatial connectivity of tourist product elements and placing these patterns in the scope of tourist experiences has become a new field of research (Leiper, 1990; Jansen-Verbeke, 1992).

In the analysis of the tourist-attraction system and its spatial implications the concept of clustering and networks has been introduced. A cluster is understood as a spatial concentration of different and complementary product elements of tourism, recreation and supporting amenities which attract specific groups of urban users. The target groups can differ in time, for instance an 'evening cluster' which combines a spectrum of opportunities for evening entertainment and hence attracts specific users.

The functional association between the elements of a cluster can also be explained from the point of view of the entrepreneurial advantages of a combination of place, product and people (Jansen-Verbeke and Ashworth, 1990). In terms of functional linkages, combining benefits of infrastructural facilities and joint promotion, spatial clustering offers advantages for entrepreneurs in tourism and related businesses. From the point of view of the customer and tourist, the spatial proximity of a wide spectrum of amenities increases the attraction of the site and as such the inclination to spend more time and money in the area (Clark and Stankey, 1979). This concept of a tourism-opportunity spectrum, previously identified as a recreation-opportunity spectrum, is now being developed into a planning tool and above all a tool for managing spatial development (Butler and Woldbrootz, 1991).

Spatial Clustering of the Tourist-opportunity Spectrum

The introduction of the concept of the 'tourist-opportunity spectrum' offers a context in which the present functioning of the system can be understood and above all in which the likely implications of development can be anticipated. The spatial analysis of the tourist-opportunity spectrum indicates a pattern of clusters. A tourist cluster is to be understood as a concentration in space of at least one core element of the tourist product and one or more supporting product elements (see Table 8.1). Spatial proximity facilitates combined use and therefore increases the opportunity spectrum in a particular site. Obviously this concept, mainly based on the distribution characteristics of the supply side, also refers to the actual pattern of use, the demand side. Not all combinations of facilities equally increase the quality of the tourist experience. A full understanding of tourist behaviour (in time and space) and motivation patterns is essential.

The spatial analysis of tourist facilities in the inner city of Amsterdam is based on the dispersion pattern of core elements and supporting elements. The search for identification of spatial clusters was carried out only from the supply-side point of view, assuming that this pattern to a large extent explains the present tourist space use of the inner city. Clusters or tourism-opportunity spectra were defined according to linear patterns, and therefore the concentration of opportunities was measured by street segments. One valid argument for this method is the fact that tourist perception of a place is segmented in a linear way; interesting street segments are easily spotted and structure the route through the city (Ankomak and Cromptom, 1992). In this way it can also be argued that a cluster ends where one comes to street segments which do not offer any additional elements of tourism or recreational value.

In order to identify the attraction of a street segment, a score has been calculated for each street segment. Street segments belong to a cluster whenever a critical value of the score has been measured and if there is a continuity of street segments containing a core element. The connectivity between 'tourist recreation street segments' is then visualized on maps, which allows for a further interpretation of the pattern. Figure 8.2 illustrates some results of the method in terms of identifying 'cinema clusters' in the inner city of Amsterdam.

Table 8.1. Tourism products of Amsterdam.

Core elements (major attractions)			
Historical	Cultural	Outdoor recreation	Secondary elements (supporting facilities)
Built environment	Museums	Canals	Shopping facilities
Urban morphology and architecture	Exhibitions	Boat trips	Street markets
	Theatres	Urban parks	Catering sector
Water and canals	Concert halls	Zoo	Pavement cafés
Historical buildings	Libraries	Botanical gardens	Bars
Monuments	Cultural programmes		Coffee shops
Churches	Cultural ambience		Restaurants
Convents	Typical lifestyle		Hotels
Béguinage	Ethnic diversity		Congress and convention facilities
Palace			
Urban history			Entertainment
Historical associations			Red-light district
Folklore			
Cultural identity			
Urban scenery			

From this analysis it could be concluded that there is a clear distinction between spatial clusters with primary attraction for tourists and clusters which have an essentially cultural attraction. The spatial connectivity pattern between clusters can at the same time explain the spatial zoning of the tourist function in Amsterdam and clearly demonstrates ribbon development along the most attractive routes.

This exercise of mapping tourist zoning in the inner city of Amsterdam offers an interesting tool for understanding and anticipating the tourist walking-routes throughout the city (Mulder, 1990, 1992). In the perspective of the waterfront development it offers useful information about the potential linkages. Above all, the possibilities for a strategic location choice are clearly demonstrated. Some locations along the waterfront can be linked with the present pattern of tourist-recreation zones, whereas other locations fall outside this pattern and would therefore need additional infrastructural adaptations and above all some strong attractions in order to become integrated into the tourist zone of Amsterdam.

Obviously the pattern of tourist space use is dynamic. Not only can changes in the supply side change the cluster map, but changing preferences or active promotion of some specific elements can also easily cause changes in the spatial-use pattern. Nevertheless, this method of mapping the tourist-opportunity spectrum can be utilized

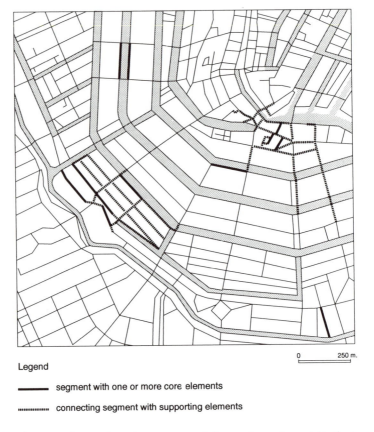

0   250 m.

Legend

—————— segment with one or more core elements

"""""""""" connecting segment with supporting elements

Fig. 8.2. Clustering of secondary elements around cinemas (core elements) in the inner city of Amsterdam.

effectively as a tool for planning tourism development in specific sites or along specific routes. It opens new perspectives for the discussion on synergetic planning.

Synergism between Tourist-product Elements

Several surveys of tourists have indicated the importance of spatial clustering of different facilities. Core elements of the tourist product need to be surrounded, within walking distance, with a wide spectrum of shops and catering facilities in order to be appreciated as an attractive site. The more facilities are clustered, the stronger the impulse to remain longer in the area. This is the basic principle of synergetic planning. However, this implies a genuine understanding of the kind of activities which urban visitors tend to combine during their stay. The challenge of synergetic planning lies in the identification of functional associations between the different elements of the urban tourist product (Law, 1992). For instance, a strategic location planning for the retail trade in relation to the major tourist attractions is of vital importance. The synergetic relationship between shops and tourist facilities has recently been researched for a specific target group – Japanese tourists in Amsterdam (Jansen-Verbeke, 1991, 1994).

Looking at tourism in this pattern of interdependency with other urban facilities holds many lessons concerning optimal locations and functional mix in redevelopment areas. Specific recommendations concerning the optimal location of new public attractions in the waterfront area resulted from the analysis (Jansen-Verbeke and van de Wiel, 1992). This survey in the inner city of Amsterdam was regarded as a first essential step in providing an integrated plan for the redevelopment area (Jansen-Verbeke and van de Wiel, 1993).

Conditions of Success

The opportunities for redeveloping the IJ waterfront into an integrated part of Amsterdam are realistic, but the conditions for implementation are complicated. Such an ambitious project of urban redevelopment requires a long and detailed planning process. All the pieces of the jigsaw puzzle need to fall into place in the right location at the right time.

Plans for an integrated development of tourism, recreation and public functions play a crucial role, not only because of the social and economic importance of these urban functions as such, but mainly because the development in this sector needs to be widely supported and critically assessed in terms of additional value to the present urban functions. In addition the perceptions of different interest groups have proved to be a critical issue in the planning process.

The success of waterfront development projects such as in Amsterdam depends not only on the social and economic climate and the political priorities, but also on the strength of the public–private partnership. Plans that are too ambitious will fail at the stage of implementation. A premature breaking-point occurred in the Amsterdam planning process for the waterfront area because the investment climate had recently changed. Views on the potentials of tourism were adapted according to the latest, more modest expectations, and political priorities changed. The impact of these changes on the external context of the project was not included in the planning. The public–private partnership may have been the only way to start innovative planning for the area, but apparently not all the conditions for success were met (Ashworth and Voogd, 1990).

Conclusions

The expectations were high, the potentials realistic, the preparatory studies in many respects strongly underpinned, but nevertheless the project for redevelopment of the Amsterdam waterfront seems to have reached a critical stage. The lessons from the Amsterdam case-study are many and the present impasse may be explained in many ways.

The interest of this experiment for urban planners lies in processing a redevelopment plan, the challenges of synergetic planning and, not least, understanding the changing role of urban planners. In many ways urban planners function as process managers and, in the particular case of tourism and recreation planning, as interpreters of the present tourist-attraction system and forecasters of future trends. Apparently, a new task of the urban planner lies in the role of a critical audit concerning the social and economic carrying capacity for new initiatives (Falk, 1989). The planning of assumed development potentials implies a thorough knowledge and understanding of the spatial implications and functioning of the tourist-opportunity spectrum.

Taking into account the limited research work done in the field of tourist behaviour and attitudes, this puts the issue at the top of the research agenda of urban planners dealing with the harmonization of tourism and recreation in the urban system.

References

Ankomak, P. and Cromptom, J. (1992) Tourism cognitive distance: a set of research propositions. *Annals of Tourism Research* 19(2), 268–286.

Ashworth, G. and Voogd, H. (1990) *Selling the City*. Belhaven, London.

Butler, R.W. and Woldbrootz, L.A. (1991) A new planning tool: tourism opportunity spectrum. *Journal of Tourism Studies* 2(1), 2–14.

Clark, R.N. and Stankey, G.H. (1979) The recreation opportunity spectrum: a framework for planning, management and research. Research Paper PNW-98, US Department of Agriculture Forest Service.

Falk, N. (1989) On the waterfront: the role of planners and consultants in waterside regeneration. *The Planner* 75(24), 11–16.

Goldberg, S. (1991) Plannen van waterfronts: bestaat er een aanpak die overal werkt? *Rooilijn* 24, 143–148.

Harmens, A., Prak, P. and Ashworth, G. (1992) The role of tourism in waterfront regeneration. *Groningen Studies* no. 50.

Hoyle, B., Pinder, D. and Husain, M. (1988) *Revitalising the Waterfront. International Dimensions of the Docklands Redevelopment.* Belhaven Press, London.

Jansen-Verbeke, M. (1991) Leisure shopping: a magic concept for the tourism industry? *Tourism Management* 12(1), 9–14.

Jansen-Verbeke, M. (1992) Urban recreation and tourism: physical planning issues. *Tourism Recreation Research* 17(2), 33–45.

Jansen-Verbeke, M. (1994) The synergism between shopping and tourism: the Japanese experience. In: Theobald, Th. (ed.) *Global Tourism: The Next Decade.* Butterworth-Heinemann, Oxford.

Jansen-Verbeke, M. and Ashworth, G. (1990) Environmental integration of recreation and tourism. *Annals of Tourism Research* 17, 618–622.

Jansen-Verbeke, M. and van de Wiel, E. (1992) *Amsterdamse Waterfrontontwikkeling, de Rol van Publiekstrekkende Functies.* Planologisch Instituut KU, Nijmegen.

Jansen-Verbeke, M. and van de Wiel, E. (1993) Tourisme et loisirs: éléments de revitalisation urbaine. Le projet de l'IJ à Amsterdam. *Hommes et Terres du Nord* 2(3), 78–84.

KPMG (1993) *Toeristische concurrentiepositie van Amsterdam ten opzichte van tien andere Europese steden.* KPMG, Amsterdam.

Law, C. (1992) Urban tourism and its contribution to economic regeneration. *Urban Studies* 29(3/4), 599–618.

Leiper, N. (1990) Tourist attraction systems. *Annals of Tourism Research* 17, 367–384.

Mulder, A. (1990) Recreatiecircuits in binnensteden, gevalstudie Amsterdam. *Recreatie en Toerisme* 22(10), 16–19.

Mulder, A. (1992) Stadswandelingen: recreatiecircuits in Europese binnensteden. *Geografie* 1(4), 16–21.

Murray, N. (1990) Castlefield's facelift. *The Surveyor*, Sept., 10–13.

Owen, C. (1990) Tourism and urban regeneration. *Cities*, Aug., 194–201.

Rietveld, P. and van der Ven, J. (1991) Waterfrontontwikkeling in New York. *Stedebouw en Volkshuisvesting* 72(3), 11–17.

9

Public Space in the Post-industrial City

J. Burgers

Faculteit Sociale Wetenschappen, Vakgroep Algemene Sociale Wetenschappen, Rijksuniversiteit Utrecht, Heidelberglaan 2, PO Box 80140, 3508 TC Utrecht, The Netherlands.

The Transformation of Public Space

Cities all over the world boast of the quality of their public spaces. People are tempted to visit museums, squares, historic buildings, pavement cafés, galleries, festivals, carnivals, sporting events, and even spaces that once were objects of embarrassment but now are deemed 'cosy': the red-light districts. This is a remarkable phenomenon. Not so long ago the city was basically in the realm of necessity; it was the place to work and shop. And when, after residential suburbanization, employment and shops were also leaving the inner city, urban life seemed doomed. That feeling was explicitly phrased by Don Martindale in his introduction to the English translation of Max Weber's work on the city: 'The age of the city seems to be at an end' (Weber, 1958, p. 62). Leisure, the social activity often explicitly associated with choice, was essentially an open-air affair, away from city life. But now the city is *en vogue* again. The going out of the city of the 1960s and 1970s has turned into the outgoing city of the 1980s and 1990s. The city seems to have migrated from the realm of necessity to the realm of freedom. One of the results of the growing popularity of the city has been a growing interest in the quality of public space. In almost all Western cities lively debates are going on about the architectural quality of important buildings and sites to be developed. Every self-respecting municipality has a committee studying the quality of public space. Whereas the cities once tried to look as suburban as possible, now even smaller towns try to look cosmopolitan. What has happened to bring this important change about? Why is it that urban public space is the object of such a profound re-evaluation?

In this chapter I will argue that the transformation of public space is rooted in more encompassing social changes. The current reappraisal of urban public space, for instance, is related to broader economic and cultural changes. Different historical types of societies develop different kinds of qualities of public space. These different qualities do not simply replace one another. Old and new qualities tend to form intricate relationships so that public space, in terms of meaning and appreciation, can best be seen as a cultural coral reef. It needs a historical-sociological analysis to unravel the different qualities which lie like a sediment on contemporary urban public space. In this chapter I will analyse changes in urban public space by relating it to different historical types of society. I intend to span a broad range of time in relatively few pages, so the societies I discuss must be seen as ideal types. The qualities of public space can be discerned in the context of cities in four different periods: the city in antiquity, the bourgeois city of late medieval Europe, the industrial city of the 19th and 20th centuries and the recently emerging postindustrial city.

Before starting this historical-sociological analysis, however, we need a definition of public space. One could use a legalistic, formal definition of public space. Public space is then the space – buildings and sites – where everyone is allowed to go: the streets, the parks, the subways, the squares. One of the problems with this formal definition of public space is that a place which is legally public is not necessarily used as such. Every guide to New York, for instance, warns one not to make use of the subways at night. It also recommends, when one does so by day, at least to avoid looking like a tourist. One way of doing this is learning the subway plan by heart so there is no need to consult the maps in the subway station. Another problem that arises when a legalistic definition of public space is used is what to do with supermarkets, cafés, shops, cinemas, opera houses and football stadiums. When they are privately owned, the owner has the right to make a decision about who may enter and who may not. In many shopping malls in American and Canadian cities people who are expected to be a nuisance to visitors are excluded. On the other hand legislation has been developed which makes it difficult for owners of cafés and discos to refuse entrance to members of ethnic minority groups. That would be an act of racial or ethnic discrimination, which is now an offence in several countries. So these places might be called semi-public.

These changes in the legislation on the relation between the private and the public sphere are very interesting and reflect, of course, changing ways of living together in modern society. Because specific legal definitions of public space ultimately reflect patterns of social integration I will use a rather broad sociological definition which can be used in different social-historical contexts. I simply define public space as the set of buildings and sites which in their use or their meaning are of importance for the urban community.

Public Space in the Ancient City

Most accounts of public space in urban sociology or the history of architecture start with the famous agora in Athens and the forum in Rome. They stress the fundamental democratic character of these central places in the city. Such analyses are a reconstruction of history which has as point of departure the character, taken for granted, of Western democratic society. The democratic character of Roman and Greek society is usually rather overestimated in these accounts. Athens, of course, had a large enslaved population and Sparta, the second most important city in ancient Greece, was really a military state. As for Rome, dictatorship was a recurrent phenomenon. The most important aspect of cities in antiquity was their sedentary agrarian base, which resulted in the symbiosis of three social classes: farmers, priests and warriors. Cities in old Mesopotamia – modern Iraq – were possible because of the economic surplus that a sedentary agricultural society generated. The priests acted as managers of a planned economy in those city-states (Starr, 1974); the temple – a very important public building – was not only a place for worship but also functioned as a store of food. There are some sociologists who contend that religion and the class of priests came into existence because of the need for control in an agricultural society (Burgers and Oosterman, 1992). Priests allegedly had a monopoly of knowledge of the calendar, which was of great importance in a sedentary agricultural society. It was crucial to start sowing at the right moment. Priests could also have had a function in holding a stock of food reserves and it is claimed by Parsons (1977) that the origin of writing is to be found in the bookkeeping of the stock of cereals in the temple. Priests might also have prevented the urban community from consuming the harvest as soon as it was harvested. That could explain the ritual which is so common to many agricultural regimes, namely having an orgiastic ritual feast after harvest, followed by abstinence. However that may be, religion and its class of priests gave a special quality to early public space – they made it *holy space.*

There was another dominant class in the early city: that of the warriors. In an agricultural regime, the output per square metre very much exceeds the output of hunter–collector societies. This higher output made possible a significant increase in population. Society became more productive, but on the other hand also more vulnerable. If the harvest were destroyed or robbed, the very basis of sedentary society would crumble. The advent of the military, the warriors, was the answer to the greater vulnerability of agricultural society. Cities were walled and defended, and public space became *safe space*. Holy space was represented by the temple, and safe space by the palace of the king. It is important to note that these public spaces – in the sense of important spaces for the entire urban community – were not accessible to the entire urban community. One can still illustrate this by the name of the ancient city centre of Peking, which is called the Forbidden City.

In summary, agricultural societies were the first to have cities. Because of the specific organization of production in these societies, two important classes emerged alongside the farmers: priests and warriors. As for public space – the set of buildings or sites of importance for the entire urban community as the term was defined – the qualities that emerged in such a society were holy space and safe space. Although society has changed dramatically since antiquity, these two qualities are still associated with public space. Churches are still holy places, of course. While the number of Christian churches may have diminished over recent years in at least some cities, the number of places of worship of other religions is growing in Western society and includes, for example, mosques. Some buildings, monuments or sites are holy in a secular way (Shields, 1991): national monuments, or houses where famous historical figures once lived – for instance the Mozart Geburtshaus in Salzburg. Even sporting accommodation can be holy – the 'holy grass' of Wembley is a case in point. The quasi-sacredness of these places shows very clearly when they are contested. Very emotional and even violent reactions can result. To give one example: in the 1970s hippies slept on the National Monument in central Amsterdam. Many people felt this to be a disgrace to the nation. Some marines, in a spontaneous action, drove them out and were applauded by large sections of Dutch society.

The safety of public space is also, of course, still a very important quality, although the fear is not of invaders from outside as in ancient society, but rather of criminals, junkies, and drunks from within the central city. Modern city guides, especially for American cities, designate neighbourhoods one should avoid, 'no-go areas', as they are aptly called.

Public Space in the Bourgeois City

I now turn to the second period which is of importance for the analysis of public space. That period can be designated as late medieval Europe, the bourgeois era. In the cities of western Europe a new class emerged, freeing itself from feudal society, the bourgeoisie (Weber, 1958; Bloch, 1961; Braudel, 1973). In the cities of late medieval Europe a social medium came to the fore which would revolutionize the world: the market. The market would in due course change the closed medieval autarchic society into an open economy. The German sociologist Bahrdt in his classic (1969) study on the origin of the public sphere saw the late medieval European city as its place of birth. When the market as organizing and integrating principle became more and more dominant, there was a need for new forms of social interaction. Bahrdt's reasoning goes as follows. In a market context people are more and more confronted with strangers, people whom they do not know. These encounters are brief and volatile. On the market the problem is that people who are strangers to one another have to come to terms in a very brief span of time. The solution for this problem, according to Bahrdt, is the stylization of interaction. People are starting to play roles, they create forms of communication to be able to interact with strangers. In this way a public sphere is created. The place connected with this sphere is, according to Bahrdt, the market-place.

The central quality of that market-place is the possibility of exchange. Everybody should have the possibility, in contrast to a feudal society, to bring one's goods as a free man to the free market. It should be socially accessible space.

Richard Sennett, an American sociologist preoccupied with the rise and fall of the public sphere, has also stressed (1978) the importance of the European bourgeoisie in the construction of public space. He does not stress the economic exchange in the market as much as Bahrdt does, but rather the exchange of opinion in the 18th-century metropolises London and Paris. He argues that the rapid urbanization in 18th-century London and Paris called for a way to live amidst people one did not know, and would never be able to know, because of their sheer numbers. This situation leads to a sharp division between a private and a public sphere. In the private sphere the more biologically perceived activities are central: procreation, the raising of children, personal care, etc. In the public sphere modern man displayed his civility, that is, the capacity, as mentioned before, to interact with people whom he does not necessarily know. For Sennett it is not so much economic exchange which is central to the public sphere, but much more political and social exchange. He focuses on the debate between free citizens in the coffee-houses and the salons, the meetings in theatres and opera houses. The central value for Sennett is heterogeneity. In this he resembles Bahrdt, because essentially this boils down to a public space which is accessible to all citizens.

So we now have a new quality of urban public space, namely

democratic space. It should be accessible to all citizens, it should be a space of free exchange, be it the exchange of goods in the market sphere, or of opinions and political standpoints in the sphere of politics and culture. This quality of public space has been emphasized down to the present day. In particular, architects and local policy-makers have stressed that city centres especially should be places where all urban groups and all urban categories can meet. The problem is that both the market and the political debate have reached a spatial scale far beyond the individual city. The market has become a world market, the political debate has scaled up to national parliaments and will probably grow beyond that too. On the level of the city, modern democratic public space means that no one is excluded from the facilities in inner-city areas. This means no ethnic discrimination in cafés and discos, and a limit to the number of shops that are so luxurious that important parts of the local population are only able to go window-shopping. In the sphere of habitation the representation of all urban groups in the inner-city housing stock is also a popular theme in local policy. In The Netherlands the urban renewal policy of the 1970s is now severely criticized because of overemphasis on housing facilities for the lower-income groups, thereby destroying the base of all kinds of urban high-quality provisions and creating ethnic ghettos and cultures of poverty and unemployment (Kruijt and Drewe, 1993).

Public Space in the Industrial City

The third important period for the analysis of the qualities of public space is that of the 19th- and early 20th-century industrial city. The industrialization of European society and the expulsion of labour from the agricultural sector led to an enormous growth of the cities. A new class developed in the slums of the industrial cities: the working class, people who worked for many hours and a low income. They had to be disciplined to work in the strict regime of industrial production. The urban élites were confronted with great masses of people who, in their perception, were a threat to their civilized way of life. There were several dimensions to that threat. First of all, there was the fear of the urban élites of being struck by contagious diseases. The 19th century was, of course, the age of cholera. Secondly, there was the fear of revolution, of a rising of the urban proletariat, fuelled by new political ideologies such as socialism, communism and anarchism. The third dimension of fear was the possibility of the urban poor degrading the moral basis of civilized society. The way the working class lived and spent their leisure time was considered a disgrace by the urban upper class. The Irish workers who migrated to London in the 18th century, for instance, kept pigs in their dwellings and had funeral rituals in which it could take weeks for the dead to be buried (George, 1976). Also the urban working classes enjoyed leisure activities that generated crowds which were rather noisy, especially when drinking was involved, which it usually was. Boxing matches, football games, dance halls and the like caused a moral panic in the urban upper classes. The answer was to complement the process of disciplining in the factory with a process of disciplining in the sphere of reproduction, the way people behaved in their leisure time. They were taught how to live in their private dwellings and taught to behave in the city. Central to this campaign was the effort to domesticate the working class, making them lead an orderly, civilized life. The public space of the city was more or less privatized; the most important goal was to keep people off the streets. This policy seems to have been rather successful in the long run. With the coming of the Welfare State and the rise in the income of the working classes after the Second World War, they seem to have accepted and internalized the bourgeois ideal of life.

In the 1960s and 1970s, people fled the city and sought suburban ways of life. Only the lowest-income groups stayed behind in the cities. The city remained a place to work: the schools, the office buildings and the industrial plants were there. But in due course employment and education were also suburbanized. Leisure became either home-oriented (everyone owned a stereo and television set) or outdoor recreation, neither being really associated with city life. The only remaining important aspect of urban public space was physical accessibility of the shopping centre. Public space was reduced to the public road. Accessibility, especially by car, was the quality related to public space. Today this aspect still plays an important role, of course. The city of Amsterdam, for instance, organized in 1992 a local referendum on the issue whether or not to reduce the number of cars allowed to park in the inner city. Local shopkeepers tend to take the stand for accessibility by car, because they expect, usually erroneously, their income to decrease if people cannot come by car to the inner city any more.

Public Space in the Post-industrial City

The debate on the nature of the post-industrial city is rather speculative because we are in the middle of it. It is always difficult to create distance from one's own society. All kinds of labels have been formulated by social scientists to make sense of contemporary society:

post-industrial, post-modern, post-Fordist, informational, etc. More important than the labels, of course, are the characteristics that have been pointed to in the literature. One of them is the change in patterns of production and consumption (Urry and Lash, 1987).

In the last phase of industrial society, mass production was combined with mass consumption, which was made possible by the growing incomes of factory workers. Today, of course, Western society is still a consumer society, but production has lost some of its 'mass' character. Tastes have multiplied; changes in consumer markets are speeding up. In 'postindustrial society', people no longer seem to rely for their status on their job, but more and more base their social identity on the way they behave in their leisure time (Featherstone, 1991). Sociologists have pointed to the fact that consumer goods have a symbolic value which is becoming more important than their use value. The display of all kinds of conspicuous consumption should express the status or desired status of people; they construct a lifestyle. The spatial correlate of this kind of society is something like a leisure city, or 'fun city'. It is the city which provides the facilities and the audiences to display a great variety of lifestyles.

The city is also the habitat of the people who are the avant-garde of lifestyle display. It is the residential milieu of the well-off modern households; the 'yuppies' (young urban professionals) and 'dinkies' (double income, no kids), as they are called. These households live in expensive inner-city neighbourhoods and apartments. Some of the low-income groups are pushed out. High-income households composed of only one or two people have much money but a lack of time. They have to buy the time of others for their reproductional activities: maintaining the house, cooking, minding their children, shopping. So they need an environment with lots of facilities and different people in the neighbourhood (Vijgen and van Engelsdorp Gastelaars, 1986). Such an environment is, of course, an urban environment. Their time order is dualistic. As Daniel Bell (1979) said of the ideal-typical personalities of post-industrial society, they are 'straight on the job and swingers at night'. They have given an impulse to urban leisure. The success of the opera house, the cinemas, the galleries, the pavement cafés, the grand cafés, the restaurants and the museums can be traced to their leisure activities. More and more, city planners try to accommodate these people in an effort to commit high-income groups to the city. Urban planners may often belong to this group themselves. That is why urban public space is made into leisure space, and its leisure quality is becoming more and more dominant. It can be read from the statistics. In Amsterdam, for instance, the number of pavement cafés grew from a few dozen in 1970 to 800 in 1990 (Burgers, 1992). Between 1980 and 1990 the number of people employed in the entertainment industry in The Netherlands increased by almost 60,000 (Kloosterman and Elfring, 1991). Because a lot of work in this sector is done on an informal basis, the real number working in this sector might easily be twice as many.

New high-income groups like yuppies or dinkies are part of a broader demographic trend in which the composition of households is changing. Up to 70% of the households in a place like Amsterdam are composed of just one or two people. As suburbia was an attractive place for the traditional couple with children to live, the city has many qualities to offer for the small household: small dwellings, some expensive and exclusive and some cheap and flexible. In addition, the leisure facilities in the city are attractive for small households: fast-food restaurants, cafés and discos, the cinema, the theatre, etc. – facilities, by the way, which have a meaning beyond their mere functional use; they are also important meeting-places for different urban groups. There they can display and exchange tastes and also look for companionship which they, unlike the 'ordinary families' of the industrial city, cannot find at home. Because of the declining importance of long-term marital relations and the emergence of what is called 'serial monogamy' the erotic function of public space – which was earlier only of importance for teenagers – becomes more important. Public space is a potential meeting-place. In this sense there have come into being a differentiation in spaces related to different kinds of sexual preferences. To give one example, the city of San Francisco offers a large number of internationally known meeting-places for male homosexuals.

Besides the demographic changes, there is another factor which makes urban reality more attractive than it was in the past. Urban renewal has changed vast areas in many cities and given them a new face. This very tangible and concrete facelift of parts of the inner city very much contributes to the impression of most people that the city is doing well again. Urban renewal has become relatively institution-alized, almost a routine operation. The political, sometimes violent conflicts between local authorities and inhabitants of the old neigh-bourhoods – especially the squatters – have decreased in number and intensity. The urban renewal process has also fed the positive image of the city in the eyes of visitors and potential inhabitants.

But all that glitters is not gold. Much of what seems to be a rebirth of the city is just image-building. This process of image-building has resulted from an important change in the relationship between city, State and market (Smith, 1991). After the Second World War, the Welfare State became the solution for the kind of economic crisis of the 1930s. Rooted in the booming economy of the 1950s and 1960s, the Welfare State provided services and income for individuals of all sorts

– the sick, the aged, the handicapped, etc. – and for all kinds of institutions, including local government. To make a successful claim on State revenues, the best legitimation for the cities was to paint their situation in as bad a light as possible. They emphasized the problems of poverty, traffic jams in the inner cities, drug abuse, and insufficient funding for necessary urban renewal. Because cities had to compete with other cities for State revenues, there was a natural tendency to exaggerate local problems (Gurr and King, 1987). What has happened since the mid-1980s is that cities have changed or at least tried to change their image, because of a more market-oriented policy. The economic recession of the 1970s and 1980s led to a crisis in the Welfare State in terms of means as well as in ideology. Making use of the democratic jargon of the 1960s and 1970s, the State decentralized some of its authority and its Welfare State regime. Cities did get more opportunities to develop their own policy, but, on the other hand, were financially curtailed by the central State. The fiscal crisis of the central State was regionalized and localized (Dear, 1981). To realize their local policy, cities were more and more forced to seek help from the market. This has had a tremendous effect on the way cities present themselves. Obviously, if a city wants to seem attractive for private capital, it should not stress local problems. It cannot say that its crime rate is the highest in the country, it cannot say that its inner city cannot be reached by car, it cannot say that it lacks cultural facilities, and it cannot say that the number of homeless people is steadily growing. On the contrary, the city must boast of its local qualities: a rich agenda of cultural happenings, famous festivals, a well-educated population, situated centrally in Europe or even the world, luxury houses and apartments, an opera house and, above all, a good business climate. So in the same way that the urban crisis of the 1970s and 1980s was exaggerated by local authorities to get the attention of the central State, now the urban renaissance is exaggerated because the cities need the attention of the market. Because of a growing importance of private capital and private initiative, cities have been forced to sell themselves. City marketing is the keyword nowadays. The city has become a product; that is why information that cities themselves provide about the local situation sometimes has the character of a commercial (Harvey, 1989; Savage and Warde, 1993).

Conflicting Claims on Public Space

It is important to note that cities stress all the qualities that history has attached to public space at the same time. Local authorities want to maintain and promote the quasi-sacred places and buildings and their monumentality; that is, they try to make the city a safe city, they try to make the city accessible to all kinds of people and economic activities, they try to promote physical accessibility in terms of traffic and, recently, they boast of the fun aspect of city life. If we are to believe local policy-makers, the modern city really seems to have every quality people want to see in it. The resemblance comes to mind with a modern television set: the city as one technical device with a multitude of channels. Modern city as 'zap city' seems an adequate metaphor. But, as always, reality is much more complicated. One does not need to be an expert on urban affairs to see that there are frictions between the several qualities of urban public space. The promotion of a leisure city, for instance, could be at odds with the promotion of safety (alcohol abuse, for instance), social accessibility (leisure activities usually attract young people and drive out the elderly) and certain kinds of shopping facilities (shops may lose their clients because they prefer shopping in peripheral areas or because they are bought out by financially stronger urban activities).

Urban sociologists and geographers, especially in the United States, have stressed that the modern city tends to become a dual or divided city (Fainstein *et al.*, 1992; Mollenkopf and Castells, 1992). The economic growth sectors of today – finance, insurance, real estate and other producer service industries – tend to cluster in the cities. In these sectors the employment and income structure has a dual character. High-income jobs and low-income jobs – sometimes called 'junk jobs' – dominate. Especially women, young men and members of minority groups do the low-paid work, with few career possibilities. Low-income employment often has an informal character, especially in the fast-food sector, the restaurants, the cafés, the discos and entertainment in general. If these jobs have a transitory character there is really no problem. They can be attractive for a short time and a certain phase in life. But when they turn out to condemn people for a long period of time to the bottom of the labour market, something is indeed wrong. In any case, they are not a solution for all the people who have lost their jobs in the traditional industries; these people are the long-term unemployed. They do not match the fun city at all: they cannot find a job in it, nor can they afford to enjoy it.

There is a tendency for cities to imitate each other. Cities all over the world seem to do the same things. They all build opera houses, megamalls, multifunctional indoor stadiums, buildings as high as possible, casinos, new town halls, waterfronts and so on. Certainly there will be winners and losers. But a policy of competition also needs a policy of complementarity, as cities operate within networks at various scales (Ashworth and Tunbridge, 1990).

References

Ashworth, G.J. and Tunbridge, J.E. (1990) *The Tourist-Historic City*. Belhaven, London.

Bahrdt, H.P. (1969) (1961) *Die Moderne Großstadt. Soziologische Überlegungen zum Städtebau*. Ellert & Richter, Hamburg.

Bell, D. (1979) *The Cultural Contradictions of Capitalism*. Heinemann, London.

Bloch, M. (1961) *Feudal Society*. Routledge & Kegan Paul, Chicago.

Braudel, F. (1973) (orig. 1967) *Capitalism and Material Life 1400–1800*. Oxford University Press, New York.

Burgers, J. (1992) Stadsgezichten. In: Burgers, J. (ed.) *Uitstad*. Jan van Arkel, Utrecht.

Burgers, J. and Oosterman, J. (1992) Het publieke domein. Over de sociale constructie van openbare ruimte. *Amsterdams Sociologisch Tijdschrift* 19(1).

Dear, M. (1981) A theory of the local state. In: Burnett, A.D. and Taylor, P.J. (eds) *Political Studies from Spatial Perspectives*. Wiley, Chichester.

Fainstein, S., Gordon, I. and Harloe, M. (1992) *Divided Cities*. Blackwell, Oxford.

Featherstone, M. (1991) *Consumer Culture and Postmodernism*. Sage, London.

George, M.D. (1976) (orig. 1925) *London Life in the Eighteenth Century*. Penguin, Harmondsworth.

Gurr, E.R. and King, D.S. (1987) *The State and the City*. Macmillan, Basingstoke/London.

Harvey, D. (1989) *The Condition of Postmodernity*. Oxford University Press, Oxford.

Kloosterman, R.C. and Elfring, T. (1991) *Werken in Nederland*. Academic Service, Schoonhoven.

Kruijt, A. and Drewe, P. (1993) Ontwikkelingen in de stedelijke economie. In: Burgers, J., Kreukels, A. and Mentzel, M. (eds) *Stedelijk Nederland in de Jaren Negentig*. Jan van Arkel, Utrecht.

Mollenkopf, J.H. and Castells, M. (1992) *Dual City. Restructuring New York*. Russel Sage Foundation, New York.

Parsons, T. (1977) *The Evolution of Societies*. Prentice-Hall, Englewood Cliffs.

Savage, M. and Warde, A. (1993) *Urban Sociology, Capitalism and Modernity*. Macmillan, Basingstoke/London.

Sennett, R. (1978) (orig. 1977) *The Fall of Public Man. On the Social Psychology of Capitalism*. Vintage Books, New York.

Shields, R. (1991) *Places on the Margin. Alternative Geographies of Modernity*. Routledge, London/New York.

Smith, M.P. (1991) (orig. 1988) *City, State, and Market. The Political Economy of Urban Society*. Basil Blackwell, Oxford.

Starr, C.G. (1974) *A History of the Ancient World*. Oxford University Press, New York.

Urry, J. and Lash, S. (1987) *The End of Organized Capitalism*. Polity Press, Cambridge.

Vijgen, J. and van Engelsdorp Gastelaars, R. (1986) *Stedelijke Bevolkingscategorieën in Opkomst: Stijlen en Strategieën in het Alledaags Bestaan*. Koninklijk Nederlands Aardrijkskundig Genootschap/Instituut voor Sociale Geografie, Universiteit van Amsterdam, Amsterdam.

Weber, M. (1958) *The City*. Free Press, New York.

From Management by Producers to Transformation by the Consumer

The focus now shifts from management by agencies, most of which are self-conscious producers, to the tourists as consumers managing their own holiday experiences.

The basic paradox here is that on the one hand this is a topic whose critical importance is clear: the effective management of the recreationist, or the recreation destination, for whatever objective, depends upon an understanding of the behaviour of visitors. On the other hand, this is one area of leisure studies where very little is known, especially at the scale of the individual destination, which is precisely where such knowledge could be most effective as a basis for place management. The four chapters here all attempt to delve deeper into the question of what tourists actually do when they are behaving as tourists. The range of possible tourism activities and thus the range of possible behavioural reactions are as wide as the human imagination. Each of the four contributions here therefore can only represent one type of tourist and one set of behavioural characteristics.

Dietvorst poses the most universally applicable question, namely how visitors arrange their space–time budgets in recreation areas. Answers are sought in small historical towns and wider recreation regions. Although the focus of the book is on the transformation of space, time is of obvious central importance, especially as tourism is generally defined in terms of the use of time and the tourism visit with its diverse activities is severely constrained by the availability of time. How tourists use space at various scales, and indeed which spaces they use, is obviously related to their management of the time at their disposal and is equally critical in placing tourism and the tourist within multifunctional urban and regional space and within the context of other non-tourist users of that space. This in turn is applied and exemplified in a way that demonstrates the direct relevance of these ideas to management intervention at the local level.

The approach of Philipsen is more generalized and conceptual as he explains some of the relationships between human behaviour and the environment that are most relevant to the recreational use of what are essentially natural landscapes (taken here to include the modification of purely natural environments by human action). Sets of environmental values are of course increasingly to be found among the objectives of recreation and tourism management plans and among the constraints of development plans and projects. These, however, are only rarely translated into detailed management of the relationship of the individual tourist to the immediate environment of the tourism place.

Active participation in sport is one catagory of special-interest tourism that is proving increasingly popular. Within this category, golf, considered by Priestley, is just one example. The value of this particular case lies not only in its increasing popularity as an activity nor in the strength of the attraction that it exercises over its aficionados over long distances, but also in its particular space requirements. Golf requires a relatively large land area for each participant and imposes particular constraints on shared use. It generally owns and manages the areas it uses, unlike some other active outdoor pursuits such as mountaineering or orienteering, which has consequences not only for the economics of the activity, but more relevantly here, for the other uses, whether recreational or not, that it precludes or allows.

If golf is one case of continuing on holiday an interest already developed at home then so is participation in an arts festival. A spectacular case, in its economic and urban impacts, is the Edinburgh Festival described by Gratton and Taylor. The significance of this festival, or more accurately, as Gratton and Taylor make clear, this cluster of different festivals serving different overlapping markets in the same city, is shown and so is its selective appeal to specific consumers. Edinburgh stands as an archetype for the well-established and well-patronized arts festival with a clear and important relevance to tourism. However, there are many hundreds of arts festivals of which only a few have such tourism significance.

A single case may illustrate the possibilities being actively considered by many places of using festival tourism as a local development strategy. Stratford, Ontario is a small Canadian town of some 26,000 inhabitants whose principal industry is the tourism and excursionism associated with the Stratford Shakespeare Festival. Its place image is so strongly associated with this theatre festival that it is difficult to realize that 40 years ago none of this existed and Stratford was an industrial town with a working-class ethos. The contraction and eventual closure of the Canadian National Railway locomotive-maintenance yards in the 1950s threatened to remove the only major economic activity in the town. The revolutionary idea (usually attributed to a local journalist called Patterson) to replace this with a cultural industry was not based on any existing cultural activity or past reputation, but solely on the coincidental associations of the place name itself with a town in another continent that had produced a playwright five centuries earlier. From that coincidence came the initiative that led to the building of three theatres, park landscaping along the Avon river and the creation of Victoria Lake with swans and associated commercial development to serve a visiting audience of more than half a million over the six-month season. The point here is that need and opportunity coincided at a particular time in a specific place, and creativity emerged to solve a problem of one economic system through the possibilities offered by another. The need for such a coincidence should modify the optimistic ambitions and hopeful expectations of places considering such developments.

10

Tourist Behaviour and the Importance of Time–Space Analysis

A.G.J. Dietvorst

Centre for Recreation and Tourism Studies, Agricultural University, Generaal Foulkesweg 13, 6703 BJ Wageningen, The Netherlands.

In the introductory chapter we referred to the processes of symbolic and material reproduction of the original resource such as the landscape and the cultural heritage by interpretation and visiting. In fact tourism and recreation are characterized by the effects of strongly differentiated spatial behaviour, as can be seen in popular destination areas. Despite the fact that spatial movements are among the most typical characteristics of tourism and recreation, attention to this phenomenon is normally restricted to the analysis of static visitor numbers and their demographic and/or socioeconomic characteristics. Such behavioural research has been used empirically to test ideas about preferences and motives in order to make strategic decisions for tourist-product development. The emphasis is rarely on the analysis of the dynamics of origin–destination flows, because of the lack of relevant and reliable statistical data. A recent report commissioned by the Dutch Physical Planning Office on the importance of tourist traffic in creating regional networks in northwest Europe (Jansen-Verbeke and Spee, 1993) demonstrates the huge number of problems related to the comparison of a wide variety of statistical figures on different spatial levels. The poor possibilities of disaggregating national data into regionally relevant figures remain an especially important hindrance to sound time–space analysis.

However, trying to realize more dynamic analysis of tourist flows by researching origin–destination figures is laudable, but not enough. The continuing differentiation in the demand for leisure goods and services is made visible in a large variety of trip possibilities on different spatial levels. The suppliers in the tourism–recreation sector have to cope with an increase in the number of market segments and the need to take into account the very divergent wishes and expectations of the different user groups. The resulting client-focused approach can be traced in the abundance of tourist products. Regional tourist boards all over the world try to get away from the image of one-sidedness (such as sand–sea–sun) and promote variety as the new brand. In a glossy brochure the *Azienda di promozione turistica della provincia di Ravenna* recommends the variety of this Italian region:

> It goes without saying that none of these attractions is in itself exclusive. The world has become a pretty small place and exotic destinations are sometimes no more than a few hours away. But ours are not scattered to the four corners of the earth: art and beaches, entertainment and history, sea, spas and hills are concentrated in an area no larger than that of a major town or city.

So in and around Ravenna they try to convince us that there is everything we could possibly wish for.

Of course Ravenna is not the only region to promote variety as the most essential product characteristic. The Spanish Basque country issued a whole series of target-group specific brochures: 'Folklore and Tradition', 'Nature and Sport', 'Towns and Villages', 'History and Art' and 'Gastronomy'. Several tourist regions in France offer all kinds of sightseeing tours, itineraries for walking and cycling, mountain-bike routes and so on. Recent research in The Netherlands revealed interesting combinations of different mobility forms: water tourists like to combine their journey on the canals and rivers with cycling possibilities on the land to enjoy the cultural heritage (de Bruin and Klinkers, 1994). What can now be learned from this handful of examples?

1. The supplier of the tourist product has to realize that it is all too easy to regard the product as homogeneous. Is there a coherence of attractive facilities offered? Are the various elements of tourism related to each other? Cohesion implies that the interests of the user are what matters. The criterion for cohesion must therefore be derived from the interrelationship between the various, and spatially separate, attractions and facilities brought together by the visitor him/herself.
2. The demands of the tourists and their differentiation in background, motives and preferences all have implications for the management of the regional and national tourist product.
3. By setting up an analysis of the real use of the supply offered, emphasis has to be laid upon the way tourists combine several attractions and facilities during their stay in a certain region. To what extent can the relationship between the product elements be described

in terms of competition, complementarity or dependency?

4. In identifying the key spatial factors of visitor behaviour, time–space analysis is essential. This conclusion seems to be obvious but one has to realize that comparatively little is known in a systematic way about the time–space patterns of tourists. Prentice (1993) noticed in his considerations on heritage tourism that visitor surveys at heritage attractions 'have been characterized by their definitional incompatibility and often their confidentiality', and this refers only to socio-demographic data as such and not to the more sophisticated time–space characteristics. The study of Light and Prentice (1994) makes clear the significance of meso-scale variations in demand for product development. In their case-study on the situation in Wales they demonstrate the advantages of having data available from a sufficient number of sites to allow examination of spatial variations within the demand for one type of heritage site. This type of analysis can, however, be further improved by application of time–space analysis.

5. In accordance with the conclusions of Light and Prentice, time–space analysis could be of considerable relevance for site development and promotion: 'If the product offered is to be matched to the characteristics and expectations of visitors then one development/ interpretation policy to be applied across all sites is clearly not suitable.... Marketing efforts can be more effectively targeted once the nature of the demand has been established.'

When the cohesion of tourism and recreation is no longer solely determined by those supplying the product, but also determined by the visitors themselves, it implies that relevant research methods must be used for the analysis.

Tourist Recreation Complexes and Time–Space Behaviour

Tourists and recreationists do not use the various possibilities in a given area at random. The various elements of a tourist–recreation product are combined according to knowledge, images, preferences and actual opportunities (Dietvorst, 1989). To the visitor the amenities appear to be related to each other and are required to be near to each other; the whole is more attractive than each separate amenity. These group-specific combinations of spatially related attractions and facilities are called complexes (Dietvorst, 1989, 1993).The tourist–recreation complex is a spatially differentiated whole and it has different spatial scales. Depending on motives, preferences and capabilities, tourists tend to combine several attractions and facilities during their holidays or daily leisure activities. Within spatially concentrated attractions and facilities (for instance the above-mentioned product elements in the Ravenna region) a variety of tourist complexes can be identified, because visitors are linking the museums, the restaurants, the shopping facilities and so on according to their own preferences and knowledge into a coherent but spatially differentiated whole. There is an indication of some sort of spatial and functional association and the positions of each of the product elements can be described as subordinate, coordinate, complementary, reinforcing and so on. Yet, in many product plans, regions and towns are seen as a simple addition of attractions, facilities and supporting infrastructure. This is just aggregation as such and insufficient for sound product development.

In looking for a theoretical base to ground the description and analysis of tourist complexes, the concept of system is very appropriate. A tourist complex can be conceptualized as a system. The different product elements such as hotels, a market-place or museums are the system elements and the relations between these elements are established by the tourist movements. Systems analysis provides the tools to obtain insight into the relations between different parts of an entity. It helps to make visible the dynamics of a region.

A system can be defined as a set consisting of the following subsets:

- a set of elements, whose identity is determined by one or more characteristics;
- a set of relations between the elements;
- a set of relations between the elements and the environment of the system.

To describe the characteristics of a system the concepts of structure and function are useful. These concepts have a long history with an often confusing series of definitions. Often these concepts are so vaguely or multifariously defined as to have little value for scientific research. However, our definition operationalizes these concepts such that their connotation is without doubt. If structure and function have to say something about the dynamics of a given system, it is necessary for the definitions of each to be exclusive, i.e. no overlap between them is allowed. Although in most definitions structure is described as the character and the composition of the systems, i.e. the elements with their relations, I prefer to reserve the concept of structure for the system elements and the connected characteristics (Table 10.1). The concept of function is reserved for the subset of relations between the system elements. These relations become tangible as tourist flows, capital flows or information flows between places or regions (Table 10.2).

Table 10.1. A structure matrix.

	Characteristic 1	Characteristic 2	Characteristic 3	Characteristic 4
Region, place or sight A				
B				
C				
D				

Table 10.2. A function matrix.

	A	B	C	D
Region, place or sight A	0			
B		0		
C			0	
D				0

Field Theory

Geographical field theory can be considered as a solution to the problems of revealing and analysing the interdependence between the structure and function of a system. The theory refers also to the most essential characteristic of a spatial system or of a tourism–recreation complex. The field theory was launched by Brian Berry as a possibility for synthesizing formal and functional regions. His ideas were partly based upon the field theory of the social psychologist Kurt Lewin (1890–1947). Lewin's research was directed at group interaction and group behaviour. These processes were considered as functions of the group structure. Berry's translation of Lewin's ideas has to do with the integration of systems theory with field theory. The quintessence of the geographical field theory lies for Berry in the interdependence between structure and function: 'a mutual equilibration of spatial structure and spatial behaviour in a state of complex interdependency. Thus in the context of ongoing spatial processes behavioural changes may call forth structural changes as well as the converse' (Berry, 1968, p. 421).

Time–Space Analysis

Structure analysis has a long tradition. Structure matrices can be analysed by well-known statistical techniques such as cross-tabulation or principal component analysis to reveal meaningful patterns. Because functional analysis presupposes much more elaborate research knowledge, we will now focus upon opportunities and problems in applying time–space analysis in tourist research.

Time–space relationships have a fairly long tradition in geographical research. Famous in this tradition and fundamental for the scientific development in this respect are the ideas put forward by Torsten Hägerstrand. Based upon spatial diffusion studies, he tried to find concepts which might integrate the basic dimensions of time and space. Since 1966 Hägerstrand and his research team at Lund (Sweden) have been working to elaborate these concepts. The approach chosen by Hägerstrand and his followers can be considered as a physicalist approach to society (Thrift, 1977), an appreciation of the biophysical, ecological and locational realities which impose constraints on human activities. It is in fact a normative approach. Capability constraints (for instance the biologically based need for sleep and food), coupling constraints (people have to do activities with others) and authority constraints (certain activities are controlled, not allowed or not possible at a given time) restrict daily activity patterns. Individuals are forced to pack their activities into specific time–space stacks. The emphasis is on constraints.

On the other hand this constraint-oriented approach is contrasted with the choice-oriented approach (Floor, 1990) making use of time-budget analysis. Activities are considered as the results of choices.

According to Chapin (1974) motives and preferences, time–space opportunities and time–space-related contexts influence specific choices, which are realized in concrete activities. In fact of course the two approaches mentioned do not exclude each other and in practice a mixture would be most appropriate.

Basic assumptions in developing time–space analysis of tourist behaviour are, paraphrasing Thrift (1977, p. 6):

- the indivisibility of a human being. Time spent at a specific location cannot be spent elsewhere at the same time
- the limited availability of time to spend on a specific day
- the fact that every activity has a duration and that movement between points in space consumes time
- the limited packing capacity of space.

The way people make their choice within the constraints of the time–space framework depends upon: (i) their motives, preferences and experience; (ii) their images and estimations of opportunities; and (iii) their material resources.

The different time–space paths of tourists, and hence the different assemblages made out of the supply of attractions and activities, were earlier researched in city-based time–space analysis in the small Dutch tourist-historic city of Enkhuizen (Dietvorst, 1994). Time–space analysis on data sets obtained from different groups of visitors revealed several typical assemblages of attractions, the so-called tourist–recreation complexes. Visitors arriving in Enkhuizen by yacht patronize several facilities in the harbour area, preferring restaurants and cafés. Some visitors with cultural interests combine a visit to the Zuiderzee Museum with a walk in the city – sightseeing or restaurant-visiting. Others can be typified as being interested in the historical or architectural aspects of the city. For them, the visit to Enkhuizen is often part of a series of visits to famous tourist-historic cities in The Netherlands.

Methods for Analysing Flow Patterns and Time–Space Behaviour

Several methods can be used for analysing the time–space behaviour of the visitors. First, principal component analysis patterns can explore patterns to reveal 'visitor preference spaces'. Second, network planning can be used in combination with geographic information systems. GIS in land-use planning gives the opportunity of adding possibilities for a translation of the real world into a model world. Often operations research is used in modelling the maximization or minimization of the effects of certain human decisions. For the analysis of time–space behaviour of visitors the route-solving capability of operations research might be very appropriate. Third, apart from the application of operations research, networks can also be analysed using mathematical graph theory. Flows of tourists can be analysed in order to discover underlying hierarchical structures within tourist–recreation complexes. The origin–destination matrix representing the network reflects the prevailing structure of linkages and dominance. Fourth, if flow data for a sequence of periods exist, Markov chain analysis is very appropriate for describing the process of change within a tourist–recreation complex. The comparison of several calculated so-called transition matrices is extremely suitable for tracing the tendencies of change in the system observed. Unfortunately, however, one seldom has the opportunity to make use of these techniques of analysis because of a lack of adequate data on a regional or a local level.

Having explained the basic notions of time–space analysis we now illustrate how different the time–space paths of individual tourists can be. This is done by presenting some results of a series of studies carried out in southern Limburg and in the Dutch theme park the Efteling.

Daily Tourists in Southern Limburg: a Case-study

For a long time southern Limburg has been a popular holiday destination area in the southern part of The Netherlands. No doubt this is due to the presence of a number of high, slightly undulating plateaux, which include dry and brook valleys. Some of the plateaux are wide and deeply cut by little rivers such as the Geul and Gulp. Although the area is known for its high population density (911 people km^{-2} compared with the Dutch average of 333), several parts have maintained natural qualities in the presence of old forests, brook valleys and small landscape elements such as thickets, lanes, springs and streams. Wide panoramas belong to the specific attractions although in other parts the relief gives a relatively small-scale impression (van Eck and van Os, 1993).

One of the best-known holiday centres in this region is Valkenburg, for decades a national holiday destination for middle-class Dutch tourists and day-trippers. Much of the accommodation in this resort dates from the second half of the 19th century, although recently a number of chalet parks and camp-sites have changed the traditional picture of middle-class hotels and boarding-houses. At the end of the

1980s Valkenburg had 300 enterprises with a total capacity of 22,000 beds. Each year approximately 1.3 million overnight stays were registered.

In recent years the municipal tourist policy aimed at upgrading the overall quality of the local tourist product and changing the nationwide stereotype image of Valkenburg as a noisy centre for mass tourism. In order to differentiate the marketing policy and to detect the weak and the strong points of the tourist product, a survey ($N = 523$) was held in 1993 to reveal the time–space patterns of camping visitors (Bergmans *et al.*, 1994). In this research each specific activity is related to a specific period and to five possible regions. For each part of a day a maximum of six activities could be mentioned. Although it is technically possible to detect the complete individual time–space paths, the SPSS/PC+ computer program used presupposes the definition of about 3000 variables. This makes the analysis too complicated. The researchers also had to cope with the complicated aggregation problem. It proved to be very difficult to form significant time–space-related tourist complexes out of the large variety of individual time–space paths. A solution was found in creating first a sound typology of camping visitors and establishing for each tourist type the most probable time–space behaviour pattern.

Three types of camping visitors could be distinguished, the nature-oriented tourist, the variety-loving tourist and the convivial tourist. These three types differ significantly in personal characteristics and activity patterns. The nature-oriented tourist on the average is more than 36 years old and prefers quiet, high-quality camp-sites, and walking and cycling belong to the main activities. The variety-loving tourist is 26–35 years old. For this tourist the attractiveness of Valkenburg is determined by the wide variety of attractions, sights, nature and events. The convivial tourist is mostly young (< 26 years) and is with a couple of friends on holiday. The presence of cafés, discos, amusements and terraces is the main reason for choosing Valkenburg as a holiday destination, as they love abundant nightlife. For each tourist type the existence of a specific tourist complex could be verified. Figure 10.1 gives a simplified representation of the time–space behaviour and thus the typical tourist complex of each of the tourists is distinguished.

The nature-oriented tourist

This type is engaged in much shopping in the morning hours, mostly in the outer regions of Valkenburg. In the afternoon walking and cycling in the immediate surroundings of the camp-site are favoured activities, demanding a relatively large amount of time (> 3 h). Shopping and sitting on terraces are also frequently mentioned activities for

(1) Nature-oriented tourist

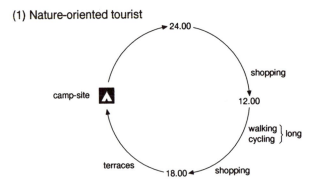

(2) Variety-loving tourist

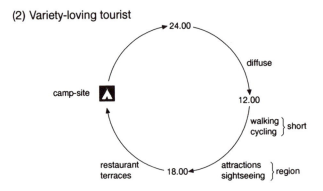

(3) Convivial tourist

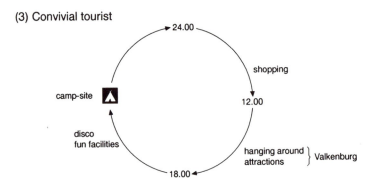

Fig. 10.1. Time–space behaviour of types of tourist.

spending the afternoon. The evening is reserved for staying on the camp-site.

The variety-loving tourist

No specific activities could be discerned during the morning. Some prefer to walk or to cycle in the afternoon but the time spent on these activities is considerably shorter compared with the nature-oriented tourist. In fact they prefer to drive to visit attractions or interesting sights in the surroundings. Restaurants and terraces in the centre of Valkenburg are frequented in the early evening.

The convivial tourist

Some shopping activities are conducted in the morning, but usually this tourist is not engaged in many activities during this part of the day. In the afternoon the activity is hanging around or visiting attractions in Valkenburg itself. In the evening relatively much time is spent in the wide variety of fun facilities (pubs, gambling, discos).

Some Conclusions of this Research

Time–space analysis proved to be succesful, because it made it possible to modify the overt stereotypical tourist picture of Valkenburg as a noisy mass tourism centre. As such the results could be used to improve the promotion and marketing of the local tourist board. Further, it is now possible for the local authorities to improve the policy of strengthening the tourist product and minimizing its negative effects. Of course, fortuitous research is not enough; in the near future a systematic monitoring of the tourist time–space behaviour is needed to evaluate the efforts of local entrepreneurs and public authorities to heighten the quality of the tourism product. The product quality will benefit from a policy of minimizing the negative effects of tourist time–space behaviour.

The Dynamics of a Theme-park: the Efteling

According to Roberts and Wall (cited by Pearce, 1988) 'Theme-parks are extreme examples of capital-intensive highly developed, user-oriented, man-modified recreational environments. The entertainment, rides, speciality foods and park buildings are usually organized around themes or unifying ideas.' Theme-parks can serve as very useful sites to experiment with time–space analysis techniques. They offer a wide variety of attractions in a relatively small area receiving several tens of thousands of visitors on peak days. From a methodological point of view a theme-park is an ideal research area because the in- and out-flow of visitors is regulated. Visitors can be easily selected and urged to participate in a time-budget survey. This kind of research is extremely useful for finding solutions for theme-park management problems. The visit sequences, the time spent in waiting and the locations selected for catering are relevant in reaching an optimal use of a theme-park.

Competition in the European market is growing for several reasons. The managers of the big theme-parks are concerned about the scale of the investment required to add new exciting attractions to their product. Normally in the past every new attraction resulted in increasing visitor numbers, but now this rule no longer seems to apply. It seems a saturation point is not far away, because the market for day-trips to theme-parks is nearly exhausted.

An interesting question is to what extent the arrival of Eurodisney is a threat to the existing theme-parks in Europe. There is a general acceptance within the industry (Lavery and Stevens, 1990) that Disney will create a market share for itself, i.e. not directly competitive with the existing theme-parks. It is assumed that Disney will set a high-quality standard which will become the market standard, so, if the others are intent on holding their positions, they have to innovate and/or improve the quality of the product. Lavery and Stevens point to the growing role of retailing in the total revenue of the parks. The admission fees constitute a relatively small proportion of the total day-visitor expenditure, so the day-visit budget offers promising possibilities for merchandising and catering. In fact a shift in eating habits is taking place (more experimental and more eating out): 'The integration of retailing and leisure is reflected in the development of indoor complexes in which the attraction component is introduced as an ancillary to the shopping experience – the reverse of the situation in an attraction' (Lavery and Stevens, 1990, p. 72). There are several parks in Europe – Metroland (UK), Aquaboulevard (France) and Brupak (Belgium) – which can be considered as forerunners of 'a new breed of integrated retail and leisure attraction, which may be located on the urban fringe or as minor city leisure developments' (Lavery and Stevens, 1990, p. 75).

Forty years ago the Efteling park was constructed in the Fairy Tale Forest designed by Anton Pieck. It could be characterized as an attraction for day tourists on the basis of an original recreation-ground for the local and regional youth at Kaatsheuvel. The first season was already very succesful: 300,000 visitors passed through the entrance. By the late 1960s the number of visitors had increased to approximately one million and then stabilized for a decade. In fact this means a decline, because a fixed number of visitors has to be seen as a decline due to rising costs.

In 1978 a new attraction, the Haunted Castle, was opened as a new direction in policy and planning of the park. It resulted in an increase of 300,000 visitors in 1979. But the great jump came in the 1980s with the introduction of a number of modern attractions characterized as 'major thrill rides' such as the Python (built in 1980 and the first super roller-coaster in Europe), the Half Moon (a swing ship) and the Pirana (rafting through swirling, wild waters). The Fata Morgana was also created, showing the way of life in a Forbidden City in the Fantasy East. At the end of the 1980s the visitors reached two million a year, and the 2.5 million mark has already been passed. The park management went on investing in big new attractions in this style.

Extension and rejuvenation of the product formula is necessary because the catchment area for day-trips to the Efteling is exhausted. To grow further, new markets have to be explored, especially with the opening of Eurodisney in 1992. The Efteling has set up a new strategic plan which has a time horizon up to 2008. The board has the intention of making huge investments in hotel and bungalow accommodation. A new hotel has already opened, a completely new holiday city and a bungalow park plus camp-site are foreseen for 1996–1997, and night recreation was planned in 1994. Besides these innovations three or four big attractions will be constructed, and even a complete second theme-park is included in the planning goals.

All these plans mean the creation of a totally new tourist-recreation product: other facilities, other time–space behaviour, new markets and/or target groups. We just mentioned the danger of an exhausted catchment area, but also inside the park the limits of growth are visible. On very busy days in the season (25,000–28,000 visitors) congestion problems are revealed. Visitors are no longer capable of moving in the park as they would perhaps prefer to do. The waiting times are growing and the spread of visitors over the different attractions is becoming unbalanced. Too long waiting times mean fewer spending possibilities, and a more ideal ratio between admission fee and spending has to be achieved. The problems mentioned in the Efteling theme-park can be adequately analysed by putting them in the framework of tourist–recreation complexes as described earlier.

The question is whether there exists insufficient coherence between the different attractions, merchandising points, shops and restaurants. For the supplier (i.e. the Efteling) it is mainly a problem of logistics (capacity, average mobility rates, routeing, spending and merchandising). For the visitor it is mainly a time-allocation problem: problem of choice within certain time–space constraints. In fact this is a matter of matching visitor preferences with time efforts (waiting time, queuing, accessibility, perception of routeing and crowding).

So the Efteling board commissioned research and formulated three objectives (Spee, 1992).

- By a better understanding of the time–space behaviour of the visitors the weak and strong elements of the product 'theme-park' should become visible.
- A more balanced diffusion of the visitor streams or a better routeing system.
- A solution for a number of logistic problems.

To analyse the coherence between the various elements in the Efteling complex, three aspects are important. First, there is the actual use of the various attractions made visible by the movements of the visitors throughout the park. This implies establishing the visit sequences, the routeing, the distances, the moments of arrival and departure and the reactions of the visitors to the spatial design of the park (path structure, landscape, buildings, entrances to attractions). Second, there are the motives for use of or non-participation in certain attractions. Are there weak links in the system? Third, there are the images visitors have of the various opportunities in the park before they arrive.

Time–space research can only be done by surveying the visitors. On seven days in the summer season and six days in the autumn season of 1991 a sample of visitors was interviewed. The questionnaire consisted of two parts. The first part included questions on personal characteristics, the image of the park and the plans for the day. The second part was a kind of time-budget filled in by the visitor during the day: which attractions and which other merchandising points or restaurants were visited, which sequence, how much time was spent on each attraction, etc. After the visits the little time-budget books were returned. In order to stimulate people to cooperate an incentive was available: 3735 questionnaires were supplied to the visitors, 2576 were returned, and because some of the returned time-budget books were unsuitable for further processing, 2378 remained. The response was 63.7% (a little lower in the summer than in the autumn). The conclusion is that this is a very high response for this type of survey.

For the analysis of the coherence between the various attractions and other elements of the park the GIS INTRANET (Interactive Route and Analysis System) was used. This is a vector-based, menu-guided program used for operations research and especially suitable for analysing network characteristics (Jurgens, 1992).

On the average a visitor spends 6–7 hours in the park visiting some seven attractions in the summer season against ten in the autumn (due to less crowding). Surprisingly, the 'white-knuckle rides' are not among the top attractions, but the 'fairy-tale attractions' such as the Fairy Tale Forest and the Fata Morgana are. Perhaps the illusion is a stronger attraction than the short (2 minutes) horrible feeling of the six or seven loops of the roller-coaster. This research verified a remarkable 'absorption capacity' of the oldest and still most popular attraction, the Fairy Tale Forest. Forty-four per cent of the visitors spent more than one hour in this part of the theme-park. This favourable position among the other product elements could be explained by the unfavourable ratio between waiting times and real attraction experience at other attractions. People do not like to wait half an hour to experience a ride of 1–4 minutes.

In the early morning and the late afternoon the footpaths are most intensively used (Figs 10.2, 10.3 and 10.4). In the summer period during the whole day many visitors are on the move. Although most of the visitors try to minimize the distances to the chosen attractions, at least 25% of the visitors are on the move in each quarter of an hour. The more visitors, the more movements between the attractions: the link intensities are high. The footpaths function as a kind of overflow for the crowded attractions. The relations between the attractions located in the same area are most clear in the autumn (there is less distortion from the 'natural pattern' due to the absorption capacity of each attraction). A fairly direct relation exists between crowding and the expenditure locations. In the summer season the small, dispersed merchandising points along the footpaths could be less intensively used than in the autumn period, whereas the expenditures related to attractions are higher in the summer period.

The survey verified a clear spatial and functional coherence between clusters of attractions and facilities created by the combination of the park infrastructure and visitor images and preferences. On peak days several parts of the Efteling show congestion. The tourist–product, the Efteling, consists of a coherent whole of primary attractions, supporting facilities and a conditioning network of paths. The time–space research verified the strong relations between each of the product elements but also the impossibility of using them efficiently on peak days. Time-consuming attractions like the Fairy Tale Forest contribute considerably to spreading the peak visitor streams. The extension of the number of attractions with a large 'absorbing capacity' could increase the 'valve' possibilities of the attraction system. Because small attractions already function as an overflow for the big attractions, carefully planned, more or less hierarchical clusters of attractions could result in relevant tourist complexes solving the congestion problem.

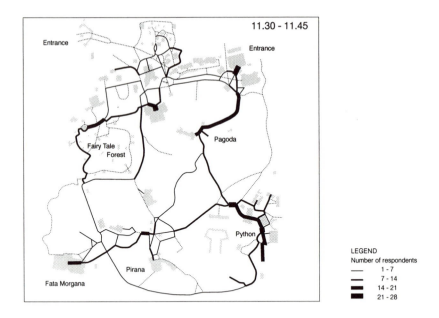

Fig. 10.2. Time–space research in the Efteling park – 11.30–11.45 hours.

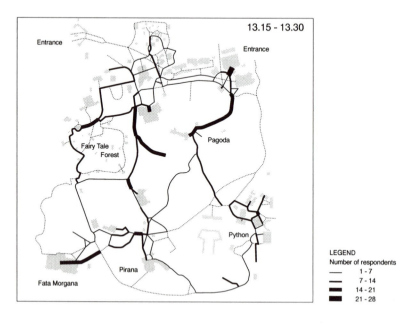

Fig. 10.3. Time–space research in the Efteling park – 13.15–13.30 hours.

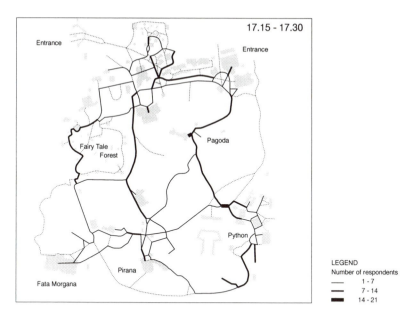

Fig. 10.4. Time–space research in the Efteling park — 17.15–17.30 hours.

More attention has to be paid to the entertainment capabilities around the path network. This could reinforce the already existing overflow function of this network. Street entertainment by 'cast members' and so-called 'characters', little events and an open-air theatre can be developed to make the path network a structural entertaining chain within the theme-park, a substitute for mere traffic.

Conclusion

Despite the fact that spatial movement is crucial for tourism and recreation, attention to this phenomenon is normally restricted to the analysis of static visitor numbers. Even more dynamic analysis of tourist flows is not enough to make visible the large variety of trip possibilities and the resulting attraction assemblages. The case-studies presented of tourist behaviour in southern Limburg and in the Dutch theme-park the Efteling show how tourists assemble the essential elements of a day-trip in quite different ways. The time–space behaviour of visitors is crucial in determining the weaknesses and strengths of an urban or regional tourist product or an internally differentiated tourist attraction such as a theme-park. It contributes to our understanding of the mutual relationships between the spatially dispersed attractions and the movement patterns of the tourists, and hence demonstrates the analytical power of field theory.

References

Bergmans, P., van Gurp, H. and Poelstra, A. (1994) *Typisch Valkenburg. Een onderzoek naar toeristentypen en het tijdruimtegedrag van campinggasten in de gemeente Valkenburg aan de Geul.* Centre for Recreation Studies, Agricultural University, Wageningen.

Berry, B. (1968) A synthesis of formal and functional regions using a general field theory of spatial behaviour. In: Berry, B. and Marble, D. (eds) *Spatial Analysis: A Reader in Statistical Geography.* Prentice-Hall, Englewood Cliffs, pp. 419–428.

Chapin, F.S. (1974) *Human Activity Patterns in the City.* Wiley, New York.

de Bruin, A.H. and Klinkers, P.M.A. (1994) *Recreatietoervaart: de Moeite Waard.* Rapport 307, Winand-Staring Centre, Wageningen.

Dietvorst, A.G.J. (1989) Complexen en netwerken: hun betekenis voor de toeristisch-recreatieve sector. Inaugural address, Landbouwuniversiteit, Wageningen.

Dietvorst, A.G.J. (1993) Planning for tourism and recreation: a market-oriented approach. In: van Lier, H.N. and Taylor, P.D. (eds) *New Challenges in Recreation and Tourism Planning.* Developments in Landscape Management and Urban Planning, 6D. Elsevier, Amsterdam, pp. 87–124.

Dietvorst, A.G.J. (1994) Cultural tourism and time–space behaviour. In: Ashworth, G.J. and Larkham, P.J. (eds) *Building a New Heritage. Tourism, Culture and Identity in the New Europe.* Routledge, London, pp. 69–89.

Floor, H. (1990) Aktiviteitensystemen en bereikbaarheid. In: Floor, J., Goethals, A.L.J. and de Koning, J.C. *Aktiviteitensystemen en Bereikbaarheid.* SISWO, Amsterdam, pp. 3–5.

Jansen-Verbeke, M.C. and Spee, R.J.A.P. (1993) *Toeristenstromen in Noordwest Europa, Een Verkennende Studie van het Regionale Kaartbeeld.* Vakgroep Planologie, Faculteit der Beleidswetenschappen, Katholieke Universiteit, Nijmegen.

Jurgens, C.R. (1992) Tools for the spatial analysis of land and for the planning of infrastructures in multiple-landuse situations. PhD thesis, Agricultural University, Wageningen.

Lavery, P. and Stevens, T. (1990) Attendance trends and future developments at Europe's leisure attractions. *EIU Travel and Tourism Analyst* 2, 52–75.

Light, D. and Prentice, R. (1994) Market-based development in heritage tourism. *Tourism Management* 15(1), 27–36.

Pearce, Ph.L. (1988) *The Ulysses Factor. Evaluating Visitors in Tourist Settings.* Wiley, New York.

Prentice, R. (1993) *Tourism and Heritage Attractions.* Routledge, London.
Spee, R.J.A.P. (1992) De Efteling, de dynamiek van een themapark. Werkgroep Recreatie, Landbouwuniversiteit, Wageningen (unpublished confidential report).
Thrift, N. (1977) *An Introduction to Time Geography.* Catmog 13, Norwich.
van Eck, W. and van Os, J. (1993) Rural development in South Limburg. Internal report, Winand Staring Centre, Wageningen.

11

Nature-based Tourism and Recreation: Environmental Change, Perception, Ideology and Practices

J. Philipsen

Department of Physical Planning and Rural Development,
Agricultural University, Generaal Foulkesweg 13, 6703 BJ Wageningen, The
Netherlands.

Introduction

In this chapter I explore developments in nature-based tourism and recreation. It will be shown that changes in the physical environment are perceived in many different ways by both visitors and resource controllers, leading to different conceptions of how environmental change should be regulated by human intervention.

As is clear from earlier chapters recreation and tourism have grown significantly over the last three decades: international tourism arrivals have increased from 70 million in 1960 to an expected 485 million in 1994 (NBT, 1993). At the same time the environmental movement has gained increased attention. Environmentalists have perceived a growing deterioration of man's physical environment. This deterioration has been attributed to widespread industrialization over the past hundred years, allied to increased material consumption by rapidly expanding populations (Pepper, 1986). Recreation and tourism have increasingly become regarded as an environmental threat alongside other external costs of economic growth like agricultural pesticides, nuclear waste and acid rain (Lowe and Goyder, 1983; Harrison, 1991). The raised environmental consciousness of people from highly developed capitalist societies not only resulted in a growing concern for the negative impacts of recreation and tourism, it also heightened the desire to experience nature all over the world. An increasing part of domestic and international tourism is nature-based.

Today, growing numbers of visitors, with ever-changing behaviour and recreational experience preferences, constitute a major problem for controllers of natural resources. They are confronted with conservation interest groups that ask for environmental protection measures, recreation groups that complain about the irresponsible behaviour of the growing number and diversity of other recreationists, and regional authorities and tourist entrepreneurs who promote revenues and jobs. A broad spectrum of environmental practices has been developed by managers of national parks, estates and nature reserves, which aim at realizing various combinations of recreation and conservation objectives, goals that also change over time.

In the first section I will consider events and processes that have determined landscape transformations of Western industrialized countries since the Middle Ages. Then I will discuss developments in environmental values and attitudes in these societies. I will also explain how these changes have affected nature experience preferences and recreational activity patterns. The last section deals with environmental decisions and practices of resource controllers. How do they change and what are the implications of these changes for recreation and tourism opportunities?

Change in the Physical Environment

Throughout the history of mankind, people have changed the environment. However, in recent decades the extent and speed of this material transformation (see Chapter 1) have been higher then ever before. Up to the Middle Ages transformations of the physical environment were largely determined by natural processes, such as sedimentation and erosion, dune formation, groundwater flows, succession and grazing, migration and dispersal of fauna. Since then the appearance of the landscape in a rapidly growing part of the world has been transformed predominantly by human intervention. Clearly, one of the most important causes of landscape change was agricultural development (Brouwer *et al.*, 1991). In most countries of the European Union agriculture takes up well over half of the total land area. Change has frequently occurred in the form of the reclamation of wilderness (such as woodland, heath, peatland and marshland), the layout of drainage systems, the extension of road patterns and increasingly intensive land use (Kerkstra and Vrijlandt, 1989). The variety in the visual character of the landscape has disappeared throughout large parts of the world as a result of uniform agricultural engineering practices. Differences in soil conditions (relief, moisture content, nutrition levels) have been levelled in order to create uniform production circumstances. Specific landscape elements, such as hedgerows, tree belts, heather fields and winding unpaved roads, have frequently disappeared, as have marked differences in the openness of the landscape.

Other important causes of landscape transformation are residential development, road building and, increasingly, tourism development. Within a free-market economy these land uses largely determine the functional arrangement of space. In general it can be said that extensive land uses with a low exchange value, such as nature management, forestry and nature-based recreation and tourism, are continually under pressure from intensive land uses with a high exchange value, such as agriculture, industry, housing or traffic. Land uses with a low exchange value are often pushed aside to whatever bits and pieces of land that may remain. Natural areas, for example, mostly exist by the grace of other activities: areas in which man is not able to withstand the powers of nature with engineering works (the sea, steep mountain slopes, river forelands), areas with poor soil conditions, where reclamation costs are unacceptably high, or peripheral areas that are located beyond acceptable distances from business centres.

Recently The Netherlands Scientific Council for Government Policy (Wetenschappelijke Raad voor het Regeringsbeleid, 1992) published the results of research on the possible consequences of alternative strategies for European Union (EU) agricultural policy on rural land use. The research outcomes show which dramatic transformations of the European landscape can be expected in the near future. Currently, the expected growth of overproduction as a result of increased agricultural productivity and the growing concern for the negative effects of agriculture on nature and environment require changes in EU agricultural policies. Different policies will have different consequences for the distribution of agricultural production throughout the EU. Current policies are focused on improvement of agricultural productivity, low prices of agricultural products, but most of all the upkeep of regional employment in agriculture. To protect existing regional production, prices of some important agricultural products are controlled by the EU. As a consequence European public expenses have increased beyond an acceptable level. If the EU decides to participate in a free world market for agricultural products, agricultural production might well concentrate in the northwest of the EU: Germany, France, The Netherlands, Belgium, eastern England and Ireland. Forestry will concentrate on the centre and south of Spain and Portugal. In other regions a large area of agricultural land will be taken out of production, although ways must then be found to finance the maintenance of the landscape of these abandoned areas. If the EU decides to decrease overproduction by the extension of present quota systems for milk or sugar to other arable products, no substantial regional shifts in agricultural production are expected. Probably, on the

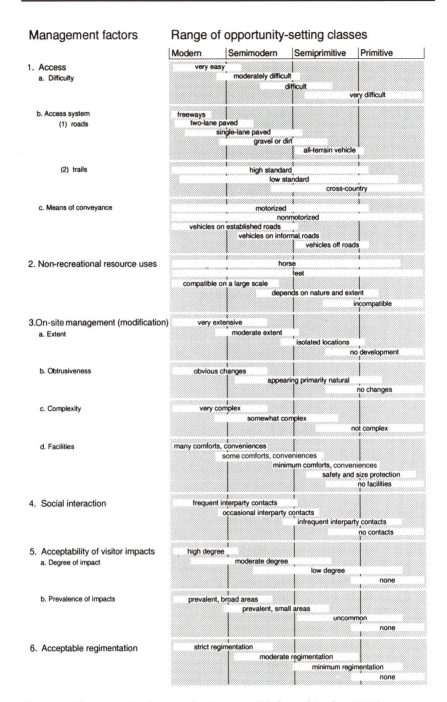

Fig. 11.1. The Recreation Opportunity Spectrum (Clarke and Stankey, 1979).

present agricultural acreage some extensification will then take place as a consequence of the improvement in production techniques.

The impact of environmental change on opportunities for nature experiences is perhaps best illustrated when using the conceptual framework of the Recreation Opportunity Spectrum (ROS; Driver *et al.*, 1987). In the ROS a range of environmental, social and managerial indicators which define recreation opportunities are combined in alternative arrangements to describe diverse recreation-opportunity settings. Figure 11.1 shows six factors which define a continuum of recreation-opportunity settings, varying from modern to primitive. Generally speaking, environmental transformations have followed a shift on the spectrum from primitive towards modern. In most former European primitive settings (such as the Alps, the Pyrenees, Scotland) tourism itself is one of the major forces causing change.

Change in Environmental Perception and Imagination

As is stated in Chapter 1, environments are not only changing in a material sense, there are also striking changes taking place in the personal interpretations of these environments: symbolic transformations. The way natural landscapes are perceived and appropriated differs from individual to individual and from one time to another. According to Zube (1991) landscapes are humanized environments that are endowed with meanings and values. To fully understand the complex relationship between man and environment, the simultaneous transformations of both personal and situational variables should be viewed in a combined way. Meaning or significance is not an attribute of the observer or the observed, but a quality of the transaction between personal needs or preferences and environmental stimuli (Boerwinkel, 1991; Hartig, 1993). Changes in environmental preferences and appreciations have been explained in several different ways. Two major perspectives can be distinguished (Hartig, 1993; Walmsley and Lewis, 1993).

From an evolutionist perspective, environmental preferences are seen as the result of evaluative capacities developed in the course of human evolution in natural environments. It is thought that properties like mystery (the promise of more information as one moves further into the environment) and legibility (the promise of being able to organize visual information from the environment as one moves into it) had adaptive significance because of their application to the acquisition and comprehension of information needed to function in a dangerous and uncertain prehistoric world.

From a cultural perspective, environmental preference is viewed as the outcome of interactions between a given culture and its physical environment. A person's response to a particular environment varies as a function of attitudes, beliefs and values shaped through personal experience and social conditioning within the context of a given culture. Interactions with a variety of environments take place because people move through the environment. They experience different landscapes not only through actual travel, but also through simulated travel as in world fairs and tourist-historical spectacles, or 'armchair' travel through looking at magazines, television programmes or other people's photographs (Urry, 1990). While moving through the environment people are aware of differences in varying degrees. They compare and contrast different landscapes and make judgements of taste. The actual selection of environments to visit largely depends upon anticipation and recall of these visits (Boerwinkel, 1991). Through daydreaming and fantasy, expectations about pleasures associated with visits to certain environments are constructed. Daydreaming is not a purely individual activity, but is socially organized. Personal judgements of taste are strongly influenced by value judgements made by friends or relatives, who tell stories about recreational or tourist experiences, or by carefully constructed images of place that are watched on television, seen in advertisements and read in literature (Urry, 1990).

Environmental judgements of taste are not fixed, but are subject to constant change, even if this change is very slow and sometimes rather difficult to detect (Jackson, 1989). Changing environmental preference goes far back in Western culture (Lemaire, 1970). Up to the 17th and 18th centuries it was generally held that wild uncultivated areas were to be deplored (Thomas, 1983). During the Middle Ages (800–1200) wilderness was experienced as threatening and devilish. Cultivated places were places of safety. These pieces of ground were regarded as withdrawn from the evil powers of demons. The regular and symmetrical forms associated with ploughing, planting, hedging and other agricultural practices were a welcome mark of civilization. In the 16th, 17th and 18th centuries, as people began to explore the world in the voyages of discovery, gradually a disenchantment with the world took place. Man began to domesticate nature on a larger scale. Slopes were cultivated, marshes were filled up, moorlands drained and heath transformed into arable land. Progress was to be achieved by taming and cultivating nature. People began to experience their environment as ordinary everyday landscapes, without any mythological reference (Lemaire, 1970). Thomas (1983) gives many examples which show that the domesticated, productive and inhabited landscapes were seen as places of beauty and that unproductive land was regarded as unattractive. The mountains of Great Britain, for example, were hated as barren 'deformities', 'monstrous excrescences' or 'the rubbish of the earth'. People complained of the 'hideous' Pennines and the 'hopeless sterility' of the Scottish Highlands. Geometrical forms were regarded as intrinsically more beautiful than irregular patterns.

By the end of the 18th century radical change took place in landscape appreciation (Lemaire, 1970; Thomas, 1983). The beginning of the romantic period marked a dramatic shift in taste. The adoration of the geometrical precision of cultivated farmland and gardens gave way to an appreciation of the randomness of wilderness. Wild barren landscape ceased to be an object of detestation and became instead a source of spiritual renewal (Pepper, 1986). Feelings of awe, fear and delight, that previously were exclusively intended for God, were now transferred to the wild nature of oceans, deserts, mountains and jungles. For the romantics the attractive features of wild nature were (Pepper, 1986): (i) wildness as opposed to domestication; (ii) an illusion of naturalness, meaning an apparent absence of human intervention: an illusion, because in many cases man-made environments were perceived as wild nature; (iii) freedom of movement through space, satisfying a desire for (iv) solitude and individuality; and (v) simplicity in the homogeneity of form.

One of the reasons for the enhanced aesthetic interest in wilderness was the fact that wild nature became less dangerous. Better means of transportation and better maps provided easier access for urban dwellers. The educated class, encouraged by easy travel opportunities and safeguarded from involvement in the agricultural production process, developed a specific interest in gazing upon landscapes. More and more the natural world was defined as scenery, views or perceptual sensations (Green, 1981). People were searching for the picturesque. This growing importance of visual consumption of landscapes gave rise to an increased concern for unspoilt nature as a spiritual sanctuary (Urry, 1992).

This brings us to a second, even more important, reason for the growing aesthetic interest in wilderness: the continuing cultivation of land. Lemaire (1970) mentions a separation of two different conceptions of nature that took place in the romantic period. On the one hand there is 'physical' nature, the nature of the natural sciences that try to discover laws explaining the functioning of nature. Knowledge of natural laws can help to cultivate the natural environment in order to attain certain human ends (e.g. agriculture, industry). On the other hand there is 'elevated' nature, the nature of the arts, the pure, free and enjoyable nature in which we wander, the refuge of spiritual experiences. Each increase in significance of 'physical' nature is accompanied by a growing desire for 'elevated' nature. The desire for encounters with pure nature expresses a dissatisfaction of the culture with itself (Lemaire, 1970). The dramatic transformation of the landscape since the end of the 19th century provoked heavy criticism of urbanization and industrialization. With the growth of the world population wild nature was seen more and more as an opportunity to escape the overfilled cities and factories. Every enlargement of industry, every technical invention was rejected as unnatural. These are phenomena that accompany an acceleration of the cultivation of the world. Cultivation is experienced as something that is getting out of control. There is a stronger than desirable feeling of uncertainty, displeasure and alienation. Harvey (1989) speaks of a crisis in our experience of space and time. As a result of the development of new technologies of transportation and communication people have access to an increasing number of different landscapes, which are compared and contrasted in order to make judgements of taste. The speed at which these landscapes change is increasing, whereas at the same time all sorts of differences between places are suppressed as a result of the increasing interdependence of events and processes that determine the character of these places. In developing perceptual equipment to make sense of these landscapes, man is not able to keep pace with the extent and speed of the spatial transformations. Or, as MacCannell (1976) argues, the world has become too big and too complex for man to know it entirely and intimately.

People who experience these feelings of uncertainty, displeasure or alienation resort to the past, in which they try to discover authentic experiences, to a utopian culture of the future or to the opposite of culture: wild nature (Lemaire, 1970). The dilemma of culture–nature has its counterpart in the dilemma of urban–rural. Romantics want to escape from the stains of civilization, which are believed to be concentrated in cities.

These conclusions are consistent with the findings of psychological research. Reviewing research on motivations for outdoor recreation and benefits from views of nature, gardens, 'nearby' nature and wilderness experiences, Hartig (1993) concludes that going to a natural setting involves both escape from features of the everyday environment, such as noise or crowding, and the pull of expectations about qualities of the given natural environment. Although some considerations temper the impression that escape to nature is necessarily motivated by urban residency, most research concludes that visits to wild nature are related to escape motives: the majority of wilderness users have proved to be from urban areas, the desire to escape crowded cities appears to be the most important motivation to be in wilderness and a strong positive relationship between size of community of residence and strength of the appeal of escape has been found.

Religious/aesthetic experiences, tranquillity, solitude and enjoyment of nature have proved to be important factors (Hartig, 1993). Ulrich *et al.* (1991) have shown that it is stressful experience rather than urban stress in particular that accounts for strong desires for nature experiences. They suggest that too high levels of stimulation in general lead to unpleasant feelings.

Today several ideological lines of thought can be distinguished regarding the way people interact, or should interact, with their natural environment. Each professes concern over the state of the natural and the built environment, and agrees that our relationship with nature has, in some way, to be improved. These ideologies strongly contribute to the development of environmental decisions and practices of both visitors and controllers (landowners and managers) of natural resources.

Arguments that are mentioned to justify environmental decisions and practices broadly relate to either a biocentric or an anthropocentric perspective (Swinnerton, 1989; Veeneklaas *et al.*, 1993). The biocentric perspective is based on an ethical principle that recognizes the intrinsic value of nature. If man were to be wiped off the face of the earth tomorrow there would still be a purpose and meaning in the continuance of life on the planet. Therefore the natural world possesses biotic rights, which are independent of any considerations of its usefulness to man. All ten million species of plants and animals with which we share this planet should be accorded legal rights. On the other hand society's right to exploit and exterminate any form of life is questioned (O'Riordan, 1981; Pepper, 1986). Because ethical arguments are difficult to comprehend and intrinsic values of nature cannot be determined as a matter of principle, in practice greater recognition tends to be given to the anthropocentric perspective. Followers of this view claim that an appreciation of nature can only be expressed in terms of a human scale of values. The justification of environmental decisions and practices is only possible in terms of society's self-interest. In the end man has to determine what a desired situation or development is. Following this 'instrumental' approach a series of benefits can be associated with natural resources. Swinnerton (1989) mentions: (i) spiritual benefits, which relate to spiritual renewal and moral regeneration; (ii) aesthetic benefits that can be derived from pleasant scenery, together with the solitude and quiet provided by natural landscapes; (iii) ecological benefits through retaining undisturbed ecological systems for maintaining natural processes upon which human life is dependent and protecting these areas as *in situ* gene banks, which is important for the survival of species of plants and animals and technological innovations in the food, fibre and pharmaceutical industries; and (iv) *in absentia* benefits, which relate to the preservation of options for future generations.

Strongly related to the biocentric and anthropocentric perspectives is the distinction made by O'Riordan (1981) between an ecocentric and a technocentric belief system. In the world conception of ecocentrics man is a part of the natural system. 'For his own sake he should not plunder, exploit and destroy natural ecosystems because in doing so he is destroying the biological foundation of his own life' (Pepper, 1986). Essentially ecocentrism is a pessimistic belief. It recognizes ecological limits in the biosphere. Economic growth should be limited and a fundamental shift in values and attitudes should be obtained, given the inevitable negative environmental consequences of the growth ethic. Examples of this line of thought are Redclift's Deep Ecology Paradigm (1981) and Lovelock's Gaia hypothesis (1979). Limits, self-sufficiency, small-scale production, recycling and zero population growth are key words in the ecocentric vocabulary. Beliefs and values of ecocentrism lie close to those of 19th-century romanticism (O'Riordan, 1981; Pepper, 1986). Technocentrism is a much more optimistic belief. Technocentrics believe that new technology will be able to counteract environmental problems. It is a matter of efficient management rather than a matter of questioning attitudes and values and the correctness of economic growth itself (Harrison, 1991). The biosphere is viewed as unlimited with regard to the supply of materials and its capacity to absorb waste and other impacts. Many authors suggest a gradual transition in cultural values of Western societies from technocentrism towards ecocentrism. This transition relates to Toffler's (1980) second and third wave (a change from the values of the industrial era into those of the postindustrial era), McCool's (1983) consumer and conserver society, or the Dominant Social Paradigm and the New Environmental Paradigm mentioned by Dunlap and van Liere (1984). With respect to environmental practices in national parks of the USA, McCool (1983) observed that park authorities put emphasis on the provision of entertainment during the industrial age and showed greater awareness of the preservation of ecological processes in the postindustrial age. Van der Zande (1989) comes to similar conclusions in reviewing the relationship between outdoor recreation and nature conservation in dune areas in The Netherlands. Between 1960 and 1973 the production of drinking-water, defence against the sea and outdoor recreation prevailed over nature conservation. After 1973 a revolutionary change of direction was set in motion by adopting the policy that all areas with nature conservation value should in principle be protected (Third Report on Physical Planning). This policy meant for dune areas that nature conservation received primacy over outdoor recreation.

Change in Environmental Decisions and Practices

Changing views on the way people should interact with their environment have led to change in environmental practices. On the one hand new environmental attitudes have affected environmental decisions and practices of controllers of natural resources. Changes have taken place in resource and visitor management. An increasing number of areas have been legally protected against human exploitation. Sometimes complete areas have been reconstructed to restore wild natural landscapes of bygone times. This has resulted in increasing nature experience opportunities of specific visitor groups. However, there is evidence that some measures have led to access limitations for other visitor groups. Philipsen *et al.* (1992) found that access to a quarter of the acreage of Dutch forest and nature areas managed by the Society for the Preservation of Nature in The Netherlands, the Dutch Forestry Commission and provincial nature conservation organizations in The Netherlands (70% of the total area) has decreased between 1971 and 1991. These trends reflect the implementation of preservation and conservation objectives that are formulated on international (e.g. Ramsar Convention, EC Birds Directive), national and local levels. They also show the growing desire of regional and local authorities to make places consistent with contemporary images of environment and place. 'Nature' has become an increasingly important marker for regions. It offers regions possibilities to make their places more attractive to capital, highly skilled prospective employees and visitors and to make them distinct from an environment that has been unified by the globalization of processes and events (Harvey, 1989; Urry, 1992).

On the other hand, raised environmental consciousness has heightened the desire to experience natural environments (Heath, 1991). Although little empirical evidence exists, there is reason to believe that transformation of environmental values and beliefs has resulted in increasing visits to quiet environments that offer an illusion of naturalness. Urry (1992) shows that changes in contemporary tourism reflect an increased environmental consciousness. The 'collective' gaze, exemplified by the package holiday to Mediterranean resorts, seems to be declining in favour of the 'romantic' gaze that characterizes participation in the vast, expanding green tourism. Referring to studies of Dunlap and Heffernan (1975), Pinhey and Grimes (1979) and van Liere and Noe (1981), Jackson (1989) concludes that much evidence supports the premiss that participation in different forms of outdoor recreational activities is related to environmental attitudes.

Swinnerton (1989) classifies environmental practices into three distinct types: preservation, conservation and exploitation (Fig. 11.2).

	Resource protection	Resource development	
	Preservation ◄——►	Conservation ◄——►	Exploitation
View of resource	Biocentric/ anthropocentric	Anthropocentric	Anthropocentric
Level of intervention	No intervention	Limited intervention	Unlimited intervention
Measures of natural value	Undisturbedness Naturalness Completeness	Biodiversity Rareness	
Land use strategy	Segregation	Combination	Segregation/ combination
Access regulations	No use Responsible use	Controlled use Responsible use	Unlimited use Abusive use
	Very small numbers	Small numbers	Big numbers Mass tourism

Fig. 11.2. Characteristics of resource protection and resource development (based on Swinnerton, 1989).

Comparison of legislation and policy notes of different reserve and park authorities throughout the world reveals a pattern of inconsistency in definitions of the terms 'conservation' and 'preservation'. Even more ambiguity exists when consequences for the type and level of recreational and tourist use have to be indicated.

In its purest sense preservation aims at self-maintenance of natural ecosystems and authenticity of natural processes (Fig. 11.3a). In order to provide opportunities for natural processes to act freely, there should be no human influence. In accordance with the biocentric perspective no fixed ultimate objectives are formulated concerning a future condition (T_1) of the resource. Humanity has to give nature the opportunity to determine its own structure. The point of reference is undisturbed nature, elsewhere or from the past, where natural processes have dominated. Human intervention is minimized in order to maximize the intrinsic value of nature. Strictly spreaking, this strategy means no intervention in the form of resource management and no human use of the resource for recreational or tourist purposes. In reality, this type of preservation is not common. In one way or another human values play a large part. Natural processes do not always result in landscapes that are highly appreciated by recreationists and tourists.

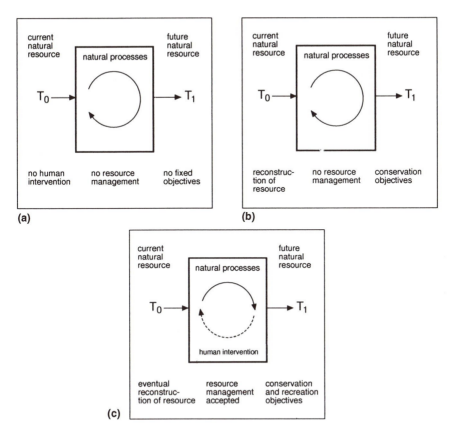

Fig. 11.3. Nature policy strategies. See text for explanation.

They very often do not contain the species that are strongly desired at a specific moment in time, such as seals, pandas, turtles, whales or colourful birds like the kingfisher, species that are used by preservationists to enhance the environmental interest and consciousness of society. Therefore, some human intervention is required.

Reid (1979) has made a distinction between the wilderness concept of preservation, which aims at the preservation of natural processes, and the natural features concept of preservation, which aims at the preservation of a specific species or ecosystem because of its social desirability. The former concept can be understood as the pure preservation concept. If the latter is the case, the area remains protected against human intervention, but additionally a more or less specific objective is formulated about a future condition of the resource (Fig. 11.3b). A commonly used objective is biodiversity or rareness of species of plants and animals. Knowledge about the functioning of natural processes can be used to forecast the future condition of the landscape (T_1) given alternative starting conditions (T_0). The area can now be reconstructed in order to achieve the desired condition at a specific moment in time in the future. Carefully contrived variations in altitude, soil type and humidity have to lead to a maximum biodiversity. However, after the reconstruction of the area human influence will be minimized. In practice, preservation strategies generally apply to nature reserves.

In those instances, where human intervention in the form of resource management is accepted in order to achieve a desired future condition, one can speak about conservation (Fig. 11.3c). Conservation aims at the protection or restoration of fixed ecological and amenity values that are linked to historical landscapes. The point of reference is the natural or cultural landscape of a previous century. The maintenance of the resource in a fixed natural condition gives rise to a considerable debate as what constitutes 'natural'. Commonly used indicators for natural value are biodiversity and rareness of species. It is not possible, however, to make objective statements on the appropriateness of certain species at a specific place. As opposed to preservation, conservation strategies mostly apply to national parks and estates.

Different ideologies on the relationship between man and environment result in different perceptions regarding the impacts of recreation and tourism on the natural resource. As we saw in Chapter 1, the mere presence of a visitor already results in a contribution to the material transformation of the natural resource. As a part of preservation or conservation strategies different solutions are suggested to reduce this perceived pressure of recreation or tourism on the natural environment. Broadly, three types of solution can be distinguished (Butler, 1991): (i) reduction of the number of visitors; (ii) change of visitor behaviour; and (iii) change of the natural resource into a form which is better able to withstand visitor pressures.

The reduction in the number of visitors would be a consistent measure when a preservation strategy is adopted. Self-maintenance of natural ecosystems can only be achieved by spatial segregation. It is necessary to create large natural areas in order to keep human influence at a distance (Veeneklaas et al., 1993). The number of visitors can be reduced either by enclosure of these areas or by increasing walking, riding or cycling distances to the most intensively protected heart of the area (Fig. 11.4a). A reduction in visitor numbers, however, is mostly extremely difficult. In regions where green tourism constitutes the major source of income or employment, the reduction in visitor numbers can result in a decline in revenue and local unemploy-

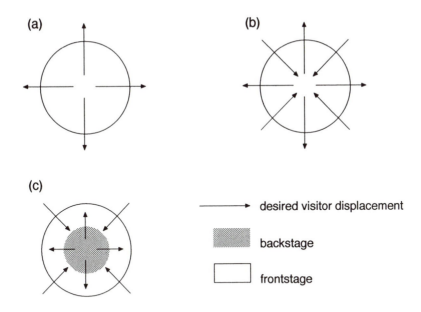

Fig. 11.4. Visitor-management practices in natural areas.

ment (Butler, 1991). Therefore, broad public support for drastic access limitations is rather difficult to acquire. Besides, the tourist industry is extremely inventive in finding ways to overcome thresholds to get access to less attainable areas. One of the reasons for the success of the mountain bike is the fact that this conveyance enables a visitor to reach ever more rare and remote, wild, quiet and undisturbed places (areas that are beyond the range of most walkers). Intensive supervision will be necessary in order to effect restrictive measures and enforce the desired use levels.

The second solution is to change the type of visitor behaviour. It is argued that access to vulnerable natural areas should be limited to those types of visitors that show responsible behaviour (Fig. 11.4b). The problem is that this solution presupposes responsible behaviour to be identifiable. Many different criteria have been mentioned to discriminate visitors on this attribute, including ecological, social and aesthetic criteria.

Assessment of undesired impacts on a natural system is one of the most common practices. However, this impact research shows a number of weaknesses. First, the selection of cause–effect relations to be studied is biased towards those relations that are important to legitimize certain policy objectives. Research is often focused on rare species of plants and animals or on visitor groups that are already stigmatized in a specific society for an abusive activity, such as fishing, hunting, downhill-skiing, or motor-boating. Certain 'responsible' activities, however, could prove to be equally disruptive, like that of bird-watchers. When a rare species has been reported, it is liable to produce an influx of hundreds or even thousands of observers to a site, each intending to see the bird in question and if possible photograph it (Edington and Edington, 1986). Second, most impact research fails to consider habituation processes of natural species. Often only etho-logical effects (the immediate behavioural response) and not ecological effects (more lasting consequences) are studied (Sidaway, 1990). Many species have proved to adjust quite well to the presence of humans. Bears, for example, develop begging habits if food is offered by visitors. Gulls seem to recognize the fact that the presence of human visitors creates an opportunity to attack the nests of shags, when they move into shag colonies (Edington and Edington, 1986). Third, it is extremely difficult to define a base level against which change induced by visitors can be measured and to determine how the environment would have changed in the absence of the impact (Wall, 1989). In most cases the causality of a cause–effect relationship has not been proved. Fourth, if relationships between increasing visitor pressure and change in a natural system are defined by impact research, the question still remains at which level change becomes unacceptable. This is a value choice. What is viewed as environmentally damaging in one era or one society is not necessarily taken as such in another. While the local extinction of a rare species could be a major problem for certain anthropocentric conservationists, at the same time this could be of minor importance to biocentric preservationists.

According to Urry (1992) in many cases the selection of visitors on the responsibility criterion is not based on their negative impact on environment. It is rather an expression of social taste. Visitor groups differ in their aesthetic judgement of the environment. As we saw earlier, romantics foster undisturbed and non-mechanical nature. Their nature experience is adversely affected by landscape features or the presence of visitors that are associated with urban life or human domestication. They complain when too many other people visit their appropriated nature area. They condemn mountain-bikers, for exam-ple, who cycle on rugged bikes, wear fluorescent skin-tight gear and leave deep wheel-tracks behind. They probably dislike this user group because they give the impression that they want to master nature by means of an efficient machine (Mortlock, 1992). They simply do not fit into the landscape desired by romantics. Sidaway *et al.* (1986) have suggested that in many cases visitor groups with a vested interest try to convert certain nature experiences to their own use by excluding newcoming visitor groups. They observed a tendency of visitors to react adversely to each novel activity as it arises. Discrimination of visitors on social criteria is in line with a conservation strategy or a natural features concept of preservation.

The third solution to reduce the pressure of visitors on the natural resource is to change the resource itself and make it more resistant. To the pure preservationist any modification of the natural resource is unacceptable, unless a false front stage is developed as a substitute for the vulnerable back stage (Fig. 11.4c). In the protected back stage, the core area, environmental change will be dominated largely by 'authentic' natural processes. The greater part of the demand for nature experiences will be satisfied in an outer zone, where 'authentic' nature is staged (MacCannell, 1976). The visitors are offered a type of nature that is more resistant to visitor pressure, but at the same time offers an illusion of naturalness. Boerwinkel (1992) found that for a large proportion of visitors to the Dutch dune area of Meijendel the back stage was not a necessary condition for the satisfaction of nature experience preferences. Not less than 70% should be able to satisfy their nature experience preferences in park settings or natural heritage landscapes. He argues that this visitor group is characterized by an aesthetic desire for the green environment in general. In other dune areas, such as Zuid-Kennemerland, the proportion, however, proved to be far less (26%; Jansen *et al.*, 1994). In the case of a conservation strategy the landscape of the entire 'natural' area can be modified by human intervention in order to realize objectives concerning both the protection of natural processes or features and the provision of opportunities for recreational experiences. If human intervention is accepted in order to realize fixed ecological goals as a principle, a variety of nature types is imaginable. In this case, it is legitimate to consider the development of a type of nature in which relatively high visitor pressure is acceptable to conservation interest groups, especially when the natural area in question is situated in the immediate environment of visitor-generating urban areas.

Summary and Implications

We have seen that both the physical environment and environmental perception change over time. An increasing number of people want to visit unspoilt wild natural environments. Yet this is more or less impossible, because these environments have become scarce as a result of landscape transformation. In the last decades the speed of landscape transformation has been higher than ever before. It seems, however, that many people are not able to make sense of this rapidly changing environment, because the development of their perceptual abilities is not able to keep pace. Not only species of plants and animals have difficulties in adapting to environmental change. The adaptability of tourists and recreationists to landscape transformation has proved to be limited as well. Human beings are afraid of change, or rather, of too much change. They are afraid that things will eventually escape. They try to capture the world in its temporal and spatial variability. This explains the growing attention of the environmental movement. It also explains why new visitor groups have to fight for access rights in natural areas. It can even explain why a true wilderness concept of preservation is difficult to implement. Conservationists simply cannot cope with the uncertainty about the species that will eventually develop in a protected area. It is the uncertainty about the future development of recreational and tourist experiences and behaviour that leads resource controllers to apply restrictive policies on recreational access.

There is a vital necessity to improve management processes with respect to natural areas. First, there should be an acknowledgement of the dynamic character of biological and social processes. There is a need for better understanding of long-lasting mutual influences between landscape characteristics and the behaviour of plant and animal species and human beings. Secondly, more fundamental differences in environmental ideologies should be taken into consideration. It is a simplification to talk about a conflict between recreation or tourism on the one hand and conservation on the other hand. In most cases certain recreational or tourist activities and experiences relate to the same basic values as certain environmental practices. Very often conflicts arise as a result of differences in ideologies between visitor groups or even between conservation parties. Thirdly, in order to minimize feelings of uncertainty and alienation people should be involved in decision-making about environmental transformations. It is the uncertainty about future policies of resource controllers that often causes distrust among recreational and tourist user groups and tourism entrepreneurs. It is important therefore to offer control over or at least visibility in the decision-making process and to make clear why certain practices are followed (Sidaway and van der Voet, 1993). To share and discuss thoughts about future environmental transformations among all interest groups seem to be an important condition in the achievement of a satisfactory relationship with their environment.

Acknowledgements

This chapter has benefited from the comments of Roger Sidaway and Frank van Langevelde.

References and Further Reading

Boerwinkel, H.W.J. (1991) *Omgevingspsychologie.* Werkgroep Recreatie, Land-bouwuniversiteit, Wageningen.

Boerwinkel, H.W.J. (1992) Influencing zone visits in forests by design: the case of the small valley of Meijendel. In: Hummel, J. and Parren, M. (eds) *Forests, a Growing Concern.* Proceedings of the XIXth International Forestry Students Symposium, Wageningen, The Netherlands, 30 Sept.–7 Oct. 1991. IUCN, Gland, Switzerland, pp. 144–154.

Brouwer, F.M., Thomas, A.J. and Chadwick, J. (1991) *Land Use Changes in Europe. Processes of Change, Environmental Transformations and Future Patterns.* Kluwer, Dordrecht/Boston/London.

Butler, R.W. (1991) Tourism, environment and sustainable development. *Environmental Conservation* 18, 201–209.

Clarke, R.N. and Stankey, G.H. (1979) The recreation opportunity spectrum: a framework for planning, management and research. USDA Forest Service Research Paper PNW-98.

Driver, B.L., Brown, P.J., Stankey, G.H. and Gregoire, T.G. (1987) The ROS planning system: evolution, basic concepts and research needed. *Leisure Sciences* 9, 201–212.

Dunlap, R.E. and Heffernan, R.B. (1975) Outdoor recreation and environmental concern: an empirical examination. *Rural Sociology* 40, 18–30.

Dunlap, R.E. and van Liere, K.D. (1984) Commitment to the dominant social paradigm and concern for environmental quality. *Social Science Quarterly* 65, 1013–1028.

Edington, J.M. and Edington, M.A. (1986) *Ecology, Recreation and Tourism.* Cambridge University Press, Cambridge.

Green, B.H. (1981) *Countryside Conservation: the Protection and Management of Amenity Ecosystems.* George Allen and Unwin, London.

Harrison, C. (1991) *Countryside Recreation in a Changing Society.* TMS Partnership, London.

Hartig, T. (1993) Nature experience in transactional perspective. *Landscape and Urban Planning* 25, 17–36.

Harvey, D. (1989) *The Condition of Postmodernity.* Basil Blackwell, Oxford.

Heath, G. (1991) *Tourism and the Understanding of Environmental Issues.* Phillips Institute of Technology, Eindhoven.

Institute for European Environmental Policy (1991) *Towards a European Ecological Network.* IEEP, Arnhem.

Jackson, E.L. (1989) Environmental attitudes, values and recreation. In: Jackson,

E.L. and Burton, L. (eds) *Understanding Leisure and Recreation: Mapping the Past, Charting the Future*. Ventura Publishing, London.

Jansen, M., Bakker, J.G. and Boerwinkel, H.W.J. (1994) Recreatie in het Nationaal Park i.o. Zuid-Kennemerland, een onderzoek naar omvang van het bezoek en het activiteitenpatroon van de bezoekers in 1993. Werkgroep Recreatie Rapport 31, Landbouwuniversiteit, Wageningen.

Kerkstra, K. and Vrijlandt, P. (1989) Landscape planning for industrial agriculture: a proposed framework for rural areas. *Landscape and Urban Planning* 18, 275–287.

Lemaire, T. (1970) *Filosofie van het Landschap*. Amboboeken, Baarn.

Lovelock, J. (1979) *Gaia*. Oxford University Press, New York.

Lowe, P.D. and Goyder, J. (1983) *Environmental Groups in Politics*. Allen and Unwin, London.

MacCannell, D. (1976) *The Tourist, a New Theory of the Leisure Class*. Schocken Books, New York.

McCool, S.F. (1983) The national parks in post-industrial America. *Western Wildlands* 9(2), 14–19.

Manning, R.E. (1986) *Studies in Outdoor Recreation: Search and Research for Satisfaction*. Oregon State University Press, Orvallis.

Mortlock, C. (1992) The aesthetics. The impact of mountain biking on the 'wilderness' experience. In: Wyatt, J. (ed.) *Mountain Biking and the Environment*. Conference report. Adventure and Environmental Awareness Group, Sports Council, Ambleside.

NBT (Nederlands Bureau voor Toerisme) (1993) *Toerisme in Cijfers*. Nederlands Bureau voor Toerisme, Leidschendam.

O'Riordan, T. (1981) *Environmentalism*. Pion, London.

Pepper, D. (1986) *The Roots of Modern Environmentalism*. Routledge, London.

Philipsen, J.F.B., Busser, M. and Valkenburg, H. (1992) Feitelijke toegankelijkheid van bosen natuurterreinen in Nederland, een onderzoek naar ontwikkelingen tussen 1950 en 1990. Werkgroep Recreatie Rapport 18, Landbouwuniversiteit, Wageningen.

Pinhey, T.K. and Grimes, M.D. (1979) Outdoor recreation and environmental concern: a re-examination of the Dunlop–Heffernan thesis. *Leisure Sciences* 2, 1–11.

Redclift, M. (1981) *Sustainable Development: Exploring the Contradictions*. Methuen, London.

Reid, R.A. (1979) The role of national parks in nature preservation. In: Nelson, J.G., Needham, S.H., Nelson, S.H. and Scace, R.C. (eds) *The Canadian National Parks: Today and Tomorrow Conference II*, vol. 1. University of Waterloo, Faculty of Environmental Studies, Waterloo, pp. 105–113.

Sidaway, R.M. (1990) *Birds and Walkers: A Review of Existing Research on Access to the Countryside and Disturbance to Birds*. Ramblers Association, London.

Sidaway, R.M. and Thompson, D. (1991) Upland recreation: the limits of acceptable change. *Ecos* 12, 31–39.

Sidaway, R. and van der Voet, J.L.M. (1993) Getting on speaking terms: resolving conflicts between recreation and nature in coastal zone areas in the Netherlands: a literature review and case study analysis. Agricultural University, Werkgroep Recreatie en Toerisme, Wageningen.

Sidaway, R.M., Coalter, J.A., Rennick, I.M. and Scott, P.G. (1986) *Access Study.* Countryside Commission, Manchester.

Swinnerton, G.S. (1989) Recreation and conservation. In: Jackson, E.L. and Burton, L. (eds) *Understanding Leisure and Recreation: Mapping the Past, Charting the Future.* Ventura Publishing, London.

Thomas, K. (1983) *Man and the Natural World: Changing Attitudes in England (1500–1800).* Penguin Books, Harmondsworth.

Toffler, A. (1980) *The Third Wave.* Bantam Books, New York.

Ulrich, R.S., Simons, R.F., Losito, B.D., Fiorito, E., Miles, M.A. and Zelson, M. (1991) Stress recovery during exposure to natural and urban environments. *Journal of Environmental Psychology* 11, 201–230.

Urry, J. (1990) *The Tourist Gaze.* Sage, London.

Urry, J. (1992) The tourist gaze and the 'environment'. *Theory, Culture and Society* 9, 1–26.

van der Zande, A.N. (1989) Outdoor recreation and dune conservation in the Netherlands. In: van der Meulen, F., Jungerius, P.D. and Visser, J.H. *Perspectives in Coastal Dune Management.* SPB Academic Publishing, The Hague.

van Liere, K.D. and Noe, F.P. (1981) Outdoor recreation and environmental attitudes: Further examination of the Dunlap–Heffernan thesis. *Rural Sociology* 46, 501–513.

Veeneklaas, F.R., van Eck, W. and Harms, W.B. (1993) *De Twee Kanten van de Snip; over Economische en Ecologische Duurzaamheid van Natuur.* DLO Staring Centrum, Wageningen.

Wall, G. (1989) Perspectives on recreation and the environment. In: Jackson, E.L. and Burton, L. (eds) *Understanding Leisure and Recreation: Mapping the Past, Charting the Future.* Ventura Publishing, London.

Walmsley, D.J. and Lewis, G.J. (1993) *People and Environment: Behavioural Approaches in Human Geography.* Longman Scientific & Technical, Harlow, UK.

Wetenschappelijke Raad voor het Regeringsbeleid (1992) *Grond voor keuzen, vier perspectieven voor de landelijke gebieden in de Europese Gemeenschap.* Sdu Uitgeverij, Den Haag.

Zube, E.H. (1991) Environmental psychology, global issues and local landscape research. *Journal of Environmental Psychology* 11, 321–334.

12

Sports Tourism: the Case of Golf

G.K. Priestley

Universitat Autonoma de Barcelona, Departament de Geografia, Edifici B,
E-08193 Bellaterra, Barcelona, Spain.

Introduction

Mass tourism has traditionally been based mainly on passive forms of recreation, but the demand for more active recreational forms of holidays has been growing steadily since the 1980s. Trends point towards an increasing interest in sports activities in particular (Redmond, 1991), including winter, water and racket sports and golf. Sport was, in fact, recommended as a stimulus to tourism development in Spain as early as 1967 (Asin López-Bermejo, 1967). This increase in demand for sports tourism is paralleled by the growth in the number of integrated resorts, where both accommodation and recreation facilities are offered on a single site (Redmond, 1991; Stanton and Aislabie, 1992).

Golf is certainly one of the major growth areas within this sector of demand, confirmed by the increasingly wide range of golf holidays offered in brochures issued by travel agencies and tour operators, and by the emergence of agencies specializing in the organization of golfing holidays. The practice of golf, long-established in the social fabric of most English-speaking countries, has expanded to a greater or lesser extent throughout the developed world in recent years. In 1993, there were almost 50 million golfers in the world and 25,400 golf-courses (see Table 12.1). The countries with the largest number of players are the USA (27.8 million in 1990) and Japan (12.4 million in 1990 rising to 14.2 million in 1993) (see Table 12.2).

Expansion during the 1980s was such that it was estimated that by the year 2000 there would be between 180 and 200 million golfers in the world (Delphi Consultores Internacionales, 1987). The exceptionally high rates of expansion registered then have not been maintained

Table 12.1. Practice of golf in the world, 1993. (Source: statistics acquired from the golf federations and associations of each country by Turespaña.)

Continent	No. of golfers	No. of golf-courses	No. of golfers per course
N America	28,700,000	16,234	1768
Asia	15,000,000*	2015	7444
Europe	3,868,250	4617	838
Australasia	1,698,434	1466	1159
S America	375,000	480	781
Africa	162,000	570	284
Total	49,803,684	25,402	1,961

*In Japan alone there are 14,200,000 golfers.

Table 12.2. Major golfing countries, 1985–1990. (Sources: Delphi Consultores Internacionales, 1987; Ortega, 1992.)

	No. of golfers					
	thousands		per 1000 inhabitants		per golf-course	
Country	1990	1985	1990	1985	1990	1985
USA	27,800	18,700	102	88	1842	1385
Japan	12,400	10,000	100	80	7142	7142
UK	3460	2600	60	40	1827	1084
Canada	2400	1000	90	44	1333	870
Australia	906	375	53	29	595	278
Sweden	290	125	34	12	1160	762
World total	48,000	35,000				

during the early years of this decade, and present expansion rates suggest that a more realistic figure for the year 2000 would be between 70 and 80 million golfers in the world, of whom between 5.5 and 6.5 million would be European (see Table 12.3). These figures include not only golf-club members but also unaffiliated golfers who use public courses (as commonly occurs in Scotland) or urban practice ranges (as occurs in Japan, where demand greatly outstrips the number of courses available). In Europe, greatest interest in golf has traditionally been shown in the United Kingdom and the Republic of Ireland. The growth of the sport has, however, been most marked in the developed countries of continental Europe, where spectacular increases were

Table 12.3. Practice of golf in Europe, 1985–1992. (Sources: Delphi Consultores Internacionales, 1987 (for 1985); European Golf Association, list of member federations unions and associations, 1992 (for 1992); French Golf Federation (France, no. of courses, 1992); Turespaña, study currently being undertaken for imminent publication (for estimates 1993–1998).)

Country	No. of players		% increase		No. of courses, 1992	
	1985	1992	1985–1992	1993–1998 (estimated)	Existing	Under construction
UK	2,600,000	3,460,000*	33	25	1975	92
Sweden	125,000	295,000	136	27	257	29
Ireland	90,000	132,000	47	27	276	40
Germany	77,000(FR)	161,400	109	65	329	60
France	76,000	194,500	156	22	210	77
Spain	31,000	64,900	109	61	131	17
Denmark	26,000	44,000	69	49	69	20
Italy	21,000	36,500	74	65	117	80
Netherlands	18,000	59,000	228	28	119	–
Switzerland	10,000	19,500	95	30	40	15**
Belgium	10,000	22,000	120	36	49	7
Finland	7,000	35,000	400	36	71	6
Norway	6,000	16,500	175	149	1	–
Austria	4,000	17,300	333	89	55	10
Portugal	3,000	4,100	37	63	26	9
Greece	1,000	750	–25	83	5	–

*Approximate estimate as figures not supplied. For England only golf-club membership was stated, and for Scotland only male players were listed.
**Courses planned.

registered between 1985 and 1992. Growth in fact began towards the end of the previous decade. For example, in France the number of golfers doubled between 1981 and 1985 and, in Spain, the number doubled between 1979 (over 17,000) and 1986 (35,000) with a similar increase in the following three years (52,000 in 1989). Similarly, between 1980 and 1985 the number of golfers increased by 60% in the German Federal Republic, 57% in Italy, 42% in Sweden and 41% in Switzerland. With the exception of Portugal and Italy, the lowest increase in Europe was 30%, registered in Denmark.

No simple, logical explanation for this rapid increase in the popularity of golf can be found, but it can certainly be associated with the coincidence in time of several interrelated phenomena. A general increase in the standard of living and socioeconomic well-being in the developed countries during the 1970s was paralleled by an increase in the practice of sport in general among the middle and older age groups. Golf was one of the most popular choices of these age groups, partly in imitation of American lifestyles, which were in vogue at the time, and partly because it was well suited to their physical capabilities, the basic requirement being the ability to walk. Those intent on improving their social status had the additional incentive of being able to practise a sport that had hitherto been considered a minority sport in these countries and, moreover for some, of making business contacts on the golf-course, like so many others before them. Increased television coverage of major golfing events and sponsorship of professional golf tournaments in many countries, mainly as a result of the presence of many first-rate golfers from countries other than the USA, UK and Ireland, all contributed to creating a worldwide phenomenon which did much to increase the popularity of golf. The hegemony of British, Irish and American golfers (Gary Player, a South African, was the main exception) on the professional golf circuit was broken by players such as Ballesteros (Spanish), Langer (German), Norman (Australian) and the Aoki brothers (Japanese).

The increasing demand for golf holidays can therefore be easily understood within the context of the expansion of the practice of golf in general, and in particular in countries with a high standard of living and harsh climates during most of the year (northern Europe) or a shortage of facilities (Japan).

Characteristics of the Golf Tourism Product

The golf tourism product is offered in four different forms, focused on the following types of facilities:

1. famous championship courses;
2. single integrated resorts;
3. golf courses associated with property developments;
4. networks of courses forming golf regions.

The resulting transformations of the physical and social structures of the area vary according to the type of development involved.

Famous championship courses

Strictly speaking these are the courses where the four 'Grand Slam' Opens are played. The US Masters is played annually at the Augusta National Golf Course, Georgia, a course which is not open to the general public. The British Open and the US Open and the PGA tournament are played on different courses in the UK and USA respectively on a rotatory basis. In Britain, there are only a few famous championship courses, which include some of the oldest courses in the world, especially those in Scotland. Indeed Scotland is the heartland of golf – the 'mecca' being the Old Course at St Andrews because it is recognized as the first true golf-course in the world, and because the rules of golf are still determined by the Rules Board of the Royal and Ancient Golf Club of St Andrews (now in collaboration with the US Golf Association). In the USA, where tradition is not deemed to be of such great importance, prestige championships are played on a larger number of different courses.

Designers of new courses, wishing to take advantage of the attraction for golfers of championship courses, usually advertise their courses as 'championship' courses. What this really means is that the courses are sufficiently long and difficult to be designated for professional competitions, although whether or not they ever will be is a different matter. The formula does, however, attract club members and tourists intent on emulating their idols.

Single integrated resorts

Although hotel accommodation has long been associated with a number of golf-courses, especially in North America, it is only in recent years that integrated golf resorts as such have become more numerous. Golf resorts may be defined as self-contained leisure complexes, which include (as minimum requirements) accommodation facilities and one golf-course, to which other golf-courses and facilities (normally sports and health centres) may be added. Such is the case of Scotland's famous Gleneagles Hotel, which, in an attempt to offer all-weather, all-season leisure activities for the whole family, has diversified its facilities to include, alongside its three 18- and one nine-hole golf-courses), riding, hunting, salmon-fishing, tennis, croquet, bowling, a health centre, an indoor swimming-pool and facilities for various indoor sports.

Such complexes have mushroomed in hotter climates, where traditional sun, sand and sea tourism could or does exist. The main aim is to offer a differentiated product and to appeal to a market sector with greater spending power and spending will, for, while the use of the beach is normally free of charge, the use of sports facilities is not. Numerous resorts exist in the sunniest areas of the USA (Florida, Hawaii and California) and on the southeast coast of Australia (Stanton and Aislabie, 1992), mainly catering for domestic markets. However, similar resorts have appeared in the Caribbean (for example, Puerto Romano in the Dominican Republic) and South Pacific and Indian Ocean Islands (Seychelles, Reunion, Bali) and in other countries where golf has not traditionally been played by the local population. Port El Kantaoui, near Sousse, designated as a key development area by Tunisian tourism authorities in 1973 and constructed after 1979, is centred on a marina with 720 apartments, 13 hotels with a total of 5000 beds, a golf-course (recently extended from 18 to 27 holes) and other sports facilities (including 50 tennis-courts). By 1987, the resort's golf facilities were attracting 5000 tourists per year.

Golf-courses associated with property developments

The benefits of the association of a property development with golf facilities are twofold: whilst the cost of the construction of the golf-course(s) can be spread evenly over the entire development project, the increase in the market value of the property development outstrips the corresponding increase in cost. A favourable return on investment is therefore ensured. These so-called 'enabling investments' afforded by the economies of scale have a considerable space-consuming impact. Two segments of demand can be satisfied: the need for select permanent residences and, depending on the location of the development, the demands of the second-home sector. The latter may in fact be considered to form part of the tourist sector. Much of the expansion of golf facilities in Languedoc–Roussillon (France), in Catalonia (Spain) and in Malaga (Spain) has been directed towards this market. In the case of southern France the demand is mostly national and in Catalonia the demand is mostly regional. However, in Malaga, demand comes from both national (basically Madrid) and foreign (mainly British) sources.

Networks of courses forming golf regions

Golf regions are obviously not planned at the outset, but rather develop from the close juxtaposition of a number of golf-courses in any of the three previously mentioned forms. Indeed, Florida and Scotland could be considered to be loosely knit golf regions on a large scale, while the Algarve peninsula (Portugal), developed as a golf region with only eight golf courses (now increased to 13), would be considered to be a golf region on a small scale. One of the best examples of a golf region is perhaps the Costa del Sol in the south of Spain, sometimes marketed as the 'Costa del Golf' (Zarca Arranz, 1990), which offers a chain of 30 golf clubs (comprising 28 courses of 18 holes and ten nine-hole courses) located along a 125-km stretch of the main coast road (N340). A certain element of conscious planning was involved in the early stages, but since then the development of golf tourism has exceeded all expectations, largely as a result of private enterprise. Both resort and property development elements have been exploited (see Fig. 12.1).

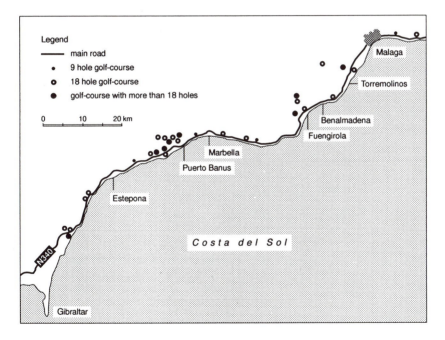

Fig. 12.1. Golf-courses on the Costa del Sol, Spain, 1993.

Characteristics of the Demand for Golf Tourism

Clearly a relationship exists between the total number of golfers in a country and the number of golf tourists generated, although this relation is not exactly proportional (see Table 12.4). Europe is the continent which generates most tourists. The unexpectedly low number of golf tourists from the USA and Canada is explained by the size of the continent, as the numerous internal flows (which consider the two countries as a single unit) are not included. The relatively low figure for Japan is a consequence of the generally low participation rate of tourism in Japan and the long distances to be travelled to suitable destinations. By way of contrast, the large number of Scandinavian and German golfers indicates the importance of climate as a generating factor.

The principal destination of North American and Japanese golf tourists is Europe, and in particular the British Isles, while that of northern European golfers is southern Europe (see Table 12.5). Golf tourism is therefore concentrated in Europe, but in two distinct climatic environments: the British Isles and the popular sun, sand and sea tourism destination regions of southern France, Spain and Portugal. In 1986, the United Kingdom received 38.7% of all European golf tourism and the Republic of Ireland a further 7.2%. Demand in continental Europe was concentrated in Spain (26.0% of the total), France (12.3%), Portugal (8.3%) and Switzerland (1.9%). The remaining 5.6% was spread over other destinations.

A more detailed analysis reveals other contrasting characteristics which further differentiate these two major destination areas. Tourist demand represents a high percentage of the total demand for golfing facilities in southern European countries, whereas in the United Kingdom, although numerically important in absolute terms, tourists

Table 12.4. Principal generators of international golf tourism, 1986. (Source: author, based on Delphi Consultores Internacionales, 1987.)

Origin	No. of golf tourists	% of total no. of players
UK	161,000	6.2
Scandinavia	62,000	39.5
German FR	47,000	61.0
France	24,000	31.6
USA/Canada	110,000	1.7
Japan	35,000	2.9

Table 12.5. Principal destinations of international golf tourism flows in Europe, 1986. (Sources: author, based on Delphi Consultores Internacionales, 1987, and Ortega, 1986.)

Origin	Destination (% of total)			
	Portugal	Spain*	France	UK
UK	74.0	62.0	33.0	–
German FR	13.0	12.0	12.6	4.6
France	4.5	5.0	–	4.6
Scandinavia	3.7	15.0	12.3	12.6
USA/Canada	1.7	**	4.0	41.4
Japan	**	**	2.7	14.7
Other countries	3.1	6.0	–	–
Unspecified	–	–	35.4	22.1

*Statistics for Spain refer to 1985.
**Included in 'other countries' for this destination.

account for only a small proportion of the total demand for golfing facilities. In 1986, foreigners played 1,230,000 rounds of golf in the United Kingdom, which represented 5.0% of all rounds played. In the same year, foreigners played 266,000 rounds in Portugal, representing 75.0% of the total, in France the figure was 394,000 (22.0% of the total), and in Spain in 1985 it was 723,000 (39.5% of the total). Tourist demand continues to increase, as indicated by figures referring to Spain, where foreign visitors played 916,000 rounds of golf in 1991, 918,000 in 1992 and 1,034,000 in 1993.

More recent but less comprehensive figures are provided in the 1993 Sports Marketing Survey, referring to organized golf holidays in the four main countries of origin of golf tourists within Europe, namely the United Kingdom, Germany, Sweden and France (see Fig. 12.3 and Table 12.6). The number of holidays surveyed was 806,383, which is estimated to represent approximately 80% of the total number of holidays taken in the four countries. The analysis of these figures confirms some of the trends identified in 1986, but also reveals new trends. Climatic factors are obviously still important, and Spain, Portugal and France continue to be the principal destinations for northern European golfers. Proximity also exerts a considerable influence, for neighbouring countries also receive a significant proportion of the total flow of tourists: 8.4% of United Kingdom golfers chose Ireland as their destination; 15.5% of Swedes went to Denmark; and 11.6% of Germans chose Austria. Internal flows within France (68.8% of the total), United Kingdom (38.9%), Sweden (17.9%) and Germany (7.0%) were also important.

In the seven-year interval between the two surveys, the total number of golf tourists increased enormously. Taking only the figures for international tourism into account, it can be estimated that the number of Swedish and British tourists doubled and the number of Germans multiplied by almost four. The number of French golf tourists rose by only 50%, a figure which was compensated by the high increase in internal tourist flows. The USA has grown as a destination for European golf tourism, especially as a result of the increase in demand from German golfers. The British Isles continue to attract a steady flow of golfers from all origins.

There is, however, a contrast in the typology of the golf-courses between destination areas in Europe: in Britain, demand is concentrated on the historically famous championship courses with a spillover to their hinterlands; in southern Europe the destinations are the golf resorts and second-home complexes on the sun periphery, where the beach and water sports play a complementary role, and demand is high in winter. Mention has already been made of the expansion of French golf facilities in the Languedoc–Roussillon region. In Spain, with the exception of 20 golf-courses located in the proximity of Madrid, the vast majority of Spanish courses are concentrated on or near the coast, especially on the Mediterranean coast. These courses

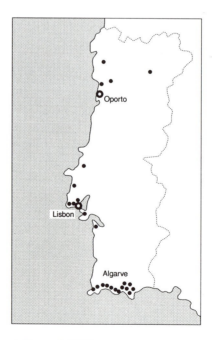

Fig. 12.2. Golf-courses in Portugal, 1993.

(except those near Barcelona) together with the Balearic and Canary Island archipelago courses serve mainly tourist demands. According to statistics provided by the Real Federación Española de Golf, foreigners play 90.0% of all rounds played in Murcia, 84.8% in the Balearic Islands, 73.5% in Andalusia, 72.9% in the Canary Islands, 33.3% in Valencia, but only 15.3% in Catalonia. In fact, 26 of the 100 Spanish courses existing in 1990 received 99% of foreign golf tourism; 58.8% chose Andalusia as a destination and 17.4% chose the Balearic Islands. Valencia, Murcia, the Canary Islands and Catalonia each received from 5 to 6% of foreign golfers. Likewise, golf-courses in Portugal are concentrated on two coasts – near Lisbon (Costa de Lisboa and Costa do Estoril) and the Algarve coast – both of which are renowned tourism destinations (see Fig. 12.2).

Relation between the Golf Tourism Product and Demand

The two major destination areas for golf tourism which have been defined serve three clearly differentiated sectors of demand. One sector consists of those golfers whose main motivation is a 'pilgrimage' to the heartland of golf, the British Isles. Although attempts to promote 'championship' courses elsewhere have been made, none can offer the atmosphere that one or more centuries of tradition can furnish on certain British courses. Hence, it is unlikely that alternative destinations capable of substituting the 'pilgrimage' product will emerge. The British Isles will therefore continue to attract a large proportion of golf tourists from diverse origins.

The other two sectors of demand comprise golfers who simply want a 'golfing holiday', price being the differentiating factor between the two. Of these two, the first seeks a relatively economical golf holiday. It must be remembered that, in the British Isles, most golfers play at relatively low prices, and even the most famous championship courses are open to non-members at relatively low cost. In 1990, charges on public golf-courses ranged between £4 and £7; similar prices were charged on most private courses in Scotland and Ireland, rising to £15 in southern England. A round of golf on a course classified as 'championship' could cost as little as £12, rising to £25 at weekends in the London region. The famous Scottish golf-courses cost between £20 and £31, the cheapest being the Old Course, St Andrews, the most famous of all. Equivalent English courses cost £30 to £47, with Wentworth as the only exception at £69 (Edmund, 1989). Using these figures as a yardstick against which to measure the cost of their golfing holiday, potential British and Irish tourists belonging to the second sector are resistant to paying higher prices, especially when the courses they are offered are unrenowned and their golfing holiday is an extra or secondary vacation, as is often the case (Priestley, 1987).

Spain and, in particular, Portugal are currently the principal destinations for British tourists in search of golfing holidays at a reasonable price. Tour operators offer a wide range of package holidays, especially in Portugal, all of which offer considerable reductions on green fees, and some even offer access to a golf-course free of charge if holidaymakers stay at an associated hotel (even when it does not form part of a resort complex). As demonstrated in Fig. 12.3 and Table 12.6, a large number of British golfers make the alternative choice of having a golfing holiday within the British Isles.

The third sector of demand is for an upmarket product – a golfing holiday with luxury trimmings – which is sought by some golfers from the British Isles, but more generally by other Europeans, Americans and Japanese, who are accustomed and, therefore, willing to pay higher prices to play golf. The pattern of tourist flows for luxury golf holidays in mild or warm winter climates and warm or hot summers is much less concentrated in spatial terms than cheaper forms. For European golfers, easy access is available to the increasing number of golf-courses of recent or imminent construction in southern France and Spain. Also within easy reach are golf facilities in Portugal (20 courses), Morocco (eight courses) and Tunisia (four courses), where the majority of courses cater for tourist rather than local demand.

However, competition from tourism destinations further afield is increasing. Such facilities are of course available in North America, although there foreign visitors mix with local players and domestic tourists. The integrated resorts which have mushroomed in recent years in subtropical and tropical destinations, where the facilities are used almost exclusively by foreign tourists, are the principal competitors of established destinations in the luxury category. Competition is such that several golf clubs on the Costa del Sol in Spain were obliged to reduce their green fees in 1991 by as much as 25% (on 1990 prices, which averaged 10,000 pesetas) as supply increased and demand fell off.

Other new destinations which are beginning to develop are to be found in eastern European countries. In 1992 in Czechoslovakia, with only 1500 golfers, there were eight golf-courses (of which only three had 18 holes) and two under construction and in Hungary, with only 295 players, there was one nine-hole course and three under construction. Obviously these destinations can only compete for summer vacationers, and are most likely to attract golfers from neighbouring countries such as Germany.

The expansion of all three sectors of demand is easily predictable,

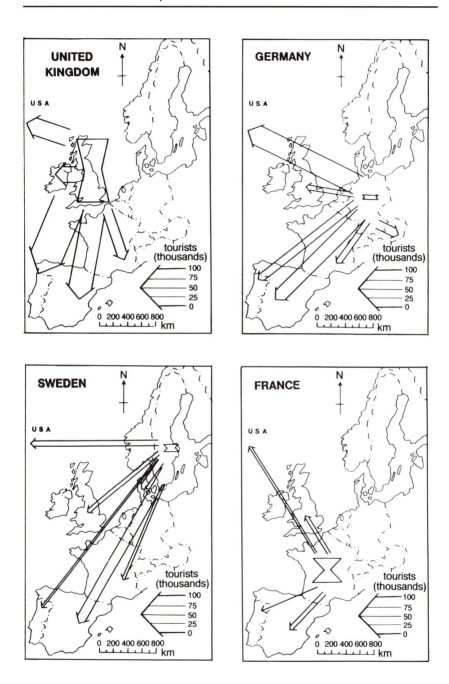

Fig. 12.3. Destinations of golf tourism flows from principal generating countries in Europe, 1993.

Table 12.6. Destinations of golf tourism flows from principal generating countries in Europe, 1993. (Source: author, based on Sports Marketing Survey 1993, 1994.)

| Destination | Country of origin | | | | Total |
	UK	Germany	Sweden	France	
All	429,285	183,817	100,045	93,236	806,383
All foreign	262,090	170,993	100,045	29,137	562,265
USA	45,188	53,435	14,292	5,827	118,742
	(10.5%)	(29.1%)	(14.3%)	(6.3%)	(14.7%)
UK	167,195	25,649	9528	10,490	212,862
	(38.9%)	(14.0%)	(9.5%)	(11.3%)	(26.4%)
Ireland	36,150	–	–	–	36,150
	(8.4%)				(4.5%)
Spain	63,263	36,336	28,585	10,489	138,673
	(14.7%)	(19.8%)	(28.6%)	(11.3%)	(17.2%)
Portugal	90,376	19,237	5955	2331	117,899
	(21.1%)	(10.5%)	(6.0%)	(2.5%)	(14.6%)
France	27,113	14,962	8337	64,099	114,511
	(6.3%)	(8.1%)	(8.3%)	(68.8%)	(14.2%)
Austria	–	21,374	–	–	21,374
		(11.6%)			(2.7%)
Sweden	–	–	17,865	–	17,865
			(17.9%)		(2.2%)
Denmark	–	–	15,483	–	15,483
			(15.5%)		(1.9%)
Germany	–	12,824	–	–	12,824
		(7.0%)			(1.6%)

bearing in mind the general trend towards active vacations, the expansion of golf in the world, particularly in countries which are major tourist generators, and the increasingly widespread supply and more efficient marketing of the golf tourism product. Moreover, the major potential markets for the product – North America, Japan and the British Isles – are relatively untapped. Golf tourism can also contribute to reducing seasonality, as it is an ideal sector of potential demand for the increasing number of retired people, who are often attracted to active off-season holidays. Moreover, the vast majority of European golfers live in regions with harsh winter climates, where golf is, at best, played in adverse weather conditions or, at worst, cannot be played at all. In these conditions many choose to take off-peak vacations, often as a secondary holiday in the form of a four- to seven-day break. In fact, many northern European golfers prefer to play in warm or even cool weather conditions rather than in strong summer heat. Golf can therefore play a complementary role at summer sun, sand and sea destinations, serving as a diversifying element.

Future Market Tendencies

The increasing demand from all three sectors of the market is paralleled by an increase in the supply of the golf tourism product. In recent years there has been a clear tendency to provide mainly the luxury-resort product. As a result of a recession in the second-home market, associated with a general stagnation of house purchasing, it is only in Spain and southern France that golf-courses with associated property developments are now being constructed in large numbers, catering largely for the domestic market. Few less costly golf facilities have been provided to cater for golfers looking for more reasonably priced products. Indeed, these golfers constitute a large percentage of the potential market, especially for southern European and North African destinations. It would be inadvisable to ignore this fact. Only the British and Irish destinations have a guaranteed market, given the unique characteristics of the product they offer.

Resulting Transformations

The environmental impact of the construction of a golf-course varies according to location and design. Certainly, in terms of surface area occupied, the physical impact of a golf-course is considerable, as an 18-hole course occupies a minimum area of 40 ha. Notable examples of the transformations occurring as a result of the development of golf are the large extensions of marshy swamps in Florida which have been transformed into golf-course fairways bounded by lakes or lined with houses, and barren, dry coastal valleys on the Costa del Sol which have likewise been converted into residential complexes set in parks.

The physical impact of a golf-course on a particular landscape can vary enormously. At one end of the scale, traditional British 'links' occupy stretches of coast in their natural state. At the other, the original landscape of many courses constructed in dry climates is often totally transformed as a result of the introduction of water sprinklers for the maintenance of grass on fairways and exotic trees and shrubs as obstacles and dividing elements. These changes have a marked effect on local soil and water management policies. Intensive use of fertilizers and pesticides affect groundwater quality. Besides, in many of the courses that have been newly designed in recent years there has also been a proliferation of artificial lakes, which create their own micro-climates. This is essentially a consequence of the model on which course design tends to be based – the lush, subtropical garden course of Augusta – undoubtedly the best-kept famous course in the world. Moreover, where a golf-course constitutes the focus of a property development, prospective purchasers expect their homes to be set in a garden.

Signs of a new trend in golf-course design are, however, apparent, moving towards styles more in keeping with the natural landscape. This is partly in response to lobbying from nature conservationists, who stress the negative visual impacts of profound transformations. Some administrative bodies (including regional golf associations and tourism planning boards) have at last realized that ecologically adapted courses constitute a differentiated tourist product. In this respect, it must be remembered that the majority of the new courses constructed along the Mediterranean coast attempt to emulate subtropical environments, instead of accentuating their natural landscapes which have been one of their principal tourist assets in the past. In some countries, legislation has prompted the modification of projects, where an environmental impact analysis is required prior to the granting of a building permit. Such is the case in the Balearic Islands where the regional government passed a law to regulate the construction of golf-courses in 1988 (Ley 12/1988).

Financial factors are also important. Not only landscape impact but also construction and maintenance costs are greatly reduced where modifications of the existing ecological structure are reduced to a minimum, where autochthonous tree and shrub species are used, and where, in the case of dry climates, dry rivers and ravines replace lakes as obstacles. In the past such courses have often been considered less attractive by golfers, but attitudes are changing. The vast majority of recently constructed courses have been financed by private funds, but, with growing participation rates and the consequent 'democratization' of the sport, the number of prospective new golfers able and willing to pay the relatively high membership fees has diminished. Speculative course construction in boom conditions has now led to an excess of supply over demand, from both the leisure and tourism sectors, at the prices charged. A number of golf-courses recently constructed in France and Spain are already in financial difficulties through a shortage of demand for membership or for use of the facilities from the tourist sector.

The situation is somewhat different in the case of golf-courses in urban or suburban locations. As already stated, these are designed to satisfy the leisure needs of the local population. Environmental conflicts usually fade into the background, as they are generally tolerated as a means of lowering the density of land occupation and increasing the extension of open spaces, albeit private not public spaces. The vast majority of courses constructed during the last two decades form part of larger-scale property developments. In this way suburban locations which otherwise might have been considered too peripheral to attract residents become poles of attraction. This is the case of the numerous complexes of this nature which surround the cities of Paris and Madrid. In fact La Moraleja golf and residential complex, developed since 1976 at 8.5 km from Madrid, is one of the most prestigious residential areas in the city. The presence of a golf-course can also contribute enormously to converting a small, insignificant village or town into a fashionable place of residence. Sometimes these become no more than dormitory towns for nearby cities, but they can have a positive impact on the conditions for the location of footloose industries and services, as decision-makers tend to choose locations with attractive living conditions (which include the existence of a golf-course) for the establishment of new plants as an incentive to attract highly qualified employees. For example, the existence of a golf-course in Sant Cugat, 20 km inland from Barcelona (Spain), has greatly contributed to its expansion from a small village where second homes predominated to a large fashionable residential town with a number of high-technology industries in its hinterland.

There is no doubt that the demand for golf as a leisure activity in general, and subsequently as a tourism product has increased sharply in recent years. Present indications suggest that this trend will continue, and investors and promoters are rapidly providing facilities to satisfy present and foreseeable demand, although in some regions supply has already exceeded present demand at the prices charged. It is therefore possible to conclude that the extent and form of development of golf is greatly influenced by the consumers. Nevertheless, the limits of growth are determined not only by demand, but also by product characteristics. These include financial factors (which condition course design, amenity provision and parallel property development); socioeconomic factors (which can affect the development of their hinterlands); and environmental considerations (which have repercussions for course design and management). Environmentally friendly, less costly golf-courses have not been a priority in the recent past, but they are likely to be much more so in the future.

References and Further Reading

Adams, R.L.A. and Rooney, J.F. (1985) Evolution of American golf facilities. *Geographical Review* 75(4), 419–438.

Asin López-Bermejo, G. (1967) *El Deporte como Promoción del Turismo.* Cuaderno Monográfico, 9. Instituto de Estudios Turísticos, Madrid.

Delphi Consultores Internacionales (1987) El turismo de golf en los países competidores de España: informe-resumen. Estudio coordinado por la Subdirección General del Instituto de Estudios Turísticos y realizado por Delphi Consultores Internacionales. *Estudios Turísticos* 96, 73–104.

Edmund, N. (ed.) (1989) *Following the Fairways,* 3rd edn. Kensington West Productions, London.

Hegarty, C. (1991) *European Golf Facilities November 1991.* Touche Ross & Co., London.

Ley 12/1988 del 17 de noviembre de Campos de golf, *BOCAIB* 145 (3 Dec. 1988).

Mazoyer, P. (1992) Resorts golfiques du sud de la Péninsule Ibérique. *Cahier Espaces* 27, 120–127.

National Golf Foundation (1991) *The Growth of US Golf.* Research Summary 12 (7/91).

Ortega, E. (1986) Presente y futuro del turismo de golf en España. *Estudios Turísticos* 90, 23–46.

Ortega, E. (1992) La economía del golf. Su evolución en el mundo y en España. *Estudios Turísticos* 114, 19–40.

Patronato Provincial de Turismo Costa del Sol (1987) Importancia del golf en el turismo selectivo: conclusiones generales. Seminario sobre la importancia del golf en el turismo selectivo, Torremolinos, 25 Sept.

Price, R. (1990) The impact of the new Scottish golf boom. Unpublished paper presented at Institute of British Geographers' Annual Conference, University of Glasgow, Jan.

Priestley, G.K. (1987) The role of golf as a tourist attraction: the case of Catalonia, Spain. Acts of the Meeting of the Commission of Geography of Tourism, Leisure and Recreation of the International Geographical Union, Sousse, Tunisia (June), pp. 288–302.

Priestley, G.K. and Sabi, J. (1990) El turismo y el deporte: el caso del golf en Catalunya. Unpublished research project undertaken in the Department of Geography, Universitat Autònoma de Barcelona.

Priestley, G.K. and Sabi, J. (1993) Le golf, pratique de loisir aux territoires périurbains de Barcelone. *Méditerranée* 77(1/2), 69–72.

Redmond, G. (1991) Changing styles of sports tourism: industry/consumer interactions in Canada, the USA and Europe. In: Sinclair, M.T. and Stabler, M.J. (eds) *The Tourism Industry: An International Analysis.* CAB International, Wallingford, pp. 107–120.

Royal and Ancient Golf Club of St Andrews Development Panel (1990) *The Demand for Golf.* RAGC St Andrews, St Andrews.

Socias Fuster, M. (1989) Los campos de golf en Baleares: la nueva oferta complementaria. In: *XI Congreso Nacional de Geografía, Comunicaciones,* vol. 3. Asociación de Geógrafos Españoles, Madrid, pp. 403–410.

Stanton, J. and Aislabie, C. (1992) Up-market integrated resorts in Australia. *Annals of Tourism Research* 19(3), 435–449.

Volle, J.P. (1989) Le golf en France: un espace en mouvement. *La Lettre d'Odile*, Groupement d'Intérêt Public R.E.C.L.U.S., Montpellier, 0, 8–9.

Zarca Arranz, A. (1986) Turismo selectivo en la Costa del Sol: importancia del golf como fenómeno económico. *Dintel* 12, 16–19.

Zarca Arranz, A. (1990) La Costa del Golf. *Dintel* 27, 37–41.

13

Impacts of Festival Events: a Case-study of Edinburgh

C. Gratton[1] and P.D. Taylor[2]

[1]*School of Leisure and Food Management, Sheffield Hallam University, City Campus, Pond Street, S1 1WB Sheffield, UK:* [2]*Leisure Management Unit, University of Sheffield, Hicks Building, Hounsfield Road, S3 7RH Sheffield, UK.*

Introduction

There is increasing interest in the role of special events (or hallmark events) in attracting tourists to cities and regions, of which the increasing literature in this area is evidence (e.g. Syme *et al.*, 1989; Getz, 1991; Hall, 1992; Richards, 1992; Weiler and Hall, 1992; and a journal launched in 1993, *Festival Management and Event Tourism*). This chapter contributes to that literature by focusing on festival tourism and specifically on the tourism impact of festivals in Edinburgh. There has been a tremendous growth in the number of festivals in the United Kingdom in recent years. Out of 527 UK arts festivals reviewed by Rolfe (1992), 56% were established in the 1980s and 1990s. Up until the 1970s the main interest in festivals was in their artistic, educational and cultural importance. However, more recently, and particularly in Britain after the publication of Myerscough's (1988) *The Economic Importance of the Arts in Britain*, it is the economic impact of arts festivals that has attracted increasing attention, and this is the focus of this chapter.

The Edinburgh festivals are unique in that two studies of their economic impact have been carried out, the first by Roger Vaughan in 1976 (Vaughan, 1977b) and the second by the present authors in conjunction with the market-research company Scotinform in 1990–1991. This chapter will concentrate on the later study though making some comparisons with the earlier one. Before considering the details of the economic-impact studies, however, the relationship between special events and tourism is discussed, paying particular attention to festivals.

Festival Events and Tourism

There are many problems in defining any specific sector of the tourism market. Different commentators have taken different approaches. Probably the broadest definition is that adopted by Weiler and Hall (1992), who use the term 'special-interest tourism' for that type of travel behaviour that involves people going somewhere because they have a particular interest that can be pursued in a particular region or at a particular destination. It is the special interest that is the motivating force behind the travel behaviour. Read (1980) has indicated that such tourism can be a rewarding, enriching, adventuresome and learning experience (hence his use of the term REAL travel). Other authors (Getz, 1991; Hall, 1992) have concentrated on special or hallmark events which attract a large part of the special-interest tourism market. Such special events may be centred around a wide range of activities including sporting and cultural activities, but festival events are clearly an important part of such event tourism.

Thus festival events and the tourism associated with them come within the scope of a wide range of tourism categories (cultural tourism, arts tourism, special-interest tourism, and event tourism). Despite the fact that festivals are only a subcategory of any of these, there is a wide variety of types of festival, as Rolfe (1992) discovered in her survey of British festivals:

> Some festivals are concerned with only one art form. Many include activities in many different art forms. In addition to almost every type of music, there are festivals of dance, drama, film, literature, poetry and puppetry and a number offering innovative combinations of art forms. Indeed, the diversity of festivals is so great that there is more than a grain of truth in one festival organiser's comment that the only thing they have in common is the 'festival' title.

Rolfe goes on to argue that despite this diversity, there is a common characteristic shared by all festivals: an intensity of artistic output and experience that can be achieved by a programme which is concentrated in time and delivered with a clear purpose and direction.

It is not only the content of different festivals that exhibits wide variety. Such diversity is also a feature of the objectives of festivals. For many festivals, the prime objective is normally the presentation of arts events themselves to the local community. For many areas it is impossible to sustain a high-quality arts venue throughout the year, but over a short period of time a festival allows the local community to enjoy such high-quality performances. Tourism is often a secondary objective to make the event financially viable both by increasing attendances and by attracting financial backing from local government and commercial sponsors. Gratton and Taylor (1986, 1987) describe a typical example of such a festival, the Hayfield International Jazz Festival.

Other festivals have a much greater emphasis on attracting tourists and some festivals are part of a broader economic development strategy based on cultural tourism. Law (1992, 1993) has indicated that many European cities in the 1980s adopted an urban tourism strategy, following the examples of such strategies in American cities such as Baltimore and Boston in the 1970s. Within such an urban tourism strategy, urban cultural policy, often with an emphasis on festivals, has become increasingly important. In Britain, the link between arts and tourism became much more important after the publication of Myerscough's (1988) study of the economic importance of the arts. In many ways, the economic arguments in favour of government support for the arts and culture changed during the 1980s away from arguments concerned with education, cultural appreciation and cultural integration, towards arguments concerned with the economic benefits generated by the arts through their attraction of tourists. This economic motivation may explain to some extent the rapid rise in the number of arts festivals in recent years.

Biancini (1990) argues that one particular group of European cities where cultural tourism is a primary objective of cultural policy are 'declining cities'. These have used cultural policy to support strategies for the diversification of their economic base and the reconstruction of their image. These cities have suffered decline due to the disappearance of their old manufacturing base. Within this category he includes Glasgow, which is of particular interest in the context of this chapter. Historically, there has been little real competition in the field of cultural tourism between the two major Scottish cities, Glasgow and Edinburgh. It was generally assumed that Edinburgh was the cultural capital, which in fact is the way Biancini classified Edinburgh. Things started to change in the mid-1980s with the promotional campaign 'Glasgow's Miles Better' together with the introduction of Mayfest, a major annual arts festival. In 1990, Glasgow became European Cultural Capital and prior to this there was massive investment in new cultural facilities. The effect of such policies was to substantially boost cultural tourism in Glasgow and make Glasgow a real competitor to Edinburgh in the cultural tourism field.

Festival Tourism in Edinburgh

Edinburgh is the capital of Scotland and is an attractive historical city and a major tourist destination in its own right irrespective of the festivals. Much of the rest of tourism outside the festival period could also be referred to as cultural tourism but is more to do with 'heritage tourism' than with 'arts tourism'. In 1976, Vaughan (1977a, b) estimated that all visitors to Edinburgh contributed £40 million of expenditure in the city and generated 7300 full-time equivalent jobs for the residents of the Lothian region. However, the majority of this inflow of money into Edinburgh was due to business and social visitors. The total expenditure by holiday visitors was about £18 million, of which about 20% was due to the festivals. Thus the festivals make up an important part of a portfolio of attractions that bring visitors to Edinburgh.

The first Edinburgh Festival, officially entitled the Edinburgh International Festival, took place in 1947. The director of this first festival was Rudolph Bing, who was also General Manager of Glyndebourne Opera Festival, and the emphasis in the first years was on music (although it is now a broadly based festival of opera, music, dance, theatre, and poetry). Richards (1992) argues that Bing, and an associated group of Edinburgh intellectuals and dignitaries, designed the Festival to be exclusive and élitist, the primary objective being to create a new European festival to compete with Bayreuth and Salzburg. Rolfe (1992) argues that the Edinburgh International Festival was one of a number of festivals in Europe established after the end of the Second World War both to celebrate European culture and to act as a vehicle of unification. Vaughan (1977b), however, states that one of the aims of the festival was clearly to extend the tourism season into September and so tourism was an important factor in setting up the festival.

The rather élitist nature of Edinburgh International Festival immediately led to a second festival taking place at the same time, the Edinburgh Festival Fringe. Many performers not invited to the official festival simply came along and performed wherever an audience could be found. By 1990, the Fringe, mainly consisting of street theatre, mime and drama, dominated the proceedings with almost 1000 events attracting over half a million visitors, compared to 245,000 visitors attending 110 events in the International Festival.

A third festival, the Edinburgh Film Festival was also established in 1947 and has now become one of the major European film festivals. By 1950, a fourth festival had been added, the Military Tattoo, which consists of pipe bands, other military bands, and armed services displays. When Vaughan carried out his study of the economic impact of Edinburgh festivals in 1976, it was these four festivals that were

Table 13.1. Events, venues, attendances, and dates of the nine Edinburgh festivals, 1990–1991.

Festival	No. of events	No. of venues	Total audience	1990–1991 dates
International Festival	110	25	245,000	10 Aug.–2 Sept. 1990
Fringe Festival	990	140	500,000	10 Aug.–1 Sept. 1990
Jazz Festival	421	20	65,000	18 Aug.–26 Aug. 1990
Film Festival	153	3	15,000	11 Aug.–26 Aug. 1990
Military Tattoo	1	1	200,000	2 Aug.–25 Aug. 1990
Book Festival	170	1	62,000	10 Aug.–26 Aug. 1990
Folk Festival	50	6	8,000	22 Mar.–31 Mar. 1990
Science Festival	290	41	201,000	1 Apr.–14 Apr. 1991
Children's Festival	12	1	30,000	28 May–2 June 1990

included. By 1990, the number of festivals taking place in Edinburgh over the August–September period had grown to six, the previous four plus the Jazz Festival and the Book Festival. In addition, three other Edinburgh festivals took place at different times of the year: the Folk Festival (March), the Science Festival (April) and the Children's Festival (June). Table 13.1 indicates the full festival programme in Edinburgh in 1990–1991.

Over the years different directors have changed the focus of the festivals. The International Festival remains the major focus for arts visitors even though the Fringe Festival attracts a higher number of visits. The International Festival has become less élitist but is still clearly much more representative of the conventional arts attractions than the more avant-garde Fringe Festival. In the 1980s, there was a stronger emphasis on promoting Scottish culture through the International Festival, and at the same time there has been a more international flavour fostered by the attraction of more foreign performers.

The Edinburgh festivals, spanning virtually the whole of August and the beginning of September, are now one of the longest running festival events held in the United Kingdom. In Rolfe's (1992) survey of 527 festivals in the UK only 5% predate the Edinburgh festivals. Taken together they have become the largest festival event in the United Kingdom, attracting more visitors than any other festival. In 1990, as well as taking more at the box office than virtually any other festival (at around £1.5 million), the festivals received support from Edinburgh District Council, the Scottish Arts Council, and commercial sponsors (each contributing around £0.6 million). Add to this the other festivals taking place at other times of the year, and Edinburgh can justly claim to be one of the main festival cities in Europe, justifying on this claim alone Biancini's (1990) description of it as a cultural capital.

The festivals thus give Edinburgh an important position in the cultural league table for European cities. What has interested policy-makers most, however, in the most recent past is what economic effects such festival events generate.

Economic Impact of Edinburgh Festivals

Edinburgh is unique in Europe in that it has been the subject of two separate economic impact assessments of the importance of festival tourism. The two studies, in 1976 and in 1990–1991, span a time period when festival tourism in European cities has supposedly increased substantially, which gives us the opportunity therefore to analyse in detail the nature of festival tourism in cities and to assess how it has changed over this period.

The first study of Edinburgh festivals (Vaughan, 1977b) was carried out in 1976 as part of a wider study of the economic impact of tourism in Edinburgh (Vaughan, 1977a). The second study was carried out in 1990–1991. The research was commissioned by the Scottish Tourist Board, Edinburgh District Council, Lothian Regional Council, and Lothian and Edinburgh Enterprise Ltd. The research was carried out by the market-research company Scotinform, with the present authors employed as economic consultants to carry out the economic-impact assessment. The detailed economic-impact calculations and method-ology are described elsewhere (Scottish Tourist Board, 1993; Gratton and Richards, 1995). Here we concentrate on the major results of the 1990–1991 study and also on comparisons with 1976.

The main data collection took place in August and September 1990, but, in order to include the other festivals, interviewing also took place in 1991 to cover a full festival year. In order to compare 1976 with 1990 most of the evidence below will concentrate on the four festivals that took place in both years, and in particular the three main festivals, the Military Tattoo, the International and the Fringe Festivals.

Table 13.2 gives the overall results of the economic-impact estima-tion in 1990–1991, reporting the additional expenditure generated by the festivals. The term 'additional expenditure' is used since it refers to that expenditure by visitors that would not take place without the festivals. Total additional expenditure due to the festivals in 1990–1991 was estimated at £43.9 million, which generated an estimated 1319 full-time equivalent jobs in the local economy. Table 13.2 shows that the three festivals that dominate the net addition to expenditure in Edinburgh

Table 13.2. The economic impact of the Edinburgh festivals.

	Edinburgh and Lothian	Scotland
Local income	£9.2m	n.a
Employment (full-time equivalent jobs)	1319	3034
Direct expenditure		
Fringe Festival	£10.36m	£11.29m
International Festival	£6.91m	£7.53m
Military Tattoo	£19.57m	£44.25m
Jazz Festival	£1.19m	£1.31m
Film Festival	£0.45m	£0.46m
Folk Festival	£0.18m	£0.19m
Science Festival	£0.69m	£0.74m
Book Festival	£1.84m	£2.41m
Children's Festival	£0.01m	£0.01m
Multiple Festival Visitor	£2.65m	£3.85m
Total direct expenditure	£43.86m	£72.00m

Note: Scottish figures include Edinburgh and Lothian.

due to the festivals are the Tattoo, International and Fringe Festivals, accounting together for 84% of additional spending due to the festivals. These three attract the highest number of visits, have the highest proportion of tourist visits (i.e. those staying at least one night in Edinburgh), and the highest average daily spending per visitor. Of the three main festivals, the Military Tattoo is the single largest contributor in terms of economic impact, contributing 45% of additional expenditure in Edinburgh and 61% of additional expenditure in Scotland.

Of the total additional expenditure, 86% was incurred by tourists spending at least one night in Edinburgh. Most of the rest (11% of additional expenditure) was by day-visitors, non-residents who visited Edinburgh for the festivals but did not stay overnight. Less than 3% of additional expenditure was due to residents. The reasons for the low contribution to additional expenditure by residents was their low average daily expenditure compared with day-visitors and tourists and the small percentage of residents' expenditure that was 'additional', in the sense that much of this expenditure would have taken place in Edinburgh anyway.

One important aspect of the 1990–1991 study was the attempt to assess the importance of the Edinburgh festivals in generating tourism and the resultant economic impact in other parts of Scotland. Visitors that create a further economic impact in the rest of Scotland are those that spend further nights elsewhere in Scotland as part of their visit to the Edinburgh festivals. These are of two types: those classed as tourists in our analysis of spending in Edinburgh (i.e. those staying at least one night in Edinburgh) who then go on to spend further nights in other parts of Scotland; and those classed as day-visitors in our Edinburgh analysis who spend tourist nights in other parts of Scotland. Edinburgh residents who visit the festivals contribute no additional economic impact in the rest of Scotland.

For those visitors to the festivals that spent at least one night in Edinburgh, the average number of nights spent in Edinburgh by festival visitors was 8.5. In addition, 30% of tourist visitors to the Fringe and International Festivals spent an average of six nights elsewhere in another part of Scotland. Also, 20% of day-trip visitors to these festivals also spent an average of seven nights in another part of Scotland. These percentages were even higher for visitors to the Military Tattoo, where one-third of day-trip visitors and nearly a half of tourist visitors spent seven nights in another part of Scotland. The evidence then from this study indicates that all festival tourism in Edinburgh does not come under the heading of 'short-break' tourism. For a significant number of visitors, it is more akin to conventional 'long-holiday' tourism where tourists combine cultural-event visiting with other tourist activities, most probably outdoor recreation, given Scotland's abundant resources, in other parts of Scotland. The short-break market is undoubtedly an important part of the visitor numbers to Edinburgh festivals, but these data show that it is not the only market, and probably not the most significant one in terms of economic impact.

Estimated additional direct expenditure in the rest of Scotland was £28.19 million. This is equivalent to a further 1190 additional full-time equivalent jobs generated by the spending of festival visitors in Scotland as a whole. The important point about these results is that about 40% of the economic impact of the festivals in Scotland as a whole is due to expenditure outside Edinburgh. This study indicates that the festivals are a major attraction of tourists to Scotland. As this result is perhaps the most unexpected from the study, there is perhaps a need for a more thorough investigation of holiday behaviour that is combined with festival visiting.

Table 13.3 compares the total impact of all the festivals for both 1976 and 1990–1991. Vaughan estimated total additional direct expenditure due to the festivals in 1976 to be £3.7 million (at 1976 prices). We estimated total additional expenditure in 1990–1991 to be £43.8 million (at 1990 prices). One major reason for the difference is that prices rose substantially between 1976 and 1990 (the average price level for the British economy in 1990 was more than three times higher than in 1976) and allowance must be made for this. However, even after allowing for this price inflation, total real additional direct expenditure on the

Table 13.3. Economic impact of Edinburgh festivals (1976 and 1990) in Edinburgh and Lothian.

	1976	1990
Additional direct expenditure	£3.7m	£43.8m
Additional local income	£0.96m	£9.2m
Additional local jobs (full-time equivalents)	n.a.	1319

Edinburgh festivals in 1990–1991 was 369% higher than in 1976, a substantial increase.

Three clear reasons can be identified for this large increase. First, looking at attendances for the four festivals that were staged in both years, in 1990 there was a 172% increase in festival visits compared to 1976. Secondly, average daily expenditure per head by staying festival-goers (i.e. those staying at least one night in Edinburgh) was twice as high, in real terms, in 1990 as in 1976. This group of staying tourists was the most significant group contributing to the economic impact of the festivals in both years and this large rise in the average real daily expenditure was the most important factor accounting for the difference in economic impact between the two years. Although expenditures increased on all items, the largest increase was for expenditure on food and drink in cafés, pubs, and restaurants.

A third reason for the increase in direct expenditure due to the festivals was the growth in the number of festivals from four in 1976 to nine in 1990–1991. The effect of this, however, was less than might be expected. This is because the major contribution to economic impact was by visitors to the Military Tattoo, International, and Fringe Festivals which were staged in both years. The new festivals attracted a large proportion of local visitors and relatively small amounts of additional expenditure, except for the Book Festival, visitors to which had one of the highest levels of average daily expenditure.

Table 13.3 indicates that festival tourism has indeed increased substantially in Edinburgh. However, Table 13.4 indicates an interesting aspect of this growth. The table shows that the share of international tourists to the festivals has in fact decreased, with a substantial decrease in the proportion of visitors from the rest of Europe (outside the UK). The biggest rise has been in visitors from the rest of the UK, and particularly England.

All festivals, except for the Military Tattoo, attract a large number of visitors from residents of the city of Edinburgh and the surrounding region. The smaller festivals attracted even higher proportions of visitors than the 42% for the International Festival in Table 13.4, with

Table 13.4. Place of residence (1976 and 1990) of festival visitors.

	Tattoo (%)		International (%)		Fringe (%)	
	1976	1990	1976	1990	1976	1990
City and Lothian	15	6	36	42	50	35
Rest of Scotland	15	13	15	19	12	10
Rest of UK	42	53	23	26	24	41
Rest of Europe	7	7	10	5	6	4
North America	10	12	11	7	6	4
Elsewhere	11	10	5	3	3	4

the Children's Festival attracting 86% of its visitors from the local region. This indicates the diversity in the types of demand that different festivals satisfy. Yet again, the Military Tattoo stands out as the exception, and the fact that only 6% of visitors are local (with the other 94% being day-visitors or tourists) is one of the major reasons additional expenditure is so high.

Another interesting feature of Table 13.4 is the decrease in the proportion of visitors from the local area, with the exception of the International Festival, which has the largest share of local visits at 42% in 1990. The reason for this is perhaps the difference in the type of festival. The Military Tattoo is a display that is broadly similar year after year. Once visited it is less likely to generate repeat visits. The Fringe is an avant-garde arts festival, perhaps appealing less to more conservative Edinburgh audiences. The conventional opera, theatre, and music performances appear in the International Festival and these are likely to appeal to a certain section of the local population who become regular visitors on an annual basis.

Tables 13.5 and 13.6 show the profile of visitors to the three main festivals by age and socioeconomic group in 1990. It is generally assumed that cultural tourists come disproportionately from the younger age groups and the older (particularly the early retired) groups since these two groups have greater leisure time availability to pursue their cultural interests. There is some support for this view in Table 13.5, but the main message from this table is that the age profile varies considerably depending on the type of festival. The Military Tattoo appeals particularly to older age groups with almost two-thirds of its audience over the age of 45. The Fringe Festival, on the other hand, appeals mainly to younger age groups with over two-thirds below the age of 35. The International Festival age profile is more even, appealing to all age groups.

Table 13.5. Profile of visitors by age.

Age group	Tattoo	International	Fringe
15–24 (%)	11	11	31
25–34 (%)	14	19	37
35–44 (%)	16	20	16
45–54 (%)	20	21	9
55–64 (%)	20	15	5
65+ (%)	13	11	2
Not stated (%)	6	3	1
Total no. of respondents	708	1770	1604

Table 13.6. Profile of visitors by socioeconomic group (base = all respondents resident in UK).

Socioeconomic group	Tattoo	International
A (%)	2	7
B (%)	10	38
C1 (%)	22	29
C2 (%)	28	4
DE (%)	18	7
Total no. of respondents	634	1678

Note: A – higher managerial, administrative or professional; B – Intermediate managerial, administrative or professional; C1 – Supervisory or clerical, and junior managerial; C2 – skilled manual workers; D – semi- and unskilled manual workers; E – state pensioners; casual or lowest-grade workers.

The socioeconomic profile in Table 13.6 relates only to festival visitors resident in the UK. It shows that, again, the profile varies depending on the type of festival. The main audience for both the Fringe and International Festivals is in the ABC1 social classes. This is perhaps not surprising since these are the main vehicles for theatre and music at the Edinburgh festivals and it is well known that audiences for this area of the arts are predominantly from these social groups. The Military Tattoo, however, has a very different socioeconomic profile with 68% of the audience coming from social classes CDE. It is interesting that this festival makes the biggest contribution to the economic impact of the festivals even though it appeals disproportionately to lower-income groups.

Table 13.7. Importance of festival/s in decision to visit Edinburgh (base = non-residents of Edinburgh and Lothian).

	Tattoo	International	Fringe
Sole reason for coming (%)	57	52	57
Very important reason (%)	18	20	20
Fairly important reason (%)	10	13	11
Only a small reason (%)	9	8	8
Of no importance at all (%)	5	6	6
Total no. of respondents	674	1054	1078

Table 13.7 shows that the festivals play an important role in bringing visitors to Edinburgh. Nearly three-quarters of festival visitors from outside the region said that the festivals were the sole reason or a very important reason for their visit to Edinburgh. What is perhaps more surprising is that a quarter of these visitors were visiting Edinburgh for the first time and over a third of all festival visitors (or two-thirds in the case of the Tattoo) were visiting the festivals for the first time. This shows that special events, such as festivals, clearly play an important role in tourist generation.

Conclusions

We began this chapter by discussing the increasing interest of tourism researchers in 'special-event tourism'. In the past, there has been some difficulty in pursuing this interest because of a lack of evidence on the size and importance of this part of the tourism market, particularly in the European context. We have tried to rectify this to some extent by looking at the case of one European city, Edinburgh, and the effects of the staging of a series of festivals on tourism to the city. Edinburgh is unusual in having had not one, but two, studies of the economic importance of cultural events on tourism: two studies which cover a period when festival tourism in Europe is supposed to have become increasingly important.

Some of the conventional hypotheses concerning cultural tourism in European cities are confirmed from the Edinburgh evidence, but others are not. In particular, there has been strong growth in the numbers of people visiting, more than a doubling of the number of visits between 1976 and 1990. The economic impact has increased substantially not only because of more visitors but also because they on average spend twice as much per head (in real terms) in 1990 than in 1976.

In general, the normal assumptions about the cultural tourist are confirmed. They come disproportionately from the better-off and better-educated groups. The festivals taking place in August are very much a 'joint product'. Not only do visitors visit several events at one festival, they also visit events at other festivals.

The Military Tattoo is very much an exception. Visitors were likely to be older (over 45) and to come from the lower socioeconomic groups: a high percentage were in parties of six or more and on a package tour. Visitors tended to have just one visit to the Tattoo and there was little interest in, or visits to, the other festivals. Because such a high proportion of visits were by tourists spending several nights in Edinburgh and even more in other parts of Scotland, the Tattoo was the festival that contributed most to economic impact. The Military Tattoo is not an arts festival but adds to the attractions on offer during the festival period, which means there is a broader spectrum of visitors to the city during this period. The lesson from Edinburgh is that providing a diverse range of attractions can be successful in broadening the market and substantially increasing the economic impact of a festival event.

Two other major conclusions follow from the Edinburgh study. The festivals are a major tourist attraction bringing tourists to the city for the first time. Also, for a significant number of tourists, visits to the festivals are only part of a wider holiday experience which includes staying an average of six to seven nights in other parts of Scotland. This combination of festival tourism with other types of tourism (e.g. outdoor recreation) has not been reflected in other studies and indicates that the overall economic impact of festival tourism may be seriously underestimated because researchers have failed to investigate links between cultural/festival tourism and related tourist activities. The 1976 Edinburgh Festival study, for instance, asked no questions about whether people combined festival visiting with other tourism within Scotland and therefore we cannot draw any conclusions as to whether this aspect of tourist behaviour has become more or less important. We can simply state that in 1990, tourists were spending significant periods of time and a substantial amount of money in other parts of Scotland directly as a result of the staging of the Edinburgh festivals.

The evidence from Edinburgh suggests that festival tourism can make a significant economic contribution to the local and regional economies of cities. Given the relatively small amount of public subsidy given to the festivals, it is a very efficient way of generating local income and employment as well as regional and national employment.

References and Further Reading

Biancini, F. (1990) Cultural policy and urban development: the experience of west European cities. Paper delivered at the conference Cultural Policy and Urban Regeneration: The West European Experience, Liverpool, 30–31 Oct.

Getz, D. (1991) *Festivals, Special Events and Tourism.* Van Nostrand, New York.

Gratton, C. and Richards, G. (1995) The economic context of cultural tourism. In: Richards, G. (ed.) *Cultural Tourism in Europe.* CAB International, Wallingford (in press).

Gratton, C. and Taylor, P. (1986) The economic impact of Hayfield International Jazz Festival. *Leisure Management* 6(10), 19–21.

Gratton, C. and Taylor, P. (1987) Hayfield International Jazz Festival: an analysis of festival sponsorship. *Leisure Management* 7(7), 29–21.

Hall, C.M. (1992) *Hallmark Tourist Events: Impacts, Management, and Planning.* Belhaven Press, London.

Law, C.M. (1992) Urban tourism and its contribution to economic regeneration. *Urban Studies* 29(3/4), 599–618.

Law, C.M. (1993) *Urban Tourism: Attracting Visitors to Large Cities.* Mansell Publishing, London.

Myerscough, J. (1988) *The Economic Importance of the Arts in Britain.* Policy Studies Institute, London.

Read, S.E. (1980) A prime force in the expansion of tourism in the next decade: special interest travel. In: Hawkins, D.E., Shafer, E.L. and Rovelstad, J.M. (eds) *Tourism Marketing and Management Issues.* George Washington University, Washington.

Richards, B. (1992) *How to Market Tourist Attractions, Festivals and Special Events.* Longman, Harlow, UK.

Richards, G. (1993) Cultural tourism in Europe. In: Cooper, C.P. and Lockwood, A. (eds) *Progress in Tourism, Recreation, and Hospitality Management,* vol. 5. Belhaven Press, London, pp. 99–115.

Rolfe, H. (1992) *Arts Festivals in the UK.* Policy Studies Institute, London.

Scottish Tourist Board (1993) Edinburgh festivals study: visitor survey and economic impact. *Festival Management and Events Journal* 1(2), 71–78.

Syme, G., Shaw, B.J., Fenton, D.M. and Mueller, W.S. (1989) *The Planning and Evaluation of Hallmark Events.* Avebury, Aldershot.

Vaughan, R. (1977a) *The Economic Impact of Tourism in Edinburgh and the Lothian Region.* Scottish Tourist Board, Edinburgh.

Vaughan, R. (1977b) *The Economic Impact of the Edinburgh Festival.* Scottish Tourist Board, Edinburgh.

Weiler, B. and Hall, C.M. (eds) (1992) *Special Interest Tourism.* Belhaven Press, London.

IV

From Transformation by the Consumer to Management of the Consumer

The focus of the above studies of visitor behaviour can now be related back to the official management agencies who are responsible for managing visitors in pursuit of various goals that are extrinsic to the tourism industry itself. Tourism is seen by almost all public-sector agencies as a means to be utilized instrumentally in the pursuit of other economic or non-economic objectives, even if these are often assumed or only vaguely formulated. Much management at the local level may even be largely defensive in character. Tourism is viewed as an incoming flow of consumers whose size, timing and expectations are determined elsewhere but whose behaviour within the destination place can to an extent be modified and their various costs reduced.

However, more positively, Dutch planning literature is currently full of accounts of how local planners have responded to, and thereby further encouraged, changes in social spatial behaviour in cities with the shaping of outdoor terraces and squares and indoor plazas. Boerwinkel explains further this idea of managing behaviour through the structuring of space, especially public space, in which the tourism consumer is now subsumed in a much broader set of uses of the same space for the same activities. This chapter mirrors in many ways the earlier chapter by Burgers although the focus has now decisively shifted from the management of the product to the management of the consumer and as a consequence the approach is through social psychology rather than spatial analysis and planning. The point is made and worth stressing that not only is management intervention especially desirable on this scale, but, more pragmatically, it is possible and relatively easily achieved, if only because in most countries the statutory instruments, organizational structures and working practices exist in public sector agencies at this level.

The importance of cultural tourism has already been demonstrated in one of its aspects by Gratton and Taylor and was the underlying motive for much of the behaviour of tourists described in cities and regions by Dietvorst.

239

Ashworth's chapter develops the proposition that managing the cultural tourist is dependent upon understanding the various ways in which culture is used both within tourism and also for other quite different purposes. From these distinctions come a variety of types of tourism, but also, most relevant here, a variety of types of consumer management problems and possibilities.

In this section the management, or at least containment, of the less welcome impacts of the tourist upon host communities is illustrated by Beke and Elands in the case of crime committed by visitors while on holiday. Recreational crime emerges from the empirical material as antisocial behaviour expressed in various ways, undertaken not only during a tourism trip but often, and disturbingly, as an essential ingredient of the tourism experience for some visitors. A range of possible measures for monitoring, surveillance, prevention and apprehension are reviewed as part of consumer management at the destination.

The study of the relationship between tourism as an activity and the natural environmental resources it uses is far too complex to be considered in detail here. This relationship and the policy implications it prompts are described in detail in a number of texts (such as Briassoulis and van der Straaten, 1992). However any attempt at an integral approach cannot neglect the links between the production and resource systems and when these resources are drawn from the natural environment then issues of such current importance are raised as to determine the pace, type and location of much tourism development. Sidaway relates recreation activities and environmental resources through the idea of acceptable change, with 'acceptable' having a separate and sometimes conflicting meaning for participating recreationists, the recreation facility suppliers and even society as a whole.

Many of the policies, industrial strategies and management techniques depend upon the obtaining, transmitting and retrieval of accurate and timely information. Intervention requires knowledge of how, when and where to intervene, togther with a continuous monitoring of the effectiveness of such intervention. A contribution to this is made by Taylor's account of aspects of tourism information systems.

Reference

Briassoulis, H. and van der Straaten, J. (eds) (1992) *Tourism and the Environment.* Kluwer, Dordrecht.

14

Management of Recreation and Tourist Behaviour at Different Spatial Levels

H.W.J. Boerwinkel

Centre for Recreation and Tourism Studies, Agricultural University, Generaal Foulkesweg 13, 6703 BJ Wageningen, The Netherlands

Introduction

The management of recreation and tourist behaviour as a conscious and deliberate approach of planners, designers and managers is quite a recent development. There are probably at least two sources of reasons why this new trend in social engineering has not been developed earlier. One is on the demand side of management of behaviour studies, the other on the supply side.

On the demand side a reason for putting more research energy into the management of tourist and recreation behaviour may be found in the change of cultural context in which recreation and tourist behaviour occurs. The old forms of social discipline into which people used to be socialized by custom, church and other authorities do not function as easily as they used to do in the past (Featherstone, 1991, p. 112). Individualization and an increased sophistication of individual participants in leisure tours reinforce the personal basis of decisions about what to do or not to do in specific places. Visitors to recreation and tourist destinations may feel less guests than rightful buyers of a recreational product. The host in such places is now, more than in the past, considered by the leisure consumer and tourist as just a provider of a recreational product (Forster, 1964), and not so much as a person with feelings of personal attachment to the site, an attachment that should be respected by the visitor. So there is now more reason for a search for behaviour management techniques directed at a visitor whose behaviour is attuned to external conditions rather than to internal discipline.

On the other hand, due to the same processes of individualization and modernity and also because of the massive character of certain recreation and tourist developments, local people may not be as able as they used to be to defend their habitat if it happens to be a recreation and tourist environment. Dogan (1989), citing Bisiliat (1979), states that 'Tourism … weakens mutual help and cooperation based on traditional norms, increases intergenerational conflicts, and destroys intimate, personal and friendly relations.' As a consequence there is also reason for the host community to look for techniques that reinforce its control over its environment against the leisure masses. Techniques often go beyond particularly socially orientated coping mechanisms, such as aggressive resistance, retreating to old traditions, just keeping a distance from a visitor, revitalizing traditional culture, or simply adopting the tourist lifestyle (Dogan, 1989).

Although in the light of the increased self-centredness of recreationists and tourists, and of the increased vulnerability of host communities, increased control, i.e. interventions and transformations, by management groups seems to be a most natural response, it will turn out that both increased and decreased control by management groups is appropriate.

On the supply side of behaviour management research, the research within the discipline of environmental psychology – which will be our main focus in this analysis of spatial management opportunities – was, at the start of the 1970s, and at least within the Anglo-American research tradition, more focused on obtaining insight into the basics of environmental and recreative experience than on manipulating this experience. This appears to be a logical line of reasoning: before a researcher contributes to the control of an experience or a certain type of behaviour he or she wants to be certain about what kind of experience or behaviour is to be controlled. To give some indications of the differential covering of the two subjects (insight in experiences and behaviour, and suggestions about management possibilities) it is revealing that in the largest single survey of the state of the art of environmental psychology, the *Handbook of Environmental Psychology*, which was published in 1987 (Stokols and Altman, 1987), there was scarcely one whole article devoted to the management of behaviour, while several articles focused on the experience of the environment.

Therefore, this short treatment of behaviour management principles stands in a thematic line of scientific analysis with a very short history. Although the focus of this text is, in the first place, to bring demand and supply of management behaviour relationships in recreation and tourism closer to one another, the impression may be quite different. The practical aim is worked out by a search for general, and evidently sometimes rather abstract, principles. But, as Kurt Lewin, one of the founders of both social and environmental psychology, is purported to have said: 'nothing is as practical as good theory'. The approach of this analysis is, however, necessarily an exploratory one; by analysing data from rather diverse sources a provisional set of control principles is put forward. The terms in which the elaboration is performed are, as far as possible, taken from the transformation model for tourism-recreation (TR) relationships as formulated by Dietvorst and Ashworth (Chapter 1). At relevant points suggestions for modification and augmentation of that model will be given.

The first step in the search for basic control principles in management of TR behaviour will not be directed forward, but in a sense backward. This necessary step is the presentation of a minimal model for the description of fundamental psychological transactions of – in terms of the Dietvorst and Ashworth model – a 'consumer' with a 'resource'. As will be explained below, the dynamic of a common principle, such as the effect of geographical distance to a destination on visit decision, or visit frequency, depends in part on the type of psychological transaction that is focused upon. The concept of transaction is used to indicate that a psychological relationship between a consumer and a resource is basically a two-way relationship. The subject is, on the basis of expectancy patterns, influenced by the charateristics of the resource. In terms of the transformation model of Dietvorst and Ashworth (Chapter 1) the subject is 'interpreting', or symbolically transforming, the resource. Consecutively, however, the subject also influences the resource by acting upon it, and lets further actions depend on the feedback from the outcome of previous actions as well as the autonomous dynamic within the resource. This notion runs parallel with the 'material transformation' by the subject in the transformation model. Transaction is thus not meant to imply what Altman and Rogoff (1987, p. 8) have in mind with transactionality, i.e. that it 'treats context, time, and processes as aspects of an integrated unity' in the sense that a researcher 'is not dealing with separate elements of a system', that 'persons, processes, and environments are conceived as aspects of a whole, not as independent components that combine additively to make up a whole'. Transactionality is in this view conceived as a supra-individual concept. In the following, transaction is consistently defined only from the psychological perspective of an individual consumer. The resource and the producer/manager are only introduced in a transactional analysis as far as they function in the interpretation by, and actions of, an individual consumer. The level of analysis is what goes on psychologically in an individual brain, and not what goes on in a sociospatial ecosystem. However, the outcome of the transactional analysis in the first paragraph and the elaboration of basic control principles in the following paragraphs are described according to the implications they have for a supra-individual – in a way 'eco-actional' – analysis, such as is implied in the transformation model.

After the presentation of the person–environment transaction model three bipolar principles for the management of TR behaviour will be described. The principle of 'positive versus negative distance' effects deals with, among other aspects, the contrast between regular visits to the same destination and visits that are only performed once or occasionally. The former type of visits require shorter distances between starting-point and destination, because larger distances operate negatively on the satisfaction of the behaviour. The latter requires larger distances, because larger distances contribute positively to the satisfaction of the behaviour.

The principle of 'simultaneous versus successive arrangements' of resource locations applies the contrast between the simultaneous arrangement of resource elements in a simultaneously available multiplexity of associative layers on the one hand and the arrangement of such elements in a simple, successive order on the other. The former contributes fundamentally to the contents of the leisure experience. The latter is required to channel a TR consumer to the location of that experience in a way that keeps the resource in a sustainable condition.

Finally, the principle of 'internal versus external control' considers the contrast between the need for control and the acceptance of the loss of control, both by the visitor, as the consumer, and by the manager and the host community, as the producers. As will be explained, the need for more control by the visitor is suggested by the core principle of freedom in leisure, and by the identity diffusion which is implied in the so-called post-modern condition. The acceptance by the visitor of having less control than wanted and expected is suggested by the illusive character of cognitive control attributions in Western culture today. The need for more control by the manager of resources and by host communities is a consequence of the massive character of TR visits to many locations. The acceptance by these groups of less control is the corollary of the greater need for control by the visitor for reasons of freedom and authenticity.

As a last step the three principles will be connected to the transformation model. It will turn out that each principle covers a different relationship between the 'coding' block and a further differentiated 'assembly' block (see Chapter 1, this volume).

A Four-level, Time-related, Person–Environment Transaction Model

Different subdisciplines of psychology not only focus on different sectors of the total life space of a person (such as clinical, environmental, managerial, social and child psychology, to name just a few specialities). Some subdisciplines may also be characterized by different positions on fundamental dimensions, such as time and space. As far as time is concerned a speciality like perception psychology focuses more on short-term transactions (seeing an object, establishing the identity, receiving semiotic associations from it, retrieval from memory, etc.). A perception psychologist is conceptually and technically equipped to process perceptual transactions that may last from only a split second to a couple of minutes. Closer to the other end of the time scale, the speciality of developmental psychology, however, focuses on processes that extend over a time span of weeks, months and years. Although there is no clear-cut criterion for the establishment of the correct type and number of time periods to be differentiated formally in psychological transactions, the following four time-based transaction levels appear to be both minimally required and useful.

Exploration

A consumer of a recreation and tourist object explores on the shortest time-scale level the distant or nearby resource. This resource may further be scanned and experienced, either directly or indirectly, by retrieving images of this resource from memory, or by perceiving representations of it, possibly coupled with a photograph or a sketch. As indicated before, an exploratory transaction may formally extend from a split second to a couple of minutes.

Instrumentation

A consumer may consecutively learn, on a longer-term basis, relationships between different parts of the resource, in order to get instrumental insight into how to get from one location in space of the resource to another, and to get access to them. Or the consumer may learn relationships between the resource in the present and the past by absorbing a historical story, so that, by orienteering in space and time, it may be possible to use the environment on a more permanent, or recurrent, basis. An instrumental transaction may extend from a split second (e.g. learning that one may burn one's skin with a flame at a barbecue) to a couple of years (e.g. learning to tackle communicative problems in the course of an increased acquaintance with tourist operations).

Existence

On a still longer time scale consumers may get familiar with, or be existentially rooted in, a particular resource, so that one may feel that a city, a landscape or a site which one lives in, spends holidays in and feels participatively involved with is from a personal point of view not exchangeable with other cities, landscapes or sites. Parting from such an environment for a longer time may cause a more or less strong feeling of uprooting and alienation. An existential transaction may extend from, again, a split second (e.g. having a sudden mystical feeling that turns one's life upside down, an experience that may even start a process of fundamental psychological transformation, either traumatic or therapeutic) to a whole lifetime (e.g. the feeling of personal identity that is subjectively connected to experiences from early and later childhood, and is anticipatorily projected into the years ahead and old age (Erikson, 1963)).

Basic cultural attitude

Finally, consumers' transactions with resources are also based on long-term psychocultural basic attitudes, or value systems, which generally exceed the lifetime of one person, and may, therefore, only partially be considered as a property of a psychological transaction. Because basic cultural attitudes generally exceed an individual lifetime, and are, therefore, by definition, also carried on by other people, this type of attitude may extend from a certain period in one person's lifetime (e.g. the 'happy sixties') to a couple of centuries in which this individual lifetime is embedded (e.g. the cultural phase of modernity, from the enlightenment to the middle of the 20th century, to which people who were born at the beginning of this century have been only partly witness).

Time–space interaction in psychological transactions

Positive and negative distance principles

As well as the time dimension, psychological specialities may be ordered along a space dimension. Specialities that perform studies in the laboratory, such as perception, learning, and test psychology, among others, conceive the environment more as 'molecular' (reduced to small-scale, broken-up transactions (Stokols, 1977)) and close to the person, whereas more application-orientated specialities, such as clinical, developmental, managerial, social and environmental psychology, among others, focus on particularly 'molar' (larger-scale, complex (Stokols, 1977)) environments, located at a – somewhat or much – larger distance from the person. Although apparently in the context of recreation and tourism, being an application field of psychology, the resource is most probably best conceived in a molar way, there is reason to differentiate, in this molar context, between smaller and larger space levels, because the central issue in space, i.e. distance, operates differently at different space levels, depending on specific time-based transaction levels that are involved.

In several separate pieces of research in the context of the direct experience of landscapes and nature – in the shorter-distance or micro-spatial range – Kaplan and Kaplan (1989), two environmental psychologists well known in their field, consistently found a dimension which they called 'mystery'. Mystery means that a visitor gets, in the course of exploring a resource, at one location in a natural resource area an impression that more distant locations, which are not yet observable, will be worthwhile to explore if one moves further into the area. This, generally labelled 'positive distance principle' on the exploratory transaction level, is, on the instrumental level, contradicted by the well-researched negative distance principle of decreasing visit frequency, when distance of a destination to a residential location or other recruitment area increases (for a short historical overview of the research performed on the so-called 'gravity' law in mobility, see for example, Erlander and Stewart (1990)). Frequent use of preferred resources is generally enhanced by short distances. Discussions about the effect of TR behaviour on increased mobility and the solution of that problem by promoting the establishment of recreation facilities close to neighbourhoods will, therefore, only affect the instrumental level and not the exploratory one. Recreationists and tourists will always strive to explore resources located ever further away. That is the positive distance principle operating in leisure exploration.

Studies covering much larger distances and existential types of transactions reveal on the time-based level, as on the instrumental level, a negative distance principle. In studies such as those performed by Gould and White (1968, 1974) in England and the United States, studies which have been followed by Hauer (1970) in The Netherlands, the differential effect of the contradictory distance principles on the existential and exploratory level are rather well illustrated. Responding to the survey question 'at what location in the country' young school-leavers or university students 'would prefer to live' two dimensions appeared to be responsible for the outcome. One dimension, operative at a relatively small distance from the present residential location, turned out to follow a decreasing function of preference with increasing distance. This dimension apparently concerned the existential feeling of rootedness in one's familiar environment, and fear of uprooting if one settles farther away from the present residential location (it is, of course, possible that an instrumental aspect is also involved, in so far as schools, shops, hospitals, recreation opportunities such as swimming-pools, and other facilities may be preferred to be close at hand; because distance operates negatively in both instrumental and existential transactions, the differentiation between the two was not possible from the data presented by the authors). The other dimension in the studies mentioned by Gould and White and by Hauer indicated a preference for settling in a region that is known for its attractive landscape, an evaluation that was most probably established on the basis of prior exploration, either personally, through hearsay or through the media. Of course, in situations where people already live at or close to a location of great landscape attractiveness the second dimension may be absorbed by the first one. This was, indeed, found by Gould and White. This is one reason why the difference between the two distance principles may not become apparent in every study on preference of residential location, or in other types of evaluations by consumers of resources located at different distances.

So far the first three of the four time-based transaction levels have become involved in the elaboration of the two distance principles. The fourth transaction level, basic cultural attitude, is perhaps more elusive in this respect. If one considers the fact that the definition of this level is based on concepts such as the European Enlightenment, one is tempted to attribute to this level a relatively large range of homogeneous distance effects, as seen from the consumer point of view. People living in Western countries will experience the same amalgam of basic cultural attitudes over a relatively large distance from their home area. Or, to put it otherwise, one has to travel far to experience a real change of basic cultural attitudes in the form of a 'culture shock' (of course, because of the rapid growth of ethnic minorities in Western countries, a smaller, but none the less perceptible culture shock may be experienced in the neighbourhood next door).

In Fig. 14.1 the different effects of distance on the time-based transaction levels are schematically represented. They do not represent, of course, the relationship between distance and time-based relationships for every single person. There are cosmopolitically oriented persons, such as some ecotourists, who will feel existentially at home all over the world, or whose instrumental transactions are dispersed over global distances, such as pilots, members of international firms and other organizations, TR researchers, etc. Figure 14.1 describes an average effect of distance on time-based transaction levels to be found

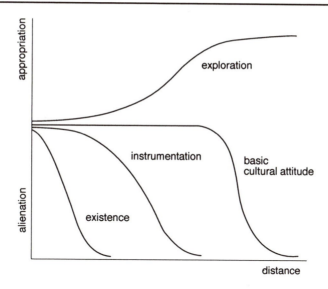

Fig. 14.1. Schematic representation of the appropriation of, and alienation from, space over a certain distance on four levels of psychological transactions.

in aggregated groups. It may be worthwhile to adapt the figure to different focus groups.

Simultaneous and successive arrangement principles

So far the resource has been conceived as an undifferentiated whole, located at a certain distance from the consumer. The resource, is however, in a complex, molar, environment, always behaviourally embedded in a relationship with other resources, or one part of a resource is connected to other parts of the same resource. For diverse reasons resource producers and managers may want to control this connection in the behaviour of a consumer. One reason may be the economic exploitation of one part by the so-called spin-off effect. Visitors to one location may become interested in a visit to an adjacent location. The mystery concept of Kaplan and Kaplan (1989) falls into this category.

Another reason for a producer/manager to want to control the relationship between parts of a resource behaviourally may rather be to counter a spin-off effect. If an attractive, and much visited, location in a natural resource area lies close to a vulnerable area that needs protection, a manager may look for measures to curb visits to that location by visitors who visit the primary attraction. Boerwinkel (1992) described possible spatial measures, such as creating a detour around the vulnerable location, a relocation of the starting-point (e.g. a parking-place) from which both parts can be approached, or presenting an alternative for the primary attraction elsewhere, inside or outside the area. In this context the routeing of visitors along marked walking trails is increasingly recognized by managers as an efficient diversion. Of course, these markings are – in the full spirit of MacCannell's (1976) sight-marking – officially intended to indicate attractive sights (vistas, special vegetation and wildlife species). But, while channelling visitors along a trail towards attractive sights, the opportunity is gratefully accepted by the manager to channel them away from ecologically vulnerable areas.

A similar approach, producing a sequence of attractive events on one location in order to protect another location, may be applied when the vulnerable system is not a subhuman ecological one, but is of a more human nature. The vulnerable system may be a local population which is unduly affected by too many visitors (Dogan, 1989). On the island of Bali, Indonesia, for example, most tourists are channelled to the south coast by Western transport, hotels, and other leisure facilities, and are kept busy by well-organized sequences of socioenvironmental events (i.e. trips to particular places where traditional rites and dances are performed), so that to a certain extent the centre and the north of the island retain their traditional peace. Without mentioning this positive spatial management objective Wood (1984) stresses the fact that in Bali this development was dictated by the central government, bypassing any real participation of the local population in the decision-making process. Both Wood (1984) and Dogan (1989) do, however, also mention some positive social outcomes of tourism in Bali: Wood indicates the opportunity for Hindu adherents to reinforce their traditional religion on the basis of the mainly Hindu-based religious rituals performed for tourists, and Dogan referred to the renewed education of the local youth in traditional crafts, such as wood-carving, dancing, and ceremonies, to prepare them for the tourism industry.

As is shown in the above examples, controlling the relationship between resource elements in time and space in a sequential order may be in the interest both of the managing producer and of interest groups other than TR consumers. The latter will, however, often be served better by less managerial control of the behavioural relationship between different parts of the resource. Leisure appears to be, psychologically, particularly connected to simultaneous presentations of resource parts rather than sequential ones.

The concepts of simultaneous and successive arrangements of information are adapted from psychophysical theories about basic brain functions. The right cerebral hemisphere is purported to function as a simultaneous processor. The identification of a complex or unfamiliar image the informational, aesthetic and associative focus upon the constructive properties and upon details are the central issue in this type of information-processing. The left hemisphere, on the other hand, is – while at birth also simultaneously orientated – during the development of the individual transformed, at least in the case of right-handed persons, into a successive information-processing system (Das *et al.*, 1975). One indication of this shift in the balance between the two processing systems is the finding (Torrance, 1975) that creativity, which is particularly connected with simultaneous processing, drops significantly in children every time they pass into the following school system. Language training is, among other aspects, an important medium for accomplishing this transformation. It appears, then, that the ability to process the resource information successively presents an advantage for cultural adaptation and survival. This conclusion, however, has to be qualified further. Taylor (1975) summed up several authors in the field of clinical psychology who stressed, in the context of 'well-being', the importance of creativity in the promotion of self-actualization and a healthy personal development. So, although creativity may not be the most central ability to pass school examinations, its adaptive functionality need not be questioned.

In the context of the spatial arrangements of resource elements the connection between simultaneous processing, creativity and leisure may be viewed as follows. The environmental conditions that foster creativity are, among other characteristics, intensive simultaneous sensory stimulation (Taylor, 1975, p. 19). Creativity is also often defined as the ability to come up with rather divergent associations (Taylor, 1975, pp. 9–11). This stimulation has also to be absorbed in a social climate that is relatively free from social pressure (Taylor, 1975, p. 19). Freedom is, further, precisely the condition that is considered as one of the core aspects of leisure (Neulinger, 1978). Leisure behaviour has, so to speak, more than other types of behaviour, a special relationship with free exploration of simultaneously ordered resources, rather than successively ordered ones.

The conclusion is that the opportunity to process simultaneously ordered TR resources by the consumer has to be a central aim for the managing producer, and must be measured against the manager's own urge to control TR behaviour by way of successive arrangements. The best way to handle this problem in practical situations is to look for opportunities to combine the two principles. The following are examples of possible combinations in two different types of TR resources, a city park and a museum.

The still very popular 19th-century city parks that were designed on the basis of the so-called English (romantic) landscape style (Fig. 14.2) may be considered as a clever combination of the two types of

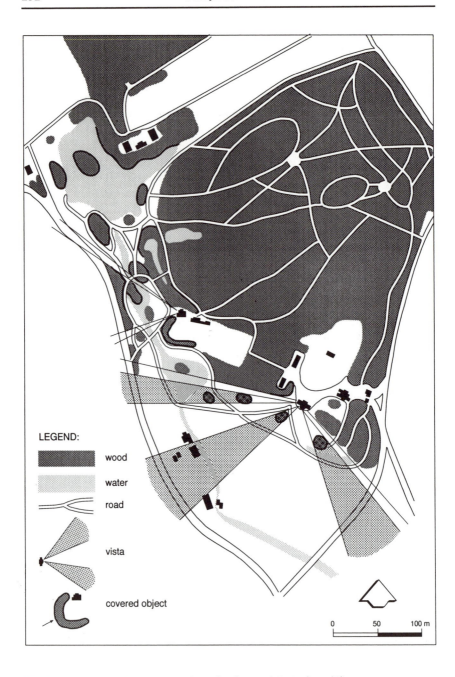

Fig. 14.2. Layout and main vistas of Sonsbeek, a park in Arnhem (The Netherlands) created in the 19th century, designed in English landscape style (after Vakgroep Landschapsarchitectuur, 1979).

order. This style is recognized (Hunt and Willis, 1975) by its open and playful use of water (ponds, brooks, waterfalls), winding paths along the borders of these elements, artificial constructions like bridges over the water and fountains in the water, grottoes (shallow but cosy, sometimes located under a waterfall), statues, follies (functionally not very useful buildings such as miniature temples, but for this reason rather intriguing), belvederes, hunting lodges, and tea pavilions. Centrally but not too conspicuously located in the area is the main residence of the former private owner. Finally, a core issue in the concept of this design style is the introduction of smaller and larger groups and lanes of trees and shrubs, positioned in such a way that both from outside the park, and from inside during a stroll in the park, the central building, the water, and the artefacts are at one moment suddenly displayed along a viewing axis, and subsequently hidden from view. The viewing axis is sometimes singular or bipolar (one can look only in one of two directions), but in many cases it is a multiple axis, so that one may choose from several directions which artefacts one wants to look at, and – because of frequent crossing of paths – also in what direction one wants to walk. Moving forward, the following moment the view of the same objects is again covered by greenery, to be uncovered again at a further location, but from a different angle and distance, when passing through another viewing axis.

The connection with the simultaneous–successive order principles can be clarified as follows. The system of stepwise covering and uncovering of sights is an example of successive environmental 'storytelling', while the application of multiple viewing axes at crossings with multiple artefacts, and multiple viewing angles and distances toward them, is an equally clever application of the simultaneous arrangement.

Comparing the liberal connotations of the English landscape style with, for example, the autocratic formality of the French gardens (Hunt and Willis, 1975, p. 7) shows a lower simultaneous complexity in the latter and a higher successive rigidity, because at any point in the garden the view of the main building had to be sustained. This gives way to a fixed main axis toward the building and smaller side alleys, combined in a strongly fixed geometrical design. The simultaneous order is, in this case, very much dominated by the successive order. As a matter of fact there is scarcely an articulated order of autonomous subspaces in this respect, because there is at any location in the garden often just one viewpoint and only one target: the main building with its many decorations, viewed over a flat garden that has also the status of decorating the main building. These decorations are just meant to mark the main building. They have no meaning on their own. Such a garden inspires more awe and respect – or resentment and jealousy –

toward the owner, through the strict hierarchy of space, than enjoyment of free associations by the visitor, through the multiplicity of spaces and objects.

The case of the museum arrangements is comparable with the case of park design. A museum consists mostly of adjoining rooms that give onto each other through a route that is indicated by the manager, often by signs (compare the marked walking trails in nature areas). This successive order is often reinforced further by ordering objects according to historical phases. So the successive order is established in the first place by the architecture, and further reinforced by management aims. This is useful for creating some sort of 'story' in which different objects may be embedded, and through which a certain climax can be established. However, at specific locations, the experiences are also triggered by a rather undifferentiated, simultaneously ordered, complex. The combination of successive and simultaneous arrangements may be illustrated with the example of the well-known *Night Watch* by Rembrandt in the Rijksmuseum in Amsterdam. The route through different rooms, and the viewing axis at the entrance of the special room for this painting, are controlled successively. However, by presenting opportunities for quietly sitting and looking at this main attraction, visitors are allowed to let their eyes wander over details of the *Night Watch*, but also toward neighbouring objects, which may not be as 'marked' in MacCannell's (1976) sense, but are still worth looking at (compare the multiple viewing axes toward multiple artefacts in the park). The museum manager creates in this situation a local simultaneous order that may give way to free associations, to experience the essential freedom of leisure. The differentiation by Melton (1972) of (attention-) 'drawing power' of museum objects and the ensuing 'holding power' (in this case to protect the primary object from distraction by surrounding objects) is closely related to the difference between the principles of the two types of order. From the above discussion, however, the conclusion may be drawn that the holding power would probably better be labelled and reinterpreted as 'radiation power'. From a leisure point of view the power of locations, however they may be wrapped up in a spatially and thematically successive 'story', allowing the exploratory focus of the consumer to radiate towards a complex, associatively rich, organized environment, must be considered an equally important part of the 'order compound' as the story itself. Or, to state it otherwise, part of the story the manager wants to present is the story that must be filled in by the consumer.

This rather post-modern approach to environmental storytelling brings us to another important principle in the management of TR behaviour. So far, the elaboration of two 'distance principles' and two 'arrangements principles' has occasionally brought up the question of the control intention of the managing producer, and its effects on the consumer. The distribution of control between a consumer and his social environment, including a managing producer, appears to present another important pair of basic control principles in TR behaviour management, namely the principles of internal versus external control.

Internal and external control principles

Rotter (1966), who introduced the concept of internal versus external control, defined internality as the extent to which a person feels that life conditions are predominantly dependent on one's own initiative and abilities, whereas externality was defined as the extent to which a person feels that external conditions, such as fate, other people in power in school and work situations, and society as it is organized, largely control one's personal life conditions. Immediately after introduction by Rotter the literature on this concept grew prolifically (Lefcourt, 1976). Unlike the two other pairs of principles this pair is well recognized in the field of psychology. There have also been some applications in the field of leisure. Kleiber (1979), for example, found that a leisure orientation was correlated with an external control experience. He interpreted this finding as indicating a rejection of the 'traditional work-oriented culture'. This interpretation is remarkable in so far as it does not implicate a feeling of deficit, as Rotter attributed to externality. In Rotter's view internality was the indication of a better adaptation to life. Rejection of a traditional work-oriented basic cultural attitude does not, however, in any way by itself imply a deficit. On the contrary, such a rejection, as a rejection of the rat-race, may, for some people, be considered as more healthy and more adaptive to their personal situation. Rothbaum *et al.* (1982) also came to the conclusion that for some people in specific situations persistent strivings for internality would not be the most adaptive option. For example, people confronted with a sudden personal accident, from which a permanent handicap resulted, would, after an initial feeling of external control as a consequence of the new situation, in a really adaptive process develop a more healthy feeling of 'secondary control'; on a lower level of ability one learns new types of internal control. Stress psychologists find also that the sheer predictability of the appearance of stressors may be as important in reducing the stress experience as the factual possibility of eliminating the stressor (Baron *et al.*, 1980, p. 707). The knowledge that one does not have real control is in itself a form of control. It may be concluded then that the principle of control in TR situations must be looked at in an equally balanced way as was the case in the two other pairs of behaviour control principles. Illustrations of such a balanced approach will now be given for all four time-based transaction levels.

On the exploratory level in the previous discussion a certain contrast has already emerged between the aim of providing some sort of a successively ordered 'story' by the managing producer and giving the opportunity to let a consumer freely ramble in a complex, simultaneously ordered, environment. With the increasing interest in historical aspects of TR environments greater stress is put upon the presentation of a story that is 'expertly' told. This means that external control by the storyteller should be at a maximum. However, because of the post-modern differentiation into rather diverse focus groups, and even into individualization beyond the focus group, the story that is told should be not a singular but a multiple one. A really expertly managed exploratory TR resource is, therefore, set up as a complex amalgam of several stories with fixed endings and with open endings, attuned to different focus groups and individuals. Post-modernism, is, in art and architecture, already associated with the eclectic presentation of several layers of meaning (Jencks, 1987, p. 22) that can be explored by a TR consumer.

On the instrumental level the balance of control is also a delicate one. Csikzentmihalyi (1975) introduced the concept of 'flow', indicating the feeling of smooth control in leisure activities, such as mountain climbing and other sports with a high level of difficulty. This suggests a high level of internal control by the recreationist. However, Goffman (1963) described in one of his perceptive analyses the dynamics of 'role distance'. A surgeon who has performed a difficult operation time and again may, out of sheer boredom, try another approach to the operation, and so create unwarranted risks for his patient. Similarly, a ticketman in an operating merry-go-round may show off his ability to keep his balance by swinging smoothly through the horses without using his hands as support. The risk is also in this case for others, namely children who may try to imitate this show.

Similarly, an expert mountaineer, particularly when preoccupied with leisure, may slip away from his usual cautiousness and so create unacceptable risks. Again, in this case, others, such as rescuers, may become involved in this role-distance hazard. It is, therefore, understandable that in TR situations, where a consumer may be inclined to go beyond his ability in order to enlarge his enjoyment of the experience, as in risk sports, externally imposed safety regulations are becoming ever more strict (e.g. see the triple Dutch slogan of 'nature-orientated, environment-friendly, and safe' as the recent hallmark for open-air sports (Daalder, 1991)). The balance between internal and external control in TR resource management of instrumental behavioural transactions is, again, a subtle one.

On the existential level the control theme has already been implicitly indicated. Local populations who may suffer from too many leisure visitors should reinstall their internal control over their neighbourhood. Just as in the case of institutions and student dormitories, where dominance may reinforce territorial claims (Brown, 1987), it appears reasonable to expect tourists to be impressed by a self-assured host community.

However, considering the literature on the environmental psychology of criminal behaviour, it is also evident that the architecture of buildings and other aspects of the spatial layout that may block viewing axes on sensitive spots in the neighbourhood may externally control the conditions for 'defensible space' (Newman, 1972). The case of Pruitt Igoe (Yancey, 1971) demonstrates how the existential space that is necessary for creating a sense of personal and communal (internally controlled) well-being may become so expelled from the direct home environment, and compressed into the internal space of apartments, that the only solution that is left lies in the external decision of the city council to literally dynamite the whole neighbourhood.

In order to avoid such developments, host communities may be stimulated to regain control over their resources by letting outsiders help them to create spatial environmental plans so that they may be able in the future to internally control that environment. This type of environmental spatial planning should not, on the other hand, lead to such an intensity of control that the host community produces a tourist 'cage', that can make a visitor feel too externally controlled and may consequently deter the tourist from further visits. Probably those visitors who are particularly sensitive to 'authenticity' (MacCannell, 1973) may be most vulnerable to this overexertion of external control by the host community. Again, the balance between internal and external control in TR behaviour management appears to be a sensitive one.

Finally, the basic cultural attitude appears also to be vulnerable to an imbalance of the two control types. The so-called post-modern condition is evidently on the one hand considered as a liberation from the too fixed external control of monofunctional modernism (Featherstone, 1991, p. 3). Post-modernism, as a basic cultural attitude in producers (i.e. planners, architects, artists, etc.), is also, being strongly connected to consumer culture (Featherstone, 1991), purported to create an increased individual control over public life. On the other hand post-modernism as a basic cultural attitude in producers and consumers also presents a new uncertainty. Toffler (1980) labelled the uncertainty of what he called the 'third-wave' personality as one of representing a 'configurational identity' (the third wave is Toffler's concept of a new historical phase that comes after the 'second wave', which is his name for the industrial phase in Western culture). People do not identify, for example, in the third-wave condition, either with male or with female role models, but create a personal mixture of both by taking from each model some aspects at will. Although Toffler considers what he subsumes under the heading of third-wave dynamics generally as positive adaptations, it is not clear whether, from an identity point of view, the term 'configurational' indicates an unequivocally positive, or sometimes negative, kind of psychological adaptation.

A similar paradox in terms of control – one may speak of an illusion of control – is rather well illustrated by what Morgenthau and Person (1978) diagnosed as the root of cultural narcissism. They stated that, while individualization suggests the rise of autonomy of the individual in a way unprecedented since the Middle Ages, the citizen today is in an equally unprecedented way dependent on society for food, shelter, safety, energy, transportation, etc. Narcissism is, according to the authors, the reaction of turning away from the uncontrollable distant world and concentrating on a still controllable proximate environment, one's own private space (Fig. 14.3). It is remarkable in this respect that one of Toffler's other examples of a new third-wave identity, the 'prosumer', concerns particularly leisure activities. The prosumer combines the role of producer and consumer, roles that were separated in the previous ('modern') 'second-wave' phase. The prosumer produces, just as in former times, the products (food, do-it-yourself furniture, etc.) that he or she is also consuming.

The function of nature in present society, as far as TR behaviour is concerned, may be interpreted in a similar, and even more paradoxical, way. The high public valuation of nature's relatively untouched status is partly interpreted by the need of modern cultural man to flee from everyday life (Knopf, 1987, pp. 786–789). This status of nature as a last free haven is based on symbolic attributes, such as 'basic vitality of life', 'capacity for growth and change', 'stability', 'timelessness', 'universality', 'imperviousness to man', 'innocent purity', 'mystery and spirituality', 'defying scientific analysis', etc. This set of attributes of nature may be summarized by a view of nature as being really autonomous and internally controlled. Considering the previous analysis of management intentions in controlling visitor behaviour in natural areas, the urban narcissist fugitive, whose narcissism is the result of an illusion within culture in the first place, is, again, illusively misled in nature areas, due to the increasingly successively ordered sociospatial network. The perception of nature as an autonomous free haven for cultural man is, therefore, in a sense, just as illusory as the notion of the individual autonomy of man in the present age of unprecedented dependence on society.

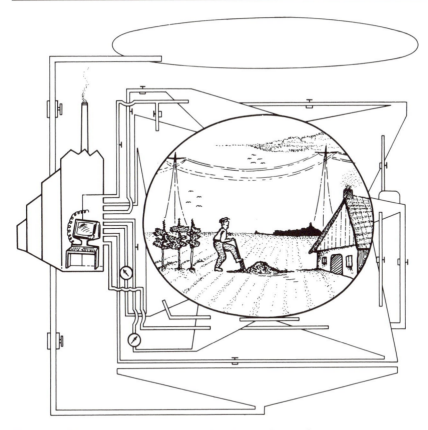

Fig. 14.3. The illusory condition of internal and external control.

The conclusion regarding the balance of the principles of the management of behaviour, particularly from the point of view of basic cultural attitudes, has to be that on this level the balance is a particularly sensitive one. The search for basic principle of the management of behaviour, being control principles with general political implications, has to be itself controlled by culture. However, the paired combination of opposites, as presented in the three pairs of principles, positive and negative distance, simultaneous and successive order arrangements and internal and external control, may, hopefully, on the one hand reinforce the notion of urgently rebalancing control if an imbalance is diagnosed, and at the same time provide tools for restoring that balance in a practical way.

Because at least some adherents of post-modernism do not want to unduly fix its identity (Jencks, 1987, p. 12), this specific form of basic cultural attitude may, in its most positive intention, foster a rather sympathetic sort of configurational self in present-day philosophers, architects, artists and TR managers. It then comes close to what Boerwinkel (1986) has analysed as being the most progressive, the most psycho-logical, basic cultural attitude, namely 'biocentrism'. This basic cultural attitude does not want to regress to a traditional authoritarian ('nomocentric') reconstruction of society, a 'traditional classicism' in basic value systems. Neither does it want to reinforce expert ('techno-centric') solutions for basic social problems. Biocentrism puts life in its multiple forms, human and non-human, in the centre, seeking a profound balance between life in one's own person (self-interest), in other people and in nature by means of achieving consensus between interest groups.

Conclusion and Discussion

Three principles of bipolar behaviour-management measures on different levels of spatial planning of recreation and tourist transactions have been described so far. Although they appear to be basic ones, there is no indication that they are exhaustive. Nevertheless, it appears also that just these three principles have a relationship with three fundamental positions in the transformation model of Dietvorst and Ashworth, presented in Chapter 1 (Fig. 14.4).

The principle of positive or negative distance is perhaps the most basic principle operating in the relationship between the interpreting consumer and the assembled resource, approached from the consumer point of view (Fig. 14.4, relationship 1).

The principle of simultaneous or successive arrangement is probably equally singularly basic in the relationship between the interpreting consumer and different objects within the assembled resource. In the version of the TR model in Fig. 14.4 these objects are represented by a minimum of two separate blocks within the assemblage block, connected by a line (relationship 2) which is traced back to the consumer.

The principle of internal versus external control is, again, very basic in the relationship between a consumer and a producer (Fig. 14.4, relationship 3), when the focus is on controlling direct relationships both between the consumer and the assembled resource and between the consumer and the structural connections between different objects within the assembled resource.

There appear to be no positions left, at least in the TR model, for which basic control principles, from the consumer point of view, should be sought further. So if the three principles are indeed as basic

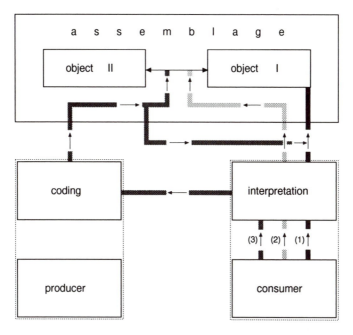

Fig. 14.4. The position of three basic principles of management of tourist and recreation behaviour in the transformation model, as put forward in Chapter 1.

to each of the positions in the TR system as is supposed, they may after all be considered as a fairly complete set. The test for this supposition is, of course, to be sought in a confrontation of this set with rather diverse concepts that are operative in the assembly process. In the previous analysis of the three principles some of these concepts have already been introduced (e.g. marker–sign relationship, drawing/ holding power of attractions, the park design principles of covering and uncovering of objects along viewing axes in parks). A further test of the supposed basic status of the three principles may, in due course, indicate necessary additions.

References

Altman, I. and Rogoff, B. (1987) World views in psychology: trait, interactional, organismic, and transactional perspectives. In: Stokols, D. and Altman, I. (eds) *Handbook of Environmental Psychology,* vol. I. Wiley, New York, pp. 7–40.

Baron, R.A., Byrne, D. and Kantowitz, B.H. (1980) *Psychology: Understanding Behavior*. Saunders, Philadelphia.

Bisiliat, J. (1979) Problèmes posée par l'expansion du tourisme dans les pays en voie de développement. *Peuples Méditerranéens* 7, 59–67.

Boerwinkel, H.W.J. (1986) *Cultuur, Psychologie, Omgevingsvormgeving en Zelfoverstijging*. Landbouwhogeschool, Wageningen.

Boerwinkel, H.W.J. (1992) Influencing zone visits in forests by design: a case of the small valley of Meijendel. In: Hummel, J. and Parren, M. (eds) *Forests: A Growing Concern*. Proceedings of the XIXth International Forestry Students Symposium, Wageningen, The Netherlands, 30 Sept.–7 Oct. IUCN, Gland (Switzerland)/Cambridge (UK), pp. 144–154.

Brown, B.B. (1987) Territoriality. In: Stokols, D. and Altman, I. (eds) *Handbook of Environmental Psychology*, vol. 1. Wiley, New York, pp. 505–532.

Csikzentmihalyi, M. (1975) *Beyond Boredom and Anxiety: The Experience of Play in Work and Games*. Jossey-Bass, San Francisco.

Daalder, R. (1991) Een keurmerk voor buitensport-touroperators. *Recreatie en Toerisme* 1(10), 27–28.

Das, J.P., Kirby, J. and Jarman, R.F. (1975) Simultaneous and successive synthesis: an alternative model in cognitive abilities. *Psychological Bulletin* 82(1), 87–103.

Dogan, H.Z. (1989) Forms of adjustment. Sociocultural impacts of tourism. *Annals of Tourism Research* 16, 216–236.

Erikson, E.H. (1963) *Childhood and Society*. Norton, New York.

Erlander, S. and Stewart, N.F. (1990) *The Gravity Model in Transportation Analysis: Theory and Extensions*. VSP, Utrecht.

Featherstone, M. (1991) *Consumer Culture and Postmodernism*. Sage, London.

Forster, J. (1964) The sociological consequences of tourism. *International Journal of Comparative Sociology* 5, 217–227.

Goffman, E. (1963) *Encounters: Two Studies in the Sociology of Interaction*. Bobbs-Merrill, Indianapolis.

Gould, P.R. and White, R.R. (1968) The mental maps of British school leavers. *Regional Studies* 2, 161–182.

Gould, P.R. and White, R.R. (1974) *Mental Maps*. Penguin Books, Harmondsworth, Middx.

Hauer, J. (1970) 'Mental maps': een onderzoek naar de woonvoorkeur van een aantal geografiestudenten. *Bulletin van de Afdeling Algemene Sociale Geografie en Sociale Geografie van Europa van het Geografisch Instituut der Rijksuniversiteit Utrecht* 8, 155–165.

Hunt, J.D. and Willis, P. (1975) *The Genius of the Place: the English Landscape Garden*. Elek, London.

Jencks, C. (1987) *Post-Modernism: The New Classicism in Art and Architecture*. Academy Editions, London.

Kaplan, R. and Kaplan, S. (1989) *The Experience of Nature*. Cambridge University Press, New York.

Kleiber, D.A. (1979) Fate, control and leisure attitudes. *Leisure Sciences* 2(3/4), 240–248.

Knopf, R.C. (1987) Human behavior, cognition, and affect in the natural environment. In: Stokols, D. and Altman, I. (eds) *Handbook of Environmental*

Psychology, vol. I. Wiley, New York, pp. 783–825.

Lefcourt, H.M. (1976) *Locus of Control: Current Trends in Theory and Research.* Erlbaum, Hillsdale.

MacCannell, D. (1973) Staged authenticity: arrangements of social space in tourist settings. *American Journal of Sociology* 79(3), 589–603.

MacCannell, D. (1976) *The Tourist: A New Theory of the Leisure Class.* Macmillan, London.

Melton, A.W. (1972) Visitor behavior in museums: some early research in environmental design. *Human Factors* 14(5), 393–403.

Morgenthau, H. and Person, E. (1978) The roots of narcissism. *Partisan Review* 45, 337–347.

Neulinger, J. (1978) *The Psychology of Leisure. Research Approaches to the Study of Leisure.* Charles C. Thomas, Springfield.

Newman, O. (1972) *Defensible Space.* Macmillan, New York.

Rothbaum, F., Weisz, J.R. and Snyder, S.S. (1982) Changing the world and changing the self: a two-process model for perceived control. *Journal of Personality and Social Psychology* 42(1), 5–37.

Rotter, J.B. (1966) Generalized expectances for internal versus external control of reinforcement. *Psychological Monographs* 80(1)/Whole No. 609.

Stokols, D. (ed.) (1977) *Perspectives on Environment and Behavior: Theory, Research, and Applications.* Plenum, New York.

Stokols, D. and Altman, I. (eds) (1987) *Handbook of Environmental Psychology*, 2 vols. Wiley, New York.

Taylor, I.A. (1975) A retrospective view of creativity investigation. In: Taylor, I.A. and Getzels, J.W. (eds) *Perspectives in Creativity.* Aldine, Chicago.

Toffler, A. (1980) *The Third Wave.* Bantam Books, New York.

Torrance, E.P. (1975) Creativity research in education. In: Taylor, I.A. and Getzels, J.W. (eds) *Perspectives in Creativity.* Aldine, Chicago.

Vakgroep Landschapsarchitectuur (1979) *Rapport over de Parken Sonsbeek, Zijpendaal en Gulden Bodem in Arnhem. Beschrijving, Waardering, Mogelijke Veranderingen.* Landbouwhogeschool, Vakgroep Landschapsarchitectuur, Wageningen.

Wood, R.E. (1984) Ethnic tourism, the state, and cultural change in Southeast Asia. *Annals of Tourism Research* 11(3), 353–374.

Yancey, W.L. (1971) Architecture, interaction, and social control: the case of a large-scale public housing project. *Environment and Behavior* 3(1), 3–18.

15

Managing the Cultural Tourist

G.J. Ashworth

Faculty of Spatial Sciences, State University, PO Box 800, 9700 AV Groningen, The Netherlands

Culture, Tourism and Places

There is a growing interest in the potential relationships between 'culture tourism' and economic development which is being manifested in government reports and academic commentaries (see for example the collection of essays in Konsola, 1993a). This is explicable quite simply because it is increasingly being perceived as furthering the interests of the three main parties involved. The tourism industry, continuously in search of diversified holiday experiences for a market that is growing in sophistication and selectivity, is aware that cultural diversity offers a wide range of potential tourism products. Secondly, city governments and other place-management authorities are increasingly conscious that they possess a usable existing resource that can be activated for commercial purposes with what appears to be potential 'windfall' economic benefits to the local economy. Thirdly, organizations engaged in the production of cultural performances, the maintenance of the stock of cultural artefacts and buildings and even the shaping and sustaining of local cultural distinctiveness are understandably being attracted to a possible available source of much-needed extra finance, especially when sources of public subsidy are becoming less certain. Thus the tourism industry, the local authorities and the cultural managers have strong motives to form a coalition of local interests that can appear to further the aims, or at least to solve the short-term problems, of all three.

Such an argument based upon the evident self-interest of the participants should be supported at this point by statistics demonstrating the growing importance of cultural tourism in general, its growing economic significance to places, especially cities, and even the growing contributions of visitors to the financial maintenance of cultural collections and performances. Unfortunately such statistics are not available and in practice the best that can be done is to infer conclusions from data sets constructed for different purposes on different criteria or to base generalizations upon a few, often randomly available, indicators. It is easy to demonstrate that 'short-break' tourism has been for some years a particularly buoyant sector of the industry (see Chapter 13), that the numbers of tourists choosing to visit cities for all or part of their trip has risen steadily (see the general visitor statistics for various cities in Costa and van der Borg, 1993) and that the number of visitors to many, but not all, cultural facilities and artistic performances has grown dramatically since the 1960s in most Western countries (see the Dutch statistics in Ministerie WVC (1992), for visitors to cultural institutions). From these not unfamiliar generalizations it is a short step to conclude that urban cultural tourism, especially to those cities of Europe which promote themselves as art, heritage and festival centres, is a sector of increasing importance within tourism and to local economies. Conversely there is some evidence that cultural tourism is as yet weakly developed in rural areas (Ministerie voor Economische Zaken, 1991).

However, some caution needs to be exercised before such a conclusion is used as the basis of local development policy. Cultural tourism exists within two contexts that are themselves growing rapidly. Travel for whatever motive shows an almost continuous annual growth, and travel to cities is motivated by a wide variety of urban functions and attractions, of which culture is only a part (Fig. 15.1). Florence may have accommodated 4.2 million visitor-nights and Salzburg 1.9 million in 1991, but then cities with far fewer cultural pretensions, such as Hamburg (4.1 million visitor-nights), Lyon (2.9 million) or Zurich (2.0 million), are also beneficiaries of the general growth in travel. (See Fig. 15.1 for statistics for a selection of major cities.) Secondly, very broad but fundamental changes in the nature of society and thus of consumer behaviour have powered the commodification of cultural products for, if not mass consumption, at least consumption by markets far larger and more varied than the small cultural élites of a generation earlier (Konsola, 1993b). Tourists consuming culture (in the form of historical architecture or artefact collections, podium performances, folk traditions and craft souvenirs) may be merely continuing their everyday activities and their consumption behaviour may be in many respects indistinguishable from that of residents. In so far as this is the case, urban cultural tourism has less distinctive meaning than might have been imagined, which accounts in part, no doubt, for the difficulty of isolating it statistically.

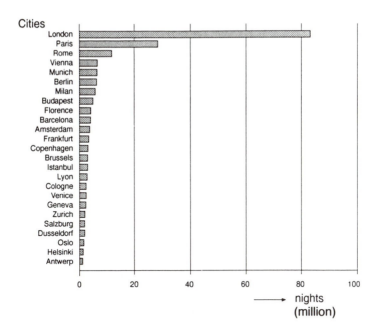

Fig. 15.1. Visitor-nights in European cities.

A long-standing and fundamental difficulty in tourism studies has been to identify segments of the tourism market. The core of the difficulty is that tourism can be segmented in a variety of different ways by different participants in the process and these classifications overlap. Relevant to the argument here are at least three different types of segmentation resulting in aspects of what is bundled together as cultural tourism. There are 'producer segmentations' (i.e. the packages of attractions and supporting services that are constructed by tourism intermediaries which can be sold as similar, interchangeable products). These are the familiar art, history or folklore packages on offer in the travel agents. There are also, however, 'consumer packages' (i.e. those activities and services actually assembled by tourists which comprise their holiday experience). These are likely to be far more varied and may include a greater or lesser element of cultural consumption within the combination. Thirdly, there are 'place-bound packages' (i.e. the functionally associated and spatially clustered selection of attractions and facilities that comprises the place product). In these packages services used by tourists may also be used by residents and tourists may comprise only a marginal addition to the total users of many cultural facilities.

We now arrive therefore at a paradox. On the one hand there is an increasing realization that the development of a diversified tourism product line, the economic well-being of places and the maintenance of local cultures, can all be related in joint policies profitable to all three groups of actors, while on the other it is all the more surprising that very little is known about these relationships in quantitative terms. In addition and more fundamentally, the idea that there exists an automatic and universal harmonious symbiosis between all three parties is assumed rather than explained, let alone seriously questioned. The relationships between each of the three apices of the triangle, tourism, culture and places, pose more questions than can currently be answered with confidence. Why and, especially relevant here, how do tourists make use of culture? What are the implications for culture of its additional use as a tourism resource? What roles does culture play in places in general and more particularly what are the impacts, economic and otherwise, on places of the use of local cultures by tourists? The management of the cultural tourist depends upon answers to these questions.

It is clear from the arguments above that if we are to manage the cultural tourist at the destination in a way that satisfies the goals of each of the three interests involved, namely the tourism industry, the culture-resource providers and the managers of the localities where such tourism occurs, then we need an understanding of some of the relationships. In particular the slippery question of what culture is, which has so far been scrupulously avoided, must be answered at least in the limited terms relevant here, namely which aspects of culture are consumed by tourists. Secondly, the various elements that comprise the cultural tourism experience need closer examination. Thirdly, the urban policy dimension must be reintroduced and cultural tourism linked to urban development strategy and management.

What Culture? Whose Culture?

One of the most fundamental difficulties in finding answers to the many questions posed above lies in the definition of culture itself but it would be unwise, as well as unnecessary, to enter here into the lengthy debate on the many different roles that the many different definitions of culture play in our society and economy (for a summary of aspects of this debate, see Beckermans, 1993). Relevant here, however, is the simple outcome of this discussion, namely that culture is capable of bearing a variety of quite different meanings, a number of which can be related to tourism. Of these, three need considering here, in an order from the more specific to the general.

Art tourism

One limited definition of culture is aesthetic productivity and certainly in popular usage culture is frequently equated with art and specifically quality artistic products and performances. This is, in many practical ways, the simplest form of culture to be commodified for tourism (that is, it can be treated as if it were a tradable commercial product on offer to customers in competition within priced markets with other products). Theatre, ballet, concert and opera performances can be sold directly in the same way as any other commercial personal entertainment service. Galleries and museums can act as major tourism attractions. Art becomes just one element in a broader package of tourism services to be assembled by the various tourism intermediaries or by the final consumer. It may be just an additional entertainment component (such as a theatre visit) while on holiday or travelling for business reasons or little more than a contributor to an artistic atmosphere as a background for other activities. Conversely art may be a primary motive for the visit as one type of 'special-interest' tourism (i.e. the pursuit while on holiday of an already existing interest or hobby). Arts festivals are a way of extending and intensifying the art component in the package by creating, at least for a limited time, a certain critical mass of performances and events which individually may not attract tourists but together may do so and which in addition create an atmosphere of a city *en fête* which can be enjoyed quite apart from the performances themselves. (The Festival d'Avignon in France is an excellent example of this phenomenon.) There is an enormous and growing variety of such festivals, many of which combine the more traditional arts with a wider range of 'ethnic' performances, spectacles and products. They not only serve for the entertainment of visitors but also support the civic consciousness and ethnic or place identities of residents. There is in practice a certain contradiction between these markets in that tourists may value the distinctively local elements as guaranteeing a genuine rather than contrived event (Newby, 1994) while their presence in any numbers threatens precisely that genuineness. Perhaps it is fortunate, and serves also as an antidote to an overenthusiastic embracing of arts festivals as an instrument of tourism policy, that in reality only a minority of arts festivals actually attract tourists at all.

However, at the other extreme the oldest, largest and most renowned arts festivals, such as Bayreuth, Salzburg or Edinburgh (see Chapter 13) are the primary attraction for large numbers of foreign, and even intercontinental, tourists and make major contributions to their particular urban economies. The link with cities is often most explicitly made with the designation of 'art city' (Costa and van der Borg, 1993) being conferred on, or adopted by, cities such as those in Tuscany or Flanders. The Council of Europe's annual designation of 'European city of culture' is a highly sought accolade, used in practice not so much as a recognition of a city's existing premier position in culture tourism but rather as a stimulus to cities such as Barcelona, Glasgow or Antwerp to develop their potential in this regard.

Heritage tourism

A wider definition of culture extends it to cover historicity transformed into heritage (Ashworth, 1991). In tourism terms this is most usually manifested in a mix of preserved buildings, conserved cityscapes and morphological patterns, as well as place associations with historical events and personalities. It may be extended to include past and even contemporary cultural products and performances defined as the cultural heritage. Thus art can be subsumed into heritage but heritage includes more than is generally considered to be art. These together are the resources that are used to create the tourist-historic city (Ashworth and Tunbridge, 1990) which is both a spatially clustered set of specific heritage tourism sites and facilities and also a more holistic idea of the heritage city as a place where tourism activities (both heritage-related and non-heritage-related) occur.

Place-specific tourism

At an even wider level of generalization, culture can be defined as the common set of values, attitudes and thus behaviour of a social group. This broad idea is at the heart of much place-specific tourism, where the tourism attraction is the total sense of place (an atmosphere, whether defined in terms of public behaviour, gastronomy and folklore, or just a place-bound exoticism) generated by the overall local culture of a Paris, a London or a Bangkok. Of course all tourism occurs somewhere and all places are to some extent unique, but only place-specific tourism uses the uniqueness of a place, rather than its more general qualities as the essential and distinctive place product saleable to tourists. Culture in all three senses described here is a major component of this distinctive identity.

This accords well with an increasingly important characteristic of tourism that Urry (1994) calls 'cosmopolitanism'. Here the tourist adopts 'an intellectual and aesthetic stance of openness towards divergent experiences from different national cultures'. This stance has consequences for the tourism product, favouring cultures that can project an easily appreciated visible distinctiveness, if not exoticism. It also makes demands upon the tourist, who, according to Urry, should possess a formidable list of attributes and skills including curiosity, risk-taking, aesthetic judgement, geographical knowledge and semiotic decoding abilities.

Cultural Tourism

Tourists therefore make use of cultures variously defined. Before these different cultural tourisms can be managed, the nature of these uses must be understood, even though any set of generalizations must be hedged about with variations and exceptions, as is clear from the above brief typology.

The nature of the culture resource

The resources used in the production of the cultural tourism products have four characteristics especially relevant here.

The first and most obvious of these in any superficial survey is variety: an enormous heterogeneity of cultural goods and services are on offer to tourists, or are consumed by tourists whether intended for them or not. An inventory of such resources would inevitably be incomplete. The occasional attempts to list at least the most patronized facilities (see for example such inventories in Vetter, 1985) ignore the many smaller and more specialized attractions but also, more seriously, overlook many more ubiquitous facilities that nevertheless are seen by the tourist as an important part of the cultural experience (the pavement café in Paris, the bazaar in Istanbul, the floating market in Bangkok and the like).

Secondly, the nature of culture renders it a ubiquitous resource. Although some places can quite obviously be associated with particularly renowned performances, more widely known historical events and personalities or galleries and museums better patronized than others, all places have a past, whether currently recorded in history or not, and all peoples a culture, whether currently presented as distinctive or not. A ubiquitous resource endows everywhere with the possibility of competing in the production of cultural products for a tourism market, and this very universal possibility intensifies the competition within that market. As the opportunity for entry increases so the chance of success for any one place narrows.

Thirdly, cultural goods and services have a wide variety of types of users other than tourists and serve a wide variety of functions other than tourism. In particular they have critically important tasks of socialization and political legitimation (Abercrombie *et al.,* 1980). The identity of a place, at scales from the local neighbourhood to the international, is strongly dependent upon its distinctive historical heritage and its characteristic vernacular culture, which is expected to convey the value and norms of that society. The relevance of mentioning this wide and well-researched field here is to stress that tourism is only one among many uses of the same cultural resources. There are many practical implications of this use by tourism of resources that were created for, and still dominantly serve other uses.

Two specific controversial cases of somewhat extreme policy options may illustrate the wider and more universal dilemmas. Egyptian tourism, for example, is highly dependent upon the Pharaonic heritage symbolized by the Giza pyramids and the Sphinx, a *sine qua non* for most visitors. This resource was accessible without charge until recently but the logic of the tourist contributing to the maintenance of the facilities used is now evident in entry fees. These in turn potentially exclude the local residents for whom the area had been a popular excursion site. The result is differential pricing of the same resource based upon nationality or, in practice, language and appearance. More generally the physical limits to the capacity of some cultural resources have led to the idea of restricting tourists in favour of 'real' cultural visitors whose credentials as art consumers are demonstrated by student or professional membership, as in many galleries and museums, or even the proposal of knowledge-testing, as has been suggested in Venice. The point in all these cases is that resource managers are recognizing different users of culture and prioritizing among them, usually at the expense of tourists, whose money is welcome but whose presence frequently is not.

Finally, and stemming directly from the previous point, tourism is generally making use of cultural resources which were not originally produced for a tourism market and which are currently owned and managed by those who are unaware of, indifferent to or even hostile towards that market. Most of those concerned professionally with the presentation and maintenance of conserved historic buildings, artefacts and past cultural products, as well as those concerned with current artistic performance, do not see themselves as serving a tourism market principally or at all, and most probably justify their work, and their selection and presentation, on aesthetic, social or even political grounds rather than as part of a commercial tourism industry. The practical implications for the tourism industry of tourists being marginal users of cultural resources are in general obvious. The fact that tourism is an industry marketing products made from resources over which it has no control leads to many detailed difficulties ranging from inconvenient opening times to inadequate interpretation or support facilities.

The nature of the cultural tourist

There are two main types of explanation for the growth of interest by tourists in culture. Each is part of a more general explanation for the growth of interest in most aspects of culture as a whole. There is an *'embourgeoisement* thesis', which relies on the idea that the consumption of cultural services and goods is part of the lifestyle of a distinctive stratum in society identifiable in terms of age, income, social status and education. In that sense art in particular, and more broadly heritage, was seen as the pursuit of a social taste-forming minority élite (one, it should be added, equipped with the skills and experience demanded by Urry's 'cosmopolitan' (Urry, 1994)). Many studies of tourists at cultural sites identify the dominance of such structural characteristics (see Hughes and Gratton (1992) for a profile of visitors to artistic performances in greater Manchester, or Prentice (1993) for a description of visitors to heritage sites on the Isle of Man). Changes in the distribution of disposable incomes and in society have successively enlarged this group and thus widened the market. In addition demographic changes in Western countries are likely to enlarge the proportion of the older age groups in society and thus the potential market for much cultural tourism (Masser *et al.*, 1994).

Two sets of statistics would seem to support this theory. First, there has been a noticeable, and occasionally spectacular, growth in museum and gallery visits and many cultural performances and the sale of cultural goods such as music recordings, art books and the like in the last 30 years in Western cultures. An attempt to at least begin to inventorize the elements contained within such a 'culture industry' is demonstrated in Wynne (1992) although it is made equally clear that the economic role of such an industry has yet to be sketched. Secondly, it is all too easy to present a profile of the average cultural tourist (NIPO, 1991; Prentice, 1993) as aged 40–60, with above-average income and education, child-free and relatively experienced in such holidays. However such generalizations conceal the large variety of submarkets which exist even within the same general field of artistic endeavour and are thus usually less than helpful in aiding management. (A seaside variety show, a local amateur production, an RSC Shakespeare, a pantomime and a London musical are all theatre but are likely to attract different audiences even from among tourists.)

An alternative theory, constructed from the supply rather than the demand side, could be called the 'democratization' thesis, in which those concerned for the preservation or creation of cultural commodities have widened the definition of their responsibilities and their product line, successively seeking out new markets using new techniques of promotion and presentation. There are various reasons for this trend, including ideas of social responsibility, but economic survival in a context of shrinking public largesse has also been prominent. In the 'new museology' (Vergo, 1989; Merriman, 1991) promotion, presentation and interpretation are the focus rather than the artefacts or products themselves. Certainly cultural tourism is no longer confined to the high art of the established classics but is offering a widening range of cultural products and broadening out the definition of culture to include the 'everyday' heritage of ordinary individuals. A consequence of this idea is that a wider proportion of the tourism market is familiar with, and can thus be attracted to, cultural events and facilities while on holiday.

The nature of the cultural tourism experience

The most important generalization about the nature of the cultural tourism experience relevant to its management is simply that culture is consumed very rapidly. Despite what has been argued about the growth in interest in culture and the widening variety of cultural products on offer, it must be remembered that any specific cultural good is rapidly consumed, especially compared with the time taken to produce it. The shift from what has been called the 'Gutenberg generation' to the 'MTV generation' (Knulst, 1993) has emphasized not only the visual elements of culture (stressing design, spectacle, fashion and the like) but also a shift towards 'instantaneous time'. The average length of stay of a visitor to even the most renowned of historic cities, whose built environment has evolved through a millennium, or art cities with art treasures accumulated over the centuries, is only two or three days (e.g. Salzburg, 2.0; Venice, 2.3) and major world cities do little better (Paris, 2.2; Berlin, 2.5; London, 5.6) (Fig. 15.2). Smaller historic or cultural centres can measure visitor stay only in hours: even visitors motivated primarily by art will spend only a matter of hours in active participation in these pursuits.

This has a number of far-reaching consequences. Few individual cultural products, however superb or unique, can sustain the interest of tourists sufficiently to allow a local tourism industry to develop. The two implications are, first, that a range of major and supporting minor elements and a considerable variety of sorts of products are generally required. A 16th-century tower at Pisa, whether leaning or not, would have little attraction as an isolated entity and less commercial value: it needs to be surrounded by other buildings in a historic town and supported by a cultural souvenir industry before a tourism diversion and stay of a few hours become possible. This underlines the critical importance of understanding the way the various elements are related through the time–space behaviour of the visitor, as Dietvorst has

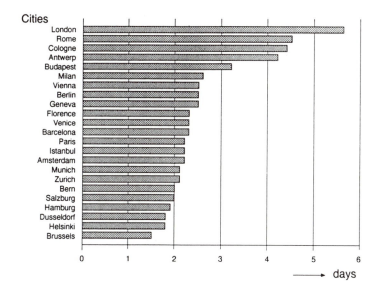

Fig. 15.2. Length of average stay of visitors in European cities.

sketched above (Chapter 10). Secondly, cities exist within networks of other places, whether cities offering similar cultural packages or regions with quite different but complementary attractions.

A commonplace observation about any discretionary activity is that fashion plays an important role. The cultural tourist, growing annually in experience and adventurousness, can exercise an increasingly fanciful, arbitrary and fickle choice from a fast-expanding supply of attractions. The established classics of the Western cultural canon whether in music, theatre, fine arts or architecture and urban design have been increasingly supplemented by an ever-widening range of cultural experiences. The reaction of producers to such shifting demands of consumers with increasingly eclectic tastes in a highly competitive market is rapid and flexible product-line diversification.

Cultural Tourism and Urban Development Policy

The three central considerations of this chapter must now be brought together. These are: culture as a tourism resource; the cities, which are both concentrations of cultural collections and performances and cultural artefacts in themselves; and thirdly, the economic development strategies of place-management authorities. The relationships between these can be explored under three relevant general headings.

Cities and the location of culture

First, the relationship of culture to cities as special forms of settlement has yet to be justified. Investigating the details of this relationship, rather than just restating it as conventional wisdom, may reveal significant points of leverage for policy instruments. It has frequently been claimed that 'the urban climate is best for the nurturing of culture' (Ministerie WVC, 1992), although why this should be so and what the planning consequences of this special relationship are have less frequently been examined.

This could in turn lead to speculation about three basic urban attributes that may have a direct bearing upon cities as cultural centres, namely size, spatial clustering and design. Underlying the assumption about cities having always played the leading role in cultural productivity is the idea that there is a certain critical volume of human interaction occurring in a spatially restricted area, and encouraged by aspects of urban form, that is crucial for the generation of artistic ideas. Thus we might expect a close correlation between urban size and cultural tourism. On an international scale this is indeed evident with the lion's share of the world's galleries, museums, concerts and the like being concentrated in a handful of major multimillion metropolitan centres which unsurprisingly also entertain most of the world's cultural tourists. (The world showcase capitals are described by Morris (1994).) There are cases of very small cities having a fortuitous and fashionable endowment (such as Cremona, with a population of 70,000, for Stradivarius violins or Sansepolchro, with a population of 15,000, for the paintings of Piero della Francesca) but these tend not only to be exceptional but of transient fame due to their inbuilt inflexibility for product-line development. In any event much cultural tourism is dependent on past rather than present artistic achievement. The lesson therefore to aspiring cultural tourism centres is not only to pursue urban growth but preferably also to become at some point in development a major national, or better imperial, artistic showcase, and success will be assured.

The other urban qualities of urban form and spatial compactness are less certain routes to success but much more easily influenced by local planning policies. The first adopts the simple propositions that culture is a product of social interaction and that such interaction is encouraged by specific urban designs, which can be shaped by planning policies. The so-called 'forum function' of cities can be encouraged by the creation of forums. The Dutch planning literature is currently full of accounts of how local planners have both responded to, and thereby further encouraged, changes in social spatial behaviour in cities with the shaping of outdoor terraces, plazas and even colonnades (see the many cases related in Burgers, 1993). The unstated environmental determinist argument is that the creation of an urban form similar to that of 15th-century Florence or Venice may have similar artistic consequences or at least can create an illusion, as far as northern European weather permits, of such a milieu. Such cultural engineering may seem far-fetched but cities endeavouring to project themselves as cultural centres are dependent to a substantial degree upon the structure and quality of their physical forms, especially in those districts which are being promoted as cultural locations. If we add that cultural performances often occur in buildings which are themselves heritage attractions (see the examples in Ashworth, 1991) or are designed as modern quality architectural structures then the link between function and form is reinforced.

Local authorities in most countries have considerable powers over land use and many cities have pursued policies that have resulted, whether intentionally or not, in a spatially compact set of cultural facility locations. The reasons for this are in part negative in that large auditoriums, museums and galleries have many of the characteristics of 'bad neighbours' and thus tend to be clustered, only partly reflecting the historic locations of many such institutions in city centres. However, despite these factors, there has also been a prevalent if generally uninvestigated idea that functional associations exist between cultural facilities so that mutual benefit is achieved through such synergies. Certainly the deliberate location of major clusters of cultural facilities, such as the Pompidou Centre (Beaubourg)–Forum/Les Halles axis in Paris or London's South Bank or Barbican complexes, did lead to the location of many smaller dependent galleries and shops (Ashworth and Tunbridge, 1990). In Amsterdam there has been a policy, sporadically implemented since the 19th century, of concentrating major national artistic showcase functions in the Rijksmuseum complex just south of the central city with the justification that they were at least architecturally mutually supporting. More recently the possible associations that might be advanced through spatial clustering have been redefined in terms of broadening the market by shaping physical links between 'high' culture and more popular facilities such as cinemas, libraries and even shops (e.g. Amsterdam). The Amsterdam 'Stopera' complex (described in detail in Dietvorst, 1994) is such a contrived location, contrasting with the Rijksmuseum complex above in its architectural appearance, linkages with other functions and targeted market.

However, when the actual behaviour of visitors is investigated, it has become increasingly clear from what detailed research exists that the role of such spatial clustering is much more complex. (See, for example, the investigation of what visitors to Norwich actually do, in Ashworth and de Haan (1986); the description of the anatomy of the museum visit in Nijmegen, in ten Tuynte and Dietvorst (1988); and, most comprehensively, the synoptic studies of visitor time–space behaviour in Enkhuizen and Arnhem, in Dietvorst (1994).) Visitors do not so much move from one museum or gallery to another as value the pervading atmosphere of a cultural district as a background to a limited number of actual visits. The functional associations on the demand side tend to be strongest between cultural and other facilities, such as catering or shopping, while associations on the supply side, i.e. between cultural institutions, are similarly limited. Thus clustering is justified to city managers for its wider planning consequences while to the tourist it plays a role very similar to what might be termed the 'Harley Street' phenomenon among medical specialists, namely not so much by providing the opportunity for making multiple visits as by identifying and justifying to the visitor that they are in the right district of town.

The relationship between cultural productivity and the facilities that display it, on the one side, and urban attributes on the other could be explored in much greater detail. The argument necessary here, however, is only that culture as an urban function cannot be separated from more general urban attributes, especially the form of cities themselves. A consequence of this is that local planning and management have, through the use of largely already existing legal instruments and practices, the means to intervene effectively. Planning for culture, including planning for one of its markets, namely cultural tourism, is thus an integral aspect of much broader urban planning. The opportunities and the capability exist at the local level: how, or even if, these are used depends upon the nature of the urban economy and the requirements of urban policy.

Culture and urban economies

Tourism is seen by most intermediaries and by tourism destinations as principally an economic activity. The economic impacts of tourism upon cities is a well-investigated topic, referred to at length elsewhere in this volume, and needs no reiteration here. Some of the distinctive attributes of cultural tourism within urban economies, however, need a brief review. Compared with other forms of tourism cultural tourism is credited with relatively high daily expenditures. This occurs principally because it is dominantly hotel-based and thus this direct economic benefit will tend to accrue to the accommodation and other services rather than to the cultural facilities themselves, which frequently have low or non-existent user charges. Thus two factors are critical determinants of the economic benefit: the number of overnight stays and the location of the cultural facilities within the same economic system as the secondary services. Day-excursion locations, for example, gain little, regardless of the volume of tourists entertained for a few hours. The economic costs, as well as the benefits, tend to be both spatially and functionally limited in their impacts as a result, in part, of the clustering argued earlier. Whether this is regarded as advantageous in its defensive concentration of negative impacts into specific areas, or disadvantageous through its exacerbation of congestion in key areas as well as its failure to spread the benefits of tourism demand over a wider city, depends on local circumstance.

As well as this direct role as a commercial activity in itself, cultural tourism can play a number of less direct but often equally important roles in the urban economy. The fact that tourism is only one use of cultural facilities and, as was argued above, usually not the most important, can enhance its secondary economic significance. To a performance, museum or gallery that already exists and will continue to exist for other purposes, the tourist is a clear gain, at least until physical capacity is reached. This argument can even be reversed. Cultural facilities created for or currently economically sustained by tourists, such as for example London theatres or famous arts festivals, can be used in addition by residents who become in that sense the 'free riders'.

The third role is even more diffuse and largely impossible to quantify. Cultural facilities which are in themselves not economically viable are often included in many multifunctional urban projects, as Snedcof (1985) and Lim (1993) amongst others have illustrated, for the sake of a whole range of externalities that they contribute to developments and districts. These can be summarized as 'animation' and 'cachet'. The former encompasses not only bringing people onto the streets, especially when other urban facilities are closed, but also introducing a liveliness that itself becomes a spectacle in which visitors become both performers and audience in public space (see for example the 'agora' function of public space described by Burgers (1993)). The latter conveys an aura of respectability, continuity and artistic patronage on other coexistent more prosaic functions in the immediate area, and even in the town as a whole, which can promote an image of cultural achievement as part of an economic development strategy. As Whitt (1987) pointed out, culture and particularly the performing arts can be used as 'a centrepiece for urban growth strategies'. The difficulty with both points is that placing the tourism experience within a wider context makes that experience more explicable but inevitably dilutes it and conceals it from analysis. In The Netherlands, as in most northern European countries, the holiday experience in Mediterranean countries, together with wider changes in the nature of society, has led to the selective import of such urban characteristics as the boulevard café and more broadly the idea of public spectacle and spectator, which, as Oosterman (1993) has described, has become in itself a major tourism attraction of cities such as Utrecht, Groningen and Maastricht. Tourist and resident are now indistinguishable. Tourists imitate residents who themselves are imitating their perceptions of the same tourists' home behaviour.

It needs stressing again that although culture is seen by many cities as a useful marginal economic activity (the 'windfall economic gain model') and even by some as the main support for their local economies, there are few cases where a town has deliberately made art the leading economic sector as a solution to economic failure in other sectors. The conditions for success can be listed as: an economic imperative with a severely limited range of options, a surplus capacity, especially of land, labour and supporting services, a fortunate location relative to the market, and also probably the timing of the initiative; all contribute to the excess of economic benefits over costs. This, more broadly, can serve as a checklist for the wisdom of any such development.

Choices

This chapter began by pointing out that culture has many different meanings. This variety was then compounded by a description of the different uses that tourism as an activity makes of culture. Finally, the third element, the cities, make use of culture and of its tourist consumers, in fulfilment of a variety of urban tasks. This threefold set of interacting variations creates an enormous diversity of possible policy reactions and implementations in specific cases.

There are many identifiably different types of city and each has quite different cultural endowments and roles that it expects culture to play. In each the balance of costs and benefits and thus planning policies are different. Consider for example the following urban cases.

- The major world showcase metropolis has an enormous concentration of cultural resources and the bulk of investment in new facilities. Such cities entertain most cultural tourists but within a large, varied and consequently flexible economic and social structure. The local, national and international functions become indistinguishable.

- The major cultural tourism magnets which are both custodians of world heritage and accommodate large flows of visitors to it. Such cities are locked into their major cultural tourism function and have little local flexibility.
- The medium-sized multifunctional multi-age cities which represent the living environments of most Europeans and which have the widest and freest range of choices about the roles they wish culture to perform.
- The small but near-perfect cultural 'gems' whose cultural role is inevitable, imposed and nearly monopolistic. They have few choices that can be exercised at the local level but accept an imposed national or international function.

The point is not only that quite different management policies are likely in each of these categories but also that few management lessons are likely to be transferable between such groups. Urban cultural policy can be used to commodify culture as a resource supporting new economic activities; to serve as an investment catalyst in physical regeneration and economic revitalization; to foster amenities which improve the competitive position; to develop local identities which can be promoted externally to attract people, enterprises and investment and internally foster civic consciousness and pride in developing extra-urban networks. The management of the cultural tourist can make a contribution to all, some or none of these.

References and Further Reading

Abercrombie, N., Hill, S. and Turner, B.S. (1980) *The Dominant Ideology Thesis.* Allen and Unwin, London.

Ashworth, G.J. (1991) *Heritage Planning.* Geopers, Groningen.

Ashworth, G.J. and de Haan, T.Z. (1986) *Uses and Users of the Tourist-historic City.* GIRUG, Groningen.

Ashworth, G.J. and Tunbridge, J.E. (1990) *The Tourist-historic City.* Belhaven, London.

Beckermans, F. (ed.) (1993) *Culture: Building Stone for Europe.* College of Europe, Bruges.

Burgers, J. (1993) (ed.) *Uitstad.* Jan van Arkel, Utrecht.

Costa, P. and van der Borg, J. (1993) *The Management of Tourism in Cities of Art.* CISET 2, University of Venice, Venice.

Dietvorst, A. (1994) Cultural tourism and time–space behaviour. In: Ashworth, G.J. and Larkham, P. (eds) *Building a New Heritage: Tourism, Culture and Identity in the New Europe.* Routledge, London, pp. 69–89.

Hitters, E. (1993) Culture and capital in the 1990s. *Built Environment* 18(2), 111–122.

Hughes, H. and Gratton, C. (1992) The economics of the culture industry. In: Wynne, D. (ed.) *The Culture Industry: The Arts in Urban Regeneration*. Avebury, Aldershot.

Jansen-Verbeke, M. (1990) *Toerisme in de Binnenstad van Brugge: een Planologische Visie*. In: Nijmeegse Planologische Cahiers 35, Katholieke Universiteit, Nijmegen.

Klerk, L. and Vijgen, J. (1993) Inner cities as a cultural and public arena. *Built Environment* 18(2), 100–110.

Knulst, W. (1993) Trends in het consumentengedrag. Conference 'Vernieuwen in toerisme', Rotterdam.

Konsola, D. (ed.) (1993a) *Culture, Environment and Regional Development*. Regional Development Institute, University of Athens, Athens.

Konsola, D. (1993b) Culture tourism and regional development: some proposals for cultural itineraries. In: Konsola, D. (ed.) *Culture, Environment and Regional Development*. Regional Development Institute, University of Athens, Athens, pp. 18–43.

Lim, H. (1993) Cultural strategies for revitalising the city: review and evaluation. *Regional Studies* 27(6), 589–595.

Masser, I., Sviden, O. and Wegener, M. (1994) What new heritage for which new Europe? Some contextual considerations. In: Ashworth, G.J. and Larkham, P. (eds) *Building a New Heritage: Tourism, Culture and Identity in the New Europe*. Routledge, London, pp. 31–46.

Merriman, N. (1991) *Beyond the Glass Case: The Past, the Heritage and the Public in Britain*. Leicester University Press, Leicester.

Ministerie voor Economische Zaken (1991) *Ondernemen in Toerisme*. SDU, The Hague.

Ministerie WVC (1992) *Investeren in Cultuur: Nota Cultuurbeleid 1993–6*. SDU, The Hague.

Morris, E. (1994) Heritage and culture: a capital for the New Europe. In: Ashworth, G.J. and Larkham, P. (eds) *Building a New Heritage: Tourism, Culture and Identity in the New Europe*. Routledge, London, pp. 229–259.

Mossetto, G. (1990) A cultural good called Venice. *Nota di Lavoro* 90(14). University of Venice.

Mossetto, G. (1993) Culture and environmental waste: an economic approach. In: Konsola, D. (ed.) *Culture, Environment and Regional Development*. Regional Development Institute, University of Athens, Athens.

Newby, P. (1994) Tourism: support or threat to heritage? In: Ashworth, G.J. and Larkham, P. (eds) *Building a New Heritage: Tourism, Culture and Identity in the New Europe*. Routledge, London, pp. 206–228.

NIPO (1991) *Vakantieonderzoek 1991: Het Bezoek aan Nederlandse Bezienswaardigheden Tijdens de Vakantie*. NIPO, Amsterdam.

Oosterman, J. (1993) Parade der passanten. De stad, het vertier en de terrassen. PhD thesis, University of Utrecht, Arkel, Utrecht.

Prentice, R. (1993) *Tourism and Heritage Attractions*. Issues in Tourism series. Routledge, London.

Snedcof, H. (1985) *Cultural Facilities in Multi-use Developments*. Urban Land, Washington.

ten Tuynte, J.G.M. and Dietvorst, A.G.J. (1988) *Musea, Anders Bekeken: Vier*

Nijmeegse Musea Bezien naar Uitstralingseffecten en Complexvorming. Werkgroep Recreatie en Toerisme. Katholieke Universiteit, Nijmegen.

Urry, J. (1994) Europe, tourism and the nation-state. In: Cooper, C.P. and Lockwood, A. (eds) *Progress in Tourism, Recreation and Hospitality Management.* Wiley, Chichester, pp. 89–98.

van der Meulen, T. (1992) *Kansen voor Cultuurtoerisme in Friesland.* Provincie Friesland, Leeuwarden.

Vergo, P. (1989) *The New Museology.* Reaktion Books, London.

Vetter, F. (1985) *Big City Tourism.* Reimer Verlag, Berlin.

Whitt (1987) Mozart in the metropolis. *Urban Affairs Quarterly* 15–36.

Wynne, D. (ed.) (1992) *The Culture Industry: The Arts in Urban Regeneration.* Avebury, Aldershot.

16

Managing Deviant Tourist Behaviour

B. Beke[1] and B. Elands[1,2]

[1]Advies- en Onderzoeksgroep Beke, Rijnkade 84, 6811 HD Arnhem, The Netherlands: [2]Centre for Recreation and Tourism Studies, Agricultural University, Generaal Foulkesweg 13, 6703 BJ Wageningen, The Netherlands

Recreational Crime: Undesired Consequence of Mass Tourism and Recreation

Although the importance of tourism and recreation to the economy is significant, this does not preclude some undesirable side-effects. Huge numbers of tourists visiting the same recreational area can cause problems such as traffic congestion, pollution and, increasingly, recreational crime. This growth in recreational crime occurs predominantly in the peak tourist season, when it is not unusual for the number of visitors in tourist areas to increase tenfold or sometimes even 30-fold.

Criminality in recreational areas has been ignored for a long time. Until recently, the inhabitants received almost no attention, which is striking because this group is often confronted with recreational crime. Apart from material claims, like bicycle theft, vandalism and burglary, local inhabitants also make important non-material claims such as the fear of being a victim, the sense of being powerless, etc. Therefore, it is not surprising that three-quarters of the local inhabitants are pessimistic about the long-term developments and expect an increase in recreational criminality in the coming five years (Beke and Kleiman, 1990). Tourists themselves have shown their disapproval by staying away from areas with high crime rates. Other groups, like tourist entrepreneurs, have noticed a decrease in revenues. Intervention is necessary in order to stop this process.

This chapter shows the results of research into the causes and the prevention of recreational crime in The Netherlands. Especially coastal

and water resorts have been involved in this study, such as the Dutch
islands and the seaside resorts of the provinces of Zeeland and Noord-
Holland.

What is Recreational Crime?

Recreational crime covers a broad area of juvenile delinquency (from
approximately 13–14 years of age), which is limited chiefly to the
recreational environment (holiday resorts, entertainment centres, etc.).
It concerns a range of criminal activities that occur mainly in leisure
time. Activities that occur frequently are vandalism, theft, traffic
offences, drug offences and violence offences. In fact, recreational crime
can be seen as a regular part of the leisure-spending patterns of young
people.

Mostly, the offenders do not have a particular aim, or it is a rather
vague aim, such as 'fighting just for fun', 'whiling away the time' or
'seeking tension and sensation'. It is precisely this aimless and unstruc-
tured behaviour that complicates the fight against, and the prevention
of, recreational crime.

Recreational crime follows naturally from all kinds of excessive
behaviour, that is, behaviour which clearly oversteps the mark:
prevailing standards are ignored. Broadly defined, we speak about
offences against moral and social codes. Excessive behaviour is usually
a precursor of frequently occurring crime, such as drunkenness,
urinating in the streets, throwing away all kinds of litter, noise
nuisance, provoking people and making improper remarks. Recreational crime is almost always accompanied by an excessive use of
alcohol and/or drugs, which is at least the facilitating factor for various
criminal manifestations.

For general orientation, we would like to stress the significance of
a growing amount of leisure time, the limited budgets and, what is
more important, the limited possibilities that are available, particularly
to young people, for spending their free time in a more useful manner.

Recreational crime can be divided into intentional and non-
intentional crime (Angenent and Beke, 1988; Beke and Leeuwenburg,
1988; Beke, 1989; Kleiman, 1989; Beke and Kleiman, 1990). Intentional
crime is crime carried out by young people who deliberately violate the
law. Crime is a 'normal part' of the behaviour of these young people.
They commit many criminal offences and heavy misdemeanours
(assault, threatening with weapons, severe forms of vandalism, burglary, etc.).

Non-intentional crime usually concerns situations that have got out of control. There is no premeditation, and later on the offenders appear completely surprised by the course of the events. Generally this concerns the minor offences such as shoplifting, drink-driving, less serious forms of vandalism and petty criminal offences.

Research, a Prerequisite for Effective Preventive Policy

For considering the above problems research was carried out with the aim of gaining insight into the motives and background of young people who are responsible for committing recreational crime. A second purpose of the research was to construct a model for the analysis of and approach to recreational crime which can be used by policy-makers for developing a preventive strategy for limiting the high occurrence of recreational crime.

For this reason a survey was directed at tourists in the entertainment centres of 14 recreational areas in The Netherlands during the summer of 1989 (Beke and Kleiman, 1990). The questionnaires were filled in by 4200 people. The main topics in the questionnaire were:

- sociodemographic data (e.g. age, educational level, lifestyle);
- personality traits (e.g. the degree of impulsiveness, locus of control, sensation-seeking, aggression);
- recreational pattern and preferences (e.g. accommodation, length of residence, company during holidays, preferences for different types of recreational activities);
- pattern and preferences of going out (e.g. frequency of going out, use of alcohol, spending pattern, preferences for different types of amusement);
- criminal behaviour (Beke and Kleiman, 1990).

The current crime statistics, i.e. police and judicial statistics, are incomplete and distorted. First of all, they do not give a correct insight into the so-called dark number, i.e. crime that has not been registered. The causes of this are a lack of notification by victims, and no registration of notifications by the police. Secondly, they distort the quality of the cases that have been registered, because the registration is not representative and selective.

Considering the aim of the research is to gain insight into the motives and backgrounds of the offenders of recreational crime, we chose a self-reporting method for offenders.

The self-reporting method was introduced by Short and Nye in 1957 and is seen as a good method of becoming acquainted with the character and the amount of hidden crime (Hirschi, 1969; Hindelang *et* al., 1981). It is a widespread research strategy, used frequently for two reasons. It offers a clear view of the dark number and it nullifies the distortion of registered crime (Bartollas, 1985). In addition, it uncovers the backgrounds of the group of offenders and segments the criminal behaviour of different sections of the population (Hood and Sparks, 1970). The self-reporting method itself has often been the subject of discussion in research. Criticism of the self-reporting method is usually directed towards the reliability and the validity of the instrument. However, the results of many recognized investigations have proved the contrary. This means that the instrument gives stable results and also records the appropriate measurements, namely the number of times the respondents are guilty of the criminal offences in the reference period (Clark and Tifft, 1966; Gold, 1966; Hirschi, 1969; Hood and Sparks, 1970; Farrington, 1973; Hardt and Peterson-Hardt, 1977; Box, 1981; Hindelang et al., 1981; Huizinga and Elliot, 1986; Bruinsma, 1991).

The 'Seattle self-reporting' instrument of Hindelang et al. (1981) was used as a base for the construction of our questionnaire. It was adapted and enlarged for the Dutch situation and the specific target groups in this investigation. The framework of the final instrument, which was called the Standard Questionnaire of Offenders, has been used in several large surveys on juvenile delinquency (Angenent and Beke, 1988; Beke and Kleiman, 1990). It has also become an officially recognized questionnaire of the Dutch Ministry of Internal Affairs (Kleiman and Beke, 1992).

Results of the Youth Research Standard Questionnaire of Offenders

The majority of the tourists in the selected entertainment centres were between 16 and 30 years of age (87%). From this it is evident that most recreationists are schoolchildren or students. The length of residence in the recreational area showed some differences. About half of the population (48%) stayed for one week or more, mostly on a camp-site, 17% stayed for one weekend and 35% came only for one evening to the recreational area.

Three main preferences for recreational activities could be distinguished: 'going out' is for 58% a primary recreational preference, 'nature and peace- and quiet-seeking' for 37% and 'sporting/activities with children' was mentioned by 5% of the respondents.

The results of the research on the criminal behaviour of recreationists are presented in Table 16.1. Six categories of criminal behaviour

Table 16.1. Results of recreational crime Standard Questionnaire of Offenders (*N* = 4200). Numbers = percentage of respondents involved in the indicated criminal offence.

Vandalism/destruction		Violent offences	
Destruction of telephone booths	4	Major mishandling:	
Destruction of sanitary facilities	7	– medical help necessary after	
Destruction of cars	7	knocking a person down	8
Destruction of mailboxes	7	– used a weapon during a fight	5
Destruction of windows	12	Public offence:	
Destruction of traffic signs	13	– fought just for fun	8
Graffiti	19	Threatening:	
Pulled plants from gardens	20	– threatened a shopkeeper	2
		– found carrying a weapon	4
		Possession of weapons:	
Offences against property		– found carrying a weapon when	
Shoplifting:		going out	10
– US$28 (or more)	5	– found carrying weapons to use	
– between US$3 and $28	14	in fights	7
– less than US$3	17		
Bicycle theft:		**Drug offences**	
– stole a bicycle	12	Used soft drugs	21
Burglary:		Dealt in soft drugs	4
– forced entry into vacation home	3	Used hard drugs	3
– forced entry into home, school,		Dealt in hard drugs	2
etc.	4		
Car burglary:		**Traffic offences**	
– forced entry into cars	4	Hit-and-run accidents:	
– stole car parts	4	– hit and run	3
– stole car radio/cassette player	3	– hit a parked car and drove away	4
Theft:		Drink-driving:	
– from tent or touring caravan	5	– drove a car while drunk	8
– sold stolen goods	4		
Received stolen goods:		**Against public authority**	
– bought goods with the knowledge		Fought with the police	3
that they were stolen	10	Refused to inform the police	12

were surveyed, and will be discussed individually. Of the total group surveyed (*N* = 4200) 48% indicated they had been involved in some form of criminal behaviour.

Vandalism is common in recreational areas and is described as deliberately destroying, damaging or making someone else's belongings unusable. Public gardens or parks are usually the objects of vandalism. One-fifth of young people destroy plants or other parts of public gardens.

The second most frequent offence is against property. Recreational areas are plagued by offences such as shoplifting and bicycle theft. Both offences seem to be accepted by people in general; at least statistics show this as a rule rather than an exception. One-eighth of young people have stolen a bicycle during a vacation, during weekends or during their evening out. Literally speaking, this is not always theft, because many young people only 'borrow' this stolen bicycle for temporary transport and after using it they leave it behind. Joyriding is a more accurate example of the offence. This does not mean that this is an acceptable form of recreational crime. Young people visiting recreational areas also appear to commit shoplifting offences during their vacation. The cheaper the stolen goods, the greater the number of young people who commit the criminal offence of shoplifting. Besides this, robbery from tents, caravans and second homes and burglary are definite forms of crime manifested in recreational areas.

Violent offences are also increasing in recreational areas, especially around entertainment centres. Even though this form of recreational crime does not happen very frequently, it is an increasing source of anxiety for the administrators responsible. Young people often meet in the various entertainment centres, which can result in public offences or fights. It is often the case that during such confrontations people have to visit a doctor after receiving a beating. Weapons (clubs, knives, etc.) are used quite often in these confrontations. A lot of people visiting recreational areas (10%) appear to carry weapons when visiting entertainment centres in recreational areas. Some of them really do have the intention of using the weapon in a fight.

The use of soft drugs is a frequent occurrence among people visiting recreational areas. On vacation or evenings out one in five young people use soft drugs, either replacing or in addition to the use of alcohol. Confirming this statement, almost 4% of the people visiting recreational areas are involved in dealing in soft drugs. Some of them are small users who sell part of their own supply; professional dealers form a minority. The use of hard drugs is small compared with the use of soft drugs. Nevertheless, hard drugs draw much attention owing to their severe consequences. Only a small proportion of the people visiting recreational areas deal in hard drugs, which are mostly handled professionally. Research shows that the entertainment centres in recreational areas are an increasing attraction for these dealers (Beke and Leeuwenburg, 1988).

The use of alcohol during recreation and going out is quite common. Drink-driving obviously has implications for traffic safety. Eight per cent of the people visiting recreational areas appear to drive with alcohol in their blood during vacations or outings. This is generally accepted by other young people, and it appears that one-quarter of them do not object to riding with someone who is driving under the influence of alcohol.

Not all the criminal activities are committed to the same degree by each individual. About 8% of the young people were guilty of 55% of the offences. These figures do not say anything about the seriousness or the gravity of the offences. A judicial index was used to rescale the offences according to their gravity. A distinction was made between 'light' and 'heavy' offences. The former category comprises offences like rape, using or dealing in drugs, violent offences and burglary. The latter category comprises offences like theft, shoplifting, bicycle theft, receiving and vandalism.

On the basis of this distinction three offender groups could be distinguished. The first group comprised the non-criminal recreationists. About 47% of the young people that visit entertainment centres, who committed only light offences, belong to this category. The second group, called the non-intentional criminals (see pp. 286–287), contained 45% of the recreationists. These adolescents committed at most one heavy offence and some also committed light offences. The last group, the intentional criminals or the so-called 'hard core', committed at least two heavy offences and a variable amount of light offences. The research showed that about 8% of young people visiting entertainment centres belong to this group. They visit entertainment centres with the intention of causing trouble. Most members of the hard core have already come into contact with the police.

Recreational Crime Related to Different Types of Recreational Areas

Pinpointing problems of recreational crime at an early stage can help to prevent escalation. Early detection increases the effectiveness of the preventive policy. Therefore, an important starting-point for the development of a preventive policy is to recognize and identify the problems and the recreational criminal offence. A method can be developed to chart the problems in a recreational area quickly and at an early stage, with the information derived from research. The possible connection between various factors and characteristics of a certain recreational area on the one hand and the recreational criminal offence on the other has been observed.

A rough inventorization showed that all recreational areas have a number of criminal activities in common, notably the non-intentional offences. This fact proves the urgency of prevention in all types recreational areas. The shared offences are vandalism, shoplifting and the lighter forms of violence offences. Apart from shared crime patterns, one can clearly establish specific crime patterns. The heavier forms of violent offences, drug offences, robbery from tents and caravans and burglary from second homes do not occur equally in

Table 16.2. Characteristics of the recreationists in the three types of recreational areas.

Type 1	Type 2	Type 3
Families with children (up to 20 years of age)	People in their thirties	Families with children (up to 17 years of age)
Young people in groups (between 14 and 20 years of age)	Young people in groups (between 17 and 20 years of age)	People in their thirties in groups
Social middle class	Social higher class	Social lower class
Reasonable income	Higher income	Moderate income
Average spending pattern (US$17)	Ample spending pattern (US$28)	Low spending pattern (US$5.5)
Overnight recreation	Much evening recreation	Weekend/evening recreation
Camp-sites	Luxurious accommodation, luxurious camp-sites	Apartments, cottages, caravans
Many nature/peace- and quiet-seeking people	Few nature/peace- and quiet-seeking, many 'going-out' people	Many peace- and quiet-seeking people
Very social	Average socializing	Little socializing
Much use of alcohol	Normal/much use of alcohol	Moderate use of alcohol
Using alcohol in private situations	Use of alcohol in cafés and bars	Use of alcohol on a quiet terrace
Higher use of alcohol during vacation	Small number drinks an excessive amount of alcohol	Small number of drunk people

holiday resorts. In other words, these criminal offences are location-specific.

At first, the shared offences were separated from the specific offences in order to differentiate between types of criminal offences and types of recreational areas. The analysis of the specific criminal offences resulted in three types of recreational areas. In the next section these types will be discussed with regard to the characteristics of the visitor groups (Table 16.2) and forms of recreational crime (Table 16.3).

Recreational area type 1: nature combined with residential recreation

Typical of the first type is a strong emphasis on the supply of residential holiday accommodation, mainly in the form of holiday homes, hotels and large camp-sites, situated in a natural environment, such as the Dutch islands. There is a mixed recreational population, mostly families with children and youths up to 20 years of age, who visit these areas for one or more weeks. The nature-oriented areas

Table 16.3. Forms of recreational crime for the three types of recreational areas.

General priority, types 1, 2 and 3	Specific priority		
	Type 1	Type 2	Type 3
Lighter and heavier forms of vandalism	Soft drugs	Criminal offences	Burglary
	Criminal offences	Traffic offences	Hard drugs
Lighter forms of shoplifting	Stealing offences	Speed	Receiving
Lighter forms of criminal offences		Soft drugs	
		Stealing offences	

contain small-scale entertainment centres, which are directed towards this group of holidaymakers. The visitors are mostly attracted by nature and the peace and quiet of these areas. A smaller group of people are attracted by the opportunity for going out and 'living it up'. The recreationists visiting this type of recreational area generally consume a lot of alcohol. The consumption of alcohol is usually restricted to private situations, i.e. near the tent or caravan.

The following criminal offences are seen in the field of recreational crime in this area. First, there are the use of and dealing in soft drugs. More than one in five recreational participants use soft drugs during their vacation and almost 5% of the recreationists deal in them. Additionally, criminal offences occur frequently in this type of recreational area. Apart from the lighter forms of abuse, heavy abuses also take place, although less frequently. One in ten of the recreationists in this type of area carries a weapon when going out. A third form of relatively frequent recreational crime is bicycle theft (14%).

Recreational area type 2: entertainment centres combined with residential recreation

This type of recreational area can be characterized by both well-developed evening recreation facilities and residential holiday accommodation. This mostly concerns recreational areas with a high degree of urbanization, such as the coastal resorts Noordwijk and Zandvoort. There are some large-scale entertainment centres which also attract local and regional inhabitants. Nature and landscape do not dominate the environment. Although the recreational population is varied, there is much segregation between families and the elderly on the one hand and young people on the other. This is in contrast to the visitor groups of the first type. More males than females visit this type of area. Most of the recreationists have high incomes and spend a lot of money on going out and on consuming alcohol.

Two visitor groups can be identified. The recreational participants in the first group, to which the majority of the visitors belong, are over 17 years of age. They usually come only for one evening and are attracted by the possibility of going out, although some of them also show an interest in nature-oriented recreation. The participants of the second group are 20 to 30 years of age, most of them are either unmarried or cohabiting, choose a more luxurious residence and are interested in nature-oriented recreation.

This type of recreational area is characterized by criminal offences which occur more often in this type of area than in the other two. This mostly accounts for abuse and possession of weapons: about one in 14 recreationists is guilty of major mishandling and more than one in ten possesses a weapon. There is also a striking number using and dealing in the drug speed (both 4%). A third characteristic offence is both frequent use of and dealing in soft drugs. More than 4% deal in soft drugs, which is done in a professional circuit. Further, traffic offences, especially drink-driving, occur frequently in this type of recreational area. The last offence that is peculiar to this area is bicycle theft (14%).

Recreational area type 3: regular weekend outings

Mostly residential recreation areas, which have a relatively long tradition in Dutch tourism and are lagging behind in tourism development, are seen in this type. One example is the Veluwe region in the centre of The Netherlands. This includes camp-sites with permanent caravans, smaller self-owned apartments and holiday cottages, which are used for weekend outings and vacational outings throughout the year. There are practically no entertainment centres in these recreational areas.

Mostly families with children up to 17 years of age and a small group of recreational participants up to 30 years of age visit this type of area. Most of the recreationists have a lower socioeconomic status. People usually visit for a weekend or for an evening and they have a preference for quiet recreational facilities. This group consumes little alcohol.

The following criminal offences characterize this recreation area. Breaking into vacation homes, tents, caravans and similar is a specific form of recreational crime. An average of one in 14 recreational participants commits this offence. Receiving stolen goods is the second form of recreational crime, which is done by 6% of the recreationists. This type clearly shows recreational areas in which somewhat heavier professional crimes take place. Also the use of and dealing in hard drugs are characteristic offences here.

Development of Preventive Programmes for Recreational Crime

Before the contents of preventive programmes can be worked out, they have to fulfil four conditions.

1. Supply and demand analysis. An adequate and accurate analysis will include an environmental and social description (composition of the holiday population, recreational facilities, etc.) plus an analysis of registered offences and the delinquency figures obtained from the self-reporting method. This will yield the various variables which constitute indications for the specific type and scale of recreational area-related crime. On the basis of these data, a set of preventive measures can be devised, which could aim at limiting or, if possible, obviating the observed forms of recreational crime.

2. Flexibility is a keyword in preventive policy. A standard package of preventive measures, which are by definition effective, cannot be given. Evaluative research is needed to measure the effectiveness of the preventive programmes (monitoring).

3. The effectiveness is determined to a large extent by the participation of the different interest groups. The cooperation between interest groups, such as entrepreneurs, camp-site owners, amusement industry, local inhabitants, the police and governmental bodies, takes shape as the so-called Preventive Platform. This recommendation has led to the establishment of about 20 Preventive Platforms in recreational areas in The Netherlands.

4. A differentiation in measures has to make sure that all criminal groups will be reached. Incidental and non-intentional criminals can be reached by referring to their feelings of responsibility by means of information and extension of social checks. Intentional criminals can be reached by measures with a more repressive character, like early identification and signalling, preventive seizure of weapons and exclusion measures.

Within the Preventive Platforms a broad spectrum of preventive measures have been developed and made effective. Some of the most important general preventive programmes will now be discussed. The topics are: activity programmes, moderation of alcohol use, 'instant punishment' and the vandalism registration project.

Activity Programmes

The development and implementation of activity programmes are very important in the whole package of measures. Such programmes ought to aim at the groups which are primarily responsible for the various forms of delinquency. These activities will have two primary characteristics. First, they will provide short-term alternatives for breaking up the negative patterns, such as alcoholism. Secondly, they will aim at achieving long-term behavioural changes. It is necessary to provide a package of activities that offers real prospects of new forms of recreation for groups which are usually absent or underrepresented (Beke, 1992).

A more balanced population is an essential part of crime prevention. Therefore, the activities should be spread out, in terms of both location/facilities and target groups. This can be reached, for example, by avoiding overly large concentrations of young people in one spot or drawing older people towards entertainment centres in the evenings (increasing social checks). Better and more varied provision of facilities would help create new patterns of recreational behaviour and thus eliminate the old ones. In a wider context, the national Dutch Foundation Centre for Recreational Work makes an increasing contribution to this subject.

Moderation of Alcohol Use

Alcohol use is a decisive variable in the cause of recreational crime and therefore it is an important issue for the Preventive Platforms. A random sample of the measures which have been developed are:

- limiting activities which stimulate the consumption of alcohol (such as 'happy hour', the selling of 'one metre of beer') within the hotel and catering industry;
- in cooperation with the various discos and the camp-sites, information was given about the use of alcohol and its effects, with an emphasis on the relationship between alcohol and traffic offences;
- clear agreements on the behavioural codes for hotel and catering industry owners to be used in cases of heavy alcohol use among young visitors (shared responsibility with the police), e.g. the creation of an adequate announcement system to warn the police;
- exclusion measures: young people who repeatedly show unacceptable behaviour will be excluded by all hotel and catering industry owners and if necessary excluded from staying at camp-sites;

- training of porters, so that they can handle conflicts and the excessive use of alcohol by the public;
- prohibiting the use of alcohol during the night on public roads and on the beach;
- better screening of terraces and pubs, and better checking of theft of glass objects (potential weapons);
- taking measures to stimulate the use of public transportation. In cooperation with hotel and catering industry owners, disco buses are being used for this reason.

Further, the programme for moderation in the use of alcohol consists of an active policy on traffic inspection. The main objective is to have frequent and intense inspection of all incoming traffic going towards entertainment centres and recreational areas. In the early evening massive inspection of incoming traffic is done to combat possession of weapons and drugs, the use of alcohol and so on. Such inspections are carried out for a number of reasons.

It seems to be an effective preventive measure to confront sober drivers with the possibility of alcohol checks. Research (Angenent and Beke, 1988; Beke, 1989) shows that slightly intensifying traffic inspections (from 5 to 15%) decreases the number of people who expect that the chance of getting caught is small or very small (30% change their minds on this issue). This is called a cumulative efficiency.

By means of traffic inspections, weapons, or objects which can be used as weapons, can be confiscated through a General Police Regulation Stipulation. Mostly, these weapons belong to the group of heavy offenders (intentional and structural criminal behaviour). During these traffic inspections a large number of weapons are prevented from being carried, such as baseball bats, clubs, knives and rifles. People arrested are, after the settlement of a fine, usually released no sooner than early in the morning. The third function of traffic inspections is to enable the early identification (through number-plate registration) of potentially suspicious groups. Two effects are expected, namely increasing the previously slight chance of getting caught and diminishing the related anonymity. This makes it possible to act faster and more effectively during arrests.

'Tit for Tat'

The public prosecutors of the province of Zeeland and Friesland both decided to expand transactional authorities of the police concerning certain violations. This means that the police can reach a settlement in the form of a fine. In these cases a direct punishment can be inflicted. This transactional policy is called 'tit for tat' or instant punishment. Dealing with these violations and offences in an efficient manner has several advantages. First, there is an immediate relationship between delinquency and punishment. This is in contrast to the usual method, in which it may take a few months before the delinquent is judged. This is the reason for the supply-and-demand policy terminology. In the second place, fines appear to be viewed as real punishments, especially among youth. A fine of US$50 is a big financial burden for them and this could mean a serious restriction in their spending pattern during their evening out. In the third place, these transactional authorities appear to work well in practice. The willingness to pay is impressive. In Zeeland, an average of 80% of all inflicted fines are paid immediately. On the Frisian Islands this percentage is even higher. Costs of collecting the fines are not as high as, for instance, the costs of collecting fines for parking violations (Beke *et al.*, 1991).

Registration of Vandalism

One of the last preventive projects, broached within this framework, concerns a vandalism registration project in 12 recreational areas. The objective of this project is to develop, carry out and evaluate preventive measures which are directed towards decreasing the occurrence of the various forms of vandalism. The second objective is to reduce the dark-number vandalism by increasing the willingness of vandalism victims to inform the police in order to get a good picture of the areas susceptible to vandalism.

In many communities at the present time it is not clear what the precise damage caused by vandalism is. Also, the costs of repair are not explicitly recorded. Working out the cost factors can be a stimulus, especially for the development of a preventive policy; furthermore it can be a definite incentive to reserve finances for preventive measures. Subsequently, it can be made clear what the benefits of certain specific measures are. Thus, there is a direct feedback of preventive measures towards financial effects.

In order to carry out this preventive project, an automatized vandalism registration system (a software program) is developed. The program offers, for example, the possibility to periodically analyse the exact locations that are susceptible to vandalism and the costs and benefits of preventive measures taken at these locations. Every community appointed one or more vandalism registrars. There has been the use of:

- posters with a phone number on them specifically to report vandalism;
- home-to-home leaflets distributed to all local inhabitants;
- special forms for institutions and entrepreneurs to inform the police;
- home visits to victims and in this way verbal advertising.

This personal attention has had an effect. Statistics show an average increase of 50–60% in the number of reports made to the police each year, which means an increase of ± 250% after two years' vandalism registration (Beke and Kusters, 1990). The registration of vandalism has resulted in recognition of a number of clusters of streets/quarters in which a concentration of incidents happened. Finally, location-oriented preventive measures have been taken.

Prevention, a Constant Care

The results of the efforts to prevent recreational crime have many aspects. In the first place there is a clearer picture of the backgrounds and the motives of the various groups of young people who commit recreational crime. Such a picture is essential for the development of an effective preventive policy. Secondly, a couple of preventive programmes have been developed focusing on the various forms of recreational crime. These programmes can be widely used in the various recreational communities. Thirdly, there is an important shift in responsibilities in the various recreational communities. The fight against and the prevention of recreational crime is no longer the exclusive responsibility of the police, the Director of Public Prosecutions and the local government officials, but a responsibility carried by a broad social group. This cooperation is not restricted to the municipal level, but is occurring increasingly on the regional level.

Integrative planning is needed for tourism. According to Gunn (1988): 'planning as a concept of viewing the future and dealing with anticipated consequences is the only way that tourism's advantages can be obtained and disadvantages can be avoided'. Therefore, the prevention of recreational crime forms an essential part of the planning process, besides the prevention of other disadvantages of tourism, such as mobility and environmental decline (Elands and Beke, 1992).

References

Angenent, H.L.W. and Beke, B.M.W.A. (1988) *Bestuurlijke Preventie van Recreatie Criminaliteit*. Rijksuniversiteit Groningen, Groningen.

Bartollas, C. (1985) *Juvenile Delinquency*. John Wiley, Chichester.

Beke, B.M.W.A. (1989) *Recreatiecriminaliteit en Alcohol*. SWP, Utrecht.

Beke, B.M.W.A. (1992) A research-project proposal for the development and application of prevention projects. In: Fleischer-van Rooijen, C.A.M. (ed.) *Spatial Implications of Tourism*. Geopers, University of Groningen, Groningen.

Beke, B.M.W.A. and Kleiman, W.M. (1990) *Recreatie, Recreatiegedrag en Recreatie-criminaliteit in Nederland. Jongeren en Recreatiecriminaliteit; de Ontwikkeling van een Analysemodel*. SWP, Utrecht.

Beke, B.M.W.A. and Kleiman, W.M. (1992) *De Harde Kern in Beeld*. SWP, Utrecht.

Beke, B.M.W.A. and Kusters, K.A.F. (1990) *Recreatiecriminaliteit en Vandalisme. Een Meersporen Beleid*. SWP, Utrecht.

Beke, B.M.W.A. and Leeuwenburg, J.W. (1988) De aanpak van recreatiecrimina-liteit in Renesse. *SEC, Tijdschrift over Samenleving en Criminaliteitspreventie* 4, 12–14.

Beke, B.M.W.A., Bunk, K., Kusters, A.F. and Riemersma, J. (1991) Herstel van de koppeling; 'lik-op-stuk'-beleid vermindert de werkdruk politie en OM. *SEC, Tijdschrift over Samenleving en Criminaliteitspreventie* 4, 22–24.

Box, S. (1981) *Deviance, Reality and Society*. Holt, Rinehart and Winston, London.

Bruinsma, G.J.N. (1991) De test-hertest betrouwbaarheid van de self-report methode. *Tijdschrift voor Criminologie* 33, 245–255.

Clark, J.P. and Tifft, L.L. (1966) Polygraph and interview validation of self-reported deviant behavior. *American Sociological Review* 31, 516–523.

Elands, B.H.M. and Beke, B.M.W.A. (1992) *Toeristisch-recreatieve Mobiliteit; een Integrale Aanpak. Kadernota Mobiliteitsplan Veluwe*. Advies- en Onderzoeks-groep Beke, Arnhem.

Farrington, D. (1973) Self-reports of deviant behavior: predictive and stable? *Journal of Criminal Law and Criminology* 64, 99–110.

Gold, M. (1966) Undetected delinquent behavior. *Journal of Research in Crime and Delinquency* 3, 27–46.

Gunn, C.A. (1988) *Tourism Planning*. Taylor and Francis, New York.

Hardt, R.H. and Peterson-Hardt, S. (1977) On determining the quality of the delinquency self-report method. *Journal of Research in Crime and Delinquency* 14, 247–259.

Hindelang, M.J., Hirschi, T. and Weis, J.G. (1981) *Measuring Delinquency*. Sage, Beverly Hills, Calif.

Hirschi, T. (1969) *Causes of Delinquency*. University of California Press, Berkeley, Calif.

Hood, R. and Sparks, R. (1970) *Key Issues in Criminology*. Weidenfeld and Nicolson, London.

Huizinga, D. and Elliot, D.S. (1986) Reassessing the reliability and validity of self-report delinquency measures. *Journal of Quantitative Criminology* 2, 293–327.

Kleiman, W.M. (1989) *Onderzoek naar Verborgen Recreatiecriminaliteit.* Katholieke Universiteit Nijmegen, Arnhem/Nijmegen.

Kleiman, W.M. and Beke, B.M.W.A. (1992) *Standaard Enquête Daders. De Ontwikkeling van een Meetinstrument t.b.v. Onderzoek naar Criminaliteit onder Jongeren.* Ministerie van Binnenlandse Zaken/Advies- en Onderzoeksgroep Beke, Den Haag.

Short, J.F. and Nye, F.I. (1957) Scaling delinquent behavior, *American Sociological Review* 22, 326–331.

17

Managing the Impacts of Recreation by Agreeing the Limits of Acceptable Change

R. Sidaway

4 Church Hill Place, EH10 4BD Edinburgh, UK

Introduction

This chapter briefly reviews the impacts of recreation on nature and considers how conflicts arise from these impacts and how such conflicts can be resolved. This perspective is based on several research reviews and case-studies on the conflicts between recreation and nature conservation (Sidaway, 1988, 1990, 1994a). This work has progressively moved from trying to assess the specifics of whether public access has any serious conservation consequences to studying environmental conflicts more generally during the course of research in Britain, the USA and The Netherlands (Sidaway, 1992). Subsequent work on conflict resolution has included a study for the Outdoor Recreation Directorate of the Dutch Ministry of Agriculture, Nature Management and Fisheries on conflicts on the Rhine Delta (Sidaway and van der Voet, 1993) and a review of the 'Limits of Acceptable Change' concept for the Countryside Commission (Sidaway, 1994b). During this time my standpoint has changed from making a professional judgement on the 'correct' solution to recognizing the merits of interests reaching their own mutually acceptable solution.

An Overview of Recreational Impacts

Like many other human activities, recreation can have a wide range of direct and indirect effects on nature. This diversity stems in part from the many different forms of leisure activity that can take place in the countryside. Whether these impacts are of any significance for conservation depends on whether they are assessed at the population level on strictly defined criteria, e.g. the decline of a breeding population or loss of habitat. When judged in this way, the crucial factors for sustaining a population are more likely to be loss of habitat and effects on food supplies due to, say, current agricultural practice (see, for example, Brindley *et al.*, 1992). In these circumstances the impacts of recreation are likely to be marginal and crucial only to species under severe stress from other factors such as grazing levels (Thompson and Horsfield, 1990).

The importance of using such criteria is to put the impacts of recreation into perspective when compared to major environmental threats, such as habitat loss from agriculture or atmospheric pollution. In comparison, the significance of recreational impacts for the conservation of wildlife is generally low. There are three important qualifications to this generalization:

- first, when sport and recreation are coupled with economic and tourism development, e.g. the development of tourist complexes or resorts, then the associated developments can result in significant loss of habitats;
- secondly, recreational impacts can be particularly acute in habitats that lack resilience. In these cases the biological system has a very long recovery cycle, e.g. alpine and certain coastal ecosystems;
- thirdly, increasing mobility and affluence, particularly among the active younger sections of the population, coupled with the introduction of new technology, provide a fertile market for new recreation activities. Examples of such new sports are jet-skiing and mountain-biking. On past experience, the effects of these activities are likely to be locally serious until management measures are developed to ameliorate them.

It is also worth remembering that some recreational activities can also have positive environmental effects such as the creation or protection of landscape features on golf-courses, which can be beneficial to wildlife. The task of the recreation manager is to balance any possible harmful effects that recreation may have on the environment against the considerable range of benefits which so many people derive from enjoying the countryside.

Impact Management

The majority of recreational impacts can therefore be reduced by good management and there is now a recognizable body of 'good conservation practice' identified in the literature (e.g. Sidaway, 1991, 1994a; Aitchison and Lloyd Jones, 1994). If impacts are to be reduced, the basic measures which managers have to consider are:

- whether to concentrate recreation activities so as to reduce disturbance to birds and mammals or to disperse the activities to spread the load;
- whether to segregate activities by zoning, thereby creating relatively undisturbed areas;
- whether to introduce time-sharing in the form of seasonal restrictions to protect sensitive species during vulnerable periods, such as the breeding season;
- how far users can be involved in management, by being responsible for regulating their own behaviour and/or in decision-making.

The development of facilities for intensive recreational use usually requires a formal process of approval in which environmental impacts are assessed. Dispersed activities, which are not concentrated at specific sites, are likely to have only local effects. Nevertheless they may require careful management. This means that the impact and the recreation activity that causes it need to be studied in some detail. But there have been few research studies which specifically examine this relationship and give clear guidance to recreation managers on what remedial action could be taken to reduce recreational impacts (Sidaway, 1994a).

Yet the more specific a management prescription can be, the greater the likelihood that users will accept regulation as necessary and will comply with it. The example of voluntary seasonal restrictions on cliff-climbing to protect nesting birds illustrates these principles. These work effectively because the nesting sites are known to the climbers and the restrictions only operate on specific climbing pitches and they are relaxed when the birds are not nesting. (Table 17.1 gives other examples.)

Table 17.1. Examples of impact management. (Based on Sidaway, 1991.)

Activity	Possible impacts	Possible solutions
Birdwatching/photography	Disturbance of migratory and nesting birds	Code of practice
Caving	Damage to features	Controlled access
Cliff-climbing	Disturbance of nesting birds	Voluntary restrictions
Fishing	Disturbance of shore-nesting birds	Restrictions in nesting season
Motor sports/off-road cycling	Damage to vegetation	Limit use to specific durable routes. Codes of practice
Orienteering	Disturbance of nesting birds	Scheduling of events
Riding	Damage to vegetation	Repair/construction of bridle-ways
Shooting	Size of cull Disturbance	Bag restriction Controlled access
Walking	Damage to vegetation Disturbance by dogs	Repair/construct paths Restrictions in nesting season
All activities	Fire damage to vegetation	Controlled access in high-risk periods

The Distinction between Impacts and Conflicts

The word conflict tends to be used very loosely, yet an important distinction can be made between impacts (a biological phenomenon), defined as a measurable physical change which may have consequences for conservation of species or habitats, and conflicts (a sociological phenomenon), defined as a disagreement between interest groups which has reached the public arena and may have political consequences, e.g. one group is trying to control the action or access of another.

How Conflicts Arise

When one examines conflicts involving nature conservation and recreation, it soon becomes clear that a recreational impact does not necessarily result in a conflict. A recreational impact may be the ostensible reason for a dispute, but whether a disagreement escalates into a conflict is more likely to depend on the relationship between different interest groups. In other words, the same impact may be handled without controversy in one situation but mishandled and lead to conflict in another. Taking two British examples, the restoration of the Basingstoke Canal has been very controversial because of its effects on wildlife, while a similar scheme for the Montgomery Canal was not; yet both contain sites of high conservation value. One part of the Rhine Delta, the Grevelingen, is successfully managed for recreation and conservation; yet in a neighbouring estuary, the Oosterschelde, and in the adjoining Voordelta, the relationship between the two interests is an unhappy one (Sidaway and van der Voet, 1993). Thus what determines whether an impact becomes contentious is the nature of the relationship between the interest groups.

Alternative explanations have been suggested as to how conflicts arise because of misunderstandings, competing interests or a clash of basic principles (Amy, 1988) but in practice all three circumstances can apply within the same conflict. By examining the nature of these

Table 17.2. A diagnostic framework to distinguish conflicts. (Source: Sidaway, 1992.)

Variables	Distinguishing features of conflicts	Distinguishing features of potential conflicts
Understanding of impact	Uncertainty and contention	Understood and uncontentious
Opposing ideologies	Competing ideologies in opposition	Ideology shared or differences respected
Advancement of principle	Issue elevated to a matter of principle	Not an issue
Environmental awareness	Interest groups insensitive to environmental impact	Interest groups sensitive to impacts and agree preventive action
Appropriateness of resource use	Use considered inappropriate	Not an issue
Communication networks	Poorly established	Well established and effective
Reaction to new claim on resource	Adverse reaction on the part of existing interests	Unclear
Negotiation strategies of interests	Confrontational	Conciliatory
Level of political organization	Highly organized	Organized
Acceptance of management aims	May/may not be an issue	Unchallenged
Type of decision-making	Adversarial	Negotiative

interactions in a series of case-studies in Britain, the USA and The Netherlands, it was possible to identify a range of contributory factors which distinguish between situations where conflicts are likely or unlikely to occur (Sidaway, 1992; see Table 17.2).

Typically, conflicts centre on a fundamental clash of principles, perhaps over 'inappropriate' use of an area, when the parties take a confrontational approach, involve the media, challenge the aims of management and resist change and the dispute is encouraged by an adversarial form of decision-making. In a cooperative situation, there is good communication between the interest groups so that information on the impact and its consequences can be understood, thereby increasing the environmental awareness of the user groups. Adversarial decision-making is replaced by negotiations, and the attitudes of the interest groups are both conciliatory and amenable to change.

Not all of these factors are amenable to change, but those that are give clues to possible ways of resolving conflicts. The understanding of the impact can be improved by research and by establishing a communication network. Information on the impact and its consequences can be disseminated, thereby increasing the environmental awareness of the user groups. By replacing adversarial decision-making with negotiations, the negotiating strategies of interest groups may change from confrontational to conciliatory.

Such negotiations tend to take place out of the full glare of the media. Negotiations can be designed to reconsider attitudes to change and reach consensus on the aims of management. Two factors from the model may prove to be stumbling-blocks to negotiation: groups are often organized around matters of principle, and those which have traditionally used an area may have strong views about the 'appropriateness' of use by newcomers.

Alternative Approaches to Conflict Resolution

Ury and his co-authors distinguish three major ways of resolving disputes: those which reconcile the disputants' underlying interests, those which determine who is right, and those which determine who is more powerful (Ury *et al.*, 1988). They argue that in general the first approach (for example, problem-solving negotiation), which identifies and recognizes interests, is less costly and more rewarding than a rights approach (such as legal action in the courts), which in turn is less costly and more rewarding than a power approach (such as strikes or wars).

In Britain we are familiar with legal processes and arbitration, particularly the planning inquiry where an inspector assesses evidence in a quasi-legal way and the result is subjected to a form of political arbitration. We are less familiar with negotiations or cooperative problem-solving using an independent mediator as an approach to resolving environmental disputes.

In the USA, in particular, as environmental problems in which large numbers of interests are involved become increasingly complex, there is growing frustration with time delays and costs of administrative and legal processes of decision-making. What mediation and a variety of 'alternative dispute resolution' (ADR) techniques try to achieve is the involvement of all the interested parties or interest groups in decision-making or negotiation on a more or less equal basis. They aim to produce a solution which is more acceptable to all of the parties and is longer-lasting than one imposed on the parties.

The benefits of using ADR procedures are claimed to be:

- the voluntary nature of the process;
- the use of less formal procedures;
- the protection and maintenance of working relationships;
- greater flexibility in designing the terms of the settlement;
- savings in time and cost;
- a greater degree of control for the interested parties resulting in more predictable outcomes;
- decisions that hold over time (based on Moore and Delli Priscoli, 1989).

The Limits of Acceptable Change: a Possible Way Forward

How then are interest groups to be involved more directly in managing the impacts of recreation on the countryside? The answer must lie with the organizations entrusted with management and their approach to that task. Their approach can be adversarial – confronting the parties in an already polarized countryside debate – or conciliatory – attempting to build trust and develop consensus.

At the moment the most promising approach for countryside problems is an American technique – the 'Limits of Acceptable Change' (LAC), which involves the interest groups in deciding what conservation measures are necessary. A recent literature review of methods of conflict resolution assessed the potential contribution of LAC, as a system of impact management, to the reduction of conflicts between nature conservation and water-recreation interests in the Rhine Delta of The Netherlands (Sidaway and van der Voet, 1993). It established a set of ideal criteria – balanced terms of reference,

Table 17.3. Stages in the LAC process. (Based on Stankey *et al.*, 1985.)

1. Broad review of issues in the area
2. Description of conditions in the area
3. Identification of change and indicators of change
4. Survey of indicators of change
5. Specification of quality standards
6. Prescription of desired conditions in each zone
7. Agreement of management action to maintain quality in each zone
8. Review of proposals for area as a whole
9. Implementation, monitoring and review

balanced representation of the interests, open access to information and continuing public involvement – common to successful methods of dispute resolution and found that the LAC process, in theory at least, conforms more closely than many of the other case-studies included in the review.

The LAC process, set out in Table 17.3, has the following merits.

1. Despite the inclusion of the word 'limits' in its title, it marks a shift in the emphasis from a negative approach to management, which characterized attempts to determine carrying-capacity, to a more positive one of managing for quality. The definition of quality is a matter of judgement and, rather than leave this to professionals alone, the LAC process involves the interested parties in a working party of, say, landowners, recreational users and conservationists, whose task is to identify the characteristic qualities of the area. This involvement should build consensus and trust, bringing with it a commitment to the process and thereby minimizing the risk of future conflict.

2. The group considers change. It recognizes that biological and social processes are both dynamic and cannot be fixed once and for all, unlike capacity. It considers changes in the area against a wider context of change. It considers the desirability of change, agreeing which changes would be unacceptable and which might be desirable. Changes are monitored on behalf of the group and when quality standards are not maintained remedial actions, which have been agreed in advance, are taken. In this way, management can respond and not stumble from crisis to crisis.

An Application of LAC in Britain

In the USA, LAC is being used in ten wilderness areas and a number of other designated areas. In Britain, the application of a modified form of the technique has been pioneered by the Institute of Terrestrial Ecology, notably at the Aonach Mor ski development near Fort William, Scotland (Bayfield *et al.*, 1988). The major impact considered is damage to vegetation, but management is also concerned with the recreational experience, measured by the length of queues at ski-tows. However, it is worth noting that the ski area is relatively small (160 ha); the use of LAC as a monitoring technique is a condition of planning permission for the development because the ski-field is within a Site of Special Scientific Interest; and the considerable costs of monitoring site conditions by an independent research institute are borne by the developer.

It seems likely that the principal benefits of using LAC at Aonach Mor have been that it encouraged a rational debate about management among the interested parties, that managers have had to be more specific about their objectives and that certain aspects of quality have been considered. Assessing change has been the underlying problem – how to distinguish natural change from that caused by recreational impacts when there is little basic understanding of the processes of change and how to ameliorate harmful impacts (Mackay, 1991).

The Strengths and Weaknesses of LAC

The LAC approach combines three components – rational planning, quality management and public involvement. The rational planning method moves logically, stage by stage, from defining objectives, analysing problems and considering options to monitoring achievement. In this respect it is similar to many other approaches to conservation or management planning. LAC differs in its attempts to identify measurable aspects of quality, to monitor whether environmental quality is maintained and the degree of interest-group involvement throughout the process.

Many of the strengths and weaknesses of LAC stem from its three component elements (see Table 17.4). For example, LAC gains considerable strengths from the clarity of purpose, the consideration of change and the clarification of uncertainty which follow from a rational analysis. Planning should have a strong positive emphasis if, for example, the quality of recreation experiences is considered as well as

Table 17.4. LAC strengths and weaknesses analysis.

Elements of LAC	Strengths	Weaknesses
The rational planning approach, which focuses on desirable future conditions	Promotes a rational debate about assessing and managing change Forces managers to be specific about objectives and standards	The costs of specifying and collecting data on biological change and recreational use are high May prove too elaborate a management system for simple impacts or widely dispersed activities
Quality management (qualities are assessed and quality indicators are selected and monitored)	Directs research and evaluation towards quality management Monitoring can be selective, management can be directed to improving quality	Qualities are difficult to define and routinely assess Undue emphasis is given to those aspects of quality that can be measured There may be practical limits on the number of impacts and/or qualities that can be handled
Public involvement throughout the process	Improves acceptance and support for conservation and recreation management in contentious situations	Difficult to find accountable representatives for informal activities that are not organized Difficult to deal with new impacts if task force is not adaptable Difficult to sustain public involvement over time

wildlife habitats and the improvement of habitats as well as their maintenance. The working relationships developed during the exercise are particularly important in resolving conflicts over access, environmental impacts and land use.

If the major strength of LAC is that it offers a powerful combination of the best of these three elements, its major weaknesses stem from the technical difficulties of assessing quality and establishing quantitative indicators, the elaborate nature of such an intensive planning process and its cost.

How can LAC be Developed?

The Limits of Acceptable Change provides a sophisticated and valuable approach to managing complex situations. It is, however, costly in terms of the skills, information and commitment that are required to operate it and any management exercise has to be commensurate with the scale and complexity of the problem it is addressing. The management of simple impacts is unlikely to be controversial and an elaborate approach like LAC will not be warranted. It is probably best applied in situations where the ecosystem dynamics are understood and there is controversy over, say, the impacts of recreational activities on wildlife. Because of its cost, the number of full applications in Britain, which strictly follow the US Forest Service model, is likely to be limited. LAC is unlikely to be a universal panacea, nor is it a soft option.

There is no reason, however, why the *principles* of LAC should not be applied more widely or why they should be limited to recreation management. They could be used in the management of water recreation (particularly in coastal-zone management of estuaries to define standards for water quality, crowding or population levels for critical species), or in the management of tourism pressures within local communities (to define levels of development and change that are acceptable to local communities). But they could also be used in ecosystem management to identify desirable future conditions as goals for management in which recreation would be one of a number of human influences. The issues of desirable and acceptable change could provide a useful focus in any situation where local communities have to understand environmental issues and adapt to new regulatory standards.

If the principles of LAC are to be more widely applied, some of the intrinsic problems of rational planning, quality management and public involvement have to be addressed. Three particular aspects will require careful attention:

- the lack of information on ecosystems, their population dynamics and the possible impacts of recreation activities;
- the problems of quantifying environmental quality;
- how to involve a wide range of interest groups in the discussion that will lead to consensus.

The recreational impacts are little researched and there is considerable debate about their seriousness. Sounder management is hampered by the lack of information on the potentially disturbing effects of recreational access, and research is required to clarify the issue. Rather than continue an abstract level of debate based on opposing principles, it will be more productive to focus on the specific problems of particular areas. Given the difficulties of trying to agree and mount elaborate programmes of definitive research, a more pragmatic experimental approach could be coupled with a LAC monitoring programme. It does not appear to be a question of choosing between research and a LAC exercise, but rather coupling the two together to solve access-management problems.

But if relatively little is known about ecosystems and impacts, even less is known about the qualities of the environment that are of importance to different types of recreational experience. LAC discussions will help to articulate important values and qualities but only those of the predominant interest groups and not those of the unorganized casual participant. Research is needed to tackle this problem but again it is not a case of research or LAC but each complementing the other, because interest-group involvement has an important role to play in conflict resolution.

Consequently, as much care has to be taken to design the LAC discussions as has to be taken in designing any research and monitoring programme. It is generally agreed that it is vital to draw conservation, recreation and land-managing interests together and to establish a constructive dialogue on management issues. For this to happen, each interest has to recognize the legitimacy of the others, decision-making has to be open and representation balanced and accountable, and information has to be treated as a common resource to ensure informed debate. There is no single model of public involvement which can be followed slavishly; local factors have to be taken into account and in the most inflamed situations professional mediation skills may well be required to establish and facilitate the discussions, at least in the initial stages.

Conclusions

In many ways it seems curious that recreation and nature conservation cannot invariably live in harmony. Indeed it is all too easy to overemphasize the relatively few conflicts and ignore the numerous instances of cooperation when the potentially harmful impacts of recreation are recognized and carefully managed in a responsible way. Certainly in those cases where conflicts do arise, it is vital to build better relationships between the interests as they have, in reality, a common cause: the protection and enjoyment of the environment. Although LAC is conceptually sound it is difficult to apply in practice. However, all too many problems of countryside management are complicated, controversial and costly. In these circumstances there does seem to be a good case for adopting the key elements of LAC – rational planning, quality management and public involvement – as basic management principles, to use them in combination and to tailor their exact application to local circumstances.

References

Aitchison, J. and Lloyd Jones, P. (1994) *A Sporting Chance for the Countryside: Case Studies of Good Practice.* Report prepared for the Sports Council for Wales and the Countryside Council for Wales. Rural Surveys Research Unit, University of Wales, Aberystwyth.

Amy, D. (1988) *The Politics of Environmental Mediation.* Columbia Press, New York.

Bayfield, N.G., Watson, A. and Miller, G.R. (1988) Assessing and managing the effects of recreational use on British hills. In: Usher, M.B. and Thompson, D.B.A. (eds) *Ecological Change: The Uplands.* Basil Blackwell, Oxford, pp. 399–414.

Brindley, E., Lucas, F. and Waterhouse, M. (1992) *North Staffordshire Moors Survey.* Royal Society for the Protection of Birds, Droitwich.

Mackay, J.W. (1991) A note on the limits of acceptable change. Unpublished paper presented to the Countryside Recreation Research Group, 14 Jan.

Moore, C. and Delli Priscoli, J. (1989) *The Executive Seminar on Alternative Dispute Procedures.* US Army Corps of Engineers, Washington.

Sidaway, R. (1988) *Sport, Recreation and Nature Conservation.* Study 32, Sports Council, London.

Sidaway, R. (1990) *Birds and Walkers: A Review of Existing Research on Access to the Countryside and Disturbance to Birds.* Ramblers' Association, London.

Sidaway, R. (1991) *Good Conservation Practice for Sport and Recreation.* Sports Council, Countryside Commission, Nature Conservancy Council and World Wide Fund for Nature, London.

Sidaway, R. (1992) *Outdoor Recreation and Nature Conservation: Conflicts and Their Resolution.* Final Report to the Economic and Social Research Council (Research Grant R 000 23 1792).

Sidaway, R. (1994a) *Recreation and the Natural Heritage: A Research Review.* Scottish Natural Heritage, Edinburgh.

Sidaway, R. (1994b) Limits of Acceptable Change in practice. Summary of an unpublished report to the Countryside Commission. *ECOS* 15(2), 42–49.

Sidaway, R. and van der Voet, J.L.M. (1993) *Getting on Speaking Terms: Resolving Conflicts between Recreation and Nature in Coastal Zone Areas in the Netherlands: A Literature Review and Case Study Analysis.* Agricultural University, Werkgroep Recreatie en Toerisme, Wageningen.

Stankey, G.H., Cole, D.N., Lucas, R.C., Peterson, M.E. and Frissell, S.J. (1985) *The Limits of Acceptable Change (LAC) of Wilderness Planning.* Forest Service General Technical Report, Int-176, US Department of Agriculture.

Thompson, D.B.A. and Horsfield, D.H. (1990) Towards an assessment of nature conservation criteria in the British uplands. In: Thompson, D.B.A. and Kirby, K.J. (eds) *Grazing Research and Nature Conservation.* R & S Report, No. 31, NCC, Peterborough, pp. 9–18.

Ury, W.L., Brett, J.M. and Goldberg, S.B. (1988) *Getting Disputes Resolved: Designing Systems to Cut the Costs of Conflict.* Jossey-Bass, San Francisco.

18

The Role of Management Information Systems in the Provision of Recreation

P.D. Taylor

Leisure Management Unit, The University of Sheffield, Hicks Building, Hounsfield Road, S3 7RH Sheffield, UK

Introduction and Context

It is vital in the transformation of a recreational resource into a valid consumption experience that the manager responsible is fully informed about the success or otherwise of the transformation. With adequate information the manager can design a recreational experience that not only fits the users' aspirations but also achieves the manager's objectives at minimum cost. Without adequate information the manager can easily make errors, such as producing an experience which consumers do not value, or incurring costs which are not covered by revenues or other returns in the appropriate time period. This chapter considers the way in which a properly designed management information system can monitor performance of a recreation organization and thus help the recreation manager to identify and resolve problems and generally seek to improve operations in the organization.

What kind of information does a management information system produce? At the heart of such a system is internal, automatically generated, quantitative information such as numbers of visits, revenues, costs and, with modern point-of-sales technology, visitor characteristics, times of visit, etc. Such information may be supplemented with the results of regular or occasional customer market research, thus revealing such qualitative dimensions as attitudes, aspirations and concerns brought about by the recreation experience.

In manufacturing industry it is relatively easy to assess the physical output and technical quality of production. Because of this it is a relatively straightforward task to monitor the effect of changing

317

inputs on the resulting output, through measures such as productivity, capacity utilization and meeting technical specifications. However, in much of recreation and tourism services, whilst there are certain tangible products which make up the visitor's experience, the services as a whole are largely intangible. They are therefore more difficult to monitor in terms of the quantity and quality of outputs. For this reason, the assessment of both process and outcome by a management information system is both important and difficult in the provision of recreation and tourism. The qualitative dimension afforded by market research is particularly important in assessing the performance of intangible recreation and tourism services (Bovaird, 1992).

Functions

Management information is important for a number of purposes, which are not unique to recreation and tourism but are as important to this industry as any other. These include the following.

The management of services

In making decisions and managing resources a well-known problem is 'crisis management', with very short time horizons and a lack of strategic direction. A properly constructed management information system facilitates the checking of key dimensions of organizational performance, the early identification of problems, the testing of different solutions and the development of production and distribution methods. This is not to deny the importance of intuitive management appraisal and decision-making. Nevertheless, no matter what intuitive decision-making skills a manager has, these can be complemented by appropriate management information which results in better decisions (Butt and Palmer, 1985).

The planning of service development

This both runs parallel to and is a precursor of crisis management. It is sadly often the case that 'crisis planning' occurs in the development of recreational services. Typically this takes the form of opportunistic rather than planned recreation development (Cowell, 1979), for example, in response to the availability of land (as from changes in property markets) or of extra funds (as at the end of the financial year). Opportunities can be exploited more effectively and with less risk if the existing management information for the organization supports the development and gives important signals about its scale, design and market direction.

Bidding for funds and credibility

It is important in both public and private organizations to present a convincing case in support of new recreation and tourism development, both within the organization and to relevant outside interests. In both the public and private sectors there is likely to be intra-organizational competition for funds. This is particularly relevant, for example, in local governments, where recreation and tourism are often discretionary areas of activity and have to compete for funds with mandatory services such as housing, social welfare and education.

Public relations

It is necessary to convince a broader set of constituencies, whether actual or potential users, the general public or the taxpayer, of the value of an organization's activities. This justification for management information systems is not an implicit endorsement of 'how to lie with statistics' but rather a recognition that such systems will enable an organization to use evidence, rather than rhetoric alone, to improve its image.

Key Elements in Establishing a Management Information System

A well-designed management information system must be based on a systematic analysis of the relationships between the objectives of the organization, the performance indicators employed in representing these objectives, and the management targets set for the performance of the organization. To some recreation managers, as indicated by Coopers and Lybrand (1981) and the Audit Commission (1989) in Britain, the differences between these terms are vague. However, rigour in separating objectives, performance indicators and targets results in clearer and more systematic answers to the question 'are we achieving our objectives?'

A precise delineation of recreation objectives, indicators and targets facilitates the structuring and specification of a whole series of performance questions in recreation organizations, such as: 'what trade-offs are apparent in the objectives and achievements of the organization?'; 'what indicators need improving?'; 'what targets need revising?'; 'what is the exact nature of any problems?'; 'what are the most probable causes of problems?'; 'what are the likely solutions to problems?'

Objectives

These should be specified so that at the close of a chosen evaluation period it is clear whether they have been achieved. This almost certainly means that objectives need to be quantifiable. Each objective should have one or more appropriate performance indicators, by which measurement of performance is possible. Objectives should be about ends not means: for example it is not an objective to 'programme specific times for use of a recreation centre by mothers with young children'; the objective here is 'to increase visits to the centre by mothers with young children' and this can be met by a number of means, of which programming is one. Intermediate objectives may be designed as a stepping-stone towards a final objective. Introducing a new computerized management information system can be seen as an example of an intermediate objective which enables the organization to better achieve a number of final objectives such as higher profits, more effective market segmentation or a larger number of visits.

The ranking of objectives must be clear as they may conflict: for example, 'increase revenue' may conflict with 'increase use of a recreation facility by the unemployed'. Where trade-offs between conflicting objectives are required, this should be explicitly recognized and where possible priorities need to be identified for appropriate contexts, such as times of the day, or particular amenities, or different customer types. Failure to specify such priorities means that unambiguous interpretation of management information is less likely, for example if the performance relating to asset utilization in a recreation service is improving while the profitability of the same service is deteriorating.

It is often the case, particularly in the public sector, that so-called objectives are either not set or are expressed in a manner which prevents anyone from assessing whether or not they have been achieved. Such wrongly termed objectives include 'achieving sport for all', 'serving the community's needs', 'providing an efficient service', 'providing a high-quality recreational experience' and 'improving the image of the attraction'. In fact these expressions of intent are really 'aims' rather than objectives, and they are more suited to mission statements than operational objectives. They are broadly based and non-measurable. They need to be supplemented with a range of more specific, measurable objectives to be monitored by management information and used for management decision-making.

In principle, objectives for public-sector recreation organizations are likely to be more complicated than those of private, commercial firms because social, non-profit objectives are of more importance to public-sector organizations. Social objectives are less easily expressed in a measurable form than financial ones. Nevertheless, it is important to attempt to encapsulate social aims in measurable objectives. Otherwise, in a period of reduced public expenditure and with conventional financial accounting systems, a public service with laudable but unprovable objectives is more vulnerable in comparison with a service which can demonstrate success in meeting objectives. Recently in Britain community recreation services and sports development have suffered more from financial stringency than have other public-sector recreation services which can more easily rely on conventional performance indicators such as revenue and visits (Taylor and Page, 1994).

Performance Indicators

A performance indicator is a measure of an objective and one of the key functions of a management information system is to provide evidence of the levels and changes in performance indicators. It provides evidence of what has been achieved and what the particular state of affairs is at a particular moment. It will usually be a quantitative measure but may be a qualitative change assessed by quantitative means, although consistency and comparability of such qualitative assessments are likely to be difficult.

The easiest indicators to understand are numbers and sometimes they portray performance accurately in relation to important objectives. However, numbers lack a reference point or perspective. For example, consider the social objective of increasing the use of a publicly subsidized recreation amenity by unemployed visitors. The simplest indicator would be to monitor the number of visits by unemployed people at a given time or, to give the indicator more perspective, their visits as a percentage of all visits. Similarly, instead of using just cash figures for, say, gross expenditure, revenue and deficit, ratios in common use in public recreation services are gross expenditure per visit, revenue per visit and deficit per visit, or deficit expressed as the ratio of revenue to expenditure, known as 'cost recovery' (Audit Commission, 1988; Hespe *et al.*, 1988). In commercial recreation, accounting ratios such as the return on capital employed (net profit to total asets), gearing ratio (borrowing to net worth) and the price/earnings ratio are in common use, along with many other standard ratios (ICC Information; Holmes and Sugden, 1986).

A management information system should be capable of reporting a representative selection of indicators, that is, those representative of the management's objectives, of different dimensions of performance such as efficiency and effectiveness as well as the quantity and quality of performance. Furthermore, this system should report the indicators' values at any time requested by management. Choosing a set of performance indicators that should be monitored by a management information system can seem deceptively straightforward. However, ideally such a set of indicators should satisfy a range of properties, which are briefly reviewed below. Many of these may seem obvious but evidence of the use of indicators in public-sector recreation services in Britain (Audit Commission, 1989, 1991a, b) suggests that the monitoring of objectives by indicators with even basic properties is often missing.

Indicators should cover all objectives; yet very often social objectives are not represented by appropriate indicators, because they are seen as difficult to monitor. However, indicators expressing the use of recreation facilities by the socially disadvantaged (for example, the unemployed, elderly, poor or disabled) or those with special recreational needs (such as the young) are fairly easy to construct and monitor. Indicators should represent their objectives accurately; yet it is often the case that an indicator is vague on such details. For example, one of the commonest indicators in recreation services is the number of visits, but this does not accurately portray the number of people who use the service – it is a composite of the number of people and the frequency of their attendance. Sophisticated membership systems employing new technology can distinguish between people and frequency, with consequent marketing benefits. Many recreation services, though, cannot monitor the changing composition of their visit figures, because of a basic deficiency in their management information system.

It is important in such a differentiated service as recreation, where there are many target markets defined by type of customer, time of day and nature of activity, that indicators monitor not only the whole service, but also the disaggregated parts of the operations. Here it is important to identify cost centres, but again the evidence, particularly in the public sector, suggests that such disaggregated indicators are infrequently monitored. In multi-use facilities such as sports centres, arts centres and parks, it may be difficult to allocate the costs which are common to the whole facility to different cost centres within the facility. However, overcoming this problem rewards the recreation manager with management information specific to the level at which some of his/her major decisions apply.

Many indicators are measured as an average over an evaluation period, usually a year. However, it is important for many management decisions to have indicators capable of incremental values, showing values for a shorter, more immediate time horizon such as a week, or in the period immediately following an important change in policy. It is often useful for managers to compare the value of indicators over time, between service elements and possibly between different organizations. The use of ratios helps to achieve such standardization so that costs and revenues, for example, can be compared between services and facilities with very different visit numbers. Finally, it is essential that indicators are administratively manageable, do not incur excessive administrative monitoring costs, and can be easily understood by their intended audience. The last of these properties is particularly relevant for public recreation services, which will be managed to a certain extent by elected and non-specialist 'lay managers' and which will be ultimately accountable to the electorate.

The choice of indicators can easily have other problems. The choice is essentially subjective, so consensus within the organization is necessary before the indicators can be seen as fair indicators of performance. Indicators are also signals to staff about what is important to the organization; they may even be associated with performance-related pay. In Britain at the moment there is some concern that the indicators used to monitor public recreation facilities which are managed under contracts are sending the wrong signals to many staff about the relative importance of financial and social objectives, to the detriment of the latter. The data needed to service performance indicators must be 'clean' and consistent.

In practice many commercial ratios are comparable across different firms, and indeed organizations such as ICC Information produce publications with the main intention of making such comparisons. The objectives of commercial firms are obviously financially orientated but they extend well beyond simple indicators of profitability. They also include indicators which are transferable to public-sector recreation services, such as productivity and the profit-to-sales ratio. In the public sector, in Britain, the main comparative evidence has been produced by the Audit Commission using mainly financial information from surveys conducted for the Chartered Institute for Public Finance and Accountancy (CIPFA). Recent Audit Commission reports have indicated substantial room for improvement in the management information systems associated with provision by local authorities in sport (Audit Commission, 1989), entertainment and performing arts venues (Audit Commission, 1991a) and museums and art galleries (Audit Commission, 1991b). The publication of such comparative public-sector performance indicators in Britain has been stimulated recently by the 'Citizen's Charter'. Under this legislation, local authorities will be required to publish data on performance indicators chosen by the government to represent performance in the whole array of public services, including recreation services. The recreation services indicators include per capita subsidy and subsidy per visit for such services as swimming-pools and other indoor facilities, and simple numbers of facilities for both indoor and outdoor facilities. The main problem with such indicators is a simple one: there are not enough of them, because the government wishes to keep the published results simple and understandable. The Audit Commission, which is responsible for making recommendations on the indicators to be used, initially suggested 20 recreation indicators. According to the Citizen's Charter legislation these indicators are to represent performance of five types – the amount of service provided, the use made of the service, the effectiveness of the services, the cost to the taxpayer and the service's value for money. Given the heterogeneity of recreation services, the likelihood of 20 indicators adequately representing recreation performance is slim.

Another stimulus to the systematic use of management information systems for delivering information on performance indicators in Britain is the implementation of compulsory competitive tendering for the management of local-authority recreation facilities. The splitting of management functions into client and contractor responsibilities imposes an implicit duty on the client authority to monitor the performance of the contractor, whether in-house or private. Only in this way will the contractor be held accountable and the client in a position to choose a contractor better at the end of the current contract period. Although there is apparently a wide variation in the seriousness with which client authorities are taking the monitoring function, one effect of this is almost certainly to improve the average management information system in local authorities.

Targets

When used in conjunction with a performance indicator, a target offers a concrete and unambiguous answer to the question 'is this objective being achieved in a particular period?' However, targets can and arguably must change through time. They should be continuously scrutinized and reviewed for relevance to the operating circumstances of the organization. A major problem, which is only resolved by expert judgement, is setting a target which is feasible but not too easy. Non-feasible targets are demotivating for staff and damage the credibility of the service to external audiences. 'Soft' targets can breed staff complacency and are not conducive to a dynamic, efficient operation.

Complementary Developments

The above discussion of the requirements of a management information system gives rise to several considerations that complement such a system. Management information integrates with other management support structures. These include the following.

Cost-centring

Many decisions in recreation management relate not to a service or facility as a whole but to constituent parts, such as activities, events or different market segments or client groups. If a management information system is to service these decisions effectively, then it needs to be able to disaggregate information to the appropriate level. The cost element of the management information presents a problem in that many costs are typically common to a range of activities and markets. To be of use to decision-makers, therefore, these costs have to be allocated to the different constituent parts of the service or facility, a process known as cost-centring or functional costing. This is not a complicated process but thought needs to be given to the way in which a management information system allocates costs to different parts of the organization.

Market research

Internally generated customer information is not adequate to express qualitative feedback. Market research conducted on a regular basis can complement the internally derived, largely quantitative management information. Market research has become a continuing feature of management information systems in large private companies and is also becoming a normal part of monitoring of recreation services in local authorities in Britain. With its variety of forms, it is the most accessible technique for revealing qualitative information on recreation experiences and services.

Budgeting

The presentation of budgets needs to be consistent with the presentation of management information; much of the latter is expressed in financial terms anyway. To be consistent, it is necessary to move away from conventional budgets towards programme budgeting and the incorporation of performance indicators, both financial and social, in budgetary documents.

New technology

This is essential for the effective and efficient collection, storage, retrieval, processing and presentation of performance data (Ridd, 1991). Only with the use of integrated management information systems software is it possible to present up-to-date information when required, estimate 'what-if?' scenarios, and make the use of management information a continual process rather than a special event.

Review procedures

The management culture necessary to encourage the continual use of management information is likely to be different from that which many recreation managers are used to. Systematizing management information is one thing, but just as important is systematizing the process of review and decision-making, using the information as a catalyst for improvement. This requires very specific initiatives, including the training of personnel, to realize the potential that management information provides. This culture also needs to encourage the shared ownership of information within the organization, so that all employees are aware of the common organizational purpose for the information and the collective responsibility to ensure that the information is accurate and helpful.

Conclusion

Management information is an investment for the organization: not just an investment in the new technology to handle the information, but more importantly an investment in the future decisions and performance of the organization. To realize the return from this investment requires very careful planning of the form that management information is to take; it also requires complementary investments in the human resources that are to use the resulting information.

It is a salutary thought that there is no such thing as a flawless management information system. All indicators, data and information systems have their limitations, so in designing a management information system it is important to minimize the deficiencies of the selected system. Increasingly, the choice of new technology determines the accessibility and usefulness of a management information system. Unfortunately it is often the case in recreation services that the primary design purpose of management information software is not a whole management information system but more particularly the function of membership and booking records. A common and fundamental defect of such software has been the failure to integrate this demand-side information with cost data.

Clearly the most significant impetus for a change to better recreation management information software would be through the demands of managers themselves. An essential precursor to investment in new technology, therefore, is investment of management time in thinking through their requirements. This involves specifying in detail the information requirements that fit the organization's objectives and indicators. By this means the management information system that is purchased will accurately inform the decisions being taken.

References

Audit Commission (1988) *Performance Review in Local Government, Action Guide and Data Supplement.* HMSO, London.

Audit Commission (1989) *Sport for Whom? Clarifying the Local Authority Role in Sport and Recreation.* HMSO, London.

Audit Commission (1991a) *Local Authorities, Entertainment and the Arts.* HMSO, London.

Audit Commission (1991b) *The Road to Wigan Pier? Managing Local Authority Museums and Art Galleries.* HMSO, London.

Bovaird, A. (1992) Evaluation, performance assessment and objective led management in public sector leisure services. In: *Leisure in the 1990s: Rolling Back the Welfare State.* Leisure Studies Association, publication 46, Eastbourne.

Butt, H. and Palmer, B. (1985) *Value for Money in the Public Sector: The Decision-Makers Guide.* Basil Blackwell, Oxford.

Coopers and Lybrand (1981) *Service Provision and Pricing in Local Government.* HMSO, London.

Cowell, D. (1979) Marketing in local authority sport, leisure and recreation centres. *Local Government Studies* 5, 31–43.

Hespe, C., Sillitoe, A. and Thorpe, J. (1988) *Measuring Performance.* Management Papers Issue 1, Sports Council, Greater London and South-East Region, London.

Holmes, G. and Sugden, A. (1986) *Interpreting Company Reports and Accounts.* Woodhead-Faulkner, Cambridge.

ICC Information Group Ltd (regular) *Business Ratio Reports,* ICC.

Ridd, S. (1991) Leisure centre computerisation. In: *Recreation Management Facilities Factfile.* Sports Council, London.

Taylor, P.D. and Page, K. (1994) *The Financing of Local Authority Sport and Recreation: a Service under Threat?* Institute of Sport and Recreation Management, Melton Mowbray.

19

Conclusion: Challenge and Policy Response

G.J. Ashworth[1] and A.G.J. Dietvorst[2]

[1]*Faculty of Spatial Sciences, State University, PO Box 800, 9700 AV Groningen, The Netherlands:* [2]*Centre for Recreation and Tourism Studies, Agricultural University, Generaal Foulkesweg 13, 6703 BJ Wageningen, The Netherlands*

Tourism Transformations and Place-management Policy

The preceding chapters were necessarily partial visions of what was presented in the introduction as a holistic model. This final chapter should provide a justification for the pursuit of the approach of this book as a whole by drawing together these specific studies of aspects of tourism in particular types of places in an integral approach to planning and management and thereby fulfilling the expectations raised in Chapter 1.

It is clear from the above chapters that not only do tourists use local resources in a bewildering variety of ways, but also places use their resource endowment for a variety of purposes other than tourism. It is these two obvious characteristics that embed local tourism policy deeply into more general place-management policy which must be addressed in this conclusion. Each tourist uses places to produce an individual recreational experience, each tourism activity or facility makes specific demands upon places while places have quite individual specific requirements of tourism in that locality. In marketing terms the simultaneous serving of many markets requires product discrimination in selling identifiably different experiences to quite separate markets and, from the viewpoint of the producer, for quite different purposes. But, equally, generalizing about the relationships of tourism, places and policies contradicts or at least has been made less convincing by the arguments advanced above in favour of variety in product and market.

However, it follows that if each place and each tourism place

329

product is thus by definition unique, then generalizations about applicable policy are not so much universally relevant and easily transferable strategies and instruments as sets of general precepts, often of either an encouraging or a minatory character. Much of the former approach can too easily degenerate into mere boosterism, or a one-sided paean of praise for the many benefits that tourism can confer on some people, in some establishments, in some sectors of the local economy, with little or no consideration of costs or of non-economic impacts upon the area. Equally misleading, if more honest, is the substantial literature on the role of tourism in specific cases of urban regeneration, where it is clear that tourism in general, and inner urban tourism in particular, have made a quantifiable contribution within more general urban regeneration policies. Law (1993) presents many good examples of this approach, but, it should be noted, draws cases principally from cities with major pre-existing problems of a severely shrinking economic base (such as the 19th-century industrial towns of northern England and the eastern USA) and few realistic alternative development strategies.

Similarly most of the above chapters have described in detail particular 'success stories' illustrating the ways in which the challenges of complexity and integration have been confronted by producer strategies that can be shown to have been successful, at least in so far as they have met the objectives set by the producers. The difficulty of such case-studies is not that they are incorrect as contextual illustrations but that they generally contain too many critical and unique characteristics to allow them to stand as archetypes, especially when transferred to a different context. It is inevitable, however regrettable, that amongst the cases of current tourism policy described in most of the literature the successes far outnumber the failures, whereas in the contemporary world of tourism place management the ratios are almost certainly reversed. When failure is only analysed, if at all, long after it has become all too apparent, while descriptions of success are frequently tinged with a premature optimism, then transferring policy experiences from one case to another is fraught with difficulty.

An opposite approach generalizes the tourist and the tourism experience and focuses upon meeting specified impacts upon the area. An extreme is the 'Golden Horde' idea, to use this expressive if derogatory term (Turner and Ash, 1976) for the rampaging mass tourist, where the impacts are specified but the demand remains largely undifferentiated. The focus is upon the place, not the tourism experience, and the task is to devise defensive policies to meet a perceived threat. Much of the detailed work using this approach is necessarily equally selective in its case material: for example, the work of van der Borg (1992) on defensive tourism policies for Venice or Jansen-Verbeke

(1990) on policies for avoiding conflict between tourists and residents in Bruges illuminates local actors, decision-making and the range of policy options but reduces the tourist to a vaguely defined homogeneous external force. In any event such place-defensive policies are generally only devised, and subsequently analysed, in cases that can be described as extreme, both in the magnitude of the problem and in its urgency. Such rescue strategies of the 'save Venice, Bruges, Bath' type inevitably contain lessons of only limited application elsewhere. Few places suffer the quite obvious but extreme difficulties posed by being committed by their worldwide reputation as tourism market leaders to the reception of very large numbers of visitors. Most place-management authorities, however, have a wide range of choices upon which to base strategy for tourism. Most places have a multifunctional economic base and a variety of economic activities and social, historic and cultural attractions to which tourism could be added but equally there is no pressing imperative for this.

Most places therefore must be cautious in deriving lessons of value to their tourism-development policies from the cases which dominate the literature and from which generally applicable conclusions are too frequently and too rapidly drawn. A central element in our argument above about the relationship of the tourism product to the resources of which it is composed is the seeming paradox that unique tourism place products (whether Venice, the Alps or the Spanish Costas) are produced from resources that we have argued are ubiquitous, in the sense that all places are endowed with culture, landscape and climate. The transformation of the resource into the product is a result of deliberate intervention in, by and for the place concerned. Thus not too long ago a 'geography of tourism' was likely to consist of a description of the spatial distribution of currently activated natural or man-made resources, while we are arguing that such a geography should more realistically consist of the spatial distribution of place-management goals and strategies that include recreation and tourism.

Integral Approaches

The term integral can be used, and is used in the chapters above, with significantly different meanings. It is clearly not enough merely to describe a pot-pourri of ingredients including a recreation and tourism element: integral implies a structural relationship between the components which contribute towards an understanding of broader issues combining different approaches. Three ways of viewing such a relationship are of particular relevance here.

- The integration of different recreational activities that occur at the same place at various spatial scales, but in the cases described above most usually cities and regions, such that they become mutually supporting, allowing combinations to be constructed, whether by producers or consumers, which are in effect new products.
- The integration of recreation functions with other functions in various functional associations or synergies. A number of such multifunctional development projects have been described above and it is worth noting that the recreation element in such integrated projects can play a variety of quite different catalytic roles.
- The integration of planning goals for particular recreation and tourism developments into the wider goals of management authorities, whether in the private or public sectors. This sort of integral planning has again been introduced in the cases above at a variety of spatial scales, but also for various types of planning goal (including policies for national tourism development, resort restructuring, rural development and the management of multifunctional cities as well as individual development projects within these). Most usually in the examples discussed the purpose of integral planning in this definition is to contribute to the excess of benefits over costs, whether economic or not, for the area discussed.

Product Life-cycle and Local Sustainability as Planning Concepts

This discussion of the use of the idea of integral development can be furthered by reconsidering its relevance within two ideas, well known in tourism analysis, namely product life-cycles and local sustainable development.

The experiences encapsulated in the chapters above have shown the importance of two main but different points of departure for new development options within regions. These are first the focus upon tourism as an economic activity, a set of products whose production can be subject to an analysis similar to that of any other product. The idea of the existence of a tourism product or even of a tourism place product has been implicit in many of the above chapters. Secondly, there is the attempt to view tourism, and recreational activities more generally, as one function of multifunctional places to be used in some quantity, in some combination, to produce some result in some locality. Two ideas may prove of value here in the attempt to reconcile these approaches and to proceed to the construction of policy. The idea of the product life cycle and the idea, or policy objective, of sustainable development have much in common: they were both introduced in the 1980s, were derived from fields of study other than tourism, have been capable of widely different interpretations in many contexts and yet have proved robust enough to have survived to become part of the conventional wisdom in the devising of local tourism strategies.

The assumption that the evolution of the tourist product in a specific region can be represented by a series of developmental market phases through which the product inevitably passes results in the well-known product life-cycle concept. This originated in microeconomics, was applied in marketing analysis and has been particularly effective in describing the typical development of the growth and decline of specific consumer goods. Its transference to tourism extended it to describe the historical vicissitudes of tourism places, most obviously resorts of one sort or another. Its utility was in describing product–market relationships through time and thus identifying critical points where intervention is appropriate.

Similarly the idea of sustainable development is based upon the existence of the time dimension and a similar idea of a progression that inevitably proceeds but is susceptible to intervention to slow or divert such progress. However, the time-scale is far wider, encompassing pasts and futures beyond the life-cycle of a product and measured not against the individual place product but against the economic, social or environmental local system as a whole. Again, however, its main utility is providing a framework for identifying the point and time of intervention.

In the most usually envisaged scenario, development starts with small visitor numbers of the explorer type looking for 'unspoilt' environments and asking for modest, 'place-authentic', facilities. At this stage the attractiveness of the place or region is that it has been as yet almost unchanged by external influences. The growth is demand-led with little consideration of a predetermined place-management strategy. Subsequently local initiatives begin to provide specific facilities for the visitors and some entrepreneurs start intervening in the market by, for example, advertising the region. The increasing number of visitors begins to take resources away from other uses and to impose new pressures upon the natural or cultural environments. The important point is reached where a transition occurs from demand-led to supply-led growth (Fig. 19.1) which in turn creates a need and an awareness for intervention, whether from inside or outside the place concerned and whether initiated by public or private agencies.

Achieving sustainability has a strong relationship with balancing processes on very different time–space axes. Economic processes are

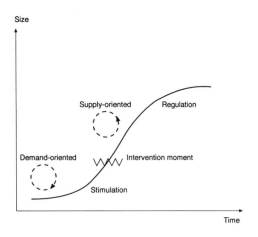

Fig. 19.1. Product life-cycle and intervention policy.

characterized by the product life-cycle mechanism and relatively short-term turnover times are typical. Spatial effects, however, do not always operate synchronously with these economic development patterns. Prominent supply-side elements (such as nature and landscape or the physical infrastructure) tend to evolve with a low growth in terms of time–space axes. Once established they are not easily wiped out, but dynamic supply-side processes, aimed at obtaining profits in the short term, can have a destructive effect. However, in the long run, supply-side elements of a dynamic nature do profit from existing spatial qualities. A subtle attuning of these processes and allocation of different elements to one another are necessary to safeguard existing regional qualities and maintain flexibility for future uses.

The determination or identification of the change-over point from demand-led to supply-led growth is of fundamental importance in achieving sustainability in the long run. As a consequence sustainable tourism planning, designing, management and operation have to respond to standards tailored to particular systems. Several experts have already formulated sets of guidelines, often strongly influenced by the management of natural ecosystems, and these are frequently restated in official policy proposals. Table 19.1, for example (derived from Grenier *et al.*, 1993), gives an impression not only of the variety of actors and objectives but also of the existence of inherent contradictions stemming from the differences of view and the near impossibility of defining or measuring the variables involved.

Such checklists of processes and policy guidelines can quickly

Table 19.1. Typical 'guidelines' for tourism planning. (Source: Grenier, 1993.)

Conceptual	Processes	Products
Define the sociocultural context of the region and identify the players with their roles	Implementation of a regional innovation centre. Patronize local business establishment. Use the wealth of local knowledge	Design sites and facilities based on design guidelines, which address appropriate scale, minimal impact on existing vegetation and habitats, the use of native plant materials, traditional building style and materials
Establish a dialogue between participants to elicit and debate the goals	Coordinate the activities of the different participants	Use local materials, building methods and local labour
Use an iterative tourism planning process as a framework for interdisciplinary coordination	Educate locals and intermediaries to the benefits of some forms of tourism as an alternative to exploitive tourism	Apply state-of-the-art environmental technology Indicate the degree of sustainability of each development project. Establish tourism standards to rank sustainability
Establish environmentally and socially sustainable goals and objectives. Specific consideration to maintain the special character of the region, local traditions, respect for ethical codes, and the use of indigenous materials, styles and plants	Conduct prior assessments in the site-selection process to minimize the impacts and secure sustainability (natural, social and cultural)	Establish a monitoring programme Establish an educational or extension programme to enhance the experience of both locals and tourists
Conceive of tourism planning as an educational process	Establish a social impact assessment procedure to evaluate the interests of the local population	Establish a marketing and promotion plan highlighting the community's commitment to care for sustainable tourism

become lengthy inventories of the goals of every agency and actor in policy formulation and thus unattainable, and often contradictory, vague and distant intentions. Tourism in particular suffers from an overloading of expectations experienced by few other economic activities. Typical is a recent study of rural tourism (Crouch, 1994) which claims as self-evident that 'any project for dynamic cultural development should seek to engage the everyday lives and changing culture of the local people who remain when the visitors have left, as well as the preferences of the visitor'. This and many similar statements in the literature attempt to combine sets of purely local objectives together with economic objectives that involve satisfying consumers. Most of the former could be analysed under the concept of sustainability while the latter involve pursuing individual satisfactions that have no ostensible relation to the pursuit of any local policy of sustainability by the provision in a competitive market of products at a particular phase of a life cycle.

A number of types of compromise, necessary for reconciling this contradiction through place-management strategy, were revealed in the local cases described above. These generally revolve around the identification of the stages in development reached, especially deciding whether, and at what moment, specific regional solutions must give way to an innovative leap to develop new qualities. The presence of local initiatives is crucial, or, if these are not forthcoming, local and regional authorities must be willing to create their own or stimulate private initiatives. The importance of this local coalition of interests is implicit in a number of the cases discussed above and the shift from national to local responsibility was explicitly related in Chapter 2. It is also important to identify the point of change-over from demand-led to supply-led growth, which requires a systematic monitoring of the rate of development of new development options. It is also necessary to take into account the different phases and phase lengths employed by the government, private enterprise and other participants in the network of regional interests. Specific points to watch out for include the different views of each partner, identifiable added value, communication, the cogency of arguments and the development of political agendas: lack of synchronization between phases can also complicate the coordination between government intervention and private-enterprise response. From the viewpoint of sustainability this pre-supposes the attainment of a reasonable balance between low and high dynamic characteristics. However, an accumulation of policy proposals can slow down the development opportunities of certain development options. This particularly applies in cases where there is a lack of clarity due to the rapid accumulation of measures, differences in legal status between policy proposals or inconsistent decentralization. The risks of this happening are particularly high at the change-over point between demand-led and supply-led growth.

The Consumer and the Place

The tourist, as a consumer freely choosing from alternative consumption patterns and exercising that choice through disposing of income within markets, is nevertheless additionally burdened with expectations deriving from the place itself. Not only is the tourist expected to provide local jobs and incomes but also to sustain local services, cultures, identities and environments. Many of the objections to current tourism developments advanced above from the viewpoint of the place were focused on the idea of the 'free ride', i.e. that the costs and benefits were so institutionally arranged that the tourism industry was free-riding upon local resources and facilities. Equally, however, the place should not expect to receive a windfall gain, whether economic or otherwise, from tourism as an economic activity. If in the booster phase of demand-led development places needed reminding that tourism development imposes local costs as well as offering local benefits, so in the later phases of the model it needs reiterating in reverse, namely that places may need to pay the costs if they wish to reap the benefits.

The necessity for understanding the relationships between the individual consumer and the characteristics of the place of consumption is by no means confined to tourism but exists, and has been studied, in many other economic activities, especially direct personal service industries. However, the necessity to consume the tourism product at the place of production, together with the nature of the tourism place as an important part of the product itself as well as the arena where tourism activities occur, makes it especially significant. It is therefore especially regrettable that the analysis of time–space behaviour, introduced in Chapter 10, is still in its infancy, despite its obvious importance as a basis for intervention.

In addition to concentrating on the 'site' as an overall package of specific regional characteristics, it is also important to take into account the 'situation', i.e. the relative position of a region within a larger whole. For example, proximity to major transport axes leading from centres of population gives many new rural development options a relative head start. Such centrally situated regions will reach the change-over point between demand-led and supply-led growth more quickly than peripheral regions, and they could also slow down the growth rate of these peripheral regions.

Without the controlled development of new options, existing qualities of regions and cities will be compromised and new initiatives will probably fail. It is vital to take into account the phase in which each region or city finds itself in terms of the product life-cycle. If a region opts for integrated, controlled development based on its existing qualities, a combination of new functions and a zoning of new functions in different intensities and qualities will usually be necessary. This creates an important task for the various levels of government. After all, although local initiatives and a local basis of support are important success factors, it is absolutely crucial that the various public and private initiatives are properly coordinated. If a decision needs to be made across various levels of government, then there is very little chance that a consistent policy will emerge which will be of any use to the region itself. It has already been pointed out that an accumulation of regulations can in itself slow down development within a region. Excessively detailed regulations made by different levels of government seriously reduce chances of success. Given that many levels of government will be involved in regional development but that local initiative is the key factor, the various authorities should simply adopt an enabling role. However, it is important that initiatives can be specifically tailored to regional needs and that local initiatives have access to a single point of consultation. Local innovation centres might be one solution. Besides, these innovation centres could play an effective extension role in developing and communicating relevant tourist guidelines for planning, designing and management in the local and regional tourist industry.

In Europe the variety of cultures and therefore planning traditions makes any detailed universal prescription for successful intervention particularly hazardous. This determines that the specific interrelationship between the facilitating roles of national governments and the initiating role of local governments and entrepreneurs will vary greatly. This, as numerous chapters above have pointed out, is an argument for the necessity for a comparative approach, not the automatic local application of a universal strategy. The central questions relevant for all regions remain: what chances can be identified, which phases are in operation, and which actors play which roles for which objectives. In the cases described above, although differing in location, scale and type of tourism activity, authors have insisted upon the presence of the same elements in the strategic plan. The process of local transformation must be recognized if it already exists, set in motion if it does not, and monitored and controlled throughout its course according to pre-imagined, but flexible, local goals.

References

Crouch, D. (1994) Home, escape and identity: rural cultures and sustainable tourism. *Journal of Sustainable Tourism* 2(1/2), 93–101.

Grenier, B. (1993) Ecotourism, landscape architecture and urban planning. *Landscape and Urban Planning* 25, 1–16.

Jansen-Verbeke, M. (1990) *Toerisme in de Binnenstad van Brugge: een Planologische Visie.* Nijmeegse Planologische Cahiers 35, Katholieke Universiteit, Nijmegen.

Law, C.M. (1993) *Urban Tourism.* Routledge, London.

Turner, L.J. and Ash, J. (1976) *The Golden Horde: International Tourism and the Pleasure Periphery.* Constable, London.

van der Borg, J. (1992) Some guidelines for sustainable tourism development. In: Briassoulis, H. and van der Straaten, J. (eds) *Tourism and the Environment.* Kluwer, Dordrecht.

Index

Accidents 99
Adventure 7, 85
  see also Sport
Advertisement 77, 78
  see also Images; Promotion
Agora *see* Urban public space
Agriculture 184–185
  see also Environment
Airlines 45, 52
Albergues 45
Alcohol *see* Tourist crime
Alpille mountains (France) 7
Alps 15, 93–105, 331
Alps d'Huez 96
Alternative tourism 84–85, 87
Amsterdam 59, 60–61, 130–144, 153, 277
Animation 108, 279
Arnhem 278
Art, city *see* Culture, city
Art tourism 269–270
  see also Culture, tourism
Arts *see* Culture
Athens 149
Audit 144, 323–324
Augusta (US) 220
Austria 93, 103
Authenticity 7, 15, 34, 70, 73, 77, 80, 88, 194, 333
  experience 190

staged 7, 82, 193, 199
Avalanche *see* Accidents
Avignon 269
Ayr 115

Balearic Islands 220
Bali 250
Bangkok 15, 69
Biocentricity *see* Environment, ideology
Bisbingen (Germany) 126
Britain *see* United Kingdom
British Isles 215–216
Bruges 331
Butlin's 111, 115

Cachet 108, 279
Canals 307
Capacity 40
Center Parcs 107, 109–110, 116, 120, 122–124, 124–125, 126
Chiang Mai 69, 71, 74
Cities *see* Urban
City marketing 156
  see also Images; Promotion
Clustering *see* Spatial clustering
Coding 4
  see also Marker

Commodification 20, 82
    see also Culture commodity
Communicative action theory
        (Habermas) 9–10, 21
Communicative staging (Cohen) 77
Conflicts 306–309, 331
    see also Tourism impacts,
        Tourism resource conflict
Cosmopolitanism 270–271, 273
Costa Brava 102,
Costa del Sol 41, 46, 219, 331
Courchevel 96
Counterstructure 10, 26–30
Crime *see* Tourist crime
Cremona (Italy) 276,
Culture 4, 7–8, 813
    city 139, 266, 269–210, 274,
        280–281, 330–331
    see also Showcase cities; Urban
        history
    commodity 80, 267, 274, 281
    see also commodification
    context 241, 246, 259–260,
        270–271
    counterculture 85
    culture capital (Bourdieu) 29
    demand 233–236, 265–266,
        273–274
    economic impacts 160, 225, 227,
        230–236, 265, 273, 275–276,
        278–280
    experience 7–8, 85–86, 274–275
    facilities 137, 141, 267, 277, 278
    festivals 160–161, 225–237, 250,
        266, 269
    industry 273
    perception 188–189
    performance 265, 275, 277
    resource *see* Tourism resource
    tourism 160–161, 226–227, 227,
        236–237, 239–240, 265–281
    see also Ethnic tourism
    tourist 273–274
    versus nature 190–191
    see also Heritage; Museums;
        Tourist-historic city
Czechoslovakia 216,

Deep ecology *see* Environment,
    ideology
Denmark 114
Den Haan (Belgium) 117, 121
Distance 246–247
    see also Spatial proximity
Docklands *see* Waterfronts
Doxa 29, 30
Drugs 84, 86, 290–291, 293
    see also Tourist crime
Durée (Bergson) 24

Ecocentricity *see* Environment,
    ideology
Edinburgh 160, 225–237
Eemhof (NL) 121
Egypt 272
El Kantaoui (Tunisia) 210
English Tourist Board 125
Enkhuizen (NL) 169, 278
Enlightenment 19
Environment
    consciousness 183, 193
    conservation 103, 193–199
    see also Tourism resources,
        conservation; Snow Plan
    friendly 256
    ideology 191–192
        biocentricity 191, 260
        deep ecology 192
        see also Romanticism
    perception 19, 187–192, 199,
        240
    physical change 89, 100, 184–187,
        200, 220
    see also Agriculture
    psychology 242–243
    practice 193–199, 240
    see also Tourism resources,
        conservation; Sustainability;
        Tourism impacts, Urban
        design, environment;
        Wilderness
Erperheide (Belgium) 120
Ethnic
    minorities 148
    tourism 69–71, 88

see also Culture, tourism; Hill
tribe trekking
Eurodisney 174, 175
European Union 5–6, 184–185,
185–186
Exoticism 15, 69, 70, 270

Field theory (Bourdieu/ Berry) 29,
167–168
Florida 219
Forum *see* Urban public space
France 93–105, 164, 217–218, 219
Friesland (NL) 297–298
Functional association 14
see also Synergies

Gaia *see* Environment ideology
Gesellschaft/gemeinschaft
(Tönnies) 56
Geographic Information Systems
(GIS) 169, 176, 298
see also Information systems
Germany 104, 114, 216, 217–218
Glasgow 227
Gleneagles (UK) 209–210
Globalization 2, 8
Golden triangle (Burma, Laos,
Thailand) 71
Golf 41, 50, 160, 205–221, 304
demand 205–208, 212–215
facilities 208–211
holiday types 215–219
networks 211
property development 210,
219
see also Real estate
Gran Dorado 109, 114, 116, 117–118
see also Holiday village

Hallmark events 38, 225, 226
Heritage 105, 137, 141, 270, 274
see also Art tourism; Culture
tourism
Hill tribe trekking 15, 69–90
see also Ethnic tourism

Historic *see* Heritage; Urban
history
Holiday camp *see* Holiday village;
Butlin's
Holiday village 109–127
definition 110
future 126–127
history 110–115
location 124–126
Households 155
Hungary 216

Images 3–4, 48, 52, 77–78, 120, 137,
155, 160, 171, 176, 193
see also Advertisement; City
marketing; Hallmark events;
Promotion
Incrementalism 14
Information systems 3, 240, 317–327
elements 319–320
functions 318–319
objectives 320–321
see also Geographic Information
Systems (GIS)
Interpretation 4, 243, 274
Italy 97

Landscape 119–124, 251–254
urban 4
see also Environment
Languedoc-Roussillon 210, 214
Lebenswelt *see* Lifeworld
Legitimation (Habermas) 20, 58–59,
271–272
Life-space 245
Lifestyle 5, 7, 8, 154–155, 208
Lifeworld 21, 22, 29
see also Communicative action
theory
Lloret de Mar 49
London 131, 153, 277

Malaga (Spain) 41, 210
Manchester 273
Marbella (Spain) 50

Marker (MacCannell) 6–7, 250, 254
　　see also Coding; Semiotics
Mediterranean 39
Meijendel (NL) 199
Minehead (UK) 115
Modernity 2
　　see also Postmodern
Moraleja (Spain) 221
Mountains *see* Alps; Sport, winter
Museums 5, 87, 154, 169, 254–255, 274, 276
　　location 277
　　see also Culture facilities; Interpretation
Mythology 188

Nature *see* Environment
Netherlands 17, 19–20, 34, 59–62, 112, 125–126, 152, 164, 192, 193, 280, 287–299
New York 130, 148
Nijmegen 129, 278
Noordwijk (NL) 293
Norwich 278

Opium *see* Drugs

Paradores 45
Paris 277
Pilgrimage 27
Pisa 274
Place-specific tourism *see* Tourism, place-specific
Ports *see* Waterfronts
Port Zeeland (NL) 117, 124
Portugal 214, 215
POS (*plan d'occupation des sols*) 103–104
Post-industrial 153–156
Postmodern 4, 31, 154, 254, 256, 257, 259
　　see also Modernity
Promotion 44, 46, 119, 141, 165, 227, 247, 274

　　see also City marketing; Images; Advertisement
Prosumer 258
Pseudo-events *see* Authenticity, staged
Public–private partnership 135–137, 143

Ravenna 164, 166
Real estate 101
　　see also Golf, property development
Recreation–opportunity spectrum 186–187
　　see also Tourist opportunity spectrum
Resorts *see* Tourism resorts
Resources *see* Tourism resources
Restaurants 5, 85, 154
Rhine delta (NL) 307
Romanticism 95, 189, 198, 251–252
Rome 149
Rotterdam 129, 131–132

Sansepolchro (Italy) 276
Sant Cugat (Spain) 221
Scotland 232
Seasonality 41, 112, 113, 127, 285
Segmentation *see* Tourism market
Semiotics 4, 6–7, 271
　　see also Coding
Sex 4, 53
Shopping 172–173
Showcase cities 276, 280
　　see also Culture city
Sitges (Spain) 50
Snow Plan 97, 99
Social organization of leisure 65–66
Socialization 271–272
Sonsbeek (NL) 251–254
Southern Limburg (NL) 170–173
Spain 15, 37–53, 164, 212, 214, 219
Space-time *see* Time–space
Spatial
　　clustering 14, 138, 139, 140–142, 165, 277–278

control 100–105
  distribution 41–43
  location 124–126
  proximity 131, 140, 244
  scale 165–166, 332
  structure 98, 118, 119, 120
  see also Zoning
Sport 8, 15, 102, 111, 164
  water sport 59–62, 112–113, 164
  surfboards 61
  winter sports 15, 93–105
  model resort 98
    see also Snow Plan
    see also Golf; Adventure
Stratford (Ontario) 160
Stress 255–256
Sun Parks 109, 114, 116, 118–119
  see also Holiday village
Sustainability 1, 18, 32
  see also Tourism, resources crisis
Sweden 217–218
Switzerland 93, 97, 103
Symbolism 3, 6–8, 21, 111
  see also Coding; Semiotics
Synergies 134, 142–143, 332

Thailand 15, 69–90
Theme parks 3, 173–179
  see also Eurodisney; Heritage
Third sector *see* Voluntary
  associations
Time 3, 17, 19, 24–25
  compression 23
  inner time 24, 26
  leisure time 19
  -space 2, 3, 165, 245, 246–260, 334
    analysis 168–169, 170–180, 337
    behaviour 171–173, 173–179,
      274–275
    budgets 159, 163–180
    constraints 168
    opportunities 169
    paths 169
    perception 190
  see also Durée; Seasonality
Tossa (Spain) 50
Tourism

accommodation 38–43, 44–45,
  50, 104, 109–127, 170–171
  apartments 97, 170
  camp-sites 40, 51, 170
  hotels 40, 97, 100, 116, 278
  second homes 50, 51, 52
  self catering 111, 114, 116
  see also Albergues; Holiday
    village; *Paradores*
attractions 6–7, 70–71, 138, 142,
  166
  see also Museums; Restaurants;
    Shopping
  complexes 166, 177
    see also Theme parks
  development 15, 37–38, 185
  experience 23–26, 70–71, 73,
    78–79, 122, 183–184, 274–275
  exploration 69, 245
    see also Adventure
  functions 139–140
  guidebooks 7, 164
  guides 75, 79–81
  growth 183, 236–237, 266–267
  impacts 18, 83–84, 303–315,
    330–331
    ecological 18, 89, 99, 100–101,
      183, 187, 196, 219–220
    economic 83–84, 88, 93,
      230–237, 330, 337
      see also Tourist crime
    management 196–197, 305–306
    sociological 89–90, 242
    wildlife 304, 305–306
    see also Conflicts
  industry 14, 163, 197, 265
    see also Tour operators
  information systems 240
    see also Geographic Information
      Systems (GIS)
  integrated 96–97, 209–210, 216
  investment 49, 96, 143
  life-cycles 332–336, 337
  market 13–14, 325
    segmentation 13–14, 267
    snow market 99–100
    see also Prosumer
  motives 86–87

Tourism *contd*
  nature-based 183–200
  place specific 270–271
  policy 18–22, 44–49, 93–100,
    104–105, 329–332, 336–338
  potential 138, 143
  producers 5–7, 13–16, 71, 102–103
    107–108, 241
    see also Prosumer
  product 13, 43–49, 141, 164, 175
  resorts 41, 49–51, 94, 100, 170–171
  resources 2, 4–10, 37–38, 243, 331
    capital resources 5
    conflict 8–9
    conservation 19, 32, 183–184,
      192
    crisis 9, 33–34
    management 249–250
    physical resources 5, 15, 160
    sociocultural 5, 15, 271, 331
    transformation 87–88
    see also Environment; Heritage
  rural, 335
    see also Agriculture
  special interest 226, 236
  taxes 49, 103
  training 79–80
  travel 2
  urbanization 6
Tourism-recreation product (TRP) 4,
    5, 6, 13–16, 43, 141, 142–143, 164
Tourist
  behaviour 140, 163–180, 197, 240,
    241–261, 278, 288–291, 292–294,
    336–337
  crime 240, 257, 285–299
    definition 286–287
    prevention 295–299
    vandalism 289–290, 293,
      298–299
    see also Alcohol; Drugs
  management 239–240, 241, 243,
    259, 335
  opportunity spectrum 140–142
    see also Recreation-opportunity
    spectrum
  perception 140, 163, 166
  preferences 166, 169, 247–249

Tourist-historic cities 159, 228, 274
  see also Culture city; Urban
    history
Tour operators 46, 70, 76
Transactionality 243–244
Transformation model 1–16,
    242–244

United Kingdom 60, 212–213,
    217–218, 219, 308–309, 311, 313,
    319, 322
United States 157, 308, 309, 311, 313
Urban
  design 276–277, 278
  development 132, 143, 275–280
  economies 278–280
  environment 135
  golf 221
  history 137, 149–153, 156
  leisure 154, 157
  networks 157, 275
  park 251–254
  policy 129, 134–137, 265
  public space 147–161, 239,
    276–277, 279
  renewal 129, 130
  revitalization 129–144, 227, 330
  tourism 129–144, 227, 236–237,
    266–267, 274–275, 275–280
    see also Culture city, festivals;
    Hallmark events; Showcase
    cities; Tourist-historic cities;
    Waterfronts

Val d'Isere 99
Valkenburg (NL) 170–171
Vallouise 98
Veluwe (NL) 294
Venice 272, 330, 331
Voluntary associations 15, 55–67
Vossemeren (Belgium) 114, 125

Wageningen (NL) 2
Waterfronts 108, 130–144, 157
Weather *see* Seasonality

Wilderness 188–189
    concept 195–196
Winter sports *see* Sports

Zandvoort (NL) 293
Zeeland (NL) 297
Zoning 97